ər

United Nations
Department of Economic and Social Development
Transnational Corporations and Management Division

United Nations Library on Transnational Corporations

Volume 5

INTERNATIONAL FINANCIAL MANAGEMENT

Note

The Transnational Corporations and Management Division (formerly the United Nations Centre on Transnational Corporations) of the United Nations Department of Economic and Social Development serves as the focal point within the United Nations Secretariat for all matters related to transnational corporations and acts as secretariat to the Commission on Transnational Corporations, an intergovernmental subsidiary body of the United Nations Economic and Social Council. The objectives of the work programme are to further the understanding of the nature of transnational corporations and of their economic, legal, social and political effects on home and host countries and in international relations, particularly between developed and developing countries; to secure effective international arrangements aimed at enhancing the contribution of transnational corporations to national development goals and world economic growth; and to strengthen the negotiating capacity of host countries, in particular the developing countries, in their dealings with transnational corporations.

General Disclaimer

The designations employed and the presentation of material in this publication do not imply the expression of any opinion whatsoever on the part of the Secretariat of the United Nations concerning the legal status of any country, territory, city or area or of its authorities, or concerning the delimitation of its frontiers or boundaries.

The articles in this series are all reprinted in their original form and country names may not be in accordance with United Nations usage.

The content, views and interpretations are those of the authors and should not be attributed to the United Nations.

United Nations Library on Transnational Corporations

Volume 5

INTERNATIONAL FINANCIAL MANAGEMENT

**Edited by Arthur I. Stonehill
and Michael H. Moffett**

General editor: John H. Dunning

INTERNATIONAL THOMSON BUSINESS PRESS
I ⓉP An International Thomson Publishing Company

London • Bonn • Boston • Johannesburg • Madrid • Melbourne • Mexico City • New York • Paris
Singapore • Tokyo • Toronto • Albany, NY • Belmont, CA • Cincinnati, OH • Detroit, MI

International Financial Management

Selection and editorial matter © 1993 United Nations

First published by International Thomson Business Press

 A division of International Thomson Publishing Inc.
The ITP logo is a trademark under licence

British Library Cataloguing-in-Publication Data
A catalogue record for this book is available from the British Library

First edition published by Routledge 1993
This edition published by International Thomson Business Press 1997

Typeset by Leaper & Gard Ltd, Bristol, England
Printed in the UK by TJ International Ltd

ISBN 0-415-14107-9

International Thomson Business Press
Berkshire House
168–173 High Holborn
London WC1V 7AA
UK

International Thomson Business Press
20 Park Plaza
13th Floor
Boston MA 02116
USA

http://www.itbp.com

Contents

Preface

The importance of transnational corporations and the globalization of production are now well recognized. Transnational corporations have become central actors of the world economy and, in linking foreign direct investment, trade, technology and finance, they are a driving force of economic growth. Their impact on the economic and social welfare of developed and developing countries is both widespread and critical.

It is one of the functions of the Transnational Corporations and Management Division (formerly the United Nations Centre on Transnational Corporations) – the focal point in the United Nations for all issues relating to transnational corporations – to undertake and promote research on transnational corporations to contribute to a better understanding of those firms and their impact. Over the past thirty years, research on this phenomenon has mushroomed, and hundreds of books and reports, as well as thousands of papers, have been published. It is the principal purpose of this twenty-volume *United Nations Library on Transnational Corporations* to distil, summarize and comment on some of the more influential of those writings on the role of transnational corporations in the world economy. In particular, the contributions in the *United National Library* deal with four main issues; namely, the determinants of the global activities of transnational corporations, their organizational structures and strategies, their interactions with the economies and legal systems of the countries in which they operate and the policies that governments pursue towards those corporations. The twenty volumes are intended to cover a wide range of topics that embrace economic, organizational and legal issues.

To accomplish that task, the Centre assembled a distinguished group of editors, who were commissioned to select the seminal contributions to their subject areas published over the past twenty to thirty years. They were also asked to prepare comprehensive bibliographies of writings on their subjects for inclusion in the volumes, and state-of-the-art introductions that summarize the development of their subjects, review the most important current issues and speculate about future work. We hope that the result in each case is a volume that provides a succinct, yet comprehensive, overview of the subject to which it is devoted.

In the early part of the post-war period, foreign direct investment was perceived to be mainly a financial activity – rather akin to portfolio investment. Even after Stephen Hymer suggested that such a phenomenon could be better explained by use of the theory of industrial organization, the subject has continued to fascinate teachers and researchers in international finance. In a sense, that is not surprising as the transnational corporation is both one of the main borrowers of capital and a leading organization agent in its allocation across national boundaries. The way in which the financial and exchange rate behaviour of firms differs according to their cross border value-added activities is of considerable interest to scholars and practitioners alike.

Arthur Stonehill is visiting Professor of Finance and International Business at Oregon State University (spring), University of Hawaii (winter), and Copenhagen Business School (fall); he is one of the doyens of international financial management, and co-author (with David Eiteman and Michael Moffett) of an influential textbook on the subject. Michael Moffett is Associate Professor of Finance and International Business in the College of Business at Oregon State University and is presently visiting Associate Professor of International Business at the University of Michigan (Ann Arbor). In the present volume the editors introduce the reader to the mainstream literature on one of the most technical aspects of transnational corporation activity embraced in this series of volumes. In the contemporary global corporation financial capital is one of the most fungible assets to cross national boundaries. The determinants of the way in which transnational corporations acquire, organize and manage those assets is of critical importance, not only to the success of those corporations, but also to the development and industrial restructuring of nation states. The 1990s are likely to pose new challenges for the international finance scholar as the demand for investment capital by the new entrants into the international market economy and the escalating costs of innovations place enormous pressures on the world demand for finance capital and its main supplying agents.

This is one of the most important reasons why a basic understanding of the management of the cross-border financial assets of companies, which probably account for one third of the world's stake of all such assets, is so important. In their introduction and selection of readings, Stonehill and Moffett seek to present the lay reader, as well as the finance specialist, with an understanding of these and related issues.

New York, July 1992

Karl P. Sauvant
Chief, Research and
Policy Analysis Branch,
Transnational Corporations
and Management Division

John H. Dunning
General Editor of
*United Nations Library on
Transnational Corporations*

Acknowledgements

The editors and publishers would like to thank the following publishers and other organizations for permission to reprint copyright material: *American Economic Review*, American Economic Association; *California Management Review*, University of California, Berkeley; *Financial Management*, Financial Management Association; *Journal of Finance*, Stern School of Business; *Journal of Financial and Quantitative Analysis*, University of Washington; *Journal of International Business Studies*, University of South Carolina; *Midland Corporate Finance Journal* (now *The Journal of Applied Corporate Finance*), Stern Stewart and Co.; John Wiley & Sons.

Introduction: International Financial Management

Arthur I. Stonehill and Michael H. Moffett

The purpose of this volume is to summarize the development of contemporary thinking on the international financial management of transnational corporations. Although textbooks on this theme typically encompass a broad definition of international financial management, this volume will maintain a somewhat more restricted definition, namely, one that is limited to the international extension of traditional corporate finance. The most important theoretical developments in international financial management, from a corporate perspective, can be captured by concentrating on the following four topic areas:

- foreign exchange management
- cost of capital
- financial structure
- capital budgeting.

Representative articles from these four areas were chosen which best depict their chronological development and contemporary thinking. The bibliography at the end of the volume highlights other articles which have made a significant contribution.

Foreign Exchange Management

Foreign exchange management is the only one of the four topic areas which has almost no domestic financial management parallel. On the contrary, most of the theoretical developments have come from the field of international economics. Nevertheless, an understanding of foreign exchange management is critical for managers of transnational corporations and must be included in any serious academic study of finance.

Historical Background

Foreign exchange exposure management did not become an important topic in corporate finance literature, or in the eyes of financial managers, until the international monetary crisis of 1971–73. Prior to that time, exchange rates were fixed in accordance with the system designed at Bretton Woods in 1944. Although periodic realignments of exchange rates occurred, the dollar's value was fixed in terms of gold at $35 per ounce, and other currencies tried to maintain par values with respect to the dollar under a gold exchange standard. A gradual deterioration of the United States balance-of-payments position during the 1960s led to a loss of confidence in the dollar, a suspension of its convertibility into gold in August 1971, and its eventual devaluation by 8.57 per cent in December 1971. After a brief return to fixed exchange rates, market pressures forced a second devaluation of the dollar by 10 per cent in February 1973. When this did not stabilize the markets, the dollar and all other currencies were allowed to float to their natural market-determined levels. Thus began the current system of managed floating rates.

Exchange rate volatility has increased sharply since 1973, with a corresponding impact on the cash flows and earnings of firms engaged in international business. This has captured the attention of business executives, investors and academics. It has led to a rich outpouring of articles and books on foreign exchange management.

The three main types of foreign exchange-risk management which are treated in academic literature of special interest to TNCs fall under the headings of *economic, transaction* and *translation*-exposure management. Because of limitations of space, this text will deal only with *economic* and *transaction*-exposure management.

Foreign Exchange Economic Exposure Management

Corporate finance literature was rather tardy in recognizing foreign exchange economic exposure as a legitimate area of concern for business students. It was not until the mid-1960s that any serious academic articles on foreign exchange management began to appear in business journals. These early articles were mainly concerned with foreign exchange transaction exposure and related hedging techniques, as well as translation exposure and related accounting principles. It was not until the early 1970s that the more important concept of economic exposure was understood. A very good summary of the early theories up to 1980 is presented in Jacque (1981; Chapter 4).

Dufey (1972; Chapter 1) had the first article in a leading corporate finance journal to explain the difference between economic (or operating) exposure and translation exposure. Although he did not coin the term "economic exposure", Dufey contrasted the "going concern" value of a foreign subsidiary with its "exposed asset" value. Shapiro and Rutenberg

(1976; Chapter 3) extended and refined the concept of economic exposure and suggested more sophisticated approaches to managing both economic and transaction exposure. Flood and Lessard (1986; Chapter 5) provide the latest summary of thinking on economic (operating) exposure management.

As it has developed, foreign exchange economic exposure is defined as the likelihood that the net present value of a firm's future cash flows will change due to an unexpected change in exchange rates. When exchange rates change unexpectedly, a transnational corporation's sales volume, prices and costs are likely to be affected.

Efforts by the firm to manage exchange rate changes are really the microeconomic version of what is happening at the macroeconomic level. International economics literature is rich in discussions of how countries adjust to exchange rate changes. For example, the concept of a "real (inflation-adjusted) exchange rate" is well understood in economics literature and by government policy makers. However, neither economic exposure nor the real effective exchange rate are well understood by top management. Instead, they often assume that any foreign exchange issue is the responsibility of the treasurer or financial vice president. In reality, managing economic exposure is best accomplished by internationally diversifying sales, production and financing by currency. These are strategic decisions that must be approved by top management and the board of directors, as well as by the financial officers.

Foreign Exchange Transaction Exposure

Foreign exchange transaction exposure is defined as the change in domestic (reporting) currency value of outstanding financial accounts which are denominated in a foreign currency. Typical accounts which are exposed are foreign currency denominated accounts receivable, accounts payable and dividends which have been declared but not yet paid from foreign affiliates. Transaction exposure can be managed by both operating policies, such as leads and lags in payments, and by contractual hedging instruments such as forward contracts, money market hedges, swaps and foreign currency futures and option contracts.

Exchange rate determination and the use of contractual hedges have long been the domain of the international economics literature. Therefore the corporate finance literature has focused more on a derivative question: are exchange rate changes predictable and, if so, can a firm (engaged in international transactions) benefit from the prediction? The answer to that question depends on whether or not foreign exchange markets are efficient. The methodology for testing this had been previously developed to determine if stock markets are efficient. The famous "random walk" studies of the United States stock market were done in the 1950s and replicated in the 1960s for other equity markets worldwide. It was therefore a logical step for Giddy and Dufey (1975; Chapter 2) to conduct tests on the foreign exchange market. Their "weak form" test of three currencies during two floating rate periods (1973–74) concluded that the foreign exchange market, at least for the data tested, is an efficient market. They concluded that exchange rate forecasting, like picking individual stocks, is not profitable in an efficient foreign exchange market. Indeed, the forward rate, which is readily available to everyone, is the best unbiased predictor of the future spot rate.

This conclusion was reinforced about the same time by Kohlhagen (1975) and Fama (1976). Kohlhagen compared the 90-day forward rate for six currencies with their spot rates 90 days later and found that any differences could be blamed on random variations. He studied both the early floating rate period 1973–74 and the preceding fixed rate period, using a sample of six currencies, three of which were the same as the ones used by Giddy and Dufey (1975). Fama (1976) also studied the early floating rate period and concluded that "when adjusted for variation through time in expected premiums, the forward rates of interest that are implicit in Treasury Bill prices contain assessments of expected future spot rates of interest that are about as good as those that can be obtained from the information in past spot rates" (Fama, 1976, p. 361).

Test results from the early floating rate years did not hold up well for longer time periods. Later tests challenged the notion that exchange markets are efficient, especially given the predilection for governments to intervene unexpectedly in the market place. The Jurgensen Report (1983) is the most comprehensive to date, using a longer time period of floating rates and more currencies. It concluded that inflation and interest rate differentials were better predictors than the forward exchange rate. Furthermore, they found that a high probability of making a profit could be achieved by consistently using certain foreign exchange trading rules. This, of course, implies that the foreign exchange markets are inefficient and it would pay for firms to spend resources on forecasting. The fact that numerous expensive forecasting services exist profitably suggests that at least some managers agree with this conclusion.

From a managerial perspective, the current thinking on whether an international firm should actively manage its transaction exposure depends on one's belief about foreign exchange market efficiency and how much risk aversion management can tolerate. Repeated hedging of all transaction exposure can be more costly than the expected loss or gain from remaining unhedged, especially if foreign exchange markets are efficient. However, if the markets are inefficient, and the size of a transaction exposure is large compared to the size of the firm, most managers would probably hedge all or some of the exposure in order to reduce variability of cash flows and earnings. Khoury and Chan (1988; Chapter 6) provide an interesting survey of how financial officers view the relative usefulness of the various types of hedging techniques and to what extent they actually use them.

Cost of Capital

A number of transnational corporations have been able to lower their cost of capital by raising funds in international capital markets and by cross-listing on foreign stock exchanges. As a result of the efforts of those firms to internationalize their cost of capital, segmented capital markets have gradually become more integrated and international portfolio investment has flourished. In addition, some scholars believe that investors may purchase the shares of transnational corporation as a proxy for not being able to acquire shares of firms which are resident in segmented capital markets. This could further lower the cost of capital of transnational firms.

Historical Background

In 1945, following the disruptions caused by the Second World War, most of the world's money and capital markets were in shambles. Investors had lost confidence in paper securities. The shortage of gold and dollar reserves outside of the United States resulted in tight restrictions on the international flow of capital and a lack of true convertibility of key currencies. The British pound sterling, which had been the most important pre-war trading currency, was in excess supply everywhere as a result of the need to finance the war. The German, Japanese and Italian capital markets had to be rebuilt from scratch.

The dollar and the United States capital market performed well as the engine of reconstruction during the early postwar years, but an overvalued dollar led to serious United States balance-of-payments problems during the 1960s. Just as foreign exchange and capital restrictions were being removed elsewhere, the United States needed to impose the interest equalization tax in 1963, followed by restrictions on foreign lending by banks and on foreign direct investment by United States firms.

With the United States capital market effectively segmented from other capital markets by the mid-1960s, the locus of international financing shifted to the newly emerging Eurocurrency market which provided an alternative source of dollars and, to a limited extent, other currencies. Moreover, the gradual improvement of European capital markets made it feasible to develop a Eurobond market as a source of long-term financing for both transnational corporations and government entities.

A more realistically priced dollar followed the move to floating exchange rates and, by January 1974, the United States was able to remove all of its previously imposed international capital controls. Since that time, the trend has been towards removal of restrictions on international capital movements by most industrial countries. In particular, the European Community has moved perceptibly towards a single capital market, where Japan has significantly opened its capital market, as well as removing restrictions on its own residents' ability to invest abroad. Thus what started as a world of segmented capital markets has gradually evolved towards a more integrated global market.

International Portfolio Diversification

In order for transnational corporations to lower their cost of capital by tapping international sources, portfolio investors must have a rationale for holding foreign securities in their portfolios. The genesis of such a rationale sprang from domestic portfolio theory as developed by Markowitz and refined by Sharpe and Lintner in the early 1960s. Grubel (1968; Chapter 7) presented the first attempt to develop an international version of portfolio theory. He showed that an efficiently diversified international portfolio should have a lower risk for a given rate of return than an efficiently diversified domestic portfolio. Furthermore, the internationally diversified portfolio should also have a higher rate of return for a given level of risk. This conclusion was confirmed by Levy and Sarnat (1970) and a number of later studies. One of the most recent studies by Eun and Resnick (1988; Chapter 11) updates these early studies by taking into account exchange rate uncertainty. They concluded that exchange rate uncertainty is essentially non-diversifiable and weakens the performance of internationally diversified portfolios. However, this can be offset by multi-currency diversification and the use of forward contracts for hedging the portfolio.

Market Segmentation and the Cost of Capital

If capital markets are partially segmented, investors cannot gain the full benefit from international portfolio diversification, and firms cannot fully lower their cost of capital by selling their securities to foreign investors. A national capital market can be segmented because of government interference and/or because of investor perceptions. An example of government interference is restrictions on the free movement of capital, either by limiting what domestic securities foreign investors can buy, or by limiting what foreign securities domestic investors can buy. Other examples are discriminatory tax policies, rationing of foreign exchange, and policies which increase transactions costs in domestic securities markets. Investor perceptions are shaped by the quality of financial disclosures, familiarity with foreign securities markets and institutions, alternative portfolio possibilities, foreign exchange risk and political risk.

Numerous empirical tests have been undertaken to determine if capital markets are segmented and, if so, whether such segmentation affects the valuation of securities and thus a firm's cost of capital. Solnik (1974) was one of the first financial analysts to test empirically whether a large sample of European and United States stocks were priced according to an international asset pricing model (an international Beta) or a domestic pricing model (domestic Beta). He found evidence that although national factors dominated the pricing of his sample firms during the period March 1966–April 1971, some of their valuation could be attributed to international factors. In other words, using domestic Beta alone in calculating a firm's cost of capital would be misleading.

Lessard (1974) also tested whether a world factor was an influence on the valuation of securities. His data base included a large number of capital markets. Although national risk was most important, world factors did have an influence on stock prices in most of the markets tested. Stehle (1977) sought to determine what level of international capital market segmentation was needed to cause strictly domestic pricing of risk assets. He tested whether stocks on the New York Stock Exchange were priced nationally or internationally during the period January 1956–December 1975. His results favoured international pricing, although they were ambiguous. International pricing implies that the stocks were traded in an integrated rather than segmented market.

Grauer, Litzenberger and Stehle (1976) hypothesized equilibrium models of international capital markets under varying degrees of segmentation, including segmentation caused by foreign exchange risk. Solnik (1977) also tested national versus international pricing of securities, while using more sophisticated definitions of different types of exchange risk (nominal, real, etc.). He concluded that it was virtually impossible to specify a theoretical model of international asset pricing that can be tested empirically.

More recently, Errunza and Losq (1985) have tested international asset pricing under mild segmentation. Rather than trying to find a general model that might explain all kinds of segmentation, which Solnik (1974) discouraged, they tested for just one type of segmentation. If domestic securities were inaccessible to foreign investors would they command a super-risk premium? They found support for such a hypothesis, using a large data base of securities from developing country markets covering the period 1976–80. Since segmentation increased the cost of capital for firms resident in segmented markets, it might be beneficial for emerging capital markets to remove most of their restrictions which prevent integration with world capital markets.

The Effect of Market Segmentation on a Corporation's Cost of Capital

If a country's capital market is segmented, investors resident in that country may not be able to hold an efficient internationally diversified portfolio, and firms resident in that country may not enjoy the lowest possible cost of capital. However, with the proper strategies, transnational firms may be able to raise their funds abroad and gain an international pricing of their securities even though their home market remains segmented. On the other hand, firms which are too small to tap international capital markets are forced to continue to accept the higher cost of

Chart 1

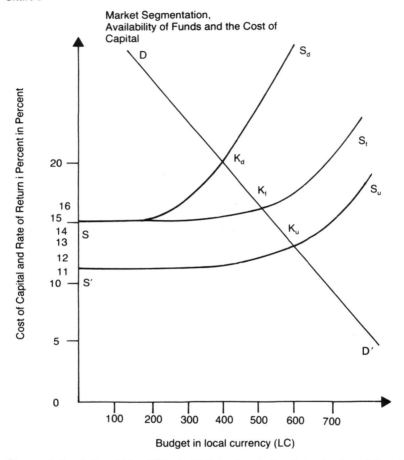

Market Segmentation,
Availability of Funds and the Cost of
Capital

Source: Arthur I. Stonehill and Kåre B. Dullum, *Internationalizing the Cost of Capital: The Novo Experience and National Policy Implications* (Copenhagen, Nyt Nordisk Forlag Arnold Busck, 1982 and New York, John Wiley & Sons, 1983), p. 28.

capital typical of their domestic markets. Chart 1 illustrates the effect of market segmentation on a firm's cost of capital and the advantages of tapping other capital markets. The diagram was originally constructed to explain how a Danish transnational corporation, Novo Industri A/S, was able to lower its cost of capital dramatically by aggressively pursuing foreign investors despite the continued segmentation of the Danish capital market.

In the diagram, a firm has given marginal return on capital at different budget levels, shown by the line *DD'*. If the firm can only raise capital in its segmented domestic market, the line *SS_d* shows its marginal cost of capital.

The optimal operating level is shown by the point K_d, where the budget is LC 400 and the cost of capital is 20 per cent. This situation would be typical of small to medium-size firms, whether they are transnational or national. What might be called a "small size bias" prevents a small firm from accepting many worthwhile projects presented by the line DD', to the right of the point K_d. From the small firm's perspective, the availability of capital is limited to what it can raise in its home market. If the firm is able to raise debt in the Euronote or Eurobond markets, it can partially escape its segmented domestic market. The new optimal level of operating is the point K_f, where its budget is increased to LC 500 and its cost of capital is reduced to 16 per cent. It should be noted that only fairly large, well-known firms have access to the Euronote and Eurobond markets. Small firms, even if they are transnational, cannot tap these markets. Finally, if a firm is allowed to sell its equity to foreign investors it has the potential to earn an international price for its equity rather than the price established in the domestic market. The optimal operating level now becomes the point K_u, where its budget is LC 600 and its cost of capital is 13 per cent. This is called the "segmentation effect". It is worth noting that at every level of the budget the firm has a lower cost of capital when it has full access to international capital markets.

The "small firm" bias is even more of a deterrent when it comes to interesting international equity investors in holding the shares of a small firm. Most institutional investors are very concerned about their ability to sell as well as to buy a firm's shares. The market for shares in a small firm is perceived as being illiquid, whether that firm is transnational or domestic.

The Transnational Corporation as a Proxy for Firms in Segmented Markets

To what extent can the shares of a transnational corporation serve as a substitute for investors who wish to diversify their portfolios internationally but cannot find or purchase the shares of firms which are resident in segmented capital markets? The answer to this question has been an important line of inquiry by scholars investigating the international aspects of the cost of capital.

The earliest theoretical work on this topic was by Adler (1974) and Adler and Dumas (1975). They modelled various scenarios of a value-maximizing firm engaging in foreign direct investment, including joint ventures, in a country with a segmented capital market. They then hypothesized under which set of assumptions a firm could lower its cost of capital (increase its value). They also modelled a case where the capital markets were not segmented but foreign exchange risk was present. The question here was whether a transnational firm could create value by efficiently diversifying exchange risk for portfolio investors who could not do this as well by themselves.

Stapleton and Subrahmanyam (1977; Chapter 8) modelled an eight-firm, 20-investor economy to investigate the theoretical impact of market segmentation on a firm's cost of capital, with and without international mergers and dual listings of shares on foreign exchanges. They concluded that three corporate financial policies could reduce the effect of market segmentation for firms resident in that market:

1. Investing in foreign securities or foreign direct investment in the segmented market on behalf of investors who cannot do this themselves;
2. Merging with foreign firms;
3. Listing the firms' shares on one or more foreign capital markets.

Lee and Sachdeva (1977; Chapter 9) analysed the role of a transnational corporation in the integration of segmented capital markets. Continuing along the lines introduced by Adler and Dumas (1975), they investigated to what extent foreign direct investment by transnational corporations can serve as a substitute for international portfolio holdings by home country investors, thereby resulting in a more optimal world-wide welfare state. They also analysed whether diversification by transnational corporations into a partially segmented capital market can result in unambiguous benefits for investors resident in the host country. They concluded that under conditions of perfect competition, a transnational corporation does make welfare-optimal decisions for its investors, thus providing a strictly financial rationale for foreign direct investment. However, under imperfect competition the strategy of foreign direct investment does not make welfare-optimal decisions and might leave investors in the host country worse off.

Agmon and Lessard (1977; Chapter 10) tested whether investors recognized the benefits of indirect international portfolio diversification by using a transnational corporation as a proxy to reach segmented capital markets. They found that investors appeared to pay a premium for the shares of firms which are heavily involved in foreign direct investment. Thus, being transnational would seem to lower a firm's cost of capital.

In summary, considerable evidence exists to suggest that transnational firms should have a lower cost of capital than their domestic counterparts. Because of that, they may receive a higher valuation by investors who are using their shares for international diversification into segmented markets that they cannot tap themselves. Listing on foreign securities exchanges has a favourable liquidity effect because more investors are available to buy the limited number of a firm's shares outstanding. Tapping foreign markets is also a way for firms which are resident in segmented markets to escape the lower valuation of their shares in that market. Normally a firm must be transnational, or at least extremely visible abroad, to succeed in attracting a significant following of foreign investors.

Financial Structure

Modigliani and Miller (1958) launched the great debate about whether or not an optimal financial structure for a firm exists. Their original contention was that, under certain very restrictive assumptions about perfect competition, financial structure was irrelevant. They later modified this assertion by recognizing that the tax advantages of debt biases the firm towards a much higher use of debt. Later theorists suggested that agency and bankruptcy costs place an upper limit on the desirable portion of debt.

The "traditionalists" always felt that an optimal debt ratio exists in the form of a U-shaped cost of capital curve. As a firm takes on debt, the weighted average cost of capital is reduced due to the tax advantages of debt; but when the debt ratio becomes too high, agency and bankruptcy costs, as well as the reticence of lenders, raises the cost of capital. Therefore, the optimal debt ratio is a flat range at the bottom of the U-shaped cost of capital curve.

A number of studies in the 1960s concluded that there were significant industry differences in United States debt ratios. This was interpreted to mean that lenders and borrowers alike recognized different business risk classes and this influenced the choice of optimal debt ratios.

Stonehill and Stitzel (1969: Chapter 12) were the first to investigate empirically the debt ratios of firms in other countries in order to determine if the domestic United States findings applied worldwide. Their conclusion was that financial structures of firms in the same industry do not adhere to any world-wide industry norm. Instead, there were significant country norms which were far more important than industry (business risk) norms. They suggested that environmental variables were the probable explanation of country norms. Environmental variables might include lack of liquidity in non-United States capital markets, differences in tax treatment, differing national attitudes towards risk and differential rates of inflation. It remained for later studies to test these and other variables.

Stonehill and Stitzel (1969) also began the debate about whether the financial structure of foreign subsidiaries of transnational corporations should conform to local norms, the parent country's norm, or somewhere in between. They concluded that conforming to local norms would be preferable for the following reasons:

- The environmental factors that influence local firms, such as inflation and taxes, should be taken into account.
- A localized financial structure would reduce criticism by host governments that foreign subsidiaries were using too much or too little debt. Too much debt implied unwillingness to take a risk locally. Too little debt meant the foreign subsidiary would be insensitive to local monetary policy.

- Management could evaluate their return on equity investment relative to local competitors in the same industry and with the same financial risk.
- Unless a foreign subsidiary can earn a return equal to or better than local competitors (with the same financial structures) it is probably misallocating scarce local capital.

The conclusion that country norms are the dominant determinant of financial structure has been confirmed by numerous studies since 1969. Remmers *et al.* (1974), Toy *et al.* (1974) and Stonehill *et al.* (1975) reported the results of a large-scale cooperative research project involving five countries. Country norms were always found to dominate tests of industry, size, growth rate and profitability as determinants of local debt ratios. Essentially the same conclusions were reached by Aggarwal (1981), Collins and Sekely (1983), Sarathy and Chatterjee (1984), Wright and Suzuki (1985), Rutterford (1985) and Kester (1986).

Shapiro (1978; Chapter 13) analysed the theoretical weighted average cost of capital for transnational corporations by costing each component; a subset of this analysis was the question of an optimal financial structure for foreign subsidiaries. He disagreed with Stonehill and Stitzel (1969) in so far as he concluded that conforming to local norms was wrong. On the contrary, a foreign subsidiary should borrow all it can locally if the cost of doing so, after considering taxes and exchange rate risk, was less than what was available to the parent firm in other capital markets. If the local cost was relatively high, the foreign subsidiary would borrow very little locally. Such policies, however, are constrained by the need to optimize the parent's consolidated worldwide debt ratio. Shapiro also hypothesized other likely variables which should influence a foreign subsidiary's financial structure. These included parent guarantees, taxes, regulatory restrictions, riskiness of foreign operations, political risk, inflation, foreign exchange risk, diversification, investor perceptions and the ownership structure of the foreign subsidiary.

Since none of these previous studies was able to establish a consistent empirical relationship between specific economic variables and country norms, Sekely and Collins (1988: Chapter 15) tested empirically the hypothesis that cultural variables were the principal determinant of country norms. They defined culture to include such variables as social institutions, belief systems, aesthetics, language and material culture. Since these elements would be difficult to test individually, they postulated that countries having similar cultural backgrounds would contain firms with similar financial structures. Using a data base of 677 companies in nine industries and 23 countries, they identified seven cultural realms (see Chapter 15), which lends some credence to their hypothesis of the importance of cultural similarities. They concluded that cultural analysis may be of value to transnational corporations when choosing financial structures for their foreign subsidiaries.

Lee and Kwok (1988: Chapter 14) have opened an interesting new line of inquiry that does not necessarily relate only to country norms or foreign subsidiary financial structures but is an extension of domestic finance theory. It has always been assumed that transnational corporations should be able to justify higher debt ratios than their domestic counterparts because of greater diversification of cash flows and greater international availability of capital. Using a large sample of United States transnational and domestic firms, Lee and Kwok (1988) found statistical support for the hypothesis that transnational corporations have higher agency costs of debt than domestic firms due to political risk, market imperfections and other international environmental variables. Furthermore, after controlling for size, transnational corporations appeared to have about the same bankruptcy risk as domestic firms. Finally, the transnational corporations actually had lower debt ratios than their domestic counterparts, presumably due to higher agency costs.

Capital Budgeting

The return of most industrial countries to currency convertibility in the 1950s, and the formation of the European Community and EFTA, led to large new capital movements in the form of foreign direct investment. The strategic, economic and behavioural motives for foreign direct investment enjoy an immense, rich literature, which is surveyed by John Dunning in a companion volume in this series. However, the analytical methods used to evaluate specific new foreign projects, or reinvestment in existing projects, is the subject of capital budgeting, which is an important topic in the corporate financial management literature.

Capital budgeting for a foreign project uses the same discounted cash-flow techniques as are used to evaluate domestic projects. In a true transnational corporation, all projects, foreign and domestic, compete on an equal footing for a piece of the capital budget. However, the analysis of a foreign project is considerably more complex than for a domestic project for the following reasons summarized by Eiteman, Stonehill and Moffett (1992, pp. 493–494)

- Parent cash flows must be distinguished from project cash flows. Each of these two types of flows contributes to a different view of value.
- Parent cash flows often depend on the form of financing. Thus cash flows cannot be clearly separated from financing decisions, as is done in domestic capital budgeting.
- Remittance of funds to the parent must be explicitly recognized

because of differing tax systems, legal and political constraints on the movement of funds, local business norms, and differences in how financial markets and institutions function.

- Cash flows from affiliates to parent can be generated by an array of non-financial payments, including payment of license fees and payments for imports from the parent.
- Differing rates of national inflation must be anticipated because of their importance in causing changes in competitive position, and thus in cash flows over a period of time.
- The possibility of unanticipated foreign exchange rate changes must be remembered because of possible direct effects on the value to the parent of local cash flows, as well as an indirect effect on the competitive position of the foreign affiliate.
- Use of segmented national capital markets may create an opportunity for financial gains or may lead to additional financial costs.
- Use of host government subsidized loans complicates both capital structure and the ability to determine an appropriate weighted average cost of capital for discounting purposes.
- Political risk must be evaluated because political events can drastically reduce the value or availability of expected cash flows.
- Terminal value is more difficult to estimate because potential purchasers from the host, parent, or third countries, or from the private or public sector, may have widely divergent perspectives on the value to them of acquiring the project.

Since the same theoretical capital budgeting framework is used to choose among competing foreign and domestic projects, a common standard is critical. Thus all foreign complexities must be quantified as modifications to either expected cash flow or the rate of discount. Although in practice many firms make such modifications arbitrarily, readily available information, theoretical deduction, or just plain common sense can be used to make less arbitrary and more reasonable choices.

Stonehill and Nathanson (1968; Chapter 16) attempted to introduce the complexities of capital budgeting for a foreign project into the corporate finance literature of the late 1960s, but it was many years before mainline financial theorists considered the problem worthy of further study. Stonehill and Nathanson (1968) suggested that a foreign project be evaluated from the viewpoint both of the parent firm and of the foreign project itself. In order to be acceptable, a project should pass muster on both counts. They also concluded that financial cash flows must be considered rather than just operating cash flows since project cash flows were not necessarily immediately available to the parent. Moreover, when they would be repatriated in the future, contingent tax and foreign exchange costs could be expected.

They suggested that an allowance for political and foreign exchange risks should be made by charging cash flows the cost of a programme of uncertainty absorption, whether or not it is actually carried out. Uncertainty could be absorbed by purchasing more information, borrowing most of the investment locally, buying hedging and investment insurance if available and negotiating the environment with the host-country government. Arbitrarily raising the discount rate for a foreign project was rejected because that does not take account of the actual amounts at risk, or for variations in the degree of risk of the project over time. Finally, Stonehill and Nathanson reported on a survey of transnational firms to determine which analytical techniques and definitions they were using for evaluating foreign projects financially. Only 48 per cent of firms used any kind of cash-flow technique and 38 per cent treated risk in a subjective way rather than attempting to quantify it. It should be noted, however, that capital budgeting was at an early stage of acceptance even for domestic projects.

Shapiro (1978; Chapter 17) reexamined the assumptions and conclusions of Stonehill and Nathanson (1968) but expanded the analysis to include more variables. In particular, he added the tax treatment of foreign-source income, the risk of expropriation, blocked funds, inflation and segmented capital markets. He agreed with Stonehill and Nathanson that all foreign risks should be incorporated as adjustments to cash flows rather than adjusting the discount rate.

Lessard (1985; Chapter 18) contributed an adjusted present-value approach to foreign project evaluation. The main difference between this approach and the traditional one lies in its separation of contractual and non-contractual cash flows. For example, the tax advantages of debt are treated separately and explicitly as is the effect of expropriation, exchange risk and other foreign complexities. The present value of each of these components can be determined separately, perhaps even with different discount rates to reflect varying risks, and then all the resulting present values are added together. The main advantage of this approach is its simplicity because it breaks up a complex simulation into more manageable pieces. Its main disadvantage is that a whole generation of managers has finally learned capital budgeting in the traditional manner, and it is difficult for them to simultaneously learn both the foreign complexities and a new approach to analysis.

During the 1980s, capital budgeting for foreign projects has attracted a respectable amount of scholarly attention compared to that of earlier years. Notable contributions have been made by Oblak and Helm (1980), Baker (1981), Gordon and Lees (1982), Kelly and Philippatos (182), Stanley and Block (1983) and Hodder (1986).

Fruitful Areas for Future Research

Since international financial management is a dynamic field of study, there will always be fertile new topics for research. The following research ideas are by no means all inclusive but instead are suggestive of lacunae in the literature.

- *Techniques to improve access to international capital markets.* As was discussed earlier, small and medium-size firms do not have access to the Eurobond or Euroequity markets. This may not be too harmful to firms resident in the industrialized countries with respectable domestic capital markets. However, such firms resident in developing countries with limited domestic capital markets are likely to be damaged. In addition, the Central and Eastern European countries are spawning an array of newly-privatized firms that have no access to international capital markets, but also virtually no domestic capital market. An important research question could be to analyse alternative techniques to enable such firms to have access to international capital markets.

With respect to firms resident in developing countries, research has already started. Lessard (1973), Errunza (1977) and Errunza and Rosenberg (1982) have made a strong case for including securities from developing country firms in an internationally diversified portfolio. Because developing country securities markets are not closely correlated with other securities markets, inclusion of shares of developing country firms can lower the risk of an internationally diversified portfolio for any given rate of return.

Despite the theoretical desirability of investing in securities of firms in developing countries, certain barriers have prevented most portfolio managers from implementing such a strategy. One barrier has been the lack of reliable and timely data. A second barrier has been the illiquid home market for such firms, thus making it difficult to transact sizeable investments at close to the existing market price. A third barrier has been perceived political risk. The "Emerging Markets Data Base", currently being published by the International Finance Corporation (a subsidiary of the World Bank), has done a great deal to remove the data barrier. And the emergence of "country funds" has helped to remove the small-size barrier. Country funds are an application of the technique of securitization which has been so successful at increasing liquidity in real estate mortgage markets. Political risk will probably remain a barrier unless some kind of international guarantee fund could be established. National guarantee funds such as the United States Overseas Private Investment Corporation, exist to protect the direct foreign investments of their home country firms. No parallel exists for international portfolio investment.

With respect to the newly-privatized Central and Eastern European firms, all three barriers still exist. Since their historical accounting systems are unique, and they have had no equity markets to provide securities data, it would be nearly impossible to add these countries to the "Emerging Markets Data Base". The possibility of their securitization into country funds exists, but some of the best firms have already been acquired by Western partners. Obviously, political risk is still a big barrier.

- *Immunization of portfolios to foreign exchange risk.* A second promising area for research is the immunization of internationally-diversified portfolios for foreign exchange risk. This would be analogous to the current practice of immunizing bond portfolios for interest rate risk. Eun and Resnick (1985) and (1988; Chapter 11) have made a good start on this line of inquiry. As mentioned earlier, they analysed this issue, using multi-currency diversification and forward contracts for hedging a portfolio. Other potential candidates are swaps, investment in real assets such as land and buildings, guaranteed investment contracts in foreign currencies, currency cocktail bonds, options, futures and other artificial or derivative instruments.

- *Applying agency theory to international financial management.* Agency theory, which is so popular in domestic finance literature, may appropriately be applied to international financial management topics. Lee and Kwok (1988; Chapter 14) have applied it to explain differences in the capital structure norms of firms located in different countries. Hodder (1986) has used it to analyse differences between capital budgeting practices of firms from the United States and Japan. Kester (1986) has done likewise for the same pair with respect to the cost of capital. Agency theory can be applied to a broader range of comparative international financial management topics and to a more diverse sample of countries.

- *Foreign exchange economic exposure management.* Although foreign exchange economic exposure has attracted a respectable amount of theoretical attention, as exemplified by four readings in the present volume, it is still not well understood by top management. In particular, strategic decisions, such as the location of production facilities, cross-border mergers and capital budgeting analyses of foreign projects, are often made without recognizing the consequences of economic exposure. A country's competitive position can change dramatically if its exchange rate is either overvalued or undervalued for a long period of time. This has an impact on all firms, foreign and domestic, operating in that country. An example of this occurred in the United States during the period 1981–85.

More applied research is needed to help firms anticipate and manage foreign exchange economic exposure. The kind of research which might be most useful should analyse how specific industries might be impacted by economic exposure and how they should react. This approach might capture the attention of top executives better than the more abstract theoretical research which has identified the problem.

Bibliography

Abuaf, Niso, "Foreign exchange options: the leading hedge", *Midland Corporate Finance Journal*, 5 (Summer 1987), pp. 51–58.
—— , "The nature and management of foreign exchange risk", *Midland Corporate Finance Journal*, 4 (Fall 1986), pp. 30–44.
Adler, Michael, "The cost of capital and valuation of a two-country firm", *Journal of Finance*, 29 (March 1974), pp. 119–132.
Adler, Michael, and Bernard Dumas, "Portfolio choice and the demand for forward exchange", *American Economic Review*, 66 (May 1975), pp. 332–339.
—— , "International portfolio choice and corporation finance: a synthesis", *Journal of Finance*, 38 (June 1983), pp. 925–984.
Aggarwal, Raj, "International differences in capital structure norms: an empirical study of large European countries", *Management International Review*, 21 (1981), pp. 75–88.
Agmon, Tamir, and Donald Lessard, "Investor recognition of corporate international diversification", *Journal of Finance*, 32 (September 1977), pp. 1049–1055.
Aliber, Robert Z., "The interest rate parity theorem: a reinterpretation", *Journal of Political Economy*, 81 (December 1973), pp. 1451–1459.
Aliber, R.Z., and C.P. Stickney, "Accounting measures of foreign exchange exposure: the long and short of it", *Accounting Review*, L (January 1975), pp. 44–57.
Babbel, David F., "Determining the optimum strategy for hedging currency exposure", *Journal of International Business Studies*, 14 (Spring/Summer 1983), pp. 133–139.
Baker, James C., "Capital budgeting in West European countries", *Issues in Financial Management*, 19 (1981), pp. 3–10.
Bilson, John F.O., "Rational expectations and the exchange rate", in Jacob A. Frenkel and Harry G. Johnson, eds., *The Economics of Exchange Rates* (Reading, Mass., Addison-Wesley, 1978), pp. 75–96.
Choi, Frederick D.S., Howard D. Lowe, and Reginald G. Worthley, "Accountors, accountants, and standard No. 8", *Journal of International Business Studies*, 9 (Fall 1978), pp. 81–87.
Cohn, Richard A., and John J. Pringle, "Imperfections in international financial markets: implications for risk premia and the cost of capital to firms", *Journal of Finance*, 28 (March 1973), pp. 59–66.
Collins, J. Markham, and William S. Sekely, "The relationship of headquarters, country, and industry classification to financial structure", *Financial Management*, 12 (Autumn 1983), pp. 45–51.
Dornbush, Rudiger, "Expectations and exchange rate dynamics", *Journal of Political Economy*, 84 (December 1976), pp. 1161–1176.
Dufey, Gunter, "Corporate finance and exchange rate variations", *Financial Management*, 1 (Summer 1972), pp. 51–57.
Dufey, Gunter, and Ian H. Giddy, "International financial planning: the use of market-based forecasts", *California Management Review*, 21 (Fall 1978), pp. 69–81.

——, "Innovation in the international financial markets", *Journal of International Business Studies*, 12 (Fall 1981), pp. 33–51.

Eaker, Mark R., "Denomination decision for multinational transactions", *Financial Management*, 9 (Autumn 1980), pp. 23–29.

Eiteman, David K., Arthur I. Stonehill and Michael H. Moffett, *Multinational Business Finance*, sixth edition (Reading, Mass., Addison-Wesley, 1992), pp. 493–494.

Errunza, Vihang, R., "Gains from portfolio diversification into less developed countries", *Journal of International Business Studies*, (Fall-Winter 1977), pp. 83–99.

Errunza, Vihang, R. and Barr Rosenberg, "Investment in developed and less developed countries", *Journal of Financial and Quantitative Analysis*, 17/5 (December 1982), pp. 741–762.

Errunza, Vihang R., and Lemma W. Senbet, "The effects of international operations on the market value of the firm: theory and evidence", *Journal of Finance*, 36 (May 1981), pp. 401–417.

Errunza, Vihang R., and Etienne Losq, "International asset pricing under mild segmentation: theory and test", *Journal of Finance*, 49 (March 1985), pp. 105–124.

Eun, Cheol S., and Bruce G. Resnick, "Currency factor in international portfolio diversification", *Financial Management*, 14 (Summer 1985), pp. 45–53.

——, "Exchange rate uncertainty, forward contracts, and international portfolio selection", *Journal of Finance*, 43 (March 1988), pp. 197–215.

Fama, Eugene F., "Forward rates as predictors of future spot rates", *Journal of Financial Economics*, 5 (October 1976), pp. 361–377.

Flood, Eugene, Jr., and Donald R. Lessard, "On the measurement of operating exposure to exchange rates: a conceptual approach", *Financial Management*, 15 (Spring 1986), pp. 25–36.

Folks, William R., Jr., "Decision analysis for exchange risk management", *Financial Management*, 1 (Winter 1972), pp. 101–112.

Folks, William R., and Stanley R. Stansell, "The use of discriminant analysis in forecasting exchange risk movements", *Journal of International Business Studies*, 6 (Spring 1975), pp. 33–50.

Garman, Mark B., and Steven W. Kohlhagen, "Foreign currency option values", *Journal of International Money and Finance*, 2 (December 1983), pp. 231–237.

George, Abraham M., "Cash flow versus accounting exposures to currency risk", *California Management Review*, 20 (Summer 1978), pp. 50–55.

Germany, J. David, and John E. Morton, "Financial innovation and deregulation in foreign industrial countries", *Federal Reserve Bulletin*, 71 (October 1985), pp. 743–753.

Giddy, Ian H., "An integrated theory of exchange rate equilibrium", *Journal of Financial and Quantitative Analysis*, 11 (December 1976), pp. 863–892.

——, "Why it doesn't pay to make a habit of forward hedging", *Euromoney* (December 1976), pp. 96–100.

——, "Exchange risk: whose view?", *Financial Management*, 6 (Summer 1977), pp. 23–33.

Giddy, Ian H., and Gunter Dufey, "The random behavior of flexible exchange rates: implications for forecasting", *Journal of International Business Studies*, 6 (Spring 1975), pp. 1–32.

Gordon, Sara L., and Francis A. Lees, "Multinational capital budgeting: foreign investment under subsidy", *California Management Review*, 25 (Fall 1982), pp. 22–32.

Grauer, Frederick A., Robert A. Litzenberger, and Richard E. Stehle, "Sharing rules and equilibrium in an international capital market under uncertainty", *Journal of Financial Economics*, 5 (June 1976), pp. 233–256.

Grubel, Herbert G., "Internationally diversified portfolios: welfare gains and capital flows", *American Economic Review*, 58 (December 1968), pp. 1299–1314.

Grubel, Herbert G., and Kenneth Fadner, "The interdependence of international equity markets", *Journal of Finance*, 26 (March 1971), pp. 89–94.

Hekman, Christine R., "Don't blame currency values for strategic errors", *Midland Corporate Financial Journal*, 4 (Fall 1986), pp. 45–55.

Hodder, James E., "Evaluation of manufacturing investments: a comparison of U.S. and Japanese practices", *Financial Management*, 15 (Spring 1986), pp. 17–24.

Hughes, John S., Dennis E. Logue, and Richard J. Sweeney, "Corporate international diversification and market assigned measures of risk and diversification", *Journal of Financial and Quantitative Analysis*, 10 (November 1975), pp. 627–637.

Ibbotson, Roger C., Richard C. Carr, and Anthony W. Robinson, "International equity and bond returns", *Financial Analysts Journal*, 38 (July–August 1982), pp. 61–83.

Jacque, Laurent L., "Management of foreign exchange risk: a review article", *Journal of International Business Studies*, 12 (Spring/Summer 1981), pp. 81–101.

Jacquillat, Bertrand, and Bruno H. Solnik, "Multinationals are poor tools for diversification", *Journal of Portfolio Management*, (Winter 1978), pp. 8–12.

Jurgensen Report, *Report of the Working Group on Exchange Market Intervention*, Washington, D.C.: U.S. Treasury, 1983.

Kelly, Marie E. Wicks, and George C. Philippatos, "Comparative analysis of the foreign investment evaluation practices by US-based manufacturing multinational companies", *Journal of International Business Studies*, 13 (Winter 1982), pp. 19–42.

Kester, W. Carl, "Capital and ownership structure: A comparison of United States and Japanese manufacturing corporations", *Financial Management*, 15 (Spring 1986), pp. 5–16.

Khoury, Sarkis J., and K. Hung Chan, "Hedging foreign exchange risk: selecting the optimal tool", *Midland Corporate Finance Journal*, 1 (Winter 1988), pp. 40–52.

Kohlhagen, Steven W., "Forward rates as predictors of future spot rates", *Journal of International Business Studies*, 6 (Fall 1975), pp. 33–39.

——— , "A model of optimal foreign exchange hedging without exchange rate projections", *Journal of International Business Studies*, 9 (Fall 1978), pp. 9–19.

Lee, Kwang Chul, and Chuck C.Y. Kwok, "Multinational corporations vs. domestic corporations: international environmental factors and determinants of capital structure", *Journal of International Business Studies*, 19 (Summer 1988), pp. 195–217.

Lee, Wayne Y., and Kanwal S. Sachdeva, "The role of the multinational firm in the integration of segmented markets", *Journal of Finance*, 32 (May 1977), pp. 479–492.

Lessard, Donald R. "International portfolio diversification: A multivariate analysis for a group of latin american countries", *Journal of Finance*, 28 (June 1973), pp. 619–633.

——— , "World, national, and industry factors in equity returns", *Journal of Finance*, 29 (May 1974), pp. 379–391.

——— , "Evaluating international projects: an adjusted present value approach", in Donald R. Lessard, ed., *International Financial Management: Theory and Application* (New York, Wiley, 1985), pp. 570–584.

——— , "Finance and global competition: exploiting financial scope and coping with volatile exchange rates", *Midland Corporate Finance Journal*, 4 (Fall 1986), pp. 6–29.

Levich, Richard M., "Tests of forecasting models and market efficiency in the international money market", in Jacob A. Frenkel and Harry G. Johnson, eds., *The Economics of Exchange Rates* (Reading, Mass., Addison-Wesley, 1978), pp. 129–158.

——— , "Analyzing the accuracy of foreign exchange forecasting services: theory and evidence", in Clas Wihlborg and Richard Levich, eds., *Exchange Risk and Exposure: Current Developments in International Financial Development* (Lexington, Mass., Heath, 1980), pp. 99–127.

Levy, Haim, and Marshall Sarnat, "International diversification of investment portfolios", *American Economic Review*, LX (September 1970), pp. 668–675.

Logue, Dennis E., and George S. Oldfield, "Managing foreign assets when foreign exchange markets are efficient", *Financial Management*, 6 (Summer 1977), pp. 16–22.

Modigliani, Franco and Merton Miller, "The cost of capital, corporation finance and the theory of investment", *American Economic Review*, XLVIII (June 1958), pp. 261–297.

Oblak, David J., and Roy J. Helm, Jr., "Survey and analysis of capital budgeting methods used by multinationals", *Financial Management*, 9 (Winter 1980), pp. 37–41.

Remmers, Lee, Arthur Stonehill, Richard Wright, and Theo Beekhuisen, "Industry and size as debt ratio determinants for manufacturing internationally", *Financial Management*, 3 (Summer 1974), pp. 24–32.

Robichek, Alexander A., and Mark R. Eaker, "Debt denomination and exchange risk in international capital markets", *Financial Management*, 5 (Autumn 1976), pp. 11–18.

Rodriguez, Rita M., "Corporate exchange risk management: theme and aberrations", *Journal of Finance*, 36 (May 1981), pp. 427–439.

Rutterford, Janette, "An international perspective on the capital structure puzzle", *Midland Corporate Finance Journal*, 3 (Fall 1985), pp. 60–72.

Sarathy, Ravi, and Sangit Chatterjee, "The divergence of Japanese and U.S. corporate financial structure", *Journal of International Business Studies*, 15 (Winter 1984), pp. 75–89.

Sekely, William S., and J. Markham Collins, "Cultural influences on international capital structure", *Journal of International Business Studies*, 19 (Spring 1988), pp. 87–100.

Shapiro, Alan C., "Exchange rate changes, inflation, and the value of the multinational corporation", *Journal of Finance*, 30 (May 1975), pp. 485–501.

——— , "Capital budgeting for the multinational corporation", *Financial Management*, 7 (Spring 1978), pp. 7–16.

——— , "Financial structure and cost of capital in the multinational corporation", *Journal of Financial and Quantitative Analysis*, 13 (June 1978), pp. 211–226.

Shapiro, Alan C., and David P. Rutenberg, "When to hedge against devaluation", *Management Science*, 20 (August 1974), pp. 1514–1530.

——— , "Managing exchange risks in a floating world", *Financial Management*, 5 (Summer 1976), pp. 48–58.

Solnik, Bruno H., "Note on the validity of the random walk for European stock market capital structure", *Journal of Finance*, 28 (December 1973), pp. 1151–1159.

——— , "The international pricing of risk: an empirical investigation of the world capital market structure", *Journal of Finance*, 29 (May 1974), pp. 365–378.

——— , "Testing international asset pricing: some pessimistic views", *Journal of*

Finance, 32 (May 1977), pp. 503–512.

Stanley, Marjorie T., "Capital structure and cost of capital for the multinational firm", *Journal of International Business Studies,* 12 (Spring/Summer 1981), pp. 103–120.

Stanley, Marjorie and Stanley Block, "An empirical study of management and financial variables in influencing capital budgeting decisions for multinational corporations in the 1980s", *Management International Review* 23 (1983), pp. 61–71.

Stapleton, Richard C., and Marti Subrahmanyam, "Market imperfections, capital market equilibrium, and corporation finance", *Journal of Finance,* 32 (May 1977), pp. 307–319.

Stehle, Richard F., "An empirical test of the alternative hypothesis of national and international pricing of risk assets", *Journal of Finance,* 32 (May 1977), pp. 493–502.

Stonehill, Arthur, and Leonard Nathanson, "Capital budgeting and the multinational corporation", *California Management Review,* 11 (Summer 1968), pp. 39–54.

Stonehill, Arthur, and Thomas Stitzel, "Financial structure and multinational corporations", *California Management Review,* 12 (Fall 1969), pp. 91–96.

Stonehill, Arthur, Theo Beekhuisen, Richard Wright, Lee Remmers, Norman Toy, Antonio Parés, Alan Shapiro, Douglas Egan, and Thomas Bates, "Financial goals and debt ratio determinants: a survey of practice in five countries", *Financial Management,* 4 (Autumn 1975), pp. 27–41.

Toy, Norman, Arthur Stonehill, Lee Remmers, Richard Wright, and Theo Beekhuisen, "A comparative international study of growth, profitability and risk as determinants of corporate debt ratios in the manufacturing sector", *Journal of Financial and Quantitative Analysis,* 9 (November 1974), pp. 875–886.

UNCTC, *World Investment Report 1991: The Triad in Foreign Direct Investment* (New York, United Nations, 1991).

Turnbull, Stuart M., "Swaps: a zero sum game?", *Financial Management,* 16 (Spring 1987), pp. 15–21.

Transnational Corporations and Management Division, *World Investment Report 1992: Transnational Corporations as Engines of Growth* (New York, United Nations, 1992).

Wheelwright, Steve, "Applying decision theory to improve corporate management of currency-exchange risks", *California Management Review,* 17 (Summer 1975), pp. 41–49.

Wright, Richard, and Sadahiko Suzuki, "Financial structure and bankruptcy risk in Japanese companies", *Journal of International Business Studies,* 16 (Spring 1985), pp. 97–110.

PART ONE: Foreign Exchange Management

Corporate Finance and Exchange Rate Variations*

Gunter Dufey

*Source: *Financial Management*, 1 (Summer 1972), pp. 51–57.

In 1962 a U.S.-based automobile manufacturing company which already had extensive foreign operations began to expand and restructure its subsidiaries in the European Economic Community (EEC). The corporation decided to concentrate most of its engine production in a new plant in Strasbourg, France. This location was chosen because of shipping economies and in response to considerable inducements offered by the French government to export-oriented industries willing to settle in that part of the country. The company had no other facilities in France; however, it owned very large manufacturing operations in Germany and smaller ones in Belgium where vehicles were assembled. The entire output of the French subsidiary was sold to these two plants. The automobiles were then marketed throughout the Common Market and beyond, although the market share of the company in France was negligible.

After the political turmoil in France during May 1968, financial managers at corporate headquarters became increasingly concerned about the weakness of the French franc. As a result, the French subsidiary was ordered to keep working balances to an absolute minimum. By early 1969, the outlook for the French franc had not improved. The new government had steadfastly refused to devalue. Instead, it had put stringent restrictions on the transfer of francs out of the country; but the threat of devaluation was still present. Faced with the probability of a 10% to 20% devaluation of the franc, financial planners viewed with concern the possibility that consolidated earnings of the corporation might be reduced thereby by $2 million to $8 million for 1969. Therefore, various "hedging" alternatives were prepared for the top corporate finance committee to consider. All of these proposals involved substantial cost.

A member of the corporate finance committee was contemplating these alternatives when a recent visit to Strasbourg came to his mind. There, the resident general manager had argued for expansion plans on the grounds that a devaluation of the franc in the region of 10% would boost returns on his operations by over 25%.

At this point, the committee member began to wonder whether there might not be some basic inconsistencies in his company's international finance policy.

"Contradictions" in Financial Policies

Similar situations have troubled financial executives of international corporations for a long time. The basic problem is that a single economic event, in this case a devaluation, is expected to have two opposing effects. In the aforementioned situation, for example, management worries that the subsidiary will show a loss, which calls for costly defensive tactics; at the same time, increased expected profitability calls for greater investment.

Although some of the circumstances surrounding this case make it an extreme example, the problem of appropriate financial policies arises, in one form or another, whenever a company has operations in more than one country and the rate of exchange between their currencies is expected to change. The extent to which corporate assets are subject to these problems has been well documented in studies of the dimensions and growth patterns of multinational investment; the magnitude of this problem needs no further comment [2].

Likewise, exchange rate changes in the postwar years have been frequent and their magnitude sometimes very large. The outlook for the international monetary system is increased frequency—if not magnitude— of situations such as the one presented here.

This article attempts to provide a clear analysis of the apparent contradictions in the financial policy of many corporations with respect to exchange rate changes. Specifically, it will first consider the effect of a devaluation on a subsidiary in terms of the cash flow. Then the policies based on the use of current accounting procedures will be retraced, and an attempt will be made to isolate the core of the issue. Finally, suggestions of appropriate financial policies will be made.

Rate Changes Alter Profitability

The problem faced by the finance committee in the illustration serves as a convenient starting point for considering the basic question, "What really happens to the subsidiary when the country in which it operates devalues its currency?" Obviously, change in the profitability of this subsidiary, and therefore in its value to the parent, will depend substantially on the effect of the devaluation on the subsidiary's future revenues and costs. It is of course necessary to draw a clear distinction between cash flows in terms of local currency (LC) and the currency in which the company calculates its results, here the U.S. dollar. To simplify matters, the following analysis disregards the possibility of exchange controls; however, they can be included by giving consideration to (a) time value of the delayed cash flows in the unit of final account and (b) the return on unremittable local funds.

A fundamental point is that local currency revenue and cost streams will *not* follow the pattern projected before the devaluation. In fact, after the devaluation these LC flows will exhibit differences that are systematic and predictable as to direction. Therefore, a uniform, indiscriminate application of the devaluation percentage to the projected predevaluation flow gives an inaccurate picture.

Devaluation should improve the LC revenues that result from a firm's export sales. The firm may either maintain its product prices in terms of foreign currency, thereby increasing its LC receipts by the devaluation percentage, or it may lower the foreign currency price and presumably increase its sales volume. It is true that the firm's revenues may not receive the full benefit of the devaluation because of increased competition from other exporters, but situations in which LC revenues do not benefit to some extent from export sales will be rare. Similarly, firms producing goods that compete with imports in the domestic market should normally see an improvement in revenues, since the devaluation adversely affects foreign competition.

If a firm is producing goods for a sector of the domestic market where import competition is not a factor, LC revenues will suffer because demand is weakened by falling real income attributable to more costly imports and the rise of domestic cost of exports benefiting from devaluation. In addition, austerity measures likely to accompany the devaluation will have the greatest effect on such a firm. It can be argued that the devaluation will have an expansionary effect on the economy of the devaluing country. However, this will cause an increase in real income only if there are readily employable resources available. If this condition does not exist, such expansionary effects will only result in further price increases which will, in turn, call for even harsher austerity measures by government. Otherwise, the benefits of the devaluation will be lost very quickly and the state of the economy will soon require another devaluation. In either case, firms producing for the domestic market will bear the brunt of the effects of a devaluation in terms of the subsequent relative decrease in income for domestic consumption and investment.

In any event, the devaluation will cause a rise in the LC cost of inputs for most firms. Obviously, those companies whose expenses include a high proportion of imported materials will be hardest hit. The price of imported inputs can increase by any percentage up to the full amount of the devaluation rate, although normally it will be somewhat less, the final level depending on competition. Even firms using primarily domestic inputs will experience a rise in costs, because the expanding export- and import-competing companies will tend to require increasing amounts of labor, material, and capital. Of course, the extent of the rise in cost of local inputs will largely depend on the employment situation before the devaluation, the effectiveness of the government's austerity program, and the speed with which productive resources can be shifted to different types of production. This analysis is obviously a simplified version of what is known in international economics as the "adjustment process" applied to the individual firm.

No two firms will be affected in exactly the same way by developments in the post-devaluation economy. Some may be better off as a result of the devaluation and some will fare worse; while for a few, the net change will be negligible. Note, however, that up to this point the analysis has been strictly in terms of LC units.

Any final effect of a devaluation on the profits received by the parent company can be computed only *after* the expected LC revenue and expense streams have been adjusted. The effect is determined by applying the new exchange rate to the predicted net LC profit. After translating the adjusted net LC cash flows into dollars, the final devaluation gain or loss can be determined. The result will depend on whether the loss arising from the new rate exceeds, equals, or is less than the change in the net LC cash flow. Thus the outlook for some subsidiaries will actually improve after a devaluation, for some it will deteriorate,while for others the net changes will be close to zero.

The Effects of Current Accounting Practices

A quick survey of corporate practices suggests that current financial policies of international corporations are *not* based on the incremental profit analysis which has just been outlined. Although their stated objective is the same, namely, to counter any negative effects of a devaluation, there is, nevertheless, a fundamental difference in the underlying concept of the loss due to exchange rate changes. A number of articles and research studies have described the reactions of corporations to changes in exchange rates [10, 1, 4].

The loss with which financial management is currently concerned is perceived as the potential reduction in reported earnings caused by the restatement, or translation, of the LC accounts of a subsidiary into dollar equivalents at a "new" exchange rate. Translation of subsidiary accounts is largely a consequence of (a) centralized management, and (b) the need to publish consolidated statements. While it is conceivable that corporate management could be educated to think simultaneously in 10 or 20 currencies, a company cannot expect its present and prospective share-holders, creditors, and governments to have the same ability. In fact, internal revenue authorities and public supervisory bodies, such as the Securities and Exchange Commission (SEC) in the United States, require that foreign subsidiary accounts be translated into domestic currency equivalents.

As a consequence, many companies with foreign operations make use of the concept of "exposure" as a basis for their international financial policies. Exposure is defined as the net LC asset base, the dollar value of which would shrink when restated at the postdevaluation exchange rate.

Two factors determine the magnitude of exposure: one is the amount of the LC accounts; the other is the method of translation. The first can obviously be controlled by the firm to a certain extent at least, and is therefore a policy variable. The second factor is presumably fixed for the individual firm by prevailing accounting principles [3].

The following is a schematic, and greatly simplified, summary of translation principles, in which C denotes the use of the current (postdevaluation) rate, and H the historical rate of exchange.

Cash (LC)	C
Marketable securities (LC)	C
Receivables (LC)	C
Inventories	C/H
Fixed assets	H
Current liabilities (LC)	C
Long-term liabilities (LC)	C/H
Capital stock	H
Preferred stock	H
Retained earnings	(residual)

Although these simplified rules may be modified in a few well-defined cases, such as long-term liabilities and receivables, the only item where accounting principles allow a choice in accord with economic realities is the

Exhibit 1.1 Projected balance sheet of subsidiary X or Y for December 31, 1969

	LCs	4LCs=$1	5LCs=$1		LCs	4LCs=$1	5LCs=$1
LC financial assets	160	$40	$32	LC liabilities	60	$15	$12
Inventory	20	5	5	Capital stock	280	70	70
Fixed assets (net)	200	50	50	Retained earnings	40	10	5
Total	380	$95	$87	Total	380	$95	$87

valuation of inventories. For example, when the local selling price of inventories is expected to rise in proportion to the devaluation, the use of the historical rate of exchange is deemed proper [3, pp. 16–25]. Exhibit 1.1. illustrates the effect of these translation principles on projected balance sheets of a foreign subsidiary, first under the assumption of no change—i.e., an exchange rate of 4 LCs = $1—and then assuming alternatively a devaluation of the foreign currency to 5 LCs = $1.

This example also serves to illustrate the exposure concept:

Financial assets	LC 160	
LC liabilities	60	
Exposure	LC 100	
Predevaluation rate	LC 100	= $25
Postdevaluation rate	LC 100	= 20
Potential foreign exchange loss		$ 5

The policies which are based on this concept can be divided into two groups. One comprises all those measures by which any positive exposure is reduced, such as decreasing LC monetary assets and/or increasing LC denominated liabilities. The other is hedging the remaining exposure through forward operations in the currency involved. In this case, for example, the company would sell LC 100 in the forward exchange market for a fixed price in terms of dollars. The cost of this transaction is given by the discount prevailing in the forward exchange market, e.g., $1 = 4.1 LCs. The difference between the current rate and the forward rate of .1 LCs can be expressed as an annual percentage rate.

Unfortunately, current accounting practices with respect to international operations are too rigid to make the conventional exposure concept very meaningful. Two examples, admittedly extreme, illustrate this point. One assumes that Subsidiary X is an assembly operation where imported parts comprise the bulk of the operating costs, while the output is sold exclusively in the domestic market of the host country. It is readily imaginable that the devaluation may so completely alter the revenue–cost relationship that the total operation becomes unprofitable, the loss far exceeding that shown when traditional translation methods are applied. The issue becomes even more obvious if it is assumed instead that Subsidiary Y, which has the *same* balance sheet, obtains a large portion of its labor and materials from sources within the country and sells in export markets. Obviously, the profitability of the subsidiary increases because of the devaluation, and there is no economic justification for the translation loss shown.

Whenever a method of measuring provides the same answer to situations which are, in effect, entirely different, it must be judged deficient as a basis for financial decision making. Where, then, are the roots of this deficiency?

Going Concern vs. Exposed Assets

Part of the problem with current accounting methods and resulting financial practices is that they are based on concepts developed to deal with the simple export-import transaction with its inherent focus on exposed receivables. Under this concept, a given export transaction results in a foreign currency receivable; the value of this asset decreases by a devaluation percentage. The same considerations apply to foreign currency loans, where repayment of principal and interest is reduced as a result of a devaluation and so, therefore, is the value of the underlying asset. To illustrate, an investment in British consols carrying a 10% coupon yields only 8% if affected by a 20% devaluation of the pound sterling.

In contrast, if an equity investment in a British enterprise is considered, devaluation loss is not automatically equal to the devaluation percentage. If this devaluation leads to an increase in the rate of return, measured in sterling, which is more than the devaluation percentage, the equity will have a higher value in terms of dollars after the devaluation of the pound.

One argument, which is based on a piecemeal approach, is erroneous; this is that certain portions of the "bundle of assets," which constitute the subsidiary, always suffer a loss in value because of the devaluation. Viewing the subsidiary realistically as an ongoing concern, one would expect that a certain minimum amount of LC cash, receivables, and other financial assets are as necessary for continuing profitable operations as the brick and mortar for its building. Therefore, it seems illogical to act as if certain parts of that bundle of assets, the subsidiary, were subject to the full devaluation loss, while other equally necessary parts are treated as automatically "self hedging." It is better to say that the change in the value of the total subsidiary must equal the sum of all changes in value of individual assets and liabilities.

This points up one truth: a loss occurs on those LC assets in excess of the minimum assets necessary for the level of operation at the time of the devaluation. Apart from those, however, the value of individual assets and liabilities will be altered only to the extent that their relative contribution to the profitability of the subsidiary changes.

Special Circumstances

Before reform of the current practices can be promoted, it must be, recognized that several factors tend to favor them. One is again related to accounting treatment. Foreign exchange losses on translation are very conspicuous in published financial statements. However, incremental costs of forward currency operations, increased interest payments on LC liabilities, and the reduction of LC monetary assets below levels necessary for continuing profitable operations are all buried somewhere in the income statement. As a result, there is an incentive to pursue the "safe" path to eliminate accounting exposure, even if it is based only on conventions inadequate for financial policy making.

A corollary is that the treasury function in many corporations developed into a profit center after the early fifties when financial managers found that aggressive fund management can yield considerable returns. Operations in foreign currency markets now provide a welcome additional opportunity to make money at the treasury. This type of operation has an added advantage: if the expectations of financial management do not materialize, the cost of these operations—high interest rates on LC borrowings and excessive discounts on foreign exchange contracts—can always be justified under the label "insurance for foreign asset protection." Thus, risk aversion, in the form of eliminating accounting exposure, and aggressive fund management can be realized simultaneously.

Another quirk must be mentioned in connection with this kind of operation. In general, present U.S. taxation practices do not allow for the deduction of translation losses in foreign operations. However, hedging profits are normally subject to the full corporate income tax rate unless the firm is able to take very special steps to present them as capital gains. In most cases, foreign exchange gains are treated as current income. Therefore, in order to compensate for a given translation loss—assuming a tax rate of 50% on current income—a company would have to hedge twice the amount of exposure in order to compensate fully for the translation loss [7].

These considerations make it clear that current accounting practices are deficient because they deter the firm from maximizing profits. They have also been criticized on other grounds. Given the large-scale operations of multinational companies, the financial flows caused by present practices can be enormous. It is sometimes said that "nowadays an international monetary crisis occurs when three large multinational corporations decide to shift around their working capital." Some evidence suggests that some very large corporations, strictly as a matter of public policy, avoid aggressive international fund management because it might possibly disturb the international payment situation of their host countries [9]. Be that as it may, if these fund flows occur for the wrong reasons, they are doubly damaging, both for the firm and the countries involved.

There is an additional point; one might wonder how often corporations pass up profitable investments in countries with unstable monetary situations just because management is worried about embarrassing write-offs caused by devaluations [6]. Certainly, unstable monetary conditions may reduce the attractiveness of an investment for other reasons, but translation losses that do not adequately reflect the change in profitability of operations are surely an unnecessary deterrent. The countries which are deprived of investments are usually underdeveloped countries—those which most need a boost in economic growth.

Towards Better Financial Policies

Mere negative criticism serves little purpose. Here, then, is an outline of what seems a preferable way to deal with the problem of changing exchange rates.

First, corporations should attempt to persuade accountants to take a more realistic approach to a revaluation of assets and liabilities after changes in exchange rates. There are indications that the accounting profession is not at all happy with present practices. The American Institute of Certified Public Accountants (AICPA) is now engaged in a wide-ranging study, the object of which is the reformation of current accounting methods for foreign operations. In the meantime, a survey of corporate reports shows that corporate managements and their public accountants have recently become somewhat more realistic, particularly with respect to the treatment of inventories. As an interim measure we might well consider the possibility of setting up a special reserve account for foreign exchange losses, a measure which occasionally seems acceptable to accounting firms. The consolidated accounts of International Telephone and Telegraph (ITT) provide a good example of this method. However, the device of an exchange reserve does not really solve the basic problem, which is the realistic valuation of assets and liabilities; this should reflect the changes in economic value occasioned by exchange rate exchanges.

Second, corporate financial management must take a stand on whether it should attempt to educate the board, shareholders, and security analysts about the real effects of a devaluation or revaluation. In essence, the problem can be stated as one of "education versus cosmetics."

Third, exchange rate changes must become integrated with all facets of decision making by the corporation; it is not enough simply to limit such considerations to working-capital policy. All variations in exchange rates can be translated into a change in the real rate of return on assets and a change in the real rate of interest cost on the liabilities of foreign operations. This fact is the guide to the direction in which appropriate policies should be developed. Obviously, virtually all such measures must be taken in anticipation of exchange rate changes as asset prices and interest rates may quickly adjust to new currency rates. There is, inevitably, a large degree of uncertainty involved, but this holds true for all business decisions.

Some of the specific considerations in developing appropriate financial policies are:

1. Prediction and forecasting of devaluations and revaluations are as important as ever. Forecasting of exchange rate changes must become integral to the function of the management of an international corporation, just as forecasting of interest rates, prices, wages, and political developments is the responsibility of management.

2. Working-capital management takes on increased importance. It has always been an essential task of financial management to keep the level of liquid assets such as cash, marketable securities, receivables, and similar items at just the level necessary for ongoing profitable operations. When there is a possibility of devaluation or revaluation, however, so-called excess liquid assets are truly exposed. Excess assets are those that should have been transferred to the parent company but for some reason or another have not.

3. The prospects for devaluations and revaluations must be taken into account in the initial foreign investment decision. Unfortunately, most firms seem to leave it at that. However, investment decisions are not one-shot deals; they must be seen as a continuous process. The firm continually decides whether to expand or curtail part of its assets or shift operations from one country to another. The possibility of monetary changes must become an intrinsic part of these decisions since, as was illustrated in the beginning of this article, exchange rate changes affect the real rate of return. In this sense asset management includes the whole package of pricing decisions, product policy decisions, and exporting and importing decisions.

4. Last but not least, the possibility of exchange rate changes directly affects the financing decision because devaluations and revaluations influence the real cost of funds. With this in mind, hedging decisions take on a new meaning. They must be clearly seen as alternatives to borrowing and lending in every way, including timing. For example, deciding on the length of a foreign exchange contract is the same as deciding whether to borrow short or long.

For illustrative purposes, this article has focused almost exclusively on the problems posed by the devaluation of foreign currencies under the "rules of the game" inherent in a past international monetary system. The basic problem will remain the major concern of financial management of international corporations. For the future, however, it will become necessary to recognize significant variations in the way the international monetary system operates. One aspect, which is of particular importance for international corporations based in the United States, is the revaluation of some major foreign currencies. The other innovation, already manifested, involves the way in which devaluations and revaluations will occur. Instead of occasional substantial changes of exchange rates, there may be increasingly frequent, but smaller, adjustments. Because of these conditions, the analysis that has been presented here is all the more important. Only those adjustments that account for the direction and frequency of change are required; the basic methods of analysis remain the same.

References

1. William L. Furlong, "Minimizing Foreign Exchange Losses," *Accounting Review* (April 1966), pp. 244–252.
2. Rainer Hellman, *The Challenge to U.S. Dominance of the International Corporation*, New York, Dunellen, 1970.
3. Samuel R. Hepworth, *Reporting Foreign Operations*, Michigan Business Studies, XII, no. 5, Ann Arbor, Michigan, Bureau of Business Research, Graduate School of Business Administration, University of Michigan, 1966.
4. Christopher M. Korth, "Survival Despite Devaluation," *Business Horizons* (April 1971), pp. 47–52.
5. Bernard A. Lietaer, "Managing Risks in Foreign Exchange," *Harvard Business Review* (March–April 1970), pp. 127–138.
6. D.R. Mandich, "Devaluation, Revaluation—Re-Evaluation?" *Management Accounting* (August 1970), pp. 27–29.
7. D.R. Ravenscroft, "Taxation of Incomes Arising from Changes in Value of Foreign Currency," *Harvard Law Review* (February 1969), pp. 772–797.
8. Robert B. Shulman, "Corporate Treatment of Exchange Risk," *Journal of International Business Studies* (Summer 1970), pp. 83–88.
9. Robert Stobaugh, Jr., "Financing Foreign Subsidiaries," *Journal of International Business Studies* (Summer 1970), pp. 43–64.
10. H.W. Allen Sweeney, "Protective Measures Against Devaluation," *Financial Executive* (January 1968), pp. 28–37.

The Random Behavior of Flexible Exchange Rates: Implications for Forecasting*

Ian H. Giddy and Gunter Dufey

*Source: *Journal of International Business Studies*, 6 (Spring 1975), pp. 1–32.

This article explores the forecasting accuracy of the "random walk" and other models of exchange rate behavior. Under present conditions of floating exchange rates, it is argued, anticipations of *future* demand and supply determine fluctuations in exchange rates. The authors present results consistent with the notion that, for the world's major currencies, the foreign exchange market is an "efficient market" and exchange rate forecasting is not profitable.

Introduction

Prediction and predictive models

Predicting exchange rates has been a favorite occupation of foreign exchange traders, business executives, and economists as long as different currencies have been in existence. Current practices rely on exchange rate forecasts as significant inputs into decisions concerning practically every aspect of international business. And speculation based on exchange rate forecasts provides the opportunity to make sizeable profits—provided, of course, that the speculator's forecasts are right more often than they are wrong.

It is hardly surprising, therefore, that a variety of exchange rate forecasting techniques is now available—some, naturally, at a price. The violent gyrations of the foreign exchange markets during the past three or four years, combined with the rapid internationalization of business activities, has resulted in a dramatic rise in interest in such methods. An institutional manifestation of this interest is the growth in the number of service organizations which sell advice on the future course of exchange rates to anyone willing and able to pay the fees (which usually are not inconsiderable). These groups range from well-established publishers of periodic currency reviews to new departments created by the most prestigious names in international banking, and they include a number of more or less experienced economic consulting firms who offer their wares in response to an apparent gap in the market for advice. Another institutional result of this interest is the International Money Market in Chicago, where private individuals of reasonable means now can buy and sell standardized future contracts in major currencies. Formerly, pressure from the Federal Reserve Board and occasional operational problems effectively prevented U.S. banks from accommodating individuals who wished to "take a view" on the future of a currency. These developments, plus the string of spectacular losses incurred by the foreign exchange trading operations of major banks which came to light during 1974, in combination with the fundamental changes in the international monetary environment that have occurred since the late 1960s, revive interest in the possibility of successfully predicting exchange rates.

In general, forecasting economic data requires the presumption of a set of relationships among variables, one of which is the variable to be forecast.[1] Economic forecasting, in other words, requires a model. Such a model may be in unspecified form in the back of the mind of a person who has been a long-term observer of the processes which generate these data. In many forecasting methods the relationships comprising the model are stated in explicit mathematical terms, as in the case of econometric models. Forecasting techniques based on formal models may rely on an assumed sequence of causal relationships (e.g., simulation models), or on the data-based development of statistical relationships between the variable of interest and past values of the same series (intrinsic models) and/or past values of various exogenous variables (extrinsic models).

The widespread availability of computer facilities, permitting huge amounts of data to be manipulated, has fostered the proliferation of statistical forecasting techniques. Exogenous models of this type usually endeavor to employ accepted economic relationships in developing a model which is then refined through statistical analysis of historical data. Typical of these models in the case of exchange rate forecasting is one that has been described by Gray.[2] The model attempts to predict changes in exchange rates by means of a two step isolation of factors. First, exchange rates are defined as the product of trade flows between countries. Second, changes in trade flows are defined to be the product of relative movements of the industrial production index and consumer price indices of the countries involved. The author also notes that "the critical question is not how many of the factors (active) in the foreign exchange market does this model incorporate?" but rather "how accurate a predictor of foreign exchange rates is the model?"

Intrinsic forecasting models, relying only on the past sequence of the same series, are less widely employed for obvious reasons. Nevertheless, recent developments in time series theory have led to the frequent use of methods which forecast by fitting some functional relation to the historical values of the series and extrapolating them into the future. "Trading rules," in stock market parlance, confirm to this class of techniques; several such techniques designed for exchange rate forecasting are now being marketed.

The international monetary environment and exchange rate forecasts

One feature common to both explanatory and causal and extrinsic and intrinsic statistical models is that their predictive ability depends crucially on the assumption that relationships established in the past will continue reasonably unchanged into the future. It makes little difference whether the nature of this relationship is specified in terms of a logical-theoretical framework or as a statistical dependence of some sort. The stability of the forecasting model, however, is not the only condition necessary for profitable forecasting. A more fundamental condition is that the actions of other forecasters do not wipe out any possible profit from successful prediction. Although this condition held under the Bretton Woods system, it is most unlikely that it holds under the present system of floating exchange rates.

The international monetary environment in which exchange rate forecasts are made has passed through several transitions. The environment in which most observers of foreign exchange markets grew up can be characterized by the feature that national monetary authorities pledged to maintain exchange rates within small margins around a target rate, called the "par value," in the form of an agreement within the International Monetary Funds. This par value could be changed whenever the balance of payments of a country moved into disequilibrium and when it became clear that various alternative policies such as internal deflation and/or controls were ineffective and/or politically not feasible. The disequilibrium condition was then defined as being of a "fundamental" nature which, according to the IMF articles, exempted a country from its obligation to defend the par value. In a process of negotiation with its trading partners, which was usually informal, the country then devalued or revalued its currency and declared a new par value.

Forecasting procedures developed in this environment consisted essentially of a three step procedure. First, from an examination of the balance of payments and other trends one derived the pressure on a currency. Second, the level of central bank foreign exchange reserves (including borrowing facilities) gave an indication of the point in time when a situation became critical. Then came the crucial step of predicting which one of the rather limited policy options economic-decision makers of a nation would resort to in a crisis: increased attempts at internal deflation, interventionism and exchange controls, or devaluation. Clearly, the success or failure of the forecasting process depended on step three, and there was no doubt that some participants did very well. Some corporations and banks, for example, spent considerable resources on analyzing both the power structure and the economic ideology of key decision makers in various countries in order to succeed in step three.[3]

Steps one and two were not terribly difficult. The data base was and is available through such organizations as the IMF and the OECD, after being publicly released by various governments and reported promptly by wire services such as Dow Jones and Reuters. The difficulty of step three in the past was considerably eased by the fact that those who decided on devaluations and revaluations were—unlike private transactors—not guided by profit maximizing objectives. The motives of monetary authorities ranged from considerations of national prestige, and domestic partisan politics, all the way to justified fears of postdevaluation inflationary pressures or post-revaluation unemployment. One particularly pleasant feature about this era of exchange rate forecasting was that the downside risk of actions taken on the basis of such forecasts was quite limited; the exchange rate either moved in the direction in which it was generally expected to move, or it stayed virtually steady. Little wonder that more and more people caught on to this game so that finally the consensus forecast became self-fulfilling. Most importantly, this occurred only after many people had taken positions during the period in which the monetary authorities tried to "stem the tide," to use one of the favorite expressions of commentators during that period, by buying and selling in the foreign exchange market.

With the advent of the 1970s, the forecasting environment has changed considerably. These changes have been analyzed and reported innumerable times, and there is little that can be added here. One important aspect of the changes, however, has had fundamental implications for forecasting: the objectives of monetary authorities in respect to their intervention in the market have become much less clear-cut. Some do not intervene at all; others intervene occasionally but on different sides of the market.[4] National governments have become ambiguous and internally divided about the objectives of exchange rate policy. Formerly, a devaluation was "bad," and defending the rate was "good." Things are not quite as clear any more. Either to let the exchange rate move down or even push it down, relative to other currencies, is "good" for the balance of trade; but it is "bad" as far as the inflationary effect is concerned. Since many governments now seem to have both problems on their hands, fundamental economic analysis will not solve this dilemma for them; and, as a result, their exchange rate policies are much less predictable.

Some central banks, of course, may have definite and persistent objectives in managing their exchange rates. To the extent that such targets can be recognized by astute forecasters and monetary authorities persist with their objectives in the face of the forecaster's speculation, the old rules of the forecasting game still pertain and provide all private transactors who "play the game" with a change for profit.

In the case of those currencies which monetary authorities abstain from buying or selling, or intervene only to improve the technical condition of the markets, or intervene but are unsure which objective to follow (and consequently their actions are more or less random), the foreign exchange market attains the characteristics of what has been called a purely speculative market. In such a market, it is argued, opportunities for monetary gain require not only the availability of a superior forecasting model but also the exclusive use of such a model.

Price Determination in Speculative Markets

Observers of security markets, commodity markets, and foreign exchange markets have long recognized the inadequacy of the conventional demand–supply framework for explaining price behavior in speculative markets.[5] Holbrook Working (1958) proposed the replacement of the original demand framework as devised by Marshall with a theory of expectations in speculative trading.[6] The premise of Working's "theory of anticipatory prices" is that speculative prices are formed according to *anticipations* of supply and demand rather than on the basis of *present* supply and demand. It is the behavior of the trader, anticipating future demand and supply, which induces price changes. Indeed, anticipatory price-setting behavior is the only type of behavior which is consistent with the unrestrained pursuit of profits in markets of this type.

Traders in speculative markets, Working argued, are rational, exceptionally skilled and extremely well-informed. These traders make their profits by continually seeking, obtain, and analyzing new information that might allow them to predict price changes. Acting immediately on this new information, traders produce frequent price changes. Price fluctuations in speculative markets thus do not occur willy-nilly: they are the results of expert appraisal of the significance of changing information. But new information which is useful for price prediction comes to traders in an unpredictable or random way (otherwise it would be neither new nor useful). Hence the price changes generated by traders are unpredictable or random.

This argument, loosely speaking, constitutes the random walk hypothesis. Samuelson[7] and Mandelbrot[8] have developed formal proofs of the theorem that, in markets where (i) prices are free to fluctuate, (ii) no single trader is able to corner the market, monopolize information or otherwise manipulate prices, and (iii) present prices are strongly influenced by expected future prices, prices will fluctuate randomly. As early as 1900, however, Bachelier[9] theorized that in the case of stock market prices, the mathematical probability of a positive price change equals that of a negative price change.

During the past two decades an impressive volume of research has accumulated in support of the theory that prices in speculative markets fluctuate randomly, and do so because all new information is rapidly and unbiasedly reflected in stock market price. Many of the important results concerning the stock market are summarized in Fama's excellent survey.[10]

Do exchange rates conform to this model? That is, do series of exchange rates under the flexible exchange rate system follow a random walk? The results of empirical investigation in securities markets have lent strong support to a modified random walk in security prices: successive price changes follow a "submartingale" with a nonzero expected value equal to the expected long-run rate of return. Any deviations from complete independence over time of price changes are small and shortlived. Studies of commodity prices such as those of Labys and Granger[11] have yielded similar conclusions. Foreign exchange is, if anything, more thoroughly analyzed and more actively traded than are many commodities and securities. Hence the random walk model would be expected to characterize the behavior of flexible exchange rates.

In a study of the floating exchange rates of the post-World War I period and the Canadian dollar (1950–1962), William Poole[12] found significant departures from the random walk model after applying three different tests of serial dependence. Poole interpreted his finding of positive first-order serial correlation as being the result of transactions costs. The application of certain trading rules, he suggested, would have yielded gross annual returns of as much as 50 percent in some instances. Grubel[13] examined patterns in the forward market of the late 1950s in an operation test of three expectations models and two investment strategies. He found evidence of significant opportunities for profitable speculation with possible returns of 15 to 30 percent. Upson,[14] in an application of spectral analysis to the dollar-sterling 90-day forward rate, also found significant nonrandomness. Upson's data (weekly forward rates, 1961–67) exhibited patterns characterized by cycles of length 32, 3.8, and 2.5 weeks, which he suggested could be used for successful trading rules. It is of note that each of these three studies found significant serial dependencies in the foreign exchange market, in apparent contradiction to the efficient market or random walk hypothesis; and in each case the author interpreted his result as implying the existence of profit-making opportunities from speculation. The findings of the present study have some bearing on these conclusions.

This paper is an attempt to specify alternative models of exchange rate determination in an efficient market and to evaluate empirical implications of these models for the predictability of foreign exchange rates. The authors' attempts to provide empirical support for their theory must be put in proper perspective since such efforts are easily subject to misinterpretation. Thus far, arguments and evidence from related empirical studies of speculative markets have been presented and doubts have been raised about the possibility of making profitable price forecasts to the extent that these markets are efficient. It is important to recognize, however, that the efficient market hypothesis essentially cannot be proven or disproven. One can never preclude the possibility that there may exist some relationship or model, the exclusive knowledge of which will enable superior predictions of future exchange rates and provide opportunities for gain. All that one can do empirically is test various forecasting models and see whether the results support (not prove) the hypothesis or whether the evidence stands in contradiction to it.

Over the years it has become customary to distinguish three versions of the efficient market hypothesis. The first, the so-called weak form, has particular implications for statistical forecasting models using intrinsic variables; it asserts that successive changes in prices are independent of the sequence of past prices. The hypothesis in its semi-strong form asserts that all public information is fully reflected in prices. Finally, the strong form maintains that not only public information but *all* information is fully reflected in prices. The authors' empirical work consists of tests which refer primarily to the weak form version of the efficient market hypothesis.

In the section of the paper that follows a model of the spot exchange rate as a simple random walk or martingale will be introduced. Next, an alternative model will be proposed in which the expected rate of change of the exchange rate is not necessarily zero but depends on interest rate differentials. The forward rate as a predictor of the future spot rate will then be discussed. The theoretical part of the paper will be concluded with an outline of time series analysis as a forecasting method. The next section reports on the empirical results. The method of Box-Jenkins[15] analysis is applied to the post-1918 floating exchange rate period to discover the existence and stability of nonrandom patterns and the possibility of profitable exploitation of such patterns. Box-Jenkins analysis and the other forecasting models are also applied to the recent period of flexible rates in order to compare their predictive accuracy. Finally, the implications of the results for the predictability of flexible exchange rates will be discussed.

The Efficient Foreign Exchange Market: Alternative Models

Principal notation:

X_t = exchange rate at time point t, in dollars per unit of foreign currency.

R_t = $\ln X_t - \ln X_{t-1} \doteq (X_t - X_{t-1})/X_{t-1}$ (See note b below). R_t may be thought of as the rate of change in the exchange rate, or the return from holding the foreign currency from $t-1$ to t.

R'_{t+n} = $\ln X_{t+n} - \ln X_t$

Φ_t = all publicly available information at time t.

$'_t$ = the series of present and past values of X_t, i.e., X_t, X_{t-1}, X_{t-2}, ...

i_{St} = yield during period t to t+1 on dollar deposits in a Eurobank, expressed in fractional form. E.g., 10% p.a. for six months becomes .05.

i_{ft} = yield during period t to t+1 on foreign currency deposits in a Eurobank.

A tilde (˜) indicates a random variable.

Efficient Markets Hypothesis 1 (Martingale)

If all new information potentially affecting exchange rates is immediately reflected in the trading actions of participants in the foreign exchange market, then any future change will be unpredictable as to direction. The probability of a currency appreciation will be exactly equal to the probability of depreciation, i.e.,

$$P(\Delta \tilde{X}_t > 0) = P(\Delta \tilde{X}_t < 0) = .5$$

These probabilities hold, whatever information the prospective forecaster has at his disposal. Hence the expected value of the exchange rate at a future date, X_{t+1}, is simply the present exchange rate irrespective of the information available to the forecaster. In other words, the exchange rate sequence $\{X_t\}$ follows a martingale with respect to any information set Φ_t (see note a):

$$\begin{aligned} E(\tilde{X}_{t+1}) &= E(\tilde{X}_{t+1}|\Phi'_t) \\ &= E(\tilde{X}_{t+1}|\Phi_t) \\ &= X_t \end{aligned} \qquad (1)$$

Stated differently, the expected return on holding a foreign currency, conditional on all available information, is zero:

$$\begin{aligned} E(\tilde{R}_{t+1}) &= E(\tilde{R}_{t+1}|\Phi'_t) \\ &= E(\tilde{R}_{t+1}|\Phi_t) \\ &= 0 \end{aligned} \qquad (2)$$

If the more stringent assumption is made that the $\tilde{R}_t$ are serially independent and identically distributed, then the above model becomes the random walk:

$$\check{R}_t = \ln \check{X}_t - \ln \check{X}_{t-1}$$
$$\ln \check{X}_t = \ln \check{X}_{t-1} + \check{R}_t$$

where $E(\check{R}_t) = 0$, cov $(\check{R}_t, \check{R}_{t-j}) = 0$, all $j \neq 0$. For the purposes of this paper, however, it is necessary to assume neither that the $\check{R}_t$ follow any particular distribution (such as the normal) nor that they are identically distributed. The assumption is made only that the variance of the $\check{R}_t$ exists and is finite. It is hoped to show that the R_t are serially uncorrelated, but this does not of course prove independence: a pair of variables can be uncorrelated yet not be independent. For these reasons, a random walk model in a strict sense is not being dealt with, but rather a martingale.

The most important consequence of a martingale in the logarithm of exchange rates is that today's exchange rate is the best predictor of tomorrow's exchange rate. (See note b.)

It follows, moreover, that today's price is the best predictor of *any* future price, and that the expected gain or loss for *any* holding period is zero. By successive substitution, from

$$\ln \check{X}_{t+1} = \ln X_t + \check{R}_t$$

we obtain:

$$\ln \check{X}_{t+n} = \ln \check{X}_t + \sum_{j=1}^{n} \check{R}_{t+j}$$

Hence

$$E(\ln \check{X}_{t+n}) = \ln X_t + \sum_{j=1}^{n} E(\check{R}_{t+j})$$

(since the $\check{R}_t$ are uncorrelated)

$$= \ln X_t$$

(since $E(\check{R}_{t+j}) = 0$, all j). Next, define

$$\check{R}'_{t+n} \text{ as } \check{R}'_{t+n} = \ln \check{X}_{t+n} - \ln \check{X}_t;$$

then

$$E(\check{R}'_{t+n}) = E(\ln \check{X}_{t+n}) - \ln X_t$$
$$= 0 \tag{3}$$

It follows that

$$E(\check{X}_{t+n}) = X_t \tag{4}$$

One implication of this result is of course that any predictive model employing some or all past exchange rates will fare no better than the simple martingale model. That is, of all possible functions $f(X_t, X_{t-1}, X_{t-2},$

...), the one that will minimize the variance of the predictive error,

$$E[(\tilde{X}_{t+n} - f)^2] \qquad n = 1 \text{ to } \infty$$

is simply

$$f(X_t, X_{t-1}, X_{t-2}, \ldots) = X_t.$$

Similarly, if we define $\tilde{R}'_{t+n} = \ln X_{t+n} - \ln X_t$, then the function $f'(\Phi'_t)$ which will minimize $E[\tilde{R}'_{t+n} - f')^2]$ is

$$f'(R_t, R_{t-1}, R_{t-2}, \ldots) = 0.$$

Since it is obviously impossible to test this hypothesis for *all* possible functions of past exchange rates, we will limit ourselves to consideration of a wide range of *linear* functions that could be used as predictors of $\tilde{X}_{t+n}$ or $\tilde{R}_{t+n}$.

Although extending one's predictive horizon into the future does not alter the best predictor, the confidence interval that one is forced to place around one's prediction widens rapidly. In other words, the variance V_n of one's predictive error will be:

V_n = variance of predictive error when forecasting n periods ahead

$$= V(\ln X_{t+n} - \ln X_t)$$

$$= V\left(\sum_{j=1}^{n} R_{t+j}\right)$$

$$= \sum_{j=1}^{n} V(R_{t+j}) \qquad (5)$$

since cov $(R_{t+i}, R_{t+j}) = 0$, all i, j, i $\neq$ j.

If we assume that in addition to being uncorrelated, the R_t are identically distributed with common variance σ_R^2, then:

$$V_n = n\sigma_R^2 \qquad (6)$$

i.e., the variance of the predictive error is directly proportional to one's forecasting horizon.

Efficient Markets Hypothesis 2 (Submartingale)

This form of the efficient foreign exchange market model says that the expected value of a future exchange rate is the present exchange rate, adjusted for the difference in yields that can be earned in each of the two currencies. Stated differently, the expected return from holding a foreign currency is equal and opposite to the expected return differential between financial assets denominated in the different currencies. The exchange rate sequence $\{X_t\}$ follows a submartingale with respect to any information set Φ_t:

$$E(\tilde{X}_{t+1}|i_{St}, i_{ft}) = E(\tilde{X}_{t+1}|i_{St}, i_{ft}, \Phi'_t)$$
$$= E(X_{t+1}|i_{St}, i_{ft}, \Phi_t)$$
$$= X_t f(i_{St}, i_{ft}) \gtreqless X_t \qquad (7)$$

And, correspondingly,

$$E(\tilde{R}_{t+1}|i_{St}, i_{ft}) \gtreqless 0 \qquad (8)$$

What is the basis of Hypothesis 2? Hypothesis 1, it may be argued, would hold true only if foreign exchange traders held specie or noninterest-bearing demand deposits at banks, and neither lending nor borrowing alternatives were available. That is clearly not the case. The submartingale form of the efficient markets hypothesis is based on the premise that foreign exchange traders who buy, sell, and hold various currencies take into account the potential returns on interest-bearing instruments denominated in the currencies traded. Hence when new information impinges on the market, the traders do not merely trade on the basis of their revised forecasts of the exchange rate at a future date, but they also consider whether holding a foreign currency will earn them or cost them a higher or lower interest rate. The present exchange rate will be at equilibrium when the spot rate and the expected future rate differ only by local-currency returns on freely-available, relatively riskless securities. Eurocurrency deposits in major Eurobanks fit this definition fairly closely, chiefly because of the total absence of restrictions on deposits in the Eurocurrency markets.

What, then, is $f(i_{St}, i_{ft})$? The derivation follows closely the derivation of the conditions for forward rate equilibrium provided by the familiar interest rate parity theorem. In place of the forward rate, we have the expected future spot rate at time t+1. The terminal value of an amount P held until time t+1 in a Eurodollar deposit at rate i_{St} is $P(1+i_{St})$. At equilibrium this must equal the terminal value, in dollars, of amount P converted into foreign currency at the spot rate X_t and earning i_{ft} until time t+1 when the deposit matures and is converted back into dollars at the expected spot rate, $E(\tilde{X}_{t+1})$. Hence at equilibrium:

$$E\{P(1 + i_{St})\} = E\{(P/X_t)(1 + i_{ft})\tilde{X}_{t+1}\}$$
$$P(1 + i_{St}) = (P/X_t)(1 + i_{ft})E(\tilde{X}_{t+1})$$

(since P, i_{St} X_t, i_{ft} are known with certainty).

Solving for $E(\tilde{X}_{t+1})$, we obtain

$$E(\tilde{X}_{t+1}) = X_t \frac{(1+i_{St})}{(1+i_{ft})} \qquad (9)$$

$$= X_t f(i_{St}, i_{ft}) \gtreqless X_t$$

This result may be expressed in terms of R_t, the expected return on holding pure currencies:

$$\begin{aligned} E(\tilde{R}_{t+1}) &= E(\ln \tilde{X}_{t+1} - \ln X_t) \\ &\doteq E[(\tilde{X}_{t+1} - X_t)/X_t] \\ &= \frac{E(\tilde{X}_{t+1}) - X_t}{X_t} \end{aligned}$$

(since the spot rate is a known, fixed value)

$$= \frac{E(\tilde{X}_{t+1})}{X_t} - 1$$

$$= \frac{1 + i_{St}}{1 + i_{ft}} - 1 \qquad \text{from (9)}$$

$$= \frac{i_{St} - i_{ft}}{1 + i_{ft}} \qquad (10)$$

The expected return series is also a submartingale.

And if i_{ft} is small, then – to a close approximation – the expected return from holding a foreign currency $E(\tilde{R}_{t+1})$ equals the interest rate differential between the two currencies $(i_{St} - i_{ft})$. Note that if the left-hand side of (10) is favorable (i.e., the foreign currency is expected to rise) then the right-hand side must be unfavorable (i.e., the interest rates available in the foreign currency are lower).

When our forecasting horizon extends beyond one period, say to t+n, we have by successive substitution in (9):

$$E(\tilde{X}_{t+n}) = X_t E \left[\prod_{j=t}^{n-1} (1 + \tilde{i}_{Sj})(1 + \tilde{i}_{fj})^{-1} \right] \qquad (11)$$

if the principal plus accumulated interest is all converted back into dollars at t+n. If successive interest rates are assumed to be independent, we obtain:

$$E(\tilde{X}_{t+n}) = X_t \prod_{j=t}^{n-1} E[(1 + \tilde{i}_{Sj})(1 + \tilde{i}_{fj})^{-1}] \qquad (12)$$

Similarly, $E(\tilde{R}'_{t+n})$, the expected change in the logarithm of the exchange rate between now and t+n, becomes:

$$E(\tilde{R}'_{t+n}) = E \left[\prod_{j=t}^{n-1} (\tilde{i}_{Sj} - \tilde{i}_{fj})(1 + \tilde{i}_{fj})^{-1} \right] \qquad (13)$$

In order to circumvent the complications of unknown future interest rates, in the empirical part of this study we shall limit ourselves to consideration of the case of simple interest at known rates i_{St+n} and i_{ft+n}, where the maturity of the foreign deposit exactly matches the forecasting horizon. With simple interest, we have

$$E(\tilde{R}_{t+n}) = \frac{i_{St+n} - i_{ft+n}}{1 + i_{ft+n}} \qquad (14)$$

Our treatment of only known, fixed interest rates is consistent with our empirical tests, which are limited to forecasting horizons of 90 days or less. Tests involving longer forecasting periods would have to deal not only with the independence assumption stated above, but also with the difficulty (perhaps impossibility) of forecasting interest rates. The empirical implication of the submartingale hypothesis is that no model based on past exchange rate data or any other available information will have greater success in predicting exchange rates than will the simple submartingale model derived above. The function $f(\Phi_t)$ that will minimize the value of the predictive error, $E\{[\tilde{X}_{t+1} - f(\Phi_t)]^2\}$, is:

$$f(\Phi_t) = X_t \frac{(1 + i_{St})}{(1 + i_{ft})}$$

We should note one obvious flaw in the submartingale form of the efficient foreign exchange market hypothesis: its neglect of the role of the expected exchange rate *variability* in determining the spot rate. Equation (9) would hold only if $\tilde{X}_{t+1}$ were known with certainty. If we assume a mean-variance framework in which risk is measured by variance, (9) would represent the equilibrium condition only when

$$\text{variance}\{P(1 + i_{St})\} = \text{variance}\{P/X_t(1+i_{jt})\tilde{X}_{t+1}\}$$

i.e.,

$$V(\tilde{X}_{t+1}) = 0$$

(since P, i_{St}, X_t, i_{ft} are known with certainty).

Of course $V(\tilde{X}_{t+1}) \neq 0$. Hence the equilibrium condition depends on the variance of $\tilde{X}_{t+1}$ and the market price of risk. Knowledge of these two will enable us to determine a *risk premium* that may be incorporated into the submartingale model. Equilibrium in the spot and Eurocurrency markets will exist when the home currency return (assumed certain) equals the expected foreign currency return *minus* a premium for exchange-rate risk. Although this proposition implies that one might not expect the submartingale model in its simple form to produce the most accurate forecasts, we shall retain the unmodified submartingale model in our empirical tests. The reasons for this are, first, that selection of an appropriate value for the "market price of risk" presents obvious conceptual and empirical difficulties, and, second, that the existence of uncertain inflation rates reduces some of the apparent attractiveness of holding domestic currency: when measured in real terms, both home and foreign currency have a non zero variance.

*　　*　　*

For the curious: if i_p is the market price of risk, that is, the additional interest rate required by the market to compensate for an additional unit of risk, then

$$i_p = \frac{dE(i)}{dV(i)}$$

where $E(i)$ is expected return and $V(i)$ is the variance of return about its expected value, and expected return is a monotonically increasing function of risk. $V(i)$ might perhaps be replaced by the more appropriate measure of riskiness, the contribution of that asset's return to the variability of the investor's total portfolio. For the purpose of this paper, however, it suffices that we assume variance to be a measure of an asset's riskiness.

Next, it is assumed that i_p is known and is constant over the range of $V(i)$ of interest. Then $E(i) = i_p V(i)$. Assume too that $V(\tilde{X}_{t+n})$ can be determined and is invariant with respect to a displacement in time: that is, $V(\tilde{X}_{t+n}) = V(\tilde{X})$, all n, where $V(\tilde{X})$, a constant, is defined to be the variance of the spot exchange rate. $V(\tilde{R})$ is defined similarly.

Equilibrium will exist when expected return on dollar deposit = expected return on foreign currency deposit − premium for riskiness of foreign currency deposit, i.e.,

$$E\left\{\frac{P(1+i_{St}) - P}{P}\right\} = E\left\{\frac{(P/X_t)(1+i_{ft})\tilde{X}_{t+1} - P}{P}\right\}$$

$$- i_p V\left\{\frac{(P/X_t)(1+i_{ft})\tilde{X}_{t+1} - P}{P}\right\}$$

hence,

$$i_{St} = \frac{(1+i_{ft})E(\tilde{X}_{t+1})}{X_t} - 1 - i_p\left\{\frac{(1+i_{ft})^2 V(\tilde{X})}{X_t^2} - 0\right\}$$

since all values except $\tilde{X}_{t+1}$ are known with certainty, and $V(\tilde{X}_{t+1}) = V(\tilde{X})$. Multiplying throughout by $X_t/(1+i_{ft})$, the result is:

$$E(\tilde{X}_{t+1}) = X_t\frac{(1+i_{St})}{(1+i_{ft})} + \frac{(1+i_{ft})}{X_t}i_p V(\tilde{X}) \tag{A}$$

According to this model, the best predictor of the future spot exchange rate at t+1 is a weighted average of the present spot rate and the variance of the exchange rate, $V(\tilde{X})$.

From (A) the expected rate of change of the exchange rate, $E(\tilde{R}_{t+1})$ is:

$$E(\tilde{R}_{t+1}) = \frac{E(\tilde{X}_{t+1})}{X_t} - 1 \text{ as before}$$

$$= \frac{i_{St} - i_{ft}}{1 + i_{ft}} + (1 + i_{ft})i_p \frac{V(\tilde{X})}{X_t^2} \qquad \text{[from (A)]}$$

$$= \frac{i_{St} - i_{ft}}{1 + i_{ft}} + (1 + i_{ft})i_p V\left\{ \frac{\tilde{X}_{t+1}}{X_t} - 1 \right\}$$

(since $V(-1) = 0$ and $V(\tilde{X}_{t+1}) = V(\tilde{X})$), i.e.,

$$E(\tilde{R}_{t+1}) = \frac{i_{St} - i_{ft}}{1 + i_{ft}} + (1 + i_{ft})i_p V(\tilde{R})$$

This result suggests that the expected rate of change of an exchange rate is approximately equal, for small i_{ft}, to the interest rate differential plus the product of the market price of risk and the variance of the rate of change of the exchange rate.

*   *   *

The Forward Rate as a Predictor of the Future Spot Rate

As an alternative to the two major forms of the efficient markets hypothesis, there is the possibility that the forward exchange rate reflects the market's prediction of the future spot rate under freely fluctuating rates. This hypothesis has been proposed by Kaserman[16] and Brown[17] and is commonly referred to in discussions of exchange rate forecasting.

Arguably, if speculators monopolize or dominate the forward market, their profit-seeking actions would ensure that the forward rate settles only at the level of the expected spot rate. The modern theory of forward exchange, however, suggests that the supply and demand for forward exchange is a function not only of speculation but also of covered interest arbitrage and possibly of net supply or demand from commercial hedgers.[18] The forward rate (F_t) thus may be represented as a function of the rate needed to wipe out the profit on covered interest arbitrage (p), the speculator's expected spot rate $E(\tilde{X}_{t+n})$, and the forward rate that would equate commercial hedgers' demand and supply of forward exchange (H). (See note c below).

$$F = f(p, S, H) \qquad (15)$$

The modern theory of forward exchange thus stands in apparent contradiction to the notion that the forward rate reflects the expected spot rate.

At this point the observation should be made that the modern theory is an *ex ante* or explanatory theory of the factors affecting the forward exchange rate. In contrast, the interest rate parity theorem is an *ex post* statement of the interest rate-forward premium conditions in equilibrium. The two approaches do *not*, therefore, contradict each other (as is commonly supposed). Strong evidence exists that forward rates and interest rates in the Eurocurrency markets are simultaneously determined.[19] Hence, even if the forward rate is in part a function of speculators' and hedgers' net demand or supply, *ex post* interest parity may be established through the effect of the forward market on relative interest rates. Indeed, forward exchange rates have remained at interest rate parity with respect to Eurocurrency interest rates throughout the recent periods of international monetary turmoil.[20] This fact in no way detracts from the validity of the modern theory of forward exchange once the simultaneous determination of forward rates and interest rates is acknowledged.

The authors' position, then, is that the forward rate reflects arbitrage and hedging activities but may also represent speculators' forecasts in an efficient foreign exchange market. The model presented for comparative purposes is simply:

$$E(\tilde{X}_{t+n}) = E(\tilde{X}_{t+n} \mid \Phi_t)$$
$$= F_t \qquad (16)$$

Stated in terms of the expected n-period rate of return, this becomes

$$E(\tilde{R}'_{t+n}) = E(\tilde{R}'_{t+n} \mid \Phi_t)$$
$$= \frac{F_t - X_t}{X_t} \qquad (17)$$

The predictive accuracy of this formulation is gauged below, along with that of the other forecasting models.

Forecasting with Time Series Analysis

Successive variables in many economic time series are statistically dependent. For example, data series relating to production and consumption often display seasonality, trends, cyclical movements and other forms of dependency. This fact has led to the recent development of a range of statistical techniques designed to identify the form of the dependence of a series for forecasting purposes. In particular, Box and Jenkins[21] have shown how a wide range of discrete time series can be represented by the family of linear integrated autoregressive moving-average processes. The versatile techniques developed by Box and Jenkins are employed in this study.

Many times series may be represented as a linear function of past observations and a randomly distributed error term, e_t:

$$z_t = \delta + \phi_1 z_{t-1} + \phi_2 z_{t-2} + \dots + e_t \qquad (18)$$

where δ and the ϕ_i are fixed parameters and e_t is a random variable with mean zero and is statistically independent of all e_{t-k}, $k \neq 0$. When $\phi_i = 0$ for $i > p$, the process is designated an autoregressive process of order p, or AR(p).

By substituting in (18) for z_{t-1}, z_{t-2} and so forth successively, it is easily seen that a linear process may similarly be expressed as a weighted sum of the current and all past disturbances:

$$z_t = \mu + e_t + \theta_1 e_{t-1} + \theta_2 e_{t-2} + \dots$$

where μ and the θ_i are fixed parameters. When $\theta_i = 0$ for $i > q$, the process is referred to as a moving-average process of order q, or MA(q).

A third set of possible processes is a mixed autoregressive-moving average process, ARMA (p,q). For example, the simplest mixed process is ARMA(1,1):

$$z_t = \delta + \phi_1 z_{t-1} + \theta_1 e_{t-1} + e_t$$

Since MA(q) and AR(p) processes are really special cases of the mixed model, the general class of such linear time series models is referred to as ARMA(p,q) models. When differencing in the series is used, the model s termed integrated and designated as an ARIMA (p,d,q) model, where "d" refers to differencing of order d in the original series. First-order differencing is often necessary to obtain stationarity in the mean of the series, an important condition for the application of Box-Jenkins analysis.

The form of any ARIMA(p,d,q) series may be roughly identified by studying the shape of the estimated autocorrelation function $\hat{\rho}_k$ of the suitably differenced series. The autocorrelation is the correlation coefficient between a number of a series and a lagged member of the same series, and bears a mathematical relationship to the model generating the series. Once an ARIMA (p,d,q) model has been (tentatively) selected, the unknown parameters may be estimated by minimizing the sum of squares $\Sigma \hat{e}_t^2$, using nonlinear least-squares methods. Given a model for a particular series, predictions may be obtained by computing the expected values of future observations, conditional on the past history of the series.

Clearly the "all available" information set Φ_t subsumes the set available to ARIMA models (Φ'_t) used to forecast exchange rates. It may well be that a larger information set, or a different method of analyzing the given information set, would succeed in reducing the variance of the predictive error below that given by Box-Jenkins forecasting. These possibilities remain open to further empirical testing. Nevertheless, forecasting with ARIMA models has yielded surprisingly accurate results when compared to other time series methods, and even when compared to sophisticated econometric models.[22] This method therefore seems well suited to an empirical test of the "weak form" of the efficient foreign exchange market hypotheses.

Exponential Smoothing

ARIMA models subsume many other time series modelling techniques such as moving-average and exponential smoothing methods. Nevertheless, for the sake of thoroughness, the accuracy of forecasts made on the basis of exponential smoothing was examined. Twenty exponential smoothing forecasts were made for the post-sample period for each currency for the 1970s floating period. The technique employed was the well-known Winters' Method.[23] The authors used an interactive program developed at the University of Michigan that enables the forecaster to adapt his modelling parameters to the time series characteristics of the sample period data.

The Data

The primary data base consists of daily exchange rates for three countries during the periods of relatively flexible exchange rates in the post-World War I period and the 1970s. The rates are noon buying rates for cable transfers of foreign exchange, certified for customs purposes by the Federal Reserve Bank of New York and published each week by the Board of Governors of the Federal Reserve System. These rates are collected daily by the New York Fed from several major New York banks.[24] The 1920s series were kindly supplied by Professor William Poole of Brown University and the recent data (spot and forward rates) by Ralph Smith of the Federal Reserve Board. The periods assumed to be floating periods were those selected by Poole[25] in the case of the post-World War I series; and for the recent series the starting points were selected on the basis of public announcements of a cessation of intervention to maintain dollar-foreign currency parities. A summary of the series is contained in Table 2.1.

The interest rates employed in tests of the submartingale model are Euro-currency deposit rates of four different maturities reported daily in

Table 2.1 Flexible exchange rate data employed in study

Series	Dates	No. of trading days
	Post-World War I Period	
Canada	4/7/19–6/28/24	1583
France	4/7/19–12/4/26	2319
United Kingdom	4/7/19–5/2/25	1837
	1970s Period	
Canada	1/1/71 –10/18/74	958
France	3/19/73–10/18/74	400
United Kingdom	6/23/72–10/18/74	582

the London *Financial Times* (call, seven day, one month and three month rates). The lower of the two reported rates was used.

Statistical Analysis

The empirical analysis of the six exchange rate series described above was directed at three objectives:

(i) An investigation of the time series dependencies exhibited by daily exchange rate change data during the 1920s and 1970s. The primary tool of this analysis was the Box-Jenkins technique.

(ii) An empirical comparison of the *ex ante* forecasting accuracy of five alternative forecasting models, based chiefly on the mean squared predictive error statistic.

(iii) An examination of the variability and distributional characteristics of the daily exchange rate changes.

Descriptive statistics relating to the variability of daily percentage changes in the six exchange rate series used in this study are displayed in Table 2.2. While the mean daily change in each case is small, it is of interest to observe the rather large standard deviations and wide ranges exhibited by almost all of the series. The range and standard deviation of all three countries' exchange rate changes has decreased since the post-World War I period, indicating less volatility. More striking, however, are the differences in variability between different currencies: changes in the Canadian dollar exchange rate tend to be smaller than those of the British pound, and both are much less volatile than the French franc. These differences may reflect patterns of trading with the United States. What they suggest is that other things being equal, an investor or businessperson should prefer to deal in Canadian dollars or Sterling than in French francs, unless the latter displays greater negative covariance with the overall

Table 2.2 Variability of daily percentage changes in exchange rates[a]

Currency series	Mean	Standard deviation	Range
Canada (1920s)	.00104	.3367	−4.419 to 2.586
France (1920s)	−.06262	1.5251	−10.810 to 9.599
U.K. (1920s)	.00204	.4970	−5.325 to 4.458
Canada (1970s)	.00295	.1277	−.636 to 1.215
France (1970s)	−.01109	.8084	−4.683 to 4.612
U.K. (1970s)	−.01690	.4222	−2.284 to 1.241

[a]Percentage changes calculated as 100 R_t, where $R_t = \ln X_t - \ln X_{t-1}$ and X_t is the exchange rate on day t.

variability of his portfolio. It should be noted, however, that the data display distinct heteroscedasticity—instability of the variance over time.

Fitting time series models to the series revealed similar differences across time and between countries. Box-Jenkins techniques were used to identify and fit ARIMA models of the type discussed above. In the case of the 1920s data, preliminary results (from separate series) suggested that the fitted ARIMA models were likely to be quite unstable over time. The presence of such instability, of course, would cast serious doubt on the value for predictive purposes of *ex post* modelling of exchange rate series. In order to test this we divided the series into segments of approximately 500 trading days each and modelled each segment separately. It would be cumbersome to report the results of every model fit; for illustrative purposes, however, the five fitted models for the floating French franc series, 1919–26, are listed in Table 2.3. It is evident that not only the models but the parameter values and the goodness-of-fit (R^2) vary dramatically from one period to the next. For example, a 10th-order moving average model was fitted to the fourth segment, while a random walk (or martingale) was the best-fitting model for the final segment. No one model fitted to the series can be said to represent its time series behavior. This conclusion is confirmed by the results for Canada and the United Kingdom.

Although the fitted models display instability over time, two aspects are common to most of the models: (1) the models are of a moving-average type, and (2) the dependencies in daily rates of return on exchange rates are significant but weak and of low order in most cases. The R^2's are low; none of the fitted models was able to explain more than 9 percent of the variance in the series. It may be concluded that serial dependence did exist in the post-World War I floating exchange rates but in weak and unstable form.

ARIMA models fitted to the flexible exchange rate period of the 1970s

Table 2.3 ARIMA models fitted to French franc series, 1919–26[a]

Segment	Model	Estimated parameter	T-statistics	Adjusted R^2
1st 498 [4-7-19 to 11-27-20]	MA(5)	$\hat{\delta} = -.002$ $\hat{\theta}_1 = .115$ $\hat{\theta}_2 = -.150$ $\hat{\theta}_5 = .919$	−1.26 2.58 −3.39 2.08	.042
2nd 498 [11-29-20 to 7-22-22]	MA(5)	$\hat{\delta} = .000$ $\hat{\theta}_3 = .085$ $\hat{\theta}_5 = .160$	1.05 1.93 3.59	.034
3rd 498 [7-24-22 to 3-17-24]	MA(1)	$\hat{\delta} = -.001$ $\hat{\theta}_1 = .215$	−1.35 4.87	.048
4th 498 [3-18-24 to 11-5-25]	MA(10)	$\hat{\delta} = .000$ $\hat{\theta}_2 = -.152$ $\hat{\theta}_3 = .123$ $\hat{\theta}_6 = .090$ $\hat{\theta}_7 = .095$ $\hat{\theta}_{10} = .095$	− .71 −3.39 2.74 2.01 2.12 2.09	.062
Last 327 [11-6-25 to 12-3-26]	ARIMA (0,0,0)	$\hat{\delta} = 0$	0	0

[a]First differences of natural logarithm of raw series used (i.e., R_t).

revealed similar instability in daily rates of return. Although serial correlation of apparent statistical significance was found for many segments of the 1970s series, the dependencies exhibited by the data were even weaker than those of the 1920s data and seemed to be even more unstable. Many of the fitted models were simply a random walk with drift: a majority in the Canadian sense. This result strongly implies a shorter and weaker "memory" in foreign exchange markets in the recent period.

The floating exchange rates of the 1970s were used to test the forecasting ability of the five methods discussed above. Using sample periods of 150 trading days' length, forecasts were produced for the post-sample period 1 day, 7 days, 30 days, and 90 days ahead. These periods correspond to the forecasting horizons of many short-term forecasters. Twenty forecasts, based on each of the various methods, were made for each country. Three countries—the same ones as were examined in the 1920s period—were studied. Forecasts were made on the basis of overlapping 150 trading day periods, with the starting point moving ahead two weeks for each successive attempt at forecasting. A total of 860 forecasts was made. The sample periods ran from March 1973 through June 1974, while forecasts were made from October 1973 through October 1974.

Forecasts were made using the following five forecasting methods, each of which is described above:

1. Martingale (random walk) Hypothesis
2. Submartingale (interest rate) Hypothesis
3. Forward Rate Hypothesis
4. Box-Jenkins Analysis (univariate)
5. Exponential Smoothing (Winters' method)

It has been noted that moving-average models frequently produced a better fit than did the random walk model to the 1970s exchange rate series. Since the R^2 of the random walk model is zero, Box-Jenkins analysis usually produced a better sample-period goodness-of-fit statistic (R^2) than did the naive random walk model. The authors, however, were more interested in the predictive accuracy of the model than in its sample period goodness-of-fit. For this reason the five forecasting techniques were compared on the basis of the mean squared predictive error,

$$MSE = \frac{1}{n} \sum_{i=1}^{n} [R'_{t+j,i} - E(R'_{t+j,i})]^2$$

$$= \frac{1}{20} \sum_{i=1}^{n} [Actual_i - Forecast_i]^2 \qquad (19)$$

for each forecasting horizon: $j = 1$ day, 7 days, 30 days and 90 days ahead. Obviously a small MSE value is preferable to a large value.

The mean squared errors for each forecasting method are shown in Tables 2.4 through 2.6. The forecasting accuracy of each method decreases rapidly as an attempt is made to predict exchange rates further into the future. It is noted that the observed mean squared error is roughly proportional to the forecasting horizon, as equation (6) suggests it should be.

By constructing 95 percent confidence intervals around the estimated mean squared errors, each of the other methods could be compared with the random walk hypothesis. Confidence intervals were constructed on the assumption that the MSEs follow a t-distribution. The MSE values that were found to be significantly different from the martingale MSE's at the 95 percent confidence level are marked with asterisks. The Canadian dollar forecasts are the most accurate ones and are the most difficult to distinguish on the basis of MSE's. This probably reflects the steadiness and low variability of the U.S./Canadian dollar exchange rate.

Of the five methods, the forward rate is consistently inferior to all the others. The Box-Jenkins and adaptive exponential smoothing forecasts fare poorly in all but a few instances, all of which are very short-term forecasts. This suggests that successive exchange rate changes do have some "memory"—but a memory that is short-lived and weak. The implication is

Table 2.4 Mean squared error comparison: exchange rate forecasts (flexible exchange rates, 1973–1974)

Canadian dollar

Forecasting horizon	Forecasting method				
	Martingale (random walk)	*Submartingale (interest rates)*	*Forward rate*	*Box-Jenkins*	*Exponential smoothing*
1 day	.0000017	.0000017	—	.0000015	.0000013
7 days	.0000131	.0000125	—	.0000141	.0000114
30 days	.0000712	.0000686	—	.0000949	.0000767
90 days	.0003404	.0003388	.0011126*	.0006413*	.0004617*

*Asterisks indicate significantly different from martingale at the 95 percent confidence level.

that for short periods, one *is* able to detect a low degree of market inefficiency in the foreign exchange market. But the longer the forecasting horizon, the more evident is the inaccuracy of time series forecasting of exchange rate changes.

The methods that produce consistently the best or close-to-best forecasts are the martingale and submartingale hypotheses. The martingale yields the greatest number of "most accurate" forecasts, but the submartingale performs only marginally worse in most instances and marginally better in the Canadian dollar case. The predictive errors that result from applying the two models are certainly not sufficient to distinguish one as a more accurate reflection of reality than the others. Indeed, it is arguable on both theoretical and empirical grounds that the most accurate model might be one in which interest rate differences are taken into account in traders

Table 2.5 Mean squared error comparison: exchange rate forecasts (flexible exchange rates, 1973–1974)

British pound

Forecasting horizon	Forecasting method				
	Martingale (random walk)	*Submartingale (interest rates)*	*Forward rate*	*Box-Jenkins*	*Exponential smoothing*
1 day	.0000307	.0000307	—	.0000311	.0000318
7 days	.0001491	.0001480	—	.0001536	.0008384*
30 days	.0006297	.0007274	—	.0009209*	.0011720*
90 days	.0023917	.0028970	.0786630*	.0048649*	.0077383*

*Asterisks indicate significantly different from martingale at the 95 percent confidence level.

Table 2.6 Mean squared error comparison: exchange rate forecasts (flexible exchange rates, 1973–1974)

French franc

Forecasting horizon	Forecasting method				
	Martingale (random walk)	Submartingale (interest rates)	Forward rate	Box-Jenkins	Exponential smoothing
1 day	.0000192	.0000194	—	.0000173	.0000309
7 days	.0000927	.0000960	—	.0001616*	.0001864*
30 days	.0020616	.0021056	—	.002989	.0034665
90 days	.0047227	.0049272	.0594910*	.0111140*	.0154760*

*Asterisks indicate significantly different from martingale at the 95 percent confidence level.

price-setting actions, but not to the full extent that would yield the parity relationship implied by (10). The correct model, therefore, might be some compromise between the random walk and submartingale models.

Finally, the statistical distribution of the daily exchange rate changes was examined for evidence of non-normality. Previous research in securities markets has shown the empirical distributions of daily rates of return to be significantly non-normal. When compared to the normal, these distributions have elongated tails and exceptionally high peaks. While the exact nature of the distribution of speculative price changes is essentially unresolved in the literature, it is generally agreed that statistical tests that rest on the normal assumption are of dubious value when applied to such series.[26] To test for non-normality, frequency distributions for the R_t of each series were compiled. In every case leptokurtosis was indeed observed although some series were closer to the normal than others. For example, a glance at Exhibit 2.1, the histogram for the British (1970s) data, will confirm the presence of an unusually large proportion of very small and very large observations. The data have been standardized by subtracting the mean and dividing by the standard deviation. In the distribution shown here, over 35 percent of the observations fall within .2 standard deviations of the mean and more than 1 percent lie beyond four standard deviations. Similar results are observed for the other series. This visual observation was confirmed in statistical tests of non-normality. In table 2.7 are shown the results of comparing the observed frequency distributions for the six series with the theoretical normal distribution. The Lilliefors test statistic, which is derived directly from the Kolmogorov-Smirnov goodness-of-fit test, has been shown to be more reliable than the more conventional chi-square test.[27] In all cases the Lilliefors test indicates significant non-normality. Once more, this casts doubt on previous results showing "significant" serial dependencies in exchange rate changes.

Exhibit 2.1 Histogram of standardized R_t for British pound, 6/23/72–10/4/74

LEFT-END	TOT%	COUNT	FOR UK-70S	(EACH x = 2)
−2.8000	.2	1	+x	
−2.6000	.2	1	+x	
−2.4000	.3	2	+x	
−2.2000	.7	4	+xx	
−2.0000	1.4	8	+xxxx	
−1.8000	1.0	6	+xxx	
−1.6000	2.1	12	+xxxxxx	
−1.4000	1.0	6	+xxx	
−1.2000	2.3	13	+xxxxxxx	
−1.0000	3.1	18	+xxxxxxxxx	
−.80000	3.3	19	+xxxxxxxxxx	
−.60000	5.2	30	+xxxxxxxxxxxxxxx	
−.40000	8.4	48	+xxxxxxxxxxxxxxxxxxxxxxxx	
−.20000	14.9	85	+xxxxxxxxxxxxxxxxxxxxxxxxxxxxxxxxxxxxxxxxxx	
.24702-14	20.5	117	+xxxxxxxxxxxxxxxxxxxxxxxxxxxxxxxxxxxxxxxxxxxxxxxxxxxxxxxxxxxx	
.20000	12.1	69	+xxxxxxxxxxxxxxxxxxxxxxxxxxxxxxxxxxx	
.40000	7.3	42	+xxxxxxxxxxxxxxxxxxxxx	
.60000	3.8	22	+xxxxxxxxxxx	
.80000	2.8	16	+xxxxxxxx	
1.0000	1.2	7	+xxxx	
1.2000	1.2	7	+xxxx	
1.4000	1.6	9	+xxxxx	
1.6000	.9	5	+xxx	
1.8000	.9	5	+xxx	
2.0000	.7	4	+xx	
2.2000	.3	2	+x	
2.4000	.3	2	+x	
2.6000	.3	2	+x	
2.8000	.2	1	+x	
...				
3.2000	.2	1	+x	
...				
3.6000	.2	1	+x	
	.9	5	< −4.0000	
	.3	2	> 4.0000	
TOTAL	100.0	572	(.20000 = INTERVAL WIDTH)	

Conclusions

The purpose of this paper was to provide an analysis of the behavior of exchange rate changes under conditions of flexible exchange rates, and of the implications of such behavior for exchange rate forecasting. The focus was on two alternatives—the martingale and submartingale models of exchange rate determination. The predictive accuracy of these models was compared with that of three alternative forecasting methods. In effect, the "weak form" of the efficient markets hypothesis was tested: that the best

Table 2.7 Goodness-of-fit tests on six exchange rate series against normal hypothesis

Series	Lilliefors test statistic[a]	Lilliefors value from table (95% sign level)	Reject H_0: distribution is normal?
Canada (1920s)	.1747	.0223	Yes
France (1920s)	.1046	.0184	Yes
U.K. (1920s)	.1426	.0207	Yes
Canada (1970s)	.0803	.0288	Yes
France (1970s)	.1276	.0449	Yes
U.K. (1970s)	.1276	.0370	Yes

[a]Lilliefors test statistic = $\sup[F(x) - S(s)]$ where $F(x)$ is theoretical cumulative distribution and $S(x)$ is observed cumulative distribution.

predictor of future exchange rates is independent of information provided by the sequence of past exchange rates. Except, possibly, for very short-term forecasts, the results provide support for the notion that trading rules are of no use in forecasting exchange rate changes. Neither of the two efficient market models, however, proved to be distinctly superior to the other.

The conclusions appear to contradict those of previous researchers who claim to have found systematic dependencies in flexible exchange rates which offered speculators profit-making opportunities. It is argued, however, that any such assertion is baseless if it is predicated solely upon an *ex post* discovery of nonrandomness in exchange rate data.[28] Nonrandom patterns are of use to the forecaster only if they can be relied upon in the future. Yet the results have demonstrated the inherent instability of fitted time series models. An *ex post* measure of goodness-of-fit such as R^2 does not necessarily tell one much about the predictive ability of the fitted model. When the actual forecasting accuracy of fitted models is tested, opportunities for profit-making speculation resulting from an analysis of past data disappear.

The empirical results have focused on the futility of forecasts based on the past exchange rate sequence. Yet the thrust of this paper is much broader: it is contended that the forecasting accuracy of the simple random walk or submartingale models is superior to forecasts based on *all* publicly available information. The authors do *not* base their belief that profitable speculation is futile merely on their empirical results, but rather on their contention that no other hypothesis is consistent with rational, profit-making behavior on the part of traders. Their selection of past exchange rates as the relevant information set is somewhat arbitrary, but then so would be the choice of any other (limited) information set or predictive model. It is hoped that this research at least has provided a stimulus to the considerable amount of further research that will be necessary to provide a solid understanding of the foreign exchange market as an efficient market.

The authors' analysis and results suggest that there are only two situations in which it is worthwhile to seek to profit from exchange rate forecasting. Since the present rate reflects the market's expectation of future rates, one might profit if one had both better information (or a better model) than the market *and* one had exclusive use of that information. Both conditions are necessary: if one obtains better information (for example, by subscribing to a highly sophisticated, and expensive, exchange rate forecasting service) but this information is sold to other market participants, forecasts derived from this information will be reflected in actual rates very rapidly. If, alternatively, one had exclusive use of a model that was not superior, forecasting would evidently not be a profitable activity.

The second situation in which forecasting might be profitable is when the other player in the foreign exchange game is the Central Bank or another trader (a) who is dominant, (b) whose behavior is not governed by the profit maximization objective, and (c) whose behavior is itself nonrandom. Again, all three conditions are necessary. This is the situation that prevailed under the Bretton Woods system and which, of course, prevails today in those countries that maintain fixed exchange rates. When exchange rates are freely floating, no such actor exists in the market, and forecasting appears to be futile. Even under a system of "managed" exchange rates, however, it may be impossible to predict the nature and stability of Central Banks' trading behavior. If the monetary authorities change their objectives fairly frequently in unpredictable ways, the expected profit from forecasting will still be zero.

Notes

1. A concise taxonomy of forecasting techniques will be found in William K. Hall, "Forecasting Techniques for Use in the Corporate Planning Process," *Managerial Planning*, Vol. 20, No. 2 (November/December 1972), pp. 5–11, 33.

2. Alan K. Gray, "Foreign Exchange Forecasting—How Far Can The Computer Help?" *Euromoney* (July 1974), pp. 36–43.

3. See, for example, Robert B. Shulman, "Are Foreign Exchange Risks Measurable?" *Columbia Journal of World Business* (June 1970), pp. 57–58; and Christopher M. Korth, "The Future of a Currency," *Business Horizons* (June 1972), pp. 67–76.

4. On U.S. policy see the quarterly reports by Charles A. Coombs in the *Federal Reserve Bank of New York—Monthly Review*: "Treasury and Federal Reserve Foreign Exchange Operations."

5. Treatment here of the foreign exchange market as a speculative market

should not be taken to imply that only "speculators" (in the derogatory sense) dominate the market. Rather, it is believed that *all* buying and selling of foreign exchange—by traders, importers, exporters, hedgers, etc.—is strongly influenced by anticipations of future exchange rate changes.

6. Holbrook Working, "A Theory of Anticipatory Prices," *American Economic Review*, Vol. 48, No. 2 (May 1958), 188–99.

7. Paul A. Samuelson, "Proof that Properly Anticipated Prices Fluctuate Randomly," *Industrial Management Review*, No. 6 (Spring 1965), pp. 41–49.

8. Benoit Mandelbrot, "Forecasts of Future Prices, Unbiased Markets and Martingale Models," *Journal of Business. Security Prices: A Supplement*, Vol. 39, No. 1, part 2 (January 1966), pp. 242–255.

9. Louis Bachelier, "Theorie de la speculation," *Annales Scientifiques de l'Ecole Normale Superieure*, ser. 3, No. 1018 (1900). Reprinted as "Theory of Speculation," in Paul H. Cootner, Ed., *The Random Character of Stock Market Prices* (Cambridge, Mass.: MIT Press, 1964), pp. 17–78.

10. Eugene F. Fama, "Efficient Capital Markets: A Review of Theory and Empirical Work," *Journal of Finance*, Vol. 25, No. 2 (May 1970), pp. 383–417.

11. Walter C. Labys and Clive W.J. Granger, *Speculation, Hedging and Commodity Price Forecasts* (Lexington, Mass.: Heath Lexington, 1970).

12. William Poole, "Speculative Prices as Random Walks: An Analysis of Ten Time Series of Flexible Exchange Rates," *Southern Journal of Economics*, Vol. 33, No. 4 (April 1967), pp. 468–478.

13. Herbert G. Grubel, "Profits from Forward Exchange Speculation," *Quarterly Journal of Economics*, Vol. 79, No. 2 (May 1965).

14. Roger B. Upson, "Random Walk and Forward Exchange Rates: A Spectral Analysis," *Journal of Financial and Quantitative Analysis*, Vol. 7, No. 4 (September 1972), pp. 1897–1906.

15. G.F.P. Box and G.M. Jenkins, *Time Series Analysis, Forecasting and Control* (San Francisco: Holden-Day, 1970).

16. David L. Kaserman, "The Forward Exchange Rate: Its Determination and Behavior as a Predictor of the Future Spot Rate," *Proceedings of the American Statistical Association* (1973), pp. 417–422.

17. W.B. Brown, "The Forward Exchange Rate as a Forecasting Tool," *University of Washington Business Review*, Vol. 30, No. 2 (Winter 1971), pp. 48–58.

18. See S.C. Tsiang, "The Theory of Forward Exchange and Effects of Government Intervention on the Forward Exchange Market," *IMF Staff Papers* (April 1959), pp. 75–106; Hang R. Stoll, "An Empirical Study of the Foreign Exchange Market under Fixed and Flexible Exchange Rate Systems," *Canadian Journal of Economics*, Vol. 1, No. 1 (February 1968), pp. 55–66; Jonathan Kesselman, "The Role of Speculation in Forward Rate Determination; The Canadian Flexible Dollar 1953–1960," *Canadian Journal of Economics*, Vol. 4, No. 3 (August 1971), pp. 279–298; and John J. van Belle, "A Neglected Aspect of the Modern Theory of Forward Exchange," *Southern Economic Journal* (July 1973).

19. Richard J. Herring and Richard C. Marston, "The Forward Market and Interest Rate Determination in the Eurocurrency and National Money Markets," unpublished working paper, 1974.

20. Richard C. Marston, *The Structure of the Euro-currency System*, unpublished Ph.D. Dissertation, Massachusetts Institute of Technology, 1972.

21. Box and Jenkins, op. cit.

22. See Charles R. Nelson, "The Prediction Performance of the FRB-MIT-PENN Model of the U.S. Economy," *American Economic Review*, Vol. 62, No. 5 (December 1972), 902–917.

23. P.R. Winters, "Forecasting Sales by Exponentially Weighted Moving Averages," *Management Science*, Vol. 6, No. 3 (1960), pp. 324–342.

24. For more details on the compilation of these data see *Supplement to Banking and Monetary Statistics*, Section 15, "International Finance" (Washington, D.C.: Board of Governors of the Federal Reserve System, 1962) and *Banking and Monetary Statistics* (Washington, D.C.: Board of Governors of the Federal Reserve System, 1943), 572–3.

25. Poole, op. cit.

26. Leading candidates for the distribution of speculative prices are the lognormal, the non-normal stable Paretian, and a scaled t-distribution. See, for example, Clive W.J. Granger and Oscar Morgenstern, *Predictability of Stock Market Prices* (Lexington, Mass.: D.C. Heath & Co., 1970; Fama, op. cit.; and Robert C. Blattberg, and Nicholas J. Gonedes, "A Comparison of the Stable and Student Distributions as Statistical Models for Stock Prices," *Journal of Business*, Vol. 47, No. 2 (April 1974), pp. 244–279.

27. W.J. Conover, *Practical Nonparametric Statistics* (New York: Wiley, 1971), Chapter 6.

28. In fairness to Grubel, op. cit., it should be pointed out that his results rely only on information available to the speculator at the time he would have made his decisions. Grubel's conclusions may, however, be erroneous because he employed weekly averages of daily rates; and as Working, op. cit., has shown, averages of a time series will display positive first-order serial correlation in the first differences of such a series even where the original series is a random chain.

a. If $\tilde{X}_t$ is a martingale, then the same holds for $\ln \tilde{X}_t$: If $E(\tilde{X}_t) = X_{t-1}$ then, dividing both sides by X_{t-1} and subtracting 1,

$$E\{(\tilde{X}_t - X_{t-1})/X_{t-1}\} = 0$$

Hence $E(\ln \tilde{X}_t - \ln X_{t-1}) = 0$

$$E(\ln \tilde{X}_t) = \ln X_{t-1}$$

b. The logarithmic form is used to eliminate the effect of scale and to facilitate comparisons between exchange rate "returns" and security returns. For small values of R_t (say, $R_t \leqslant .15$), $\ln X_t - \ln X_{t-1}$ is equal to the rate of return:

$$\text{Define } R_t = (X_t - X_{t-1})/X_t = X_t/X_{t-1} - 1$$

$$\text{Then } \ln X_t - \ln X_{t-1} = \ln (X_t/X_{t-1})$$

$$= \ln (R_t + 1)$$

$$= R_t - \tfrac{1}{2}R_t^2 + \tfrac{1}{3}R_t^3 - \ldots$$

(by a Taylor series expansion)

$$\doteq R_t \text{ when } R_t \text{ is very small}$$

In this study, R_t is of the order .0001 to .001. As a check, a comparison was made of values of $\ln X_t - \ln X_{t-1}$ with values of $(X_t - X_{t-1})/X_t$; they were almost always identical at the fourth decimal place.

c. A common formulation of the modern theory puts (15) in linear form:

$$F = aP + bS + cH$$

In this model, the forecasting accuracy of the forward rate would depend in part on the values assigned to a, b, and c. It is argued, however, that it is most misleading to regard these weights as constants: they are likely to vary significantly over time and should be regarded as functions of, say, capital controls and currency uncertainties.

3

Managing exchange risks in a floating world*

Alan C. Shapiro and David P. Rutenberg

*Source: *Financial Management*, 5 (Summer 1976), pp. 48–58.

Managing the risks associated with exchange rate changes is one of the most pervasive problems faced by financial executives in the multinational corporation (MNC) today. Now that most major currencies are floating, the problem is visible as never before.

Daily currency fluctuations almost guarantee that the foreign-currency-denominated assets and liabilities of MNCs will continually change value. Compounding this problem is the new ruling by the Financial Accounting Standards Board (FASB) that companies must handle foreign exchange gains and losses (accounting exposure) in a uniform way. This ruling eliminates the reserves many companies previously used to smooth fluctuations in reported earnings due to exchange rate changes. Now all gains and losses must flow through to the profit and loss statement. Furthermore, selling and pricing, as well as buying, decisions are made more complex due to the continually changing currency values. No matter which currency is used, at least one party to any international transaction is bearing exchange risk. In addition, the value of a given foreign investment may be highly dependent on future changes in exchange rates.

In this paper we present a comprehensive view of exchange risk management and offer alternative decision criteria to those normally advocated for use in hedging. A workable approach is provided for managers trying to cope with the problem of when and how much to hedge in the face of highly uncertain exchange rate fluctuations. This approach only requires estimates of the maximum and minimum values of future exchange rates; it does not require the specification of currency change probabilities. Companies willing to specify these probabilities, though, are shown how they can be used to reduce their overall hedging costs (provided these estimates generally outperform the market's forecasts).

Additional topics covered in this paper include traditional hedging strategy and techniques, currency forecasting, the value of hedging,

Exhibit 3.1 Basic hedging strategy

	Assets	Liabilities
Hard curencies Unlikely to devalue)	Increase	Decrease
Soft currencies (Likely to devalue?	Decrease	Increase

accounting and economic concepts of exchange risk, and tax effects of exchange rate changes.

Our major thesis is that firms engaged in traditional financial hedging actions can expect, at best, to break even in the long run. Instead, the new emphasis by financial management should be on smoothing earnings fluctuations by setting maximum loss limits, analyzing impact of exchange rate changes on cash flows from existing and proposed investments, taking advantage of tax differentials in sourcing exchange gains and losses, and planning operations in countries with blocked currencies and other market imperfections.

Financial Hedging—The Traditional Approach

The traditional concept of exchange risk management is based on reducing accounting or balance sheet exposure. This approach assumes that only financial items on the current balance sheet, whose dollar (or some other base currency) value will be adversely affected by a devaluation or revaluation, are exposed to exchange risk.

The basic hedging strategy for reducing accounting exposure is shown in Exhibit 3.1. Essentially, it involves increasing hard-currency assets and decreasing soft (liable to devalue) currency assets, while simultaneously decreasing hard-currency liabilities and increasing soft-currency liabilities. If a devaluation appears likely, for example, the basic hedging strategy would be executed as follows: reduce the level of cash, tighten credit terms to decrease accounts receivable, increase local borrowing, delay accounts payable, and sell the weak currency forward. Any excess cash should be shifted out of the country, either directly or indirectly.

The indirect methods include adjusting transfer prices between affiliates, speeding up the payment of dividends, fees and royalties, and adjusting the leads and lags on intersubsidiary accounts [17]. The latter method, which is the one most frequently used by multinationals, involves speeding up the payment of intersubsidiary accounts payable and delaying the collection of intersubsidiary accounts receivable. These hedging procedures for devalu-

Exhibit 3.2 Basic hedging techniques

Devaluation	Revaluation
Sell local currency forward	Buy local currency forward
Reduce levels of local currency cash and marketable securities	Increase levels of local currency cash and marketable securities
Tighten credit (reduce local receivables)	Relax local currency credit terms
Delay collection of hard currency receivables	Speed up collection of soft currency receivables
Increase imports of hard currency goods	Reduce imports of soft currency goods
Borrow locally	Reduce local borrowing
Delay payment of accounts payable	Speed up payment of accounts payable
Speed up dividend and fee remittances to parent and other subsidiaries	Delay dividend and fee remittances to parent and other subsidiaries
Speed up payment of inter-subsidiary accounts payable	Delay payment of intersub-sidiary accounts payable
Delay collection of inter-subsidiary accounts receivable	Speed up collection of intersubsidiary accounts receivable
Invoice exports in foreign currency and imports in local currency	Invoice exports in local currency and imports in foreign currency

ations would be reversed for revaluations since they present exactly the opposite problems (see Exhibit 3.2).

Currency Forecasting

To apply these traditional financial hedging techniques, currency forecasts are required. Most researchers in the area of currency forecasting have attempted to find some key economic indicators of when a currency is in trouble. Some of these indicators are balance of payments deficit, reserves of gold and hard currencies, borrowings (S.D.R.'s, official swap agreements) and rate of inflation relative to that of the U.S.

The use of these statistics usually relies on a non-systematic application of the purchasing-power parity (PPP) doctrine. This doctrine states that under a freely-floating exchange rate regime, a relative change in purchasing-power parity for any pair of currencies, calculated as a price ratio of traded goods, would tend to be approximated by a change in the equilibrium rate of exchange between these two currencies. Thus, according to PPP, if the U.S. had a yearly rate of inflation equal to 7%, while Germany's yearly rate of inflation equalled 4%, the dollar should be devaluing by approximately 3% per annum relative to the mark. There is still debate over the appropriate price index to use in measuring PPP, although economists tend to work with wholesale price indices [9], [23].

Under a fixed-rate system, the difference between the forecasted and actual rates of exchange provide a measure of a currency's basic disequilibrium. Political and other economic factors must then be considered in determining how long the political leaders can and will persist with this particular level of currency disequilibrium.

A number of authors including Gaillot [9], Treuherz [24], Thomas [23], and Hodgeson and Phelps [10] have shown that this theory explains changes in exchange rates quite well both in fixed as well as floating rate regimes. In analyzing the present floating rate system, though, significant departures from purchasing-power parity are apparent for most developed countries' currencies. One possible explanation is continued central bank intervention in the currency markets *i.e. dirty floating.*

Other economic variables relevant to exchange rate forecasting include relative interest rates and national incomes [23]. Interest rate differentials are important because they stimulate short-term capital flows by affecting the profitability of interest arbitrage. Changes in national incomes also exert a powerful influence on a nation's balance of payments. The more rapidly a nation's economy grows relative to other national economies, the more rapidly its imports will increase relative to its exports and vice versa.

A number of currency forecasting models are now available either in academic journals or commercially. Proponents of these models claim various degrees of forecasting success. Ultimately, however, a forecasting model is only good to the extent that its predictions will lead to *better decisions. Unfortunately, none of the currency forecasting models currently available have been tested in a decision-making context.* This does not mean, though, that profitable predictions are impossible.

Successful forecasting is possible where a lagged relationship exists between changes in the underlying economic determinants of currency values and the actual exchange rate change, e.g., a fixed rate system or where there are market imperfections that do not allow interest rates and/ or forward rates to fully adjust to new information. However, where market imperfections are not significant, forecasting models will probably not be useful. This, of course, has not stopped currency forecasts from being made.

Why Hedge?

According to U.S. accounting rules, exchange rate losses must be footnoted in a U.S. corporation's annual report. The costs of hedging are buried in the aggregates of the profit and loss statement. Therefore, hedging is justified by ethnocentric treasurers on the grounds that the erratic appearance of exchange rate losses will depress the corporation's stock price. However, the Sharpe-Lintner-Mossin capital asset pricing model suggests that the cost of equity to a firm is dependent on the firm's systematic risk. If foreign currency diversification can be accomplished by the investor, then corporate hedging becomes superfluous.

Some indirect evidence of the value of hedging to individual investors is available from a study by Agmon and Lessard [1] on the price behavior of U.S.-based multinational corporations on the New York Stock Exchange. They note that neither individuals nor mutual funds are geographically diversified; multinational corporations are the major suppliers of international diversification to NYSE investors. Their regression analysis supports the hypothesis that individuals *recognize and reward* the international composition of the activities of U.S.-based corporations. (In technical terms, β was found to be a decreasing function of the percentage of foreign to overall sales).

If NYSE investors pay to diversify out of the U.S., it is ironic that corporate treasurers are paying substantial hedging fees to avoid diversifying out of U.S. dollar assets. Hedging to reduce overall foreign exchange costs is sensible only if markets are not perfect. Otherwise, prices will adjust to reflect expectations of future exchange rate changes.

One source of market imperfection often cited is that individual investors may not have equal access to capital markets. For example, since forward exchange markets only exist for the major currencies, hedging often requires local borrowing in heavily regulated capital markets. As a legal citizen of many nations, the MNC normally has greater access to these markets. Even where forward markets exist, it is usually cheaper for a corporation to hedge than for the individual investor to do so because of the margin requirements on individuals' forward contracts compared to their absence for corporate customers. However, while hedging may be cheaper for the corporation, its cost can still be high. For example, bid-ask spreads on spot and forward transactions of approximately 1/8 to 1/4 of 1% can increase hedging costs significantly, especially when decisions are continually being revised.

Does Hedging Work?

The value of hedging in the absence of market imperfections, in fact, is questionable since evidence now exists that firms engaged in these hedging strategies can expect at best to *break even in the long run.* On average, the costs of protection appear to be slightly greater than the benefits derived. The cost of hedging by borrowing locally, for example, is the higher interest rate invariably associated with a soft currency loan. Even shifting funds from one country to another is not a costless means of hedging. The net effect of speeding up remittances while delaying receipt of intracompany receivables is to force a subsidiary in a devaluation-prone country to increase its local currency borrowings to finance these additional working capital requirements. As mentioned above, this involves paying higher interest rates.

A study by Robbins and Stobaugh [16] indicates that the cost of hedging using forward contracts over a 3 year period in 7 countries averaged about .7% more than a do-nothing policy. More recent estimates by Kohlhagen [11] of forward contract costs in six major currencies during the floating-rate period April 1973—December 1974 put this average excess cost at about .65%. In addition, even though the British government supported sterling futures in the past, an internal Ford Motor Company study shows that through the years 1946 to 1969 a policy of always hedging was appreciably more expensive than one of never hedging but taking losses when devaluation occurred.

Mandelbrot's [14] theoretical view that prices in speculative markets behave as a martingale (that patterns in price movements are so weak as not to justify transaction costs) has been confirmed by Giddy and Dufey [5]. They used 1973–74 data to predict the U.S. prices of the Canadian dollar, British pound, and French franc for 1, 7, 30 and 90 days ahead. They concluded that it is a random walk—an even tighter property than martingale that says it is profitless to predict even if transaction costs were zero. As a result, the best estimate of a currency's future appreciation or depreciation is its forward premium or discount. According to Solnik, though, "[T]he forward rate is a biased estimate of the future spot rate. The bias is due to risk diversification arguments" [21, p. 369]. Therefore, unless capital market imperfections exist and persist, a treasurer or anyone else engaged in selective hedging (or speculative) activities will not be able to earn consistent foreign exchange profits (or reduce total costs) in excess of those due to risk-taking.

Where market imperfections exist and are significant, exchange risk management policies may be useful. Suppose, for example, that a subsidiary is located in a country that restricts profit repatriation. A forecasted local currency (LC) devaluation can provide this firm with an opportunity to shift excess funds elsewhere where they will earn a higher rate of return. This can be accomplished by invoicing exports from that subsidiary to the rest of the corporation in the local currency at a contracted price. As the local currency deteriorates, profit margins are squeezed in the subsidiary, compared to what they would have been with hard currency billing, but improved elsewhere in the system. In effect, cost savings from the devaluation will be shifted elsewhere in the system. If that subsidiary were exporting $1 million worth of goods monthly to its parent, for example, then a 10% LC devaluation would involve a monthly shift of $100,000 to the parent. Thus, where market imperfections such as currency controls, restricted access to capital markets, etc. do exist, there is the possibility of successful forecasting. However, the very nature of these imperfections severely restricts a company's ability to engage in profitable financial operations.

In deciding on an appropriate exchange risk management strategy, it is necessary to determine what is at risk. The following section contrasts the difference between the accounting and economic approach to measuring exposure (the degree to which a company is exposed to exchange risk).

Exposure

Under the new FASB ruling, companies are required to measure their foreign exchange exposure as the difference between current assets (except inventories and marketable securities) and virtually all short and long term liabilities [7]. This is one variant of the balance sheet approach which assumes that only financial items on the current balance sheet whose dollar value will be affected by exchange rate changes are exposed. Fixed assets are considered to maintain their dollar value after a devaluation because their local currency value is expected to rise in proportion to the extent of any devaluation (another example of the purchasing-power parity doctrine). However, this approach only considers a devaluation's effect on current year *accounting income*. In that the value of a firm is equal to the discounted sum of future after-tax *cash flows*, it is obvious that the balance sheet approach allows the first year's flow to dominate adjustments to the value of a firm. Furthermore, unless the firm can revalue its fixed assets, the dollar value of local currency cash inflows from depreciation will decline.

The myopia of acting on the basis of balance sheet exposure rather than economic impact has been scathingly portrayed by Dufey [4] in the Summer 1972 issue of *Financial Management*. In that article the French subsidiary of an American multinational corporation was instructed to reduce its working capital balances in light of a forecasted French franc devaluation, which would have forced the subsidiary to curtail its operations. However, the French subsidiary was selling all of its output to two other subsidiaries located in Germany and Belgium. Since the dollar value of its output would remain constant while franc costs expressed in dollars would decline, a 10% franc devaluation was expected to increase the dollar profitability associated with the French subsidiary by over 25%. Thus, the French manager argued, correctly, that the plant should begin expanding its operations, rather than contracting them, to take advantage of the anticipated devaluation.

The assumption that local currency sales and costs remain constant after an exchange rate change does not permit an evaluation of the typical adjustments consumers and firms undertake. In fact, Dufey [4] and Shapiro [18] have shown systematic and predictable changes to local currency cost and revenue streams, predictable both as to direction and magnitude. Discussion of some of the typical demand and cost effects of a devaluation follow.

Local Demand. If strong import competition exists, local currency prices increase, although not to the full extent of the devaluation. If import competition is weak or non-existent, local prices increase little, if at all (with weak competition, prices would have already been increased as much as possible). Demand could actually decrease if the government undertakes austerity measures in conjunction with the devaluation.

Foreign Demand. Foreign prices, expressed in dollars, remain the same or decrease, depending on the degree of competition from other exporters.

Cost of Local Inputs. Local currency costs rise although not to the full extent of the devaluation. This increase is positively associated with the import content of local inputs as well as the availability of these inputs. Inputs used in the export or import-competing sectors increase in price more than other domestic inputs. Labor costs, expressed in LC, may increase but this increase is usually less than the devaluation percentage. Hence, the greater the value added by local labor, the more dollar production costs should decline.

Cost of Imported Inputs. Dollar costs of imported inputs remain the same or decrease somewhat. The decrease depends upon the elasticity of demand for these imported goods as well as on the size of the local market relative to the world market.

Firms with world-wide production systems can be expected to increase production in a nation whose currency has devalued and decrease production in a country whose currency has revalued, all other things being equal. The greater the local labor content of a product and the percentage of local purchase, the greater the adjustment that can be expected.

All too frequently, firms neglect these effects when *analyzing proposed foreign investments.* A common mistake made is to multiply the projected local currency cash flows by the forecasted (expected) exchange rates. For example, Stonehill and Nathanson [22, p. 46] advise firms that the appropriate way to "allow for uncertainty in the multinational case would be to charge each period's incremental cash flows the cost of a program of uncertainty absorption for the period, whether or not the program was actually undertaken." For example, suppose a cash inflow of LC 1000 is expected during the current year. If the present exchange rate is LC1 = \$1, while the one year forward rate is LC1 = \$.80, then the Stonehill-Nathanson approach would charge the \$1000 cash inflow (at current rates) the \$200 cost of hedging, which would leave an adjusted cash flow of \$800. As we have seen, though, such a policy disregards the effects an exchange rate change has on the actual local currency cash flows. The appropriate technique, then, is to make these cash flows contingent on future exchange rates. The expected dollar cash flows are then found by weighting each of these contingent dollar cash flows by the probability that the exchange rate upon which each is based will actually prevail.

Let $L(f)$ be the present value of local currency cash flows with a given exchange rate f (\$ value of one unit of local currency). Suppose there are 3 possible exchange rates, f_1, f_2, f_3, with probabilities of p_1, p_2, p_3, respectively. In diagram form this would appear as:

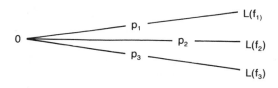

The expected present value of dollar cash flows then equals $p_1L(f_1)f_1 + p_2L(F_2)f_2 + p_3L(f_3)f_3$. For example, suppose that the proposed investment involves a plant whose entire output is to be exported. The plant's capacity is rated at one million units per annum. With a selling price of \$10 per unit, the yearly revenue from this investment equals \$10 million. This revenue is not expected to vary with the LC exchange rate. At the present rate of exchange, dollar costs of local production equal \$6 per unit. A devaluation of 10% is expected to lower unit costs by \$.30, while a 15% devaluation will reduce these costs by an additional \$.15. If a devaluation of either 10% or 15% is likely with respective probabilities of .4 and .2 (the probability of no currency change is .4), then the expected value of yearly dollar cash inflows equals .4 (\$10,000,000 − \$6,000,000) + .4 (\$10,000,000 − \$5,700,000) + .2 (\$10,000,000 − \$5,550,000) = \$4,210,000. Assuming that the forward discount equals 7% (.4 × 10% + .2 × 15%), the Stonehill-Nathanson method would instead have recognized a yearly cash inflow of \$3,720,000 (\$4,000,000 − .07 × \$4,000,000).

The diagram becomes more complex as additional periods in which exchange rates could change are added, but the basic notion is the same—local currency cash flows branch in each period in which exchange rates are expected to change. In addition, one must not neglect the higher rate of inflation that precedes a given devaluation. In general, the effects of inflation on the dollar value of a given firm or investment are the reverse of the effects of a devaluation.

It is clear that firms cannot cover their economic exposure by traditional financial hedging. Hence, instead of attempting to minimize the short-run balance sheet impact of an exchange rate change, managers should concentrate their efforts on the production and marketing adjustments and investment decisions necessary to ensure and increase profitability in the long run [22].

We realize, however, that managers are evaluated on the balance sheet impact of a devaluation. As Business International [3, p. 7] wryly observes:

> By U.S. accounting rules [d] evaluation losses are singled out in a U.S. firm's annual report. The costs of hedging are buried in aggregates in the P & L .... If after a devaluation, a finance officer could say that the company was covered—he is a hero. If the devaluation loss was not hedged, his position may be in jeopardy. On the other hand, top executives and shareholders rarely complain about the cost of hedging—even if continued over a long period—the expense is a cost of doing business.

The authors do not agree with the asymmetrical reward structure implied by this quote. For those firms that insist upon hedging their balance sheet exposure, though, the next section presents a reasonable strategy designed to avoid yearly fluctuations in income caused by exchange rate changes.

Decision Criteria

The choice of how much a treasurer should hedge and the hedging costs he should be willing to pay are heavily dependent upon his decision criteria. For example, the more risk averse a treasurer is, the more that treasurer should be willing to pay to cover his exposure.

Several authors have developed models to determine the optimal amount and type of hedging that should be done using different utility-theoretic approaches. Liaeter [13], for example, assumed a one-period portfolio theory view of the problem, and presented a classical quadratic programming formulation to calculate an efficient risk-return frontier. Other writers such as Folks [8] and Wheelwright [25] take the more general approach of maximizing expected utility (or minimizing expected disutility). However, developing exchange risk management policies by applying utility theory to a subset of a firm's assets results in suboptimiz-

Table 3.1

Optimal strategy if future exchange rate is between:	Revenue if actual future exchange rate equals:						
	$1.99	$2.00	$2.01	$2.02	$2.03	$2.04
$1.99–2.01 Hedge	$2,010,000	$2,010,000	$2,010,000	$2,010,000	$2,010,000	$2,010,000
$2.01–2.04 Don't Hedge	$1,990,000	$2,000,000	$2,010,000	$2,020,000	$2,030,000	$2,040,000
Difference	$20,000	$10,000	$00	–$10,000	–$20,000	–$30,000

ation, since that approach ignores both the covariances between asset returns and the effects of exchange rate changes on the firm's systematic risk.

In addition, these approaches all require the specification of probabilities for future currency values. A new approach presented by Kohlhagen [12] requires only an estimate of reasonable ranges of future exchange rates. It involves selecting the optimal hedging actions for each possibly currency value within the range presented. The value of a given set of hedging actions is then studied for each different exchange rate. For example, suppose a firm has a 90 day net exposure of £1,000,000 in accounts receivable as of January 20, 1976. On that date the spot price of sterling was $2.03 while a 90 day forward pound sold for $2.01. A reasonable range for sterling 90 days hence was assumed to be $1.99–$2.04. To maximize the dollar value of these receivables, the firm should sell sterling forward only if the future spot price of sterling were to be less than $2.01. The payoff matrix for such a strategy is shown in Table 3.1.

Without hedging, the maximum exchange loss equals $40,000 (1,000,000 × $.04). There is also the potential of a $10,000 exchange profit (1,000,000 × $.01). On the other hand, a cash flow of $2,010,000 is assured with hedging. (If the forward rate were an unbiased predictor of the future spot rate, expected revenue with no action would remain $2,010,000.)

In actuality, the firm's decision problem would be more complex since these receivables could probably be factored (sold at a discount) now and the proceeds used to purchase dollars. The optimal strategy would then depend on the relative cost of selling the expected proceeds forward versus selling the receivables immediately (see [19] for a detailed analysis of the receivables problem).

A worried treasurer working for a worried finance officer had better decide on a maximum exposure they dare take, and constantly hedge the rest. If a company has a net exposure of E dollars in a currency liable to devalue with a maximum potential devaluation of extent d, the firm's maximum possible exchange loss is dE. By varying E, then, the firm can limit its maximum loss to any set amount L. In the above example, if $25,000 is the maximum loss that would be tolerated, the treasurer should hedge at least £375,000 in the forward market (maximum exposure equals 25,000/.04 = £625,000).

At present, though, there is no way for the assistant treasurer to be absolutely certain of never losing more than the target (unless he hedges totally). That is to say, so long as the corporation has some exposure, there is always a chance that the exchange rate will drop so much that the losses will drop below the assumed set floor. The assistant treasurer can hedge enough to reduce the chance of that happening to, say, one year in ten.

What the assistant treasurer really wants is a foreign exchange options market. Suppose his sterling exposure is such that he would exceed his loss floor if sterling sank to parity with the dollar (£1 = $1). There is very little chance of that happening in 1976, so it would be inexpensive to buy an option to convert pounds to dollars at parity on December 31, 1976. Probably the pound will not sink so low, so he won't exercise his option. But if it does devalue that much, the option protects him from exceeding the floor on losses. Although no such options are regularly available at present, they are needed, and we predict they will be available soon.

In the above example, even though a loss of $25,000 is possible, it may not be very probable. There are two possible approaches to take account of the probabilities associated with the various possible losses. One would be to limit the expected loss. If $\bar{d}$ is the expected devaluation, then the expected devaluation loss is $\bar{d}E$. By varying E, a firm's expected loss can be constrained to any desired level. Suppose a firm operating in a country whose currency is expected to devalue by an average of 10% over the coming year wishes to limit its expected exchange loss during the year to $1,000,000. This can be achieved by setting a maximum LC exposure limit of $1,000,000/.10 = $10,000,000.

The other method directly considers the various probabilities via chance-constraints, which limit the probability of losing more than L dollars in any one time period to a level of α or less. Restricting the probability of having exchange losses totalling more than $1,000,000 in a year to less than 5% would be an example of chance-constraint. This approach is useful if a company feels that it is highly desirable to limit losses to a certain level, but is also mindful of the costs involved. The following procedure can be used to construct these constraints. Let p_i be the probability of a devaluation of extend d_i where the d_i's are ranked such that $d_1 > d_2 > d_3$, etc. For a given level of α, select that k such that

$$\sum_{i=1}^{k} p_i \leq \alpha < \sum_{i=1}^{k+1} p_i$$

Then, by setting an exposure limit of L/d_k the probability of a firm losing more than L dollars is no greater than α. For example, suppose that a firm estimated the following probability distribution function for a devaluation: no change with probability .20, 2% change with probability .25, 3% change with probability .20, 4% devaluation with probability .15, 5% devaluation with probability, .10, 7% devaluation with probability .05, 10% devaluation with probability .05. If this firm wishes to limit to 25% the probability of having exchange losses that exceed $100,000, then its total exposure must not be greater than $100,000/.05 = $2,000,000.

These constraints can still cost a firm a sizeable amount. The manager should be presented with various α and L, so as to ponder his expected savings from relaxing these exposure constraints. These savings equal the difference between the expected savings in hedging costs and the expected devaluation losses associated with an increase in exposure.

Multiple Currencies

The procedures presented above deal with the case where exposure is in only one currency. Determining possible exchange losses when several currencies are involved depends on the correlations between these currencies.

A study of currency correlations during the present floating rate system suggests that these correlations may be sufficiently unstable that extrapolation of past currency relationships may not be possible. Exhibit 3.3 presents the correlation coefficients among the English pound, French franc, Swiss franc, German mark, and Japanese yen versus the dollar. The first row for each currency refers to estimates based on exchange rate data taken daily from August 1, 1973 through August 21, 1973. The second row is computed from daily exchange rate movements between December 2, 1974 and December 20, 1974, while the bottom row provides the correlation coefficients for monthly exchange rates from March 1, 1973 through August 1, 1975 (taken on the first trading day of each month).

In general, the correlations based on longer-term data appear to be less positive or more negative than the shorter-run correlations. This suggests that the more diversified the currency portfolio of a multinational corporation, the fewer long-term fluctuations there should be in the dollar value of its foreign cash balances.

To provide some indication of the value of currency diversification, $100 was placed in each of the above 5 currencies on April 2, 1973. The dollar values of each of these holdings were then tracked for the next 9 quarters and compared with a naive portfolio consisting of $20 placed in each of the 5 currencies. Exhibit 3.4 presents these quarterly values.

The means and variances of these figures were then computed and are shown in Exhibit 3.5.

As can be seen, the variance of the portfolio is significantly below the variances of the French franc, Swiss franc, and German mark holdings. In addition, while the portfolio has somewhat smaller variance than the pound and yen holdings, its mean value is significantly higher than either of these currencies' dollar values. This naive portfolio ignores the strong correlations existing between the French, Swiss, and German currencies. To minimize variance, these currencies would have to be assigned a lower proportion in any currency portfolio. To the extent, then, that longer-run currency correlations are stable, a multinational corporation should hold its excess cash in a diversified portfolio of currencies, with the portfolio weight for each currency determined by its degree of correlation with the overall portfolio. The more positively correlated a given currency is with other currencies in the portfolio, the smaller the proportion of that currency that should be in the total portfolio. Conversely, a currency whose dollar value is negatively correlated with the dollar value of the portfolio should

Exhibit 3.3 Currency correlation coefficients

	£	fr(F)	fr(S)	Dm	$\bar{Y}$	
£	1.0000	0.9563	0.9344	0.9681	0.8945	Daily movements (8/1/73–8/21/73)
	1.0000	0.1902	0.2499	0.3963	0.0000	Daily movements (12/2/74–12/20/74)
	1.0000	0.1977	-0.2571	0.0209	0.7231	Monthly movements (3/1/73–8/1/75)
fr(F)		1.0000	0.9802	0.9870	0.8129	Daily movements (8/1/73–8/21/73)
		1.0000	0.9206	0.8642	-0.2300	Daily movements (12/2/74–12/20/74)
		1.0000	0.5935	0.6500	0.1340	Monthly movements (3/1/73–8/1/75)
fr(S)			1.0000	0.9786	0.7677	Daily movements (8/1/73–8/21/73)
			1.0000	0.9439	-0.2242	Daily movements (12/2/74–12/20/74)
			1.0000	0.8047	-0.5140	Monthly movements (3/1/73–8/1/75)
Dm				1.0000	0.8271	Daily movements (8/1/73–8/21/73)
				1.0000	-0.2991	Daily movements (12/2/74–12/20/74)
				1.000	-0.1874	Monthly movements (3/1/73–8/1/75)
$\bar{Y}$					1.000	Daily movements (8/1/73–8/21/73)
					1.0000	Daily movements (12/2/74–12/20/74)
					1.0000	Monthly movements (3/1/73–8/1/75)

Exhibit 3.4 Quarterly dollar values of foreign currency holdings: April 2, 1973–
July 1, 1975

Date	£	fr(F)	fr(S)	Dm	Y	Portfolio
4/2/73	$100.00	100.00	100.00	100.00	100.00	100.00
7/2/73	104.36	109.70	111.54	117.30	99.47	108.47
10/1/73	99.29	104.71	107.13	117.72	99.21	105.61
1/2/74	93.76	96.55	99.74	105.74	94.21	97.88
4/1/74	96.65	95.01	107.75	112.50	95.39	101.46
7/1/74	96.53	93.74	108.14	111.53	92.66	100.52
10/1/74	94.37	95.83	110.51	107.27	88.29	99.25
1/2/75	94.75	102.13	127.43	117.86	87.50	105.93
4/1/75	97.16	107.75	127.92	121.96	89.63	108.72
7/1/75	88.41	112.06	129.57	120.48	89.05	107.90

comprise a greater percentage of the final portfolio.

Even in the absence of knowledge about future values of these currency
correlations, it is possible to obtain very crude bounds on possible
exchange losses by studying extreme situations. Suppose that a currency A
is presently valued at $.25 but that its exchange rate can vary from $.23 to
$.26. At the same time, currency B's exchange rate is $.40 with a possible
range of $.38 to $.42. A firm that has $1,000,000 worth of exposure in
currency A (LC 4,000,000) and $500,000 (LC 1,250,000) in currency B
will have the following range of possible exchange effects in each currency.

A— −$80,000 to +$40,000
B— −$25,000 to +$25,000

Thus, the impact of this firm's exposure in A and B can range from a
maximum loss of $105,000 to a maximum gain of $65,000. If $.24 and
$.39 are the forward rates for A and B, respectively, then all potential
profit fluctuations due to exchange rate changes can be eliminated for
$52,500 (4,000,000 × $.01 + 1,250,000 × $.01).

As before, fractional hedging can eliminate as much earnings variability
due to exchange rate changes as is desired. The choice of the appropriate

Exhibit 3.5 Means and variances of foreign currency holdings

	£	fr(F)	fr(S)	Dm	Y	Portfolio
Mean	96.14	101.94	114.41	114.64	92.82	103.97
Variance	16.60	48.86	105.96	30.34	18.54	15.54

hedging quantity is dependent on the corporation's degree of risk aversion, the cost of hedging in different currencies and currency expectations.

This approach can easily be extended to n currencies. The maximum possible exchange loss for a firm with exposure in n currencies can be found by calculating the maximum possible exchange loss in each currency and summing. Setting probabilistic limits on total losses can be achieved by varying exposure in selected currencies. In general, the quantity hedged in each currency to satisfy a given chance-constraint will not be unique. Thus, by selectively hedging its accounting exposure, a firm can limit fluctuations in its current reported earnings due to exchange rate changes. As was pointed out previously, such a policy may be beneficial to the treasurer and other corporate officers; its value to stockholders is less clear. In fact, we will show in the next section that it is not obvious that continual hedging will reduce long-run earnings fluctuations due to exchange rate changes as compared with a policy of never hedging.

Long-Run vs Short-Run Earnings Fluctuations

Assume that a firm has anticipated yearly local currency earnings equal to C which are not expected to vary with the exchange rate. Let e_1 be the unknown dollar value of one unit of local currency in year i. Then, the variance in the dollar value of LC earnings in year i, in the absence of hedging, equals C^2 Var (e_1). Suppose now that this firm decides to hedge all of its LC earnings.

Since a forward contract of maturity greater than one year is very expensive in any currency, we assume that the firm's hedging strategy involves selling C units of LC forward for dollars at the beginning of each year. If S_1 is the forward exchange rate at the beginning of year i for local currency delivered at the end of year i, then the dollar value of year i's LC earnings equals S_1 C. Then the variance in the dollar value of these hedged earnings equals C^2 Var (S_1). Dufey and Giddy [5] have shown that at any given moment spot and forward rates are very highly correlated. Thus, var (S_1) is likely to be approximately equal to var (e_1). Hence, unless S_1 is any easier to predict than is e_1, a policy of always hedging is not likely to reduce fluctuations in reported earnings beyond the first year where these fluctuations are due to exchange rate changes.

Recommendations

Since it is unlikely that firms can consistently earn abnormally large profits from currency speculation, the goal of any hedging strategy should be at most to avoid fluctuations in the current year's reported income caused by exchange rate changes. Spending time on currency forecasting and selective hedging techniques is likely to be a misdirection of a firm's efforts. Instead, the financial officers should decide on a maximum exposure they dare take and constantly hedge the rest. Tax factors must be taken into account in deciding where and for how much to hedge (see the appendix).

References

[1] Tamir Agmon and Donald Lessard, "International Diversification and the Multinational Corporation: An Investigation of Price Behaviour of the Shares of U.S. Based Multinational Corporations on the N.Y.S.E.," Working Paper #804–75, Sloan School of Management, Massachusetts Institute of Technology, 1975.

[2] Gerald M. Blank, "Currency Devaluation: A Guide to Income Tax Consequences in 14 Countries," *The Journal of Taxation* (July 1971), pp. 15–19.

[3] Business International Corporation, "Hedging Foreign Exchange Risks," Management Monograph No. 49, New York, 1971.

[4] Gunter Dufey, "Corporate Finance and Exchange Rate Variations," *Financial Management* (Summer 1972), pp. 51–57.

[5] Gunter Dufey and Ian Giddy, "The Random Behavior of Flexible Exchange Rates: Implications for Forecasting," *Journal of International Business Studies* (Spring 1975), pp. 1–3.

[6] Edward L. Farrell Jr., "Tax Planning and the Multinational Corporation," *Pennsylvania CPA Spokesman* (February 1974), pp. 11–15.

[7] Financial Accounting Standards Board, "Accounting for the Translation of Foreign Currency Transactions and Foreign Currency Financial Statements," Statement of Financial Accounting Standards No. 8, Stamford, Connecticut, October, 1975.

[8] William R. Folks Jr., "The Optimal Level of Forward Exchange Transactions," *Journal of Financial and Quantitative Analysis* (January 1973), pp. 105–110.

[9] Henry J. Gaillot, "Purchasing Power Parity as an Explanation of Long-Term Changes in Exchange Rates," *Journal of Money, Credit and Banking* (August 1970), pp. 348–357.

[10] John S. Hodgeson and Patricia Phelps, "The Distributed Impact of Price-Level Variations on Floating Exchange Rates," unpublished working paper, University of Oklahoma, 1973.

[11] Steven W. Kohlhagen, "Evidence on the Cost of Forward Cover in a Floating System," *Euromoney* (September 1975), pp. 138–141.

[12] Steven W. Kohlhagen, "Optimal Hedging Strategies for the Multinational Corporation Without Exchange Rate Projections," paper presented at Academy of International Business Annual Meeting, Dallas, Texas, December 29, 1975.

[13] Bernard A. Liaeter, "Managing Risks in Foreign Exchange," *Harvard Business Review* (March–April 1970), pp. 127–128.

[14] Benoit Mandelbrot, "Unbiased Markets and Martingale Models," *The Journal of Business,* Vol. 39 (1966), pp. 242–244.

[15] Gordon J. Nicholson, "Tax Problems Resulting from Devaluation," *The Tax Executive* (January 1969), pp. 31–39.

[16] Sidney M. Robbins, and Robert Stobaugh, *Money in the Multinational Enterprise: A Study of Financial Policy*, New York, Basic Books, 1972.

[17] David Rutenberg, "Maneuvering Liquid Assets in a Multinational Corporation," *Management Science* (June 1970), pp. 671–684.

[18] Alan C. Shapiro, "Exchange Rate Changes, Inflation and the Value of the Multinational Corporation," *Journal of Finance* (May 1975), pp. 485–502.

[19] Alan C. Shapiro, "Optimal Inventory and Credit-Granting Strategies Under Inflation and Devaluation," *Journal of Financial and Quantitative Analysis* (January 1973), pp. 37–46.

[20] Alan C. Shapiro and Thomas S. Robertson, "Managing Foreign Exchange Risks: The Role of Marketing Strategy," University of Pennsylvania Working Paper, 1975.

[21] Bruno H. Solnik, "The International Pricing of Risk: An Empirical Investigation of the World Capital Market Structure," *Journal of Finance* (May 1974), pp. 365–378.

[22] Arthur Stonehill and Leonard Nathanson, "Capital Budgeting and the Multinational Firm," *California Management Review* (Summer 1968), pp. 39–54.

[23] Lloyd B. Thomas, "Behavior of Flexible Exchange Rates: Additional Tests from the Post-World War I Episode," *Southern Economic Journal* (October 1973), pp. 167–182.

[24] Rolf M. Treuherz, "Forecasting Foreign Exchange Rates in Inflationary Economies," *Financial Executive* (February 1969), pp. 57–60.

[25] Steven C. Wheelwright, "Applying Decision Theory to Improve Corporate Management of Currency-Exchange Risks," *California Management Review* (Summer 1975), pp. 41–49.

Appendix

Only after-tax costs are relevant to a hedging decision. So before deciding *when* to hedge against exchange risk, the treasurer of a multinational corporation must decide which of its many subsidiaries to use as an intermediary. The most suitable subsidiary depends upon: the national tax treatment of foreign exchange losses and hedging costs and gains; the individual tax status of the national subsidiary in that year, and how the government of the headquarters nation will tax the gain or loss in this particular nation.

There are differences in national tax treatments of foreign exchange gains, but unfortunately the law is not clearcut in any nation. In practice the question revolves around whether exchange gains may be categorized as capital gains and what their tax rate is. Blank [2] sketches the income tax consequences in 14 countries emphasizing when gains and losses are recognized for tax purposes. In the U.S.A. there are conflicting interpretations as to whether selling for 6 months and buying for 9 (so as to cover those months that are 6 months hence) would result in a long or short term gain.

On an after tax basis we can see how erroneous is the conventional wisdom that a dollar loan provides no protection if a local currency (LC) devalues. Suppose LC 1 = $.25 when a subsidiary borrows $1 million in the Eurodollar market for one year at 10% (hence must repay $1,100,000). If the exchange rate drifts down to LC 1 = $.20 by year end, the subsidiary must repay LC 5,500,000 instead of LC 4,400,000. The interest plus exchange loss totals LC 1,500,000. (This example would not apply for a U.K. subsidiary. Andreas Prindl of Morgan Guarantee has noted that the U.K. Inland Revenue does not allow exchange losses on foreign currency borrowings to be offset against income.) If the subsidiary's marginal tax rate is 50%, its taxes are reduced by LC 750,000 (now $150,000). To the U.S. corporation the effective after-tax dollar cost of the loan is the interest cost of $100,000 less the tax saving of $150,000, which equals −$50,000 or −5%.

The tax status of each particular subsidiary affects after tax income; hence, two corporations with the same risk aversion and exposure may differ on whether to hedge. Hedging can be done through a loss subsidiary. The gains from devaluation would be taxable income if there were any, but due to the losses they are not taxed. We have interviewed many treasurers who hedge part of their exposure from one subsidiary and the remainder from another, because the first had only limited foreign tax credits. In general a corporation can rank subsidiaries by after-tax hedging cost and start at the top of the list consuming excess foreign tax credits. As Nicholson [15, p. 37] explains:

> Many companies today have credits available in excess of the foreign tax credit limitations. This arises because a creditable tax cannot exceed the "effective" tax rate times the net foreign source income.... To the extent that the loss on devaluation is a foreign source loss, the deductability of the loss may in effect be forfeited completely due to this limitation. If the gain is foreign source gain, the effect may be to receive the gain tax free under shelter of excess foreign tax credits.

For example, suppose the treasurer expects a $2,000,000 gain from a futures contract against the devaluation of the U.K. pound. Had he taken out the contract in New York, the gain would be domestic source income taxed at 48% of $2 million, or $960,000. If he had taken out the contract in Lichtenstein, zero tax rate, the $2,000,000 would be foreign source income in the eyes of the U.S. Internal Revenue Service. If the corporation operates profitably in any nation with a higher rate of tax than the USA, it produces excess tax credits. Such tax credits can only be applied to foreign source income, which includes this $2 million from Lichtenstein, which therefore becomes tax free.

The U.S. government may tax speculative gains abroad through the minimum distribution requirements of the Internal Revenue Code's Sub-Part F. Sub-Part F income consists of nonmanufacturing income (rents, royalties, licensing fees, dividends), income from services performed for related persons outside the nation, and income from the sale of property to related persons outside the nation. Rutenberg [17] discusses some of the tax implications of subpart F of the U.S. Internal Revenue Code.

If monetary fluctuations cause translation losses, sourcing these losses in a subsidiary having subpart F income or in a subsidiary which is included in a group or chain minimum distribution election will accelerate a corporation's foreign tax credits [6]. If gains result, these rules should be avoided.

4

Management of foreign exchange risk: a review article*

Laurent L. Jacque[†]

*Source: *Journal of International Studies*, 12 (Spring/Summer 1981), pp. 81–101.

Abstract. This paper reviews the literature on Foreign Exchange Risk Management (FERM) which has burgeoned during the last decade. Scholars' and practitioners' emerging interest in Foreign Exchange Risk Management was spurred by the advent of fluctuating exchange rates in the early seventies as well as by the pronouncement of the infamous FASB Statement No. 8 in 1976 which laid down unambiguous guidelines for consolidating financial statements of multinational corporations. A normative (rather than a market) view of Foreign Exchange Risk Management is taken and accordingly the author reviews first the two key informational inputs necessary for any Foreign Exchange Risk Management program: forecasting exchange rates and measuring exposure to exchange risk. Available decision models for handling transaction and translation exposures are reviewed next. A concluding section identifies gaps in the existing literature and suggests directions for future research.

Introduction

> So much of barbarism, however, still remains in the transactions of most civilized nations, that almost all independent countries choose to assert their nationality by having, to their own inconvenience and that of their neighbors, a peculiar currency of their own.
>
> John Stuart Mill, 1894

Of all the winds of change that have buffeted multinational corporations (MNCs) in recent years, none has had a more pervasive impact upon their risk profile than the demise of the international monetary system of quasi-fixed exchange rates that had prevailed until March 1973 under the Bretton Woods agreement (1944–1971) and, later, under the short-lived

Smithsonian accord (1971–1973). A somewhat chaotic system of floating exchange rates has emerged in its stead.

The resulting heightened volatility in currencies' prices has severely disrupted the steadiness of multinational corporations' foreign income streams. The recent implementation of the controversial and inflexible FASB Statement No. 8 has further exacerbated this seemingly erratic earnings pattern by doing away with the former widely used practice of *reserving* for foreign exchange gains and losses and forcing upon MNCs the periodic disclosure of such gains and losses even though no cash flows may be involved.

This unprecedented situation has stirred a considerable amount of interest among both academics and practitioners in Foreign Exchange Risk Management. This article reviews the literature on Foreign Exchange Risk Management published in the last decade to identify the conceptual weaknesses underlying the normative Foreign Exchange Risk Management decision models currently available and to suggest fruitful directions for future managerially oriented research.

Management of Foreign Exchange Risk: Whose View?

Foreign Exchange Risk is commonly defined as the additional variability experienced by a multinational corporation in its worldwide consolidated earnings that results from unexpected currency fluctuations. It is generally understood that this considerable earnings variability can be eliminated – partially or fully – at a cost, the cost of Foreign Exchange Risk Management. Is such a cost warranted or, in other words, should corporate treasurers be concerned with the smooth period-to-period earnings pattern so cherished by security analysts, because a volatile earnings pattern is commonly believed to affect the firm's price–earnings ratio and, in turn, its ability to raise funds at a reasonable cost?

Modern capital market theory, which defines foreign exchange risk as "the systematic risk associated with a foreign currency denominated return (or cost) stream and measured by the covariance between the rate of change of the exchange rate and the domestic market return" [80, p. 25], answers in the negative. It argues that under certain assumptions of market efficiency (to be spelled out below) Foreign Exchange Risk Management is totally superfluous. This somewhat extreme point of view, detailed in Logue and Oldfield [48], holds that a firm's risky prospects are valued directly by the market on the basis of their expected profitability and their systematic risk (that is, the risk which cannot be "diversified away"); thus, it should make "no difference to the valuation of either the total market portfolio or the individual firm whether exchange risks ... are passed through to the capital market as part of the risk of the firm's shares, or 'laid off', or transferred directly to the market through forward exchange or foreign currency debt contracts."[1] In this somewhat hypothetical world, MNCs' treasurers abdicate the initiative of Foreign Exchange Risk Management whose responsibility is fully transferred to the firm's shareholders who, in turn, will manage the unsystematic portion of exchange risk through efficient portfolio diversification. The relevant question for scholarly investigation thus becomes that of exchange risk diversification from the viewpoint of the investor selecting claims on firms located in different countries or operating across national boundaries (MNCs), claims which are clearly denominated in different currencies. Normative research efforts in this direction are aimed at extending the Capital Asset Pricing Model to a multicurrency world; however, existing International Capital Asset Pricing Models are based on extraordinarily restrictive assumptions. To wit, Fama and Farber [24] and Grauer, Litzenberger, and Stehle [33] assume away international capital market segmentation (that is, international capital markets are fully integrated). The former model presumes further that investors consume only one homogeneous good and that Purchasing Power Parity holds at all times. Solnik [72 a & b] similarly assumes full integration of international capital markets but allows for different consumption goods across countries; however, exchange rates are assumed to be uncorrelated with the corresponding local currency market returns, certainly a convenient simplifying premise. In sum, all three models acrobatically dispose of the exchange risk factor in their pricing of foreign currency denominated assets.

How to diversify exchange risk effectively at the investor level remains an unanswered question because existing International Asset Pricing Models require satisfaction of a strict set of conditions which are far removed from the current multicurrency institutional environment facing international investors. Therefore it should come as no surprise that most theoretical models of Foreign Exchange Risk Management and certainly all of current management practice have considered exchange risk from the viewpoint of a firm's treasurer aiming at minimizing the impact of exchange rate fluctuations upon earnings measured in some relevant numeraire, thus upholding the fundamental hypothesis behind foreign Exchange Risk Management stated at the beginning of this section. Adoption of the firm total risk viewpoint is further warranted, as Makin [50b, p. 521] argues, when

consideration is given to the time horizon of a typical manager which is likely to be considerably shorter than the time period required for the impact of exchange market disturbances on firm's profit to net to zero. Further, costs of capital can be influenced by the perceived riskiness of claims on multinationals and that perceived riskiness, relative to other multinationals, could be altered in the short run by heavy exposures in foreign currencies.

In a similar vein, Aliber [3, pp. 134–155] writes: "The question is whether the firm or individual investor can do a more effective job of diversifying against exchange risk ... The firm may have superior knowledge, and may be able to protect itself against these risks at lower costs."

Indeed, to the extent that individual investors face exchange controls, high transaction costs, and taxation, MNCs, because they can lessen the burden of such market imperfections, are superiorly equipped to carry out currency diversification on behalf of their shareholders.

Having explained the logic behind the relevance of corporate Foreign Exchange Risk Management, this discussion next proceeds with a review of available methodologies for generating the two key informational inputs for effective Foreign Exchange Risk Management; namely, reliable probabilistic forecasts of future spot exchange rates as well as a projection of corporate exposures on a currency-by-currency basis.

Forecasting Exchange Rates

Although tremendous resources have been directed at forecasting exchange rate changes or establishing the irrelevance of such forecasting efforts (Market Efficiency hypothesis), little attention has been focused on the managerially more relevant issue of relating the forecastability of foreign exchange rates to Foreign Exchange Risk Management proper. Accordingly, this section will consider first, at some length, the general question of exchange rates forecasting independently from the praxis of Foreign Exchange Risk Management before attempting to reconcile the two.

The quantitative dimension of foreign exchange rate forecasting – that is, predicting expected future spot exchange rates – is traditionally emphasized by most forecasting models. However, the operational value of such predictions can be greatly enhanced if they can be supplemented by a qualitative forecast. Historically, parity changes have, in most cases, been tightly intermingled with a complex history of exchange restrictions running the gamut from selective controls on capital account transactions to indiscriminate controls on all exchange transactions.

The task of the currency forecaster is therefore twofold: (1) quantifying the magnitude of expected exchange rate changes (devaluations or revaluations in the context of pegged exchange rates; depreciation or appreciation in the context of floating exchange rates), and (2) anticipating the likelihood of imposition of exchange controls.

Forecasting Pegged Yet Adjustable Exchange Rates

The current international monetary system is best described as a system in which currencies within major trading blocs maintain their former pegged yet adjustable relationships with each other, but fluctuate continuously – or float in unison – against the currencies of other major blocs. The European Monetary System, for example, is very much resurrecting, on a regional basis, the Bretton Woods system of quasi-fixed exchange rates through its tightly knit grid of par values.

Under such conditions, forecasting discrete change in parities is a relatively easy task, at least in direction if not in magnitude or timing. Jacque [39a, chapter 4] developed a four-step forecasting model.[2] First, through a review of selected economic indicators, the forecaster will identify which countries have balances of payments that are in fundamental disequilibrium. Second, for the currencies of such countries, the forecaster will measure the pressure that market forces are exercising on prevailing exchange rates. Third, the level of central banks' foreign exchange reserves gives an indication of the future point in time at which the central bank will no longer be in a position to defend the prevailing exchange rate. The fourth and crucial step is to predict the type of corrective policies that politically motivated decision-makers are likely to implement: will the country under pressure adjust through a manipulation of its exchange rate (devaluation or revaluation) or, instead, initiate, essentially for political reasons, deflationary or inflationary policies combined with exchange controls and extensive international borrowing?

An interesting attempt by Folks and Stansell [28] and Murenbeeld [53], based on the use of multivariate discriminant analysis, was made at identifying the likelihood and direction of potential changes in par values of countries maintaining pegged exchange rates (steps one and two of the above forecasting procedure); however, the forecasting outputs of such models is of limited value because they fail to provide any information as to the timing or magnitude of a potential exchange rate change.

For controlled exchange rates, black market rates will prove to be helpful leading gauges of subsequent devaluation of official (controlled) exchange rates. As a rule, the black market rate (generally available from *Pick's Currency Yearbook and Reports*) depends on the extent to which the official exchange rate overvalues the equilibrium exchange rate as well as on the extent to which illegal transactors (black marketeers) are apprehended and prosecuted. Indeed Culbertson [14] has shown that for an overvalued (controlled) exchange rate, the hypothetical equilibrium exchange rate will fall somewhere between the official and the black market rate.

Forecasting Floating Exchange Rates: Market-Based Forecasts

The return in early 1973 to floating exchange rates by a number of major currencies has generated considerable interest about the general question of whether foreign exchange markets do indeed constitute efficient markets. If clearly established, the Market Efficiency hypothesis would have far-ranging forecasting implications and could possibly establish the irrelevance of building elaborate forecasting models, but, before this critical last point is further elaborated, a careful statement of the efficient markets hypothesis is in order.

A foreign exchange market in which exchange rates always fully reflect all available information is said to be efficient.[3] Three degrees of Market Efficiency are customarily distinguished:[4] (1) the weakly[5] efficient market hypothesis says that series of historical exchange rates contain no information which can be used to forecast future spot exchange rates; (2) the semistrong version of market efficiency holds that a large and competitive group of market participants have access to all publicly available information relevant to the formation of expectations about future rates; finally, (3) if the set of available information also includes private or insiders' information, the market is said to be strongly efficient.

Let us now review the evidence for and against the efficiency of the foreign exchange market and explain the forecasting implications of the hypothesis. Tests of market efficiency have been characterized by the heterogeneity of the statistical tools used as well as of the sample periods and currencies selected. Furthermore, the testing methodologies used have generally been directly borrowed from analogous empirical studies of the stock markets and commodity futures markets, although it is not clear that they are appropriate for testing the efficiency of foreign exchange markets given the presence of major, nonprofit-maximizing participants, namely central banks. Finally, the lack of a comprehensive testing of an exhaustive and uniform data basis clearly precludes reaching clear cut conclusions for or against the efficiency hypothesis.[6]

Weak-form tests have received the most attention, probably because they are the easiest to carry out. These tests are concerned with two major issues: the extent of statistical dependence of successive changes in exchange rates and the profitability of trading rules. In essence, what is being investigated is whether past series of exchange rates contain useful information for the prediction of future spot prices, thus implying that general patterns would repeat themselves at regular intervals.

The assertion that current exchange rates reflect all publicly available information, as called for by the semistrong form of Market Efficiency, is so general that it has proven a difficult hypothesis to test empirically. Accordingly, empirical evidence for or against this form of market efficiency has been scant except for one recent study by Rogalski and Vinso [63] which provided conclusive evidence in its support.

Another forecasting model that has lately received increasing attention and that is intuitively consistent with the semistrong form of the Market Efficiency hypothesis concerns the predictive accuracy of forward exchange rates. Speculators who think that the forward rate is above their expectation of the future spot exchange rate will sell the foreign currency forward, thus bidding down the forward rate until it equals the expected future spot rate. Conversely, speculators who see the forward rate under-valuing the expected future spot rate will buy foreign currency forward, thus bidding the forward rate up until forward and expected future spot exchange rates become equal. If speculative demand for forward contracts were infinitely elastic and all speculators held homogeneous expectations with respect to the future spot exchange rate, the current forward exchange rate would be equal to the expected future spot exchange rate.

A number of theoretical arguments have been developed to establish that the forward exchange rate must necessarily be a biased predictor of the future spot exchange rate.[7,8] For instance, this simple forecasting model stands in apparent contradiction to the Modern Theory of forward exchange rates determination,[9] which generally suggests that the specula-tors' schedule is less than infinitely elastic and that, as a result, the equilib-rium forward rate of exchange would be different from the future spot exchange rate. Only in the polar case (somewhat unrealistic) of risk-neutral speculators should the forward exchange rate be considered as an unbiased predictor of the future spot exchange rate.[10]

Extensive empirical testing of the Market Efficiency hypothesis, very ably surveyed by Kohlhagen [41a], has generally suffered from the joint hypothesis problem identified by Levich [45a]. Prominent studies include those of Poole [60], Dooley and Shafer [15], Giddy and Dufey [31], Logue and Sweeney [49], Cornell and Dietrich [13], Roll and Solnik [64] and Kohlhagen [41c], whose detailed critical evaluation is beyond the scope of this paper.

For fairly obvious reasons little attention has been devoted to the problem of long-term foreign exchange rate forecasts which are a much needed informational input into the selection of an optimal currency denomination for long-term debt financing or the even more puzzling question of debt refunding/debt refinancing in a multicurrency context.

The relationship between the term structure of interest rates and exchange rate expectations was explored by Porter [61]. The theoretical framework developed in this seminal study showed how the term structure of international interest rates can be used to make inferences as to the expected time path of the exchange rate adjustment between two curren-cies. This approach was subsequently operationalized very elegantly by Dufey and Giddy [17].

Econometric Modelling Approaches

Exchange rates econometric forecasting models are a systematic effort at uncovering a functional relationship between a set of explanatory (exogen-ous) variables – such as, price levels differential, interest rates differential, or differential in the rate of growth in money supplies – and a dependent (endogenous) variable – namely, the exchange rate. The functional relationship may involve only the current period values of the exogenous variables or may be of a lagged nature; that is, incorporate past periods values taken on by the exogenous variables. In this latter case econometric modelling is clearly inconsistent with the Market Efficiency hypothesis whereas in the former case it is not necessarily so. As a matter of fact, one may be tempted to argue that econometric forecasting disregarding lagged functional relationships is assisting the market in correctly interpreting all currently available information, thus making it more efficient.

The specification of the model itself – that is, the nature of the functional relationship (not necessarily linear) – as well as the choice of exogenous variables included generally blends economic theory (for example, a combination of the Purchasing Power Parity and Fisher theories) with the model builder's experience and intuition. In that sense, econometric building is as much an art as a science and accordingly the reader should expect the various forecasting services to be idiosyncratic.

Structural equations however (usually one for each currency forecasted) are extracted from time series of exogenous or endogenous variables – that is, from past observations. This means that if a drastic change in the structural relationship between independent and dependent variables were to occur and be disregarded in specifying functional relationships, the econometric model forecasting value would be adversely affected. Thus, if one accepts that the behavior of private and public market participants was markedly affected by the advent of floating exchange rates, it is perhaps too early to forecast currency prices in the context of a floating exchange rates regime. The reason is that the observations available are still too few and far between (spanning only the 1973–1979 period) to derive meaningful functional relationships between exogenous and endogenous variables. Yet a number of econometricians have apparently felt otherwise because there are at least a dozen major econometric forecasting services that can be subscribed to for a fee.

One last additional feature of econometric forecasting models worth commenting upon is the random error term that is always incorporated in this type of model.[11] The inclusion of such a stochastic element allows probability statements to be made about the forecasted variable. This is indeed an attractive feature compared with a point estimate (as provided, for instance, by forward exchange rates) especially when it is recalled that the information is to be used in a risk management context. However, for econometric forecasting to be theoretically correct, several requirements must be met.[12] The major theoretical flaw of current forecasting efforts is probably the normality assumption (of exchange rates probability distribution) which is generally made. That exchange rates are not normally distributed has been established beyond doubt with Westerfield [77] and Vinso and Rogalski [76] providing empirical evidence to the effect that exchange rates are best described as non-normal members of the Pareto–Levy class of probability distribution.

As could be expected, there is some controversy as to the reliability of such econometric forecasts: in a recent examination of the track record of 6 major econometric forecasting services, Goodman [32] found that

> The predictive accuracy of most – not all – of the economics-oriented foreign exchange rate forecasting services is so poor that they are likely to be of little use for corporations trying to manage their foreign exchange exposure.

> The results are quite different for the technically-oriented services. Their consistently very strong predictive performance supports the view that speculative runs do occur in the exchange market and that the foreign market is not efficient.

However, Goodman's testing methodology is questionable given that his comparative criterion allows subscribers to economics-oriented forecasts to act only on the last day of the month; by contrast, subscribers to technically-oriented forecasting services are assumed to act on the day the forecast is received.

By contrast, a thorough and up-to-date appraisal of 9 forecasting advisory services by Levich [45c] indicates that some services have consistently beaten the forward rate and that the record of forecasting accuracy was too good to be explained by chance. These results are all the more interesting as they were established by a Chicago-trained economist whose doctoral effort was largely focused on establishing the efficiency of the foreign exchange market [45b].

Addressing himself to the more fundamental question of why a small but vigorously successful forecasting industry is competing with "free" market-based forecasts available daily from the financial press, Makin [50c] appropriately remarks that such ex post empirical evaluation of the accuracy of forecasting services is redundant. Indeed, the true market test is whether forecasters can coexist with the "free" market forecast and incur positive information gathering and processing costs while charging for their services a fee which allows them to earn a competitive rate of return. However, it would be surprising that the output of a permanently superior forecasting model be available commercially; in fact, a recent survey by Evans, Folks, and Jilling [21] indicated that 58.4 percent of the respondents felt that currency forecasting was the weakest link in their exchange risk management programs. One suspects that treasurers place only limited faith in commercially available forecasts but find them helpful for bureaucratic hedging purposes.

Forecasting and Foreign Exchange Risk Management

In sum, the lack of decisive answers to the general question of forecasting exchange rates remains probably the single most potent justification for undertaking costly, and at times highly constraining, protective policies against foreign exchange risk. More specifically, Dufey and Giddy [17] distinguish between two basically different forecasting situations:

(1) The foreign exchange market is efficient (floating exchange rates); the use of market-based forecasts is advocated. However, it should be recognized that the market's expected value will seldom be attained (that is, the actual exchange rate will generally differ from the one actually predicted by the forward exchange rate) hence the need to plan or attempt to forecast errors which are expected to occur. Further, it becomes imperative to assess what would be the impact of such unanticipated deviations from the expected rate on the net cash flows of the firm. (See the section on Managing Economic Exposure.)

(2) The foreign exchange market is inefficient because of stifling government controls on interest rates and exchange rates (pegged yet adjustable exchange rates); multinational corporations should aim at capitalizing on the profit opportunities available because of market distortions in order to offset the cost of operating under government controls in real factor markets.

Measuring Exposure to Foreign Exchange Risk

An operationally viable – if conceptually weak – measure of exposure to foreign exchange risk is provided by accounting rules. A convenient dichotomy generally distinguishes between transaction and translation exposures.

Transaction Exposure

Wihlborg [79b] defines transaction exposure as an uncertain domestic currency value of an open position denominated in a foreign currency with respect to a known transaction; that is, a future foreign currency denominated flow. As expected, fluctuations in the exchange rate relationship over the life of the contract will result in windfall cash flow gains or losses with tax implications which are not necessarily symmetrical between gains and losses nor consistent across different types of underlying transactions. Jacque developed a simple exposure netting algorithm [39a, chapter 5] on an after-tax basis for subsidiaries of a multinational corporation which are not subjected to homogeneous tax laws with respect to exchange gains and losses.[13]

Translation Exposure

Foreign market entry through direct investment, by contrast, results in so-called translation exposure which Wihlborg [79b] defines as the uncertain domestic value of a net accounting position denominated in a foreign currency at a certain future date: that is, a future foreign currency denominated stock. The practice of periodically consolidating or aggregating parent's and affiliates' balance sheets will generally entail exchange gains or losses of a non-cash flow (paper) nature as exchange rates fluctuate over the accounting horizon. At the core of this consolidation process which allows multinational corporations to disclose earnings valued in a single numeraire (reference currency) lies the controversial question of how balance sheet accounts of foreign subsidiaries ought to be translated. Should the accounts of foreign subsidiaries be treated as exposed or non-exposed items – with exposed items translated at current exchange rates and non-exposed items translated at historical rates? Until 1976 (which marks the implementation of FASB Statement No. 8) multinational corporations were left free to use whatever methods they believed reflected most accurately their true economic performance. Most firms used either the current/non-current, monetary/non-monetary, or current method of translation, and there is an over abundance of accounting literature debating the merits and demerits of each method (cf. Hayes [36], Barrett and Spero [7], Olstein and O'Glove [57], and Pakkala [58], among the most prominent papers).

The mandatory translation guidelines put forward by Statement No. 8 (and subsequently No. 20) eliminated much of the flexibility that U.S.-based multinational corporations previously had in translating their foreign affiliates' financial statements into the reference currency. The most dramatic and perhaps most controversial ruling of Statement No. 8 is that exchange gains or losses resulting from both the conversion and translation processes are to be included in the net income for the accounting period in which the exchange rate change actually occurred. The distinction between realized and unrealized gains and losses was thus unequivocally discontinued as was the use of reserve accounts aimed at mitigating the erratic impact of exchange gains or losses on the earning profile. (For constructive suggestions on how such accounts could be reenacted see Ankrom [4a].) Also controversial are the provisions calling for the treatment of long-term debt as an exposed item (which led a number of U.S.-based MNCs' affiliates to shun local currency long-term funding in favour of dollar-denominated financing) whereas inventory would generally be considered as non-exposed. As a whole, Statement No. 8 has been severely criticized in a flurry of articles appearing in accounting magazines and journals. (See for instance Shank [67], Rodriguez [62a], and Aggarwal [1] for a limited but representative sample of the literature.) If Statement No. 8 has generally been received with skepticism by accountants, treasurers of U.S. multinational corporations have vehemently opposed it as surveys conducted by Choi, Lowe, and Worthley [11] and Stanley and Block [73] clearly establish. A major study commissioned by the FASB (Evans, Folks, and Jilling [21]) further reports that the implementation of Statement No. 8 resulted in increased Foreign Exchange Risk Management activities especially by firms which relied on translation methods most at variance with the guidelines laid down by the new ruling.

The logical consistency of segmenting foreign subsidiaries' financial statements between exposed and non-exposed categories has been questioned by Aliber and Stickney [2] who argue that if the Fisher effect holds, monetary items (generally treated as exposed items) are essentially non-exposed as cumulative interest revenue (exposure) over the maturity of the monetary asset (liability) and would offset the exchange loss (gain) from changes in the exchange rate. By contrast, treating non-monetary items as non-exposed items essentially assumes that Purchasing Power Parity will hold, which will generally not be true in the short term.

At the close of 1980, new controversy is about to be injected into this ongoing debate about what constitutes the optimal set of translation rules as the FASB is considering for adoption a new exposure draft which would supersede Statement No. 8. The new proposal would (1) impose the use of an all-current (or closing) rate method and (2) differentiate between transaction and translation gains or losses.

The first proposal would require all balance sheet accounts to be translated at the exchange rate prevailing at the time the consolidation is carried out; income statements would be translated at the average exchange rate for the reporting period.

Second, only transaction gains and losses (both realized and unrealized) would be charged to current income. By contrast, translation gains and losses would be accumulated in "a separate component of stockholders' equity." This is a major departure from FASB No. 8 rule and should reduce considerably the volatility in reported earnings. Although the new exposure draft should be welcome by U.S. multinationals, it is in clear contradiction with the concept of historical cost accounting. Finally, the use of an all-current rate method for translating the balance sheets of overseas subsidiaries operating in hyperinflationary economies which do not use inflation accounting would clearly lead to exchange losses distorted beyond reason; overall, Giannotti and Walker [29] expect the new exposure draft to have a positive impact on the financial practices of multinational corporations as corporate attention is diverted from translation to transaction exposure management and foreign affiliates' financing is sourced from local currency denominated sources (rather than dollar denominated sources).

Economic Exposure

Although widely used, this accounting concept of exposure to foreign exchange risk is, by definition, misleading, because it fails to incorporate the longer-term impact of exchange rate changes on the economic valuation of the multinational corporation. Accordingly, Heckerman [37] outlines a net discounted cash-flow approach to the economic valuation of the foreign subsidiary of a multinational corporation but fails to recognize that future cash flows are themselves a function of exchange rates. A seminal paper by Dufey [16a] showed that exchange rate changes will predictably affect the nominal cash flows of the subsidiary of a multinational corporation; however, the net impact of such a devaluation or revaluation will not necessarily match in direction nor in magnitude the percentage change in the exchange rate. For example, a subsidiary operating in a devaluing country may find itself benefitting rather than suffering from such a devaluation if part of its revenues are derived from export sales.

A more systematic analysis of the impact of exchange rate changes on the foreign subsidiary's sourcing costs and sales revenue is found in Shapiro [68a]. On the revenue side, he distinguishes between domestic and foreign sales cash-flows whereas on the cost side he identifies three partially substitutable inputs: namely, non-traded domestic goods and services, traded inputs, and imported goods.

Shapiro correctly concludes that economic exposure will be determined by the sector of the economy in which the subsidiary operates. As expected, the impact of changing domestic rates will markedly differ for export-oriented subsidiaries, strictly domestic-oriented subsidiaries facing no import competition, or subsidiaries meeting the challenge of stiff import-competition.[14]

Both Dufey's and Shapiro's papers fail to incorporate in their analyses the financial sector nor do they envision the potential use of currency denomination of debt for the purpose of neutralizing the economic exposure stemming from the real sector. Furthermore, the concept of economic exposure is strictly applied to the foreign subsidiary of a multinational corporation and generally assessed in nominal rather than real terms. The concept of economic exposure is obviously just as applicable to a strictly domestic firm (that is, selling to and procuring from domestic markets) which may find itself exposed, in spite of itself, to the vagaries of the international economy.

In a largely taxonomic paper, Wihlborg [79b] questions the relevance of an indiscriminate concept of economic exposure to foreign exchange risk by noting that there is no exposure when inflation is neutral and exchange rates are determined by the Purchasing Power Parity hypothesis. Indeed, real exposure will occur when inflation is not neutral (relative prices change with inflation and/or relative prices change with the exchange rate) and exchange rates deviate from their Purchasing Power Parity equilibria. The case of relative prices (including terms of trade) changing with the exchange rate is examined in depth by Shapiro [68a].

Cornell [12] concurs with this dichotomy between nominal and real cash flows by showing that, in a world in which exchange rates adjust instantaneously (Purchasing Power Parity holds at every point in time), there is, in real terms, no exchange risk as long as relative prices remain constant; thus, if contractual commitments in nominal terms are avoided (that is, contracts are written in terms of the price index), the firm will no longer be exposed to foreign exchange risk. By contrast, relative price risk remains the fundamental source of risk to which firms are exposed and it is equally faced by domestic and multinational corporations. Whether Purchasing Power Parity does hold is an empirical and controversial issue which has been extensively tested as illustrated in the comprehensive review article by Officer [56]. However, this theoretically attractive concept of economic exposure is difficult to turn into an operational index of exposure to exchange risk which could be readily used for Foreign Exchange Risk Management purposes.

The Management of Foreign Exchange Risk

Normative models for Foreign Exchange Risk Management are few and far between and one cannot help but contrast the sparsely populated research space of international corporate finance (of which Foreign Exchange Risk Management is only one albeit major subset) with the overly prolific research effort in Market Efficiency testing (as applied to the foreign exchange market). The dichotomy between transaction exposure covering and translation exposure hedging will again provide a convenient framework for organizing our review.

Covering Transaction Exposure

Transaction exposure can be covered either through the use of forward contracts (available only for major trading currencies) or a combination of spot and money market transactions. If Interest Rate Parity fails to hold,[15] each option should be computed and the optimal covering route should be compared with the expected cost/revenue of retaining as uncovered the transaction exposure. This naive expected value criterion is discussed in Jacque [39a, chapter 7] and somewhat elaborated by Calderon-Rossel [10] who fails to recognize that both covering routes are fully consistent with the Interest Rate Parity theorem and certainly entail no residual randomness. If covering is to be undertaken on a recurring basis, Giddy [30b] questions the wisdom of such a practice as – over the longer run – the forward rate tends to be an unbiased predictor of the future spot exchange rate.

The case of contingent transaction exposures (resulting from competitive bidding) denominated in foreign currency is examined by Feiger and Jacquillat [26] who suggest covering such exposures through a combination of a forward sale contract and a foreign exchange call option; however, a market for call and put foreign exchange options has yet to materialize.

For the management of a vector of i transaction exposures, Kohlhagen [41b] develops a decision-theoretic payoff $(N)^{i-1} \times (N)^{i-1}$ matrix of profits over all sets of possible exchange rates (each currency can take N different values) and over all strategies (each of which is optimal for one set of future exchange rates). From such a payoff matrix, for a "conservative" firm aiming at protecting cash flows, a simple maximum strategy will be derived whereas a more aggressive firm will pursue a maximax strategy. Although theoretically inferior (no formal treatment of decision-makers' risk preference, no attempt at recognizing the statistical relationships among the exchange rates in which the transaction exposures are denominated), this model is appealing from a managerial point of view because it requires for informational inputs only estimates of reasonable ranges of future exchange rates rather than specific exchange rate projections with associated probability distributions.

In a seminal paper, Folks [27b] questions the validity of the cover/not cover paradigm and suggests that an optimal level of retained uncovered exposure can be found analytically by postulating a utility function as describing the risk preference of the decision-maker.[16] In a similar vein, Wheelwright [78] discusses the practical transaction exposure problem faced by a "big-ticket" item exporter. A preference curve is developed that explicitly shows the tradeoffs that the decision-maker is willing to make between the risk surrounding an uncertain situation and an amount to be received with certainty. The reader is left uncertain, however, as to how this preference curve should be derived; namely, what choice of a utility function is to be made for encoding the risk preference of the decision-maker? Preliminary empirical evidence on risk-preference of treasurers of MNCs is provided by Rodriguez [62b] who found asymmetrical attitudes toward foreign exchange risks.

Apportioning of exchange risk in bilateral transactions is generally thought to be achieved better by denominating the transaction in a third currency or mix of third currencies (artificial currency units) rather than by resorting to a combination of the domestic currencies of the two contracting parties. Using an expected utility framework of nominal return (cost), Schwab and Lusztig [65] show that the contracting parties will always achieve a superior sharing of exchange risk by limiting themselves to a combination of their own currencies. Thus, the use of a third currency or of artificial currency units such as SDRs, EURCOs, EUAs, or ARCRUs should be discouraged.[17] Only if the variability of real (rather than nominal) returns (costs) is to be minimized should bilateral transactions be denominated in third currencies or so-called "currency cocktails."

For a set of transaction exposures denominated in different currencies, Makin [50b] derives an efficient frontier of optimal portfolios of shares of exposures to be covered in a traditional mean-variance framework. Exchange rates are assumed to be normally distributed and the matrix of variance–covariance for future exchange rates available and stable. Although not stated, this model assumes the utility of the decision-maker to be quadratic. In a theoretical paper Levi [44a] shows that in a world where the matrix of cross-elasticities between exchange rate changes is fully known at the outset of the exposure horizon it is possible to fully cover the entire portfolio of transactions exposure through only one forward contract; this may perhaps explain why forward markets appear at times to be underutilized. Yet cross-elasticities between foreign currency movements are stochastic rather than deterministic thereby limiting the operational value of this approach.

The economic exposure problem of a trading firm which imports commodities for local sale is investigated by Hodder [38]. The mean-variance model developed by that author traces the optimal level of forward cover to be sought by the importer to the correlation between the local currency price of the imported commodities (in inventory) and the exchange rate (in which the accounts payable are denominated). This is the question of "currency pass-through" which economists are concerned with in attempting to explain balance of payments adjustment (or lack thereof) to changing exchange rates.

For affiliates of multinational corporations operating in hyperinflationary economies (underdeveloped countries), foreign short-term financing will generally result in major transaction exposure management challenges. Effective costs formulae reflecting anticipated exchange rate devaluations were developed by deFaro and Jucker [25] and Shapiro [68b] on an expected cost basis generally allowing for selection of the optimal source of financing on the basis of linear simulations of exchange rates devaluations. The technique of swap loans popular with a number of Latin American central banks allows the borrower to shelter loan principles from potentially large devaluation (see Eiteman and Stonehill [20]). None of these studies consider, on a risk adjusted basis, what would be the optimal portfolio of short-term financing sources as opposed to the cheapest borrowing source as determined on an expected cost basis.

Hedging Translation Exposure

The essence of hedging is to substitute, at the outset of the exposure horizon, a known cost of buying protection against foreign exchange risk for an unknown translation loss. In a sense, the hedger is trading the uncertainty of an accounting loss which may never materialize for the certainty of the cost of eliminating translation risks – a cost that bears some resemblance to an insurance premium. Thus, the rationale behind the concept of hedging is to substitute for exchange losses, footnoted in reported earnings statements, normal business costs (such hedging costs may include a substantial cash flow loss/gain component) that flow through the income statement.

The mechanics of hedging are set forth in Jacque [39a, chapter 9] who shows that, contrary to the widely held view, hedgers are not speculators but covered interest arbitragers in disguise. Liaeter [47a & b] developes a mean-variance framework which allows the hedger to find "a combination of financing and hedging operations that minimizes expected costs and strategy risk and does not violate a set of recognized operational constraints." Strategy risk is a combination of two types of risk – the business risk measures the risk generated from relying on future financing and hedging possibilities which are not known with certainty. The second strategy risk, the devaluation risk, is a combination of risks arising from "the possibility of wrong estimates in devaluation probabilities and devaluation amounts." This one-period (extended by Liaeter to a multiperiod model in [47b]), two-currency world model fails to recognize explicitly the possibly onerous cash flow cost component of pursuing an optimal hedging policy. Last but not least, Liaeter makes two assumptions in flagrant violation of accepted international financial economics: interest rates are independent of expected parity changes and exchange rates in various currencies are assumed to be uncorrelated. The former assumption ignores the Interest Rate Parity hypothesis whereas the latter assumption contradicts the underlying rationale of the portfolio approach to Foreign Exchange Risk Management.

Folks [27a] compares a mean-variance, minimax, expected monetary value and expected utility criteria as a basis for deriving an optimal hedging strategy when available Foreign Exchange Risk Management techniques are adjustment of fund flows, forward contracts, and exposure netting. None of these studies recognize that if the total cost of hedging is known with certainty at the outset of the exposure horizon, the mix of translation gains/losses plus cash flow losses/gains remains stochastic. An attempt at remedying this flaw is provided by Jacque [39b] who formulates an expected utility theoretic hedging model under an explicit chance constraint on the maximum cash-flow cost of hedging.

The only serious attempt at considering the set of translation exposures denominated in various currencies (held by a multinational corporation in the normal course of business) as a portfolio of statistically interdependent (correlated) elements is found in Gull [35] who formulated the optimization problem in a one-period mean-variance framework which fails to distinguish the (random) cash-flow component of hedging costs from unrealized (paper) translation losses. The major difficulty with such portfolio models is in generating the key informational input; namely, the variance–covariance matrix of exchange rate changes. Gull uses historical information to derive such a matrix in order to generate the optimal vector of pro forma residual exposures, thus implicitly assuming that the covariability structure of past exchange rate changes can be safely extrapolated into the next period. Finally, as with all normative hedging models no attempt is made at capturing the randomness of pro forma translation exposures which may be potentially as serious a source of risk as exchange risk itself.

The problem of selective hedging in a multi-period setting is solved by Shapiro and Rutenberg [69a]. The stochastic dynamic programming algorithm is formulated under somewhat restrictive assumptions. Given current hedging costs, expectations of future hedging costs (both of which are assumed to be linear) should a treasurer hedge a future period or should he wait? Hedging of a future period can be achieved by selling the suspect currency forward for τ periods and buying it forward for $(\tau - 1)$ periods. One or several (discrete) devaluations are assumed throughout the exposure horizon. An expected value criterion, thus assuming risk neutrality on the part of the decision-maker, is used. No attention is paid to the cash-flow cost of deriving an optimal hedging path.

Managing Economic Exposure

As a general rule, economic exposure management should aim at neutralizing the impact of unexpected exchange rate changes on net cash flows; this will generally be achieved by striving for a balanced currency mix of cash flows between the cost and revenue side.

An operational approach for implementing this concept of economic exposure management was developed by Nauman-Etienne [54]: (1) identify managerial policies, operational characteristics, and environmental parameters to which economic exposure is sensitive; (2) define protective steps to minimize adverse effects of unexpected exchange rate changes on future cash flows.

Optimally, the sales-inputs currency mix should be adjusted so that changes in future sales revenue will be neutralized by changes in the cost of inputs; however, such changes in the real sector of the firm will seldom bring about by themselves a neutral economic exposure. Generally, manipulation of the currency risk of short-term and long-term financing will be needed and this is generally the easier to implement of the two prescriptions because the currency composition of financing can be altered independently from the sources of inputs and destination of sales; as such, it plays a natural residual and offsetting role in equating sales revenue and input costs on a currency-by-currency basis. Carrying this argument to its logical conclusion Dufey [16b] summarized it as "finance in the currency where your profits are." The obvious flaw in this approach is that it fails to incorporate the dynamics of the currency composition of cash flow which generally respond to a variety of exogenous factors which are difficult to anticipate. Also disregarded in these studies is the simultaneous and offsetting change in price levels; that is, the analysis is strictly conducted in normal terms rather than in real terms.

The Praxis of Foreign Exchange Risk Management

Last but not least, exposure measurement and exposure management have to be coordinated and integrated with an internally consistent set of guidelines acceptable to both subsidiaries' and headquarters' treasurers. Foremost is the question of apportioning equitably the responsibility of Foreign Exchange Risk Management without distorting the control/evaluation process of foreign operations [Korth 42b]. Lessard and Lorange [43] address the dilemma faced by MNCs attempting to reconcile the organizational decentralization necessary for an effective planning/control system in a large multinational/multidivisional corporation and the centralization imperative which is at the core of effective Foreign Exchange Risk Management. Specifically, the authors consider the possible combination of exchange rates – to be used in (1) setting the operating budget for a particular time period and (2) tracking realized performance relative to budgeted ones. The authors suggest that the dilemma can be resolved through the use of "internal forward rates"; that is, rates which are guaranteed by the corporate treasury irrespective of what actual exchange rates may turn out to be.

Organizational and control considerations will undoubtedly play a crucial role in setting up such a Foreign Exchange Risk Management program which will generally have to be centralized at the helm of the corporate treasurer if the synergistic benefits of multinationalism are to be taken advantage of [Ankrom 4b]. This is indeed one of the major findings of a survey of corporate Foreign Exchange Risk Management practices by Jilling [40].

One unresolved question remains: How to insure a consistent attitude toward risk (both over time and across currencies) which wouldn't reflect exclusively the treasurer's preferences but which would be firmly grounded in senior management's outlook toward risk.

Long-Term Debt Financing

This review would not be complete without mentioning promising yet embryonic research efforts aimed at the determination of the optimal currency (or artificial currency unit) of denomination in long-term debt financing. Jacque [39a, chapter 8] develops a break-even analysis methodological framework based upon expected net present value formulae (thus implicitly assuming risk neutrality on the part of the decision-maker). Using a similar framework Giddy [30d] derives a number of simplifying formulae expressing the effective cost of foreign currency denominated debt financing as a function of its nominal cost. Both approaches fail to recognize the dependency (in a probability sense) of the vector of exchange rates to prevail when interest and principal repayment will be made. Thus, future exchange rates ought to be modelled as belonging to a joint multivariate probability distribution and necessary parameters of such variates be computed accordingly.

Foreign exchange risk management and the market efficiency hypothesis

The emerging, yet embryonic, consensus among financial theoreticians is that exposure to foreign exchange risk may matter less than is commonly believed by multinational corporations' corporate treasurers, financial analysts, and investors. This jaundiced view of Foreign Exchange Risk Management is upheld by Logue and Oldfield [48] who argue that in efficient markets Foreign Exchange Risk Management is irrelevant and also relatively harmless. Theirs is loosely referred to as the Market Efficiency hypothesis and can be summarized in two propositions: in efficient capital markets, all available information is correctly impounded or reflected in stock prices. More specifically, investors are knowledgeable and sophisticated enough to be able to read beyond conventional accounting reports (balance sheets and income statements) to correctly assess the true economic value of the firm. This would mean, among other things, that hedging translation exposure to reduce or eliminate earnings variability is pure accounting gimmickry that shouldn't fool efficient investors.

Thus, in an efficient market, the multinational corporation's earning variability (resulting from translation gains or losses) would be placed in a proper economic perspective by investors and, therefore, should not affect its stock's price nor its cost of capital. However, such clearsightedness on the part of the market would require extensive and systematic disclosure by multinational corporations of their foreign subsidiaries' transaction, translation, and economic exposures. This practice is clearly not yet accepted because multinational corporations generally disclose only consolidated financial statements.

This hypothesis seems to be contradicted in a recent empirical study by Makin [50a] which suggests (but doesn't necessarily prove) that, for instance, the first set of earnings reports prepared under FASB Statement No. 8 resulted for at least one group of firms (out of five) in the decline of their share prices that was not associated with overall market behavior. Thus, the market would not be omniscient, and additional, albeit limited and imperfect, information (as that disclosed under FASB Statement No. 8) would lead investors to reevaluate their pricing of shares of corporations exposed to exchange risk. These preliminary results, however, failed to be upheld by the comprehensive study commissioned by the Financial Accounting Standards Board [Dukes, 18] which concluded that the issuance and implementation of FASB Statement No. 8 did not appear to have had significant detectable effects on the security returns of multinational firms.

Second, in efficient foreign exchange markets, currencies' prices adjust instantaneously to the inflation rates differential (Purchasing Power Parity hypothesis), thus leaving unchanged the true economic exposure to foreign exchange risk of a multinational corporation or of its foreign affiliates. The prescription in this case is simple: elaborate assessment of a firm's exposure to the inflation-cum-devaluation cycle is redundant and, a fortiori, managing economic exposure is about as irrelevant as managing accounting exposure. This point of view is elaborated upon by Aliber [3] and Giddy [30c].

Obviously, the operational value of such an extreme policy prescription will depend on the nature of the exchange rate system and the degree to which exchange rates reflect the relative internal purchasing power of any pair of currencies. Under a system of pegged yet adjustable exchange rates, par value adjustments may significantly lag price inflation differentials and the competitive position of the firm will be significantly and lastingly affected, thus calling for a strategic overhaul of the production and marketing policies. In the case of a domestic or an exporting company, an exchange rate adjustment that fails to reflect the true cost constraints of the sector in which the firm is operating will open new market horizons that would have been missed had the firm failed to recognize and/or anticipate correctly its true economic exposure.

Even in a world of floating exchange rates, which are being increasingly characterized as efficient, managing economic exposure may be a less dubious undertaking than implied by this second version of the Market Efficiency hypothesis. Instantaneous exchange rates adjustment to price levels differential will generally fail to capture the discrepancies among various sectorial price level movements that may indeed affect the true economic exposure of the firm. The sensitivity of the firm's cash flows to sectorial price movements should be carefully monitored and incorporated in marketing, production and financial plans. Even under strict conditions of foreign exchange market efficiency and positive bankruptcy costs, Dufey and Giddy [17] still prescribe that Management of Foreign Exchange Risk should aim at "structuring the firm's liabilities in such a way that any *unanticipated* change in the return on assets is offset, as far as possible, by a change in the effective cost of liabilities."

Foreign Exchange Risk Management: Directions for Further Research

Nearly all normative research efforts in the area of foreign exchange risk management have focused exlusively on short-term decisions involving accounting exposure components of a firm's working capital and one may wonder why the case of stochastic transaction and translation exposures has altogether been ignored. Consider, for instance, the case of captive insurance companies which diversify their portfolio of underwriting activities by reinsuring a "layer" of foreign risk; clearly, the magnitude of the transaction exposure is unknown (stochastic).

Bidding on foreign projects or acquisitions of foreign companies will similarly entail stochastic exposures whose magnitude can be characterized at best by a subjective probability distribution. Similarly, hedging translation exposure always assumes that the translation exposure is known with certainty whereas, in fact, it is extracted from pro forma statements and, thus, should be considered as a random variable for Foreign Exchange Risk Management purposes.

Furthermore, the longer-term dimension of Foreign Exchange Risk Management – that is, long-term debt financing and debt refunding in a multicurrency world – has hardly been considered.

In addition, most research undertakings – with two exceptions [Gull 35 and Makin 50b] – were limited to a two-currency world (foreign currency in which the exposure is incurred and reference currency [$] in which the MNC's financial statements are disclosed) thereby ignoring the diversification effect of holding a portfolio of exposures denominated in currencies whose prices are correlated.

Moreover, transaction and translation exposures were handled separately with no attempt at reconciling the two constructs into an operationally meaningful single aggregate index of real exposure to foreign exchange risk.

Finally, all decision models – with one exception [Shapiro and Rutenberg 69a] – were one-period models, thereby disregarding the sequential nature of Foreign Exchange Risk Management problems. The creation of new financial instruments such as interest rate futures, however, is opening new opportunities for research in this area as it provides information on future forward exchange rates – indeed a critical informational input for such decision models.

Notes

[†] Laurent L. Jacque's research interests center on multinational financial management. He is the author of *Management of Foreign Exchange Risk: Theory and Praxis* (Lexington Books, 1978). The author gratefully acknowledges the helpful comments from Gunter Dufey and Alan Shapiro.

1. Donald R. Lessard, *International Financial Management* (Boston: Warren, Gorhan and Lamont, 1979), p. 353.

2. For an analogous, but strictly qualitative four-step sequence see Korth [42a].

3. This concept of market efficiency should be clearly distinguished from the concept of market perfection. Market perfection is certainly a sufficient condition of market efficiency but is not a necessary one. As long as transactors take into account all available information, even large transaction costs that inhibit the flow of trans-

actions do not in themselves imply that when transactions do take place, exchange rates will not "fully reflect" all available information.

4. This three-tier categorization of Market Efficiency was suggested by Eugene Fama [23] for empirical testing purposes in the context of stock prices.

5. Failure to establish the weak form of Market Efficiency would lend credence to the Price Dynamics view of exchange rates behavior. One version of the Price Dynamics hypothesis (the so-called "bandwagon" theory) asserts that a subset of market participants (market leaders) are known or simply perceived by the rest of market participants (market followers) to have earlier access to more timely and more accurate information concerning factors affecting future spot exchange rates and/or to have the use of more sophisticated forecasting models. Thus when the price of a currency begins to fall (to rise) market followers will "jump on the band-wagon"; that is, join in the selling (buying) pressure as they attribute the price change to a signal that market leaders (who know better) have themselves begun to sell (to buy). In so doing, market followers will be pushing the currency price down (up) further until it overshoots its equilibrium level and the trend eventually reverses itself. Clearly this view of exchange rates behavior supports the hypothesis that past exchange rates contain useful information in forecasting future exchange rates as information only disseminates itself slowly among market participants, thus disproving the Market Efficiency hypothesis.

6. For a critical evaluation of testing methodologies see Kohlhagen [41a, pp. 32–34]:

7. A dissenting and somewhat unconventional opinion is offered by Papadia [59] who challenges the view that the forward exchange rate is equal to the future spot exchange rate and argues that:

> one of the two currencies which is exchanged in a forward transaction is riskier than the other. This implies that the party buying forward the riskier currency will require a premium to enter the contract. Such a premium will necessarily be expressed as a difference between the forward and the expected spot rate. The two parties could agree on a future price and still enter the forward contract with a different one.

8. See for example Siegel's paradox [71] based on Jensen's inequality; McCulloch [52] suggests however that the bias introduced by looking at only one side of the market is negligible.

9. For an in depth discussion of the Modern Theory see Grubel [34] and Stoll [74].

10. Such an attitude toward risk by speculators would result into an infinitely elastic speculators' schedule.

11. An econometric model must contain a stochastic element to permit statistical inference from the data. The usual procedure is to hypothesize a model of varying degree of sophistication that should account for the phenomenon under review and then to add, almost as an after-thought, a disturbance or random error term to which convenient statistical properties are ascribed. This residual random error term represents in an undeterminate way all the factors that are ignored in the systematic part of the model.

12. Concerning the error term, $e(t)$, the following six conditions for a correct use of multiregression analysis are all too often ignored: (1) $E[e(t)] = 0$, (2) $Var[e(t)]$ is constant and finite (homoscedasticity), (3) zero covariance between any two dependent variables (multicollinearity), (4) $Cov[e(t), e(t-k)] = 0$, (5) $Cov[e(t),$ dependent variable$] = 0$, and finally, (6) the error term is normally distributed $e(t) = N(0,s^2)$.

13. For a more limited attempt, see the model developed by Chemical Bank and discussed in Teck [75].

14. The concept of economic exposure is really the microeconomic analog of the well-known macroeconomic problem of balance of payments adjustment (or lack of) to changing exchange rates.

15. For reasons why the Interest Rate Parity theorem may fail to hold, see the comprehensive review monograph by Kohlhagen [41a], especially Section II. A primary explanation for observed deviations from Interest Rate Parity is transaction costs. For an attempt at measuring these costs, based on an ingenious device (trilateral arbitrage), see Levich [45b]. Levi [44a] shows that asymmetrical tax treatments of exchange capital gains/losses and interest income generally result in different after-tax Interest Rate Parity equilibria from the before-tax equilibria generally tested for in existing empirical work.

16. However no specific utility function model is used, which leaves the decision rules devoid of any operational content.

17. For a comprehensive discussion of artificial currency units, see Archeim and Park [5]. An empirical assessment of risk reduction provided by denominating contracts in artificial currency units is provided in Aubey and Cramer [6] as well as in Severn and Meinster [66] with the later study focusing exclusively on the use of SDRs.

References

[1]   Aggarwal, Raj. "FASB No. 8 and Reported Results of Multinational Operations: Hazard for Managers and Investors." *Journal of Accounting, Auditing and Finance*, Spring 1978, pp. 197–217.

[2]   Aliber, Robert Z., and Stickney, Clyde P. "Accounting Measures of Foreign Exchange Exposure: The Long and Short of It." *The Accounting Review*, January 1975, pp. 44–57.

[3]   Aliber, Robert Z. *Exchange Risk and Corporate International Finance.* New York: John Wiley and Sons, 1979.

[4a] Ankrom, Robert. "Why a Reserve is Cheaper than a Hedge." *Euromoney*, February 1979, pp. 56–61.

[4b] ——— "Top-Level Approach to the Foreign Exchange Problem." *Harvard Business Review*, July–August 1974, pp. 70–90.

[5]   Archeim, J., and Park, Y.S. "Artificial Currency Units: The Functional Currency Areas." *Essays in International Finance* 114, Princeton, NJ: Princeton University, International Finance Section, April 1976.

[6]   Aubey, R.T., and Cramer, R.H. "The Use of International Currency Cocktails in the Reduction of the Exchange Rate Risk." *Journal of Economics and Business*, Winter 1977, pp. 128–134.

[7]   Barrett, Edgar M., and Spero, Leslie L. "Accounting Determinants of Foreign Exchange Gains and Losses." *Financial Analysts Journal*, March–April 1975.

[8]   Biger, Nahum. "Exchange Risk Implications of International Portfolio Diversification." *Journal of International Business Studies*, Fall 1979, pp. 64–74.

[9]   Burns, Joseph M. *Accounting Standards and International Finance*, Washington, DC: American Enterprise Institute for Public Policy Research, 1976.

[10]   Calderon-Rossel, Jorge, R. "Covering Foreign Exchange Risk of Single Transactions: A Framework for Analysis." *Financial Management,* Autumn 1979, pp. 78–85.

[11]   Choi, Frederick D.S.; Lowe, Howard D.; and Worthley, Reginald G. "Accountors, Accountants and Standard No. 8." *Journal of International Business Studies,* Fall 1978, pp. 81–87.

[12]   Cornell, Bradford, "Inflation, Relative Price Changes, and Exchange Risk." *Financial Management,* Autumn 1980, pp. 30–35.

[13]   ———., and Dietrich, J. Kimball, "The Efficiency of the Market for Foreign Exchange Under Floating Exchange Rates." *Review of Economics and Statistics,* February 1978, pp. 111–120.

[14]   Culbertson, William P. "Purchasing Power Parity and Black Market Exchange Rates." *Economic Inquiry,* June 1975, pp. 287–296.

[15]   Dooley, Michael P., and Shafer, Jeffrey R. "Analysis of Short-Run Exchange Rate Behavior: March 1973 to September 1975." *International Finance Discussion Papers.* New York: Federal Reserve System, 1976.

[16a]   Dufey, Gunter. "Corporate Finance and Exchange Rates Variations." *Financial Management,* Summer 1972, pp. 51–57.

[16b]   ———. "Corporate Financial Policies and Floating Exchange Rates." Address delivered to the Seventh Congress of the International Fiscal Association, 14 October 1974, Rome, Italy.

[17]   ———, and Giddy, Ian H. "International Financial Planning: The Use of Market Based Forecasts." *California Management Review,* Fall 1978, pp. 69–81.

[18]   Dukes, Ronald. *An Empirical Investigation of the Effects of Statement of Financial Accounting Standards No. 8 on Security Return Behavior,* Stamford, CT: Financial Standards Board 1978.

[19]   Eaker, Mark R. "Denomination Decision for Multinational Transactions." *Financial Management,* Autumn 1980, pp. 23–29.

[20]   Eiteman, David K., and Stonehill, Arthur I. *Multinational Business Finance.* 2d ed. Reading, MA: Addison-Wesley, 1978.

[21]   Evans, Thomas, G.; Folks, William R., Jr.; and Jilling, Michael. *The Impact of Statement of Financial Accounting Standards No. 8 on the Foreign Exchange Risk Management Practices of American Multinationals: An Economic Impact Study,* Stamford, CT: Financial Accounting Standards Board, 1978.

[22]   Everett, Robert M.; Georges, Abraham M.; and Blumberg, Aryeh. "Appraising Currency Strengths and Weaknesses: An Operational Framework for Calculating Parity Exchange Rates." *Journal of International Business Studies,* Fall 1980, pp. 80–91.

[23]   Fama, Eugene. "Efficient Capital Markets: A Review of Theory and Empirical Work." *Journal of Finance,* December 1979, pp. 1129–1139.

[24]   ———., and Farber, Andre. "Money, Bonds and Foreign Exchange." *American Economic Review,* September 1979, pp. 639–649.

[25]   deFaro, Clovis, and Jucker, James V., "The Impact of Inflation and Devaluation on the Selection of an International Borrowing Source." *Journal of International Business Studies,* Fall 1973, pp. 97–104.

[26]   Feiger, George, and Jacquillat, Bertrand. "Currency Option Bonds, Puts and Calls on Spot Exchange and the Hedging of Contingent Foreign Earnings." *The Journal of Finance,* December 1979, pp. 1129–1139.

[27a]   Folks, William R., Jr. "Decision Analysis for Exchange Risk Management." *Financial Management,* Winter 1972.

[27b] ——— . "The Optimal Level of Forward Exchange Transactions." *Journal of Financial and Quantitative Analysis*, January 1973.

[28] ——— ., and Stansell, Stanley R. "The Use of Discriminant Analysis in Forecasting Exchange Rate Movements." *Journal of International Business Studies*, Spring 1975, pp. 33–50.

[29] Giannotti, John B., and Walker, David P. "How the New FASB 8 Will Change Exposure Management." *Euromoney*, November 1980.

[30a] Giddy, Ian H. "An Integrated Theory of Exchange Rate Equilibrium." *Journal of Financial and Quantitative Analysis*, December 1976, pp. 863–892.

[30b] ——— . "Why it Doesn't Pay to Make a Habit of Forward Hedging." *Euromoney*, December 1976.

[30c] ——— . "Exchange Risk: Whose View." *Financial Management*, Summer 1977, pp. 23–33.

[30d] ——— . "The Effective Cost of Foreign Currency Borrowing." *Journal of Financial and Quantitative Analysis*, forthcoming.

[31] ——— ., and Dufey, Gunter. "The Random Behavior of Flexible Exchange Rates: Implications for Forecasting." *Journal of International Business Studies*, Spring 1975, pp. 1–32.

[32] Goodman, Stephen H. "Foreign Exchange Rate Forecasting Techniques: Implications for Business and Policy." *The Journal of Finance*, May 1979, pp. 415–427.

[33] Grauer, F.L.A.; Litzenberger, R.H.; and Stehle, R.H. "Sharing Rules and Equilibrium in an International Capital Market Under Uncertainty." *Journal of Financial Economics* 3 (1976), pp. 233–256.

[34] Grubel, Herbert G. *Forward Exchange, Speculation, and the International Flow of Capital.* Palo Alto: Stanford University Press, 1966.

[35] Gull, Don S. "Composite Foreign Exchange Risk," *Columbia Journal of World Business*, Fall 1975, pp. 51–69.

[36] Hayes, Donald, J. "Translating Foreign Currencies." *Harvard Business Review*, January–February 1972, pp. 6–18, 159–161.

[37] Heckerman, Donald. "The Exchange Risks of Foreign Operations." *The Journal of Business*, January 1972, pp. 42–48.

[38] Hodder, James. "Hedging of Exposure to Exchange-Rate Movements." Ph.D. dissertation, Stanford University, 1978.

[39a] Jacque, Laurent L. *Management of Foreign Exchange Risk: Theory and Praxis.* Lexington, MA: D.C. Heath, 1978.

[39b] ——— . "Why Hedgers are not Speculators." *Columbia Journal of World Business*, Winter 1979.

[40] Jilling, Michael. "Foreign Exchange Risk Management: Current Practices of U.S. Multinational Corporations." Ph.D. dissertation, University of South Carolina, 1976.

[41a] Kohlhagen, Steven W. "The Behavior of Foreign Exchange Markets: A Critical Survey of the Empirical Literature." *Monograph 1978-3.* Salomon Brothers Center for the Study of Financial Institutions: New York University.

[41b] ——— . "A Model of Optimal Foreign Exchange Hedging Without Exchange Rate Projections." *Journal of International Business Studies*, Fall 1978, pp. 9–21.

[41c] ——— . "The Performance of the Foreign Exchange Markets: 1971–74." *Journal of International Business Studies*, Fall 1975, pp. 33–39.

[42a] Korth, Christopher M. "The Future of a Currency." *Business Horizons*, June 1972, pp. 67–76.

[42b] ———— . "Devaluation Dichotomy: Headquarters vs. Subsidiary." *MSU Business Topics*, Autumn 1972, pp. 52–58.

[43] Lessard, Donald R., and Lorange, Peter. "Currency Changes and Management Control: Resolving the Centralization/Decentralization Dilemma." *Accounting Review*, July 1977, pp. 628–637.

[44a] Levi, Maurice D. "Underutilization of Forward Markets or Rational Behavior," *Journal of Finance*, September 1979, pp. 1013–1017.

[44b] ———— . "Taxation and 'Abnormal' Capital Flows." *Journal of Political Economy*, June 1977, pp. 635–646.

[45a] Levich, Richard M. "On the Efficiency of Markets for Foreign Exchange." In *International Economic Policy*, edited by Rudiger Dornbusch and Jacob A. Frankel. Baltimore: the Johns Hopkins University Press, 1978.

[45b] ———— . *The International Monetary Market: An Assessment of Forecasting Techniques and Market Efficiency*. Greenwich, CT: JAI Press, 1979.

[45c] ———— . "Analyzing the Accuracy of Foreign Exchange Forecasting Services: Theory and Evidence." Forthcoming in *Exchange Risk and Exposure: Current Development in International Finance Development*, co-edited with Clas Wihlborg, Lexington, MA: D.C. Heath, Lexington Books, 1980.

[46] Levy, H., and Sarnat, M. "International Diversification of Investment Portfolios." *American Economic Review* (1970), pp. 668–675.

[47a] Liaeter, Bernard A. "Managing Risks in Foreign Exchange." *Harvard Business Review*, March–April 1970, pp. 127–138.

[47b] ———— . *Financial Management of Foreign Exchange*. Cambridge, MA: The M.I.T. Press, 1971.

[48] Logue, Dennis E., and Oldfield, George S. "Managing Foreign Assets When Foreign Exchange Markets are Efficient." *Financial Management*, Summer 1977, pp. 16–22.

[49] ———— ., and Sweeney, Richard J. "White Noise in Imperfect Markets: The Case of the Franc–Dollar Exchange Rate." *The Journal of Finance*, June 1977, pp. 761–768.

[50a] Makin, John H. "Flexible Exchange Rates, Multinational Corporations and Accounting Standards." *Federal Reserve Bank of San Francisco Economic Review*, Fall 1977, pp. 44–45.

[50b] ———— . "Portfolio Theory and the Problem of Foreign Exchange Risk." *Journal of Finance*, May 1978, pp. 517–534.

[50c] ———— . "Techniques and Success in Forecasting Exchange Rates: Should it Be Done? Does it Matter? The Long and Short of It." Paper presented at the New York University Conference on Internationalization of Financial Market and National Economic Policy, 10–11 April 1980, New York, NY.

[51] Malek, Talaat Abdel. "Managing Exchange Risks Under Floating Exchange Rates: The Canadian Experience." *Columbia Journal of World Business*, Fall 1976, pp. 41–52.

[52] McCulloch, J. Huston. "Operational Aspects of the Siegel Paradox." *Quarterly Journal of Economics*, February 1975, pp. 170–172.

[53] Murenbeeld, Martin. "Economic Factors for Forecasting Foreign Exchange Rates." *Columbia Journal of World Business*, Summer 1975, pp. 81–95.

[54] Nauman-Etienne, Ruediger. "Exchange Risk in Foreign Operations of Multinational Corporations." Ph.D. dissertation, University of Michigan, 1977.

[55] Norr, David. "Currency Translation and the Analyst." *Financial Analysts Journal*, July–August 1976, pp. 46–54.

[56] Officer, Lawrence H. "The Purchasing Power Parity of Exchange Rates: A

Review Article." *I.M.F. Staff Paper 23*, no. 1, March 1976.

[57] Olstein, Robert A., and O'Glove, Thorton L. "Devaluation and Multinational Reporting," *Financial Analysis Journal*, September–October 1973, pp. 65–84.

[58] Pakkala, A.L. "Foreign Exchange Accounting of Multinational Corporations." *Financial Analysts Journal*, March–April 1975, pp. 32–41.

[59] Papadia, Francesco. "It's Not an Error When the Forward Rate Differs from the Expected Spot." *Euromoney*, September 1979, pp. 94–96.

[60] Poole, William. "Speculative Prices as Random Walk: An Analysis of Ten Time Series of Flexible Exchange Rates." *Southern Economic Journal*, April 1967, pp. 468–478.

[61] Porter, Michael M. "A Theoretical and Empirical Framework for Analyzing the Term Structure of Exchange Rate Expectations." *International Monetary Fund Staff Papers*, November 1971, pp. 613–645.

[62a] Rodriguez, Rita M. "FASB No. 8: What Has It Done For Us?" *Financial Analysts Journal*, March–April 1977, pp. 40–48.

[62b] *Foreign Exchange Management in U.S. Multinationals.* Lexington, MA: D.C. Heath, 1980.

[63] Rogalski, Richard J., and Vinso, Joseph D. "Price Level Variations as Predictors of Flexible Exchange Rates." *Journal of International Business Studies*, Spring/Summer 1977, pp. 71–82.

[64] Roll, Richard W., and Solnik, Bruno H. "A Pure Foreign Exchange Asset Pricing Model." *European Institute for Advanced Studies in Management*: Working Paper No. 75, August 1975.

[65] Schwab, B., and Lusztig, P. "Apportioning Foreign Exchange Risk Through the Use of Third Currencies: Some Questions on Efficiency." *Financial Management*, Autumn 1978.

[66] Severn, Alan K., and Meinster, D.R. "The Use of Multicurrency Financing by the Financial Manager." *Financial Management*, Winter 1978, pp. 45–53.

[67] Shank, John H. "FASB Statement No. 8 Resolved Foreign Currency Accounting – or Did It?" *Financial Analysts Journal*, July–August 1976, pp. 55–61.

[68a] Shapiro, Alan C. "Exchange Rate Changes, Inflation and the Value of the Multinational Corporation." *The Journal of Finance*, May 1975, pp. 485–502.

[68b] ——— . "Evaluating Financing Costs for Multinational Subsidiaries." *Journal of International Business Studies*, Fall 1975, pp. 25–32.

[68c] ——— . "Defining Exchange Risk," *Journal of Business*, January 1977, pp. 37–39.

[69a] ——— , and Rutenberg, David P. "When to Hedge." *Management Science*, August 1974, pp. 1514–1530.

[69b] ——— ., and Rutenberg, David P. "Managing Exchange Risks in a Floating World." *Financial Management*, Summer 1976.

[70] Shulman, Robert B. "Are Foreign Exchange Risks Measurable?" *Columbia Journal of World Business*, May–June 1970, pp. 55–60.

[71] Siegel, Jeremy. "Risk, Interest, and Forward Exchange." *Quarterly Journal of Economics*, May 1972, pp. 303–309.

[72a] Solnik, B.H. "International Pricing of Risk: An Empirical Investigation of World Capital Market Structure." *Journal of Finance*, December 1973, pp. 1151–1159.

[72b] ——— . "An Equilibrium Model of the International Capital Market."

Journal of Economic Theory, August 1974, pp. 500–524.

[73]   Stanley, Marjorie T., and Block, Stanley B. "Response by United States Financial Managers to Financial Accounting Standard No. 8." *Journal of International Business Studies*, Fall 1978, pp. 89–99.

[74]   Stoll, Hans. "An Empirical Study of the Forward Exchange Market Under Fixed and Flexible Exchange Rate Systems." *Canadian Journal of Economics*, February 1968, pp. 55–78.

[75]   Teck, Alan. "Using Computers for Foreign Exchange Tax Planning." *The International Tax Journal*, Fall 1975, pp. 5–27.

[76]   Vinso, Joseph D., and Rogalski, Richard J. "Empirical Properties of Foreign Exchange Rates," *Journal of International Business Studies*, Fall 1978, pp. 69–80.

[77]   Westerfield, Janice M. "Empirical Properties of Foreign Exchange Rates Under Fixed and Floating Rate Regimes." *Journal of International Economics*, June 1977, pp. 181–200.

[78]   Wheelwright, Steven C. "Applying Decision Theory to Improve Corporate Management of Currency-Exchange Risks." *California Management Review*, Summer 1975, pp. 41–49.

[79a]   Wihlborg, Clas. *Currency Risks in International Financial Markets.* Princeton Study in International Finance, No. 44, December 1978.

[79b]   ——— . "Currency Exposure: Taxonomy and Theory," forthcoming in *Exchange Risk and Exposure: Current Development in International Financial Development*, co-edited with Richard M. Levich. Lexington, MA: D.C. Heath, Lexington Books, 1980.

[80]   Wurster, Thomas S. "The Firm in the International Economy." Ph.D. dissertation, Yale University, 1978.

5

On the measurement of operating exposure to exchange rates: a conceptual approach*

Eugene Flood, Jr. and Donald R. Lessard[†]

*Source: *Financial Management*, 15 (Spring 1986), pp. 25–36.

Contractual Exposure and Operating Exposure

In theory, it is straightforward to define a firm's exposure to exchange rates. If we choose to define the exposure in terms of the firm's value (as opposed to, say, a single period's cash flow or earnings) then the firm's exposure is the extent to which the value of the firm changes with a change in the exchange rate.[1] As a practical matter, it is much more difficult to find agreement on a definition and means to compute foreign exchange exposure. For example, since 1976 the United States Financial Standards Accounting Board has changed the rules twice for consolidating foreign investments for accounting purposes. The heart of the question that they have wrestled with is whether current or historic exchange rates should be used to translate the value of various foreign assets and liabilities into U.S. dollars. This article does not attempt to resolve this valuation dilemma for accountants, but focuses instead on the effects of exchange rate changes on the firm's operating cash flows, that is, its operating exposure.[2]

An understanding of the implications of exchange rate changes on a firm's cash flow is important for management for a variety of reasons. For example, Lessard and Sharp [20] have pointed out that performance evaluation of the management of divisions that are heavily influenced by global competition can be properly conducted only if the impacts of exchange rate changes on the operations and international competitiveness of the firm are well understood. Consider also the capital budgeting problem of an internationally active firm. A sensitivity analysis of the profitability of a project with respect to exchange rate changes may play a key role in the decision-making process.

For the purposes of this discussion of exposure, the cash flows of the firm can be grouped into two broad classes: those cash flows that are fixed in nominal terms in a particular currency (*e.g.*, accounts receivable and most debt) and the firm's operating cash flows.[3] The sensitivity of these two classes of cash flows to changes in exchange rates can be quite different. The value of contractual flows in their currency of denomination is, to a first approximation, independent of the exchange rate.[4] Thus, the dollar value of contractual flows moves one-for-one with the exchange rate. In contrast, the local currency value of operating cash flows is likely to be a function of the exchange rate. Therefore the dollar value of these flows may move more or less than one-for-one with changes in the exchange rate.

It is useful to separate the exposure of operating flows into two components: a *competitive effect* and a *conversion effect*.[5] The competitive effect is the sensitivity of the local currency cash flows to changes in the exchange rate, which is shown to depend on the competitive structure of the markets in which the firm sells its products and the sources of its inputs. The conversion effect is purely the one-for-one mapping of the resulting local currency cash flows into dollars. While dollar cash flows are, by definition, not subject to the conversion effect, they may be subject to a competitive effect.

This difference in sensitivity is often obscured in the firm's financial statements. To see this, consider a U.K.-based firm which sells manufacturing equipment domestically in competition with West German firms and which exports equipment to West Germany. In an attempt to assess the firm's foreign exchange exposure to the deutsche mark (DM) many managers would be tempted to consider only the contractual items found on the company's balance sheet, such as DM denominated accounts payable and receivables and debt denominated in DM. However, the firm may also have other contractual items that are equally exposed but that may not appear on the balance sheet, such as orders booked but not yet shipped, take or pay contracts or possibly some forward exchange rate contracts denominated in DM. A 5% change in the pound/DM exchange rate causes a 5% change in the recorded value of these items. An expanded approach to measuring the firm's exposure, then, would also include these off-balance-sheet items. But even the expanded approach is largely historical in perspective. It is a "snap shot" of the firm's cumulative contractual activities, which may capture only a small part of the impact of the exchange rate change on the firm's cash flows. As a result of the exchange rate shift (or a series of exchange rate shifts) the firm's international competitiveness may have been substantially altered. It may adjust its pricing and marketing strategies so as to effect a change in its market share. The exchange rate change could also affect its sourcing and ultimately its location of production. An examination of a firm's operating exposure is an attempt to go a step further than exposure estimates based on the company's books. The results of an operating exposure analysis can be thought of as coming from a sensitivity analysis to exchange rate changes performed on a pro forma income statement. It is a forward-looking approach to exposure.

As suggested in the preceding brief example, the response of operating cash flows to a change in exchange rates is determined by many groups within the firm: strategy, marketing, purchasing, and production. Clearly, the actions undertaken by each of these groups will be influenced by competitive forces in the markets in which the firm operates. For expository purposes this discussion will treat the firm as a single operating unit to focus on the firm's interaction with the competitive environment.

Deviations from Purchasing Power Parity

When studying operating exposure one has to be careful to properly define exchange rate changes. Only those changes that result in a change in (real) dollar operating cash flows are relevant.

Consider two different types of exchange rate changes: First, consider a change that is in line with purchasing power parity (PPP). Suppose price inflation in the United Kingdom during the year is 10% and inflation in West Germany is 5%. Suppose also that the pound depreciates by 5% relative to the DM. A U.K.-based firm, broadly speaking, would see prices in the U.K. market (and the cost of inputs sourced in the U.K.) expressed in pound sterling up by 10% at the end of the year. As it looks at Germany, it sees DM prices up by 5% at the end of the year; in addition, the DM is 5% more expensive, so expressed in pounds, the prices (and the cost of inputs sourced in Germany) would be a total of 10% higher (5% inflation plus 5% currency move). Thus, from the standpoint of the U.K.-based firm prices and costs have remained stable across countries, because they have moved in parity with the exchange rate. This is an example of the familiar condition of PPP. From the standpoint of a West German-based firm it can be seen that (when expressed in DM) the prices and costs in Germany and in the U.K. will increase by 5% during the year. Once again, there is no change in relative prices and costs across countries.[6]

If, on the other hand, in the same inflation environment considered heretofore, the pound appreciates by 7% during the year instead of depreciating by 5% then what will the British firm perceive? It will see U.K. prices and costs up by 10% at the end of the year. However, as it looks to Germany, it will see DM prices and costs up by 5% but the "price" of the DM is down by 7%, so effective German prices and costs are down by 2%. Compared to the beginning of the year, the U.K. has become a relatively more attractive market in which to sell and West Germany has become a relatively more attractive location from which to source.[7] Obviously, this type of change in exchange rates is one where exchange rates and prices have not moved in parity with each other, *i.e.*, relative prices have changed across countries. This is referred to as a change in the "real" exchange rate. The inflation-adjusted or real exchange rate, RX, can be written in equation form as follows:

$$RX = S \left(\frac{P^*}{P} \right) = \text{nominal exchange rate} \times \frac{\text{foreign price level}}{\text{domestic price level}}$$

where the nominal exchange rate is expressed as the home-currency price of foreign exchange. Notice that if the nominal exchange rate moves to offset changes in inflation across countries (*i.e.*, PPP holds) then RX remains unchanged. The real exchange rate can also be thought of as the *terms of trade*, or the relative price (across countries) of a composite good.[8]

Exhibit 5.1 plots the real exchange rate for the United Kingdom and West Germany during the period 1974 through 1983. As can be seen from the top graph, the rate of price inflation in the U.K. was more than twice as great as the rate in West Germany. However, the pound only depreciated by roughly 50% relative to the mark. Consequently, as can be seen in the bottom graph, when the pound appreciated in real terms relative to the mark (*i.e.*, during the period), goods in the U.K. became relatively more expensive than goods in West Germany.[9]

As emphasized heretofore, changes in the real exchange rate (i) will affect the relative attractiveness of the two markets and hence may affect the firm's competitive position on the revenue side, and (ii) may affect the cost of the firm's inputs relative to its competitors and hence may affect its competitive position on the cost side. It is through these factors that the exchange rate change can affect the operating cash flow of a firm.[10]

Determinants of Operating Exposure

As noted previously, operating exposure differs in two important respects from contractual exposure. First, it incorporates both a competitive and a conversion effect. Second, it responds to shifts in the real as opposed to the nominal exchange rate. These differences imply distinctive approaches to evaluating the two types of exposures.

In the case of contractual exposures, most inputs necessary to measure the exposure can be found in the company's accounting statements and the estimation of the impact of exchange rate movements on the exposed items is straightforward. Now think about operating exposure. The exposed items are the firm's future revenues, costs, and profits, which are not captured in present accounting statements. Further, the estimation of the responsiveness of these items to exchange rate changes includes the competitive effect, which depends upon the structure of the markets in which the firm

Exhibit 5.1a Prices and exchange rates, the U.K. and W. Germany

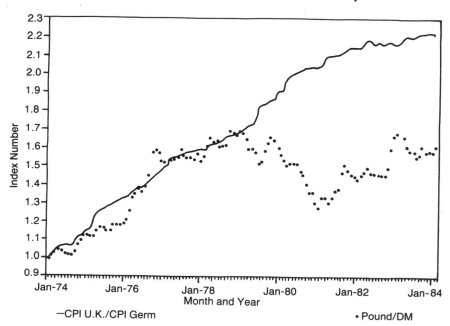

−CPI U.K./CPI Germ   • Pound/DM

operates, as well as the conversion effect, which is common to both classes of exposures. Clearly, assessing these exposures requires an analysis of the firm's competitive environment and cannot be based solely on accounting information. This section focuses on the determinants of the competitive effects.

The impact of the firm's competitive position on its operating exposure is a very important one. A firm's operating exposure is largely determined by

(i) the structure of the markets in which the company sells its products, and
(ii) the structure of the markets in which the company (and its competitors) purchase their inputs.

Market structure will, in turn, determine

(i) the currency habitat of the price of goods, and
(ii) quantity impacts (unit sales or purchases).

When the first factor, which describes the price movements, is combined with the second factor, quantity impacts, this fully describes the revenues, costs, and profits. The following section discusses explanations of these two factors.

Exhibit 5.1b Nominal and real exchange rates, the U.K. and W. Germany

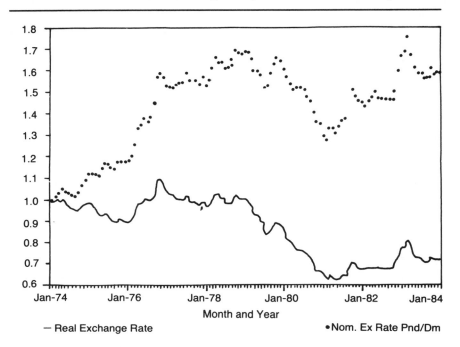

- Real Exchange Rate   •Nom. Ex Rate Pnd/Dm

Currency Habitat of Price

The currency habitat of a good is simply defined as the currency in which the price of the good tends to be most stable. The reason that this piece of information is of interest is because we need to know if a price will move or remain stable when exchange rates move. Let us first examine this issue when there is perfect competition and a unified world price for a good and then move to the more complicated case when the price of a good can differ across countries and where there may be fewer producers.

In order to motivate this concept of currency habitat when there is a unified world price, consider the following hypothetical example. Suppose the law of one price holds for lumber in the United States and Canada.[11] If the Canadian dollar weakens by 10%, how does the U.S. dollar price of lumber move? The answer to this question is determined by two factors: (i) the producers and consumers that dominate that market and (ii) the demand and supply elasticities. There are two relevant extremes. If the market is primarily composed of U.S.-based producers and consumers, changes in exchange rates will have little impact on the U.S. dollar price and the Canadian dollar price will need to rise by 10%. This "stickiness" in U.S. dollars is further compounded if the U.S. producers and consumers are the marginal producers and consumers, that is, if they are relatively

Exhibit 5.2 General case of Canadian dollar depreciation: Canadian dollar perspective

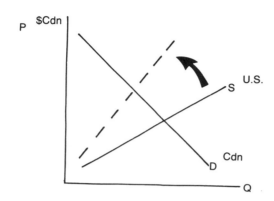

sensitive to changes in the price of the product as compared to the Canadians.[12] The other extreme is a market that is primarily composed of Canadian producers and consumers who are relatively sensitive to price changes. In this case exchange rate changes will have very little impact on the Canadian dollar price of lumber and the U.S. dollar price of lumber will fall by 10%.

What are the implications of price habitat for exposure? Notice that in the former case a U.S. company that prices and invoices in Canadian dollar prices could have *no* operating exposure (assuming that the quantity of lumber sold did not change) even though it might be doing "foreign" business. Notice also that in the latter case a U.S. company that prices and invoices in U.S. dollars could have an operating exposure, because its (U.S. dollar) prices fluctuate strongly when the exchange rate changes.

To illustrate the importance of elasticities graphically consider an even simpler example. Suppose that there are only U.S. producers of coal who export coal to only Canadian consumers (there is no U.S. coal consumption) and that the market is characterized by perfect competition. Exhibits 5.2 and 5.3 illustrate the impact of a real depreciation of the Canadian dollar on the Canadian dollar price and the U.S. dollar price of coal exported to Canada and the equilibrium quantity demanded and supplied. The exhibits illustrate the same exchange rate shift, but Exhibit 5.2 is from the Canadian dollar perspective and Exhibit 5.3 is from the U.S. dollar perspective.

Examine Exhibit 5.2. When the Canadian dollar depreciates. U.S. suppliers want to supply less coal at every Canadian dollar price (per ton). In other words, the supply curve shifts back. Consequently, there is upward pressure on the Canadian dollar price. Exhibit 5.3 shows that when the

Exhibit 5.3 General case of Canadian dollar depreciation: U.S. dollar perspective

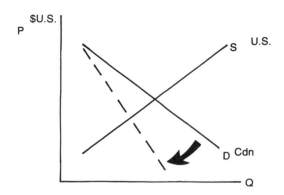

Canadian dollar depreciates Canadian consumers want less coal at every U.S. dollar price (per ton), that is, the demand curve shifts down. Consequently, there is downward pressure on the U.S. dollar price. Both graphs show that the quantity of coal sold falls. To see how elasticities impact operating exposure, consider three cases.

In the first case, shown in Exhibit 5.4, Canadian demand is perfectly inelastic so any changes in the exchange rate are passed directly on to the Canadian consumers and the U.S. dollar price is stable. Since there is no change in quantity, U.S. dollar revenues are fixed. *i.e.*, there is no exposure from the U.S. perspective.

Exhibit 5.4 Canadian dollar depreciation, infinitely elastic Canadian demand: Canadian dollar perspective

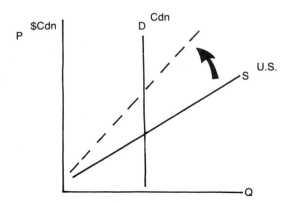

Exhibit 5.5 Canadian dollar depreciation, perfectly elastic U.S. supply: U.S. dollar perspective

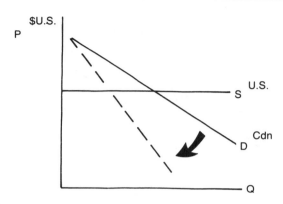

In the second case, shown in Exhibit 5.5, U.S. supply is perfectly elastic so the U.S. dollar price is once again fixed. However, this time changes in the exchange rate lead to changes in the quantity sold, so U.S. dollar revenues are exposed.

In the third case, shown in Exhibit 5.6, Canadian demand is perfectly elastic so the Canadian dollar price is stable. When the Canadian dollar depreciates the U.S. dollar price declines by the full amount and the quantity sold falls, so U.S. dollar revenues are *highly* exposed.

To this point the analysis of currency habitat has been considered in an environment in which the law of one price is a reasonable approximation.

Exhibit 5.6 Canadian dollar depreciation, perfectly elastic Canadian demand: Canadian dollar perspective

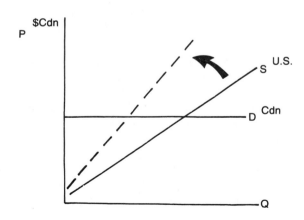

Exhibit 5.7 Indexes of relative prices, nominal and real exchange rates, the U.S. and W. Germany

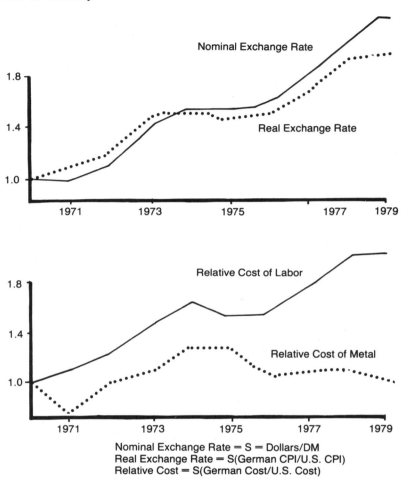

Nominal Exchange Rate = S = Dollars/DM
Real Exchange Rate = S(German CPI/U.S. CPI)
Relative Cost = S(German Cost/U.S. Cost)

For which classes of goods does the law of one price work? And, for those for which it does not work, how is the currency habitat determined? To get a sense of when the law of one price holds best, consider the appreciation of the DM relative to the U.S. dollar during the 1970s. Note that if the law of one price holds for a good, the relative price (expressed in the same currency) of that good across countries is not affected by exchange rate changes. Now answer the following question: How did the U.S. dollar price of products in the U.S. change relative to the (effective) U.S. dollar price of the similar products in West Germany? The answer to this question differs for different commodities. In spite of the fact that the DM appreciated

Exhibit 5.8 Determinants of currency habitat of cost/price

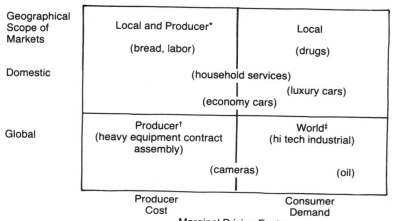

*Strictly local if recurring costs of production are local.
†Currency of marginal firm/price leader depending on industrial structure.
‡A basket income and elasticity weighted by relative importance of consumers. As a first approximation, think of this as a basket comprising special drawing rights (SDRs).

sharply in nominal terms relative to the U.S. dollar, the relative price of metal was not greatly affected, as shown in Exhibit 5.7. On the other hand, the relative price of labor in West Germany versus that in the U.S. was heavily influenced by the change in the nominal exchange rate. Why is this true? Recall that the law of one price is driven by goods market arbitrage. According to the theory, when the price of a good in one country is higher than the price of the same good in another country, consumers will shift purchases of the good to the lower price country until the price of the good is the same in both countries. Clearly, this will take place best for easily transportable goods that are widely traded by many producers. Furthermore, the smaller the extent of product differentiation across countries, the better the theory will hold. When manufacturers are able to bundle service contracts with equipment such as automobiles or computer hardware, they are able to sell essentially identical pieces of equipment to different classes of buyers at very different prices. And finally, the absence of barriers to trade, such as tariffs and quotas, improves the usefulness of the law of one price as a real world description.

These observations regarding the factors that give rise to the currency habitat of price for particular products or inputs are illustrated in Exhibit 5.8. The two dimensions depicted are (i) the geographical scope of the product market and (ii) the relative influence of producer costs and characteristics of consumer demand on price in a given market. The *geographical* scope of the market reflects barriers to transshipment including transportation costs and tariffs, differences in tastes, and so on. The *marginal pricing factor* reflects the relative importance of producer cost and consumer demand considerations that depend on, among other things, the competitive structure of the industry, the price elasticity of demand, the range of complements and substitutes and the relevant cross elasticities, and the structure of costs, in particular, the level of nonrecurring costs. If nonrecurring costs (*e.g.,* "up-front" capital investment including R & D and capital equipment) are a large proportion of total costs, then the marginal unit costs of production will be small and pricing will be dictated primarily by demand considerations.

In those cases where firms can effectively segment national markets through their own market power and with the collaboration of regulatory authorities (see the upper half of Exhibit 5.8), they face local currency-denominated marginal revenue curves. If recurring costs determined in other markets are low they will tend to maintain constant local prices in the face of exchange rate adjustments. We will refer to these as *local prices*, in that they are primarily influenced by local as opposed to international supply and demand conditions. In contrast, if costs determined in other markets are high, firms will adjust both local price and volume. In this case the currency habitat will be some combination of the local currency and the currency habitat of the producer's costs. Manufacturers of patented drugs represent one extreme in this regard, where one would expect virtually no link between local prices and exchange rates, while producers of mid-range autos, such as Toyota and Nissan, are at the other extreme. Producers of luxury cars, with greater product differentiation and higher margins of sales price over recurring costs, tend to maintain more stable local prices in the face of exchange rate shifts.

In contrast, in cases where transshipment cannot be barred, either because of the portability of the product, the inability of manufacturers to control distribution channels, or the power of key customers, prices will tend to a single world level (see lower half of Exhibit 5.8). The camera

Exhibit 5.9 Operating impact of real exchange rate shift: Case 1 (sales and costs expressed in Swiss francs)

	Case 1: Base case Nominal exchange rate: SF 1 = LC 1			
Firm descriptor:	Exporter	Local market	Importer	World market
Sales	100(world	100(local)	100(local)	100(world)
Costs	80(local)	80(local)	80(world)	80(world)
Contribution margin	20	20	20	20

industry is a case in point, with gray marketeers denying manufacturers the ability to fully segment national markets. The same is true of industrial equipment and components that are sold to sophisticated buyers who themselves are multinational. The currency habitat of these *world prices* will reflect the weighted importance of customers from various countries and costs incurred in various currencies.

Quantity Impacts

The second ingredient needed to describe the structure of the market for an operating exposure audit is the extent to which unit sales and purchases respond to real exchange rate changes. To illustrate this point, consider the example of U.K. Airlines cited by Lessard and Lightstone [19]. As a charter airline whose primary business is to fly British vacationers to the U.S., it faces potentially drastic fluctuation in rates of utilization which it cannot overcome by varying its price. In deciding where to travel, vacationers will consider the relative price of a vacation in one country compared to the price in another. Given that travel costs typically represent roughly 30% of the total vacation expenses, the relative cost of a vacation in one country compared to another can largely be described by the real exchange rate. During the 1970s, the number of travelers from the U.K. to the U.S. bore a clear relationship to the real dollar/pound exchange rate. Clearly, this would have a large impact on the airline's revenues.

As can be seen from this section, there is an important distinction between the traditional exposure analysis and an operating exposure analysis. Unlike the traditional exposure approach, where the currency of the item under consideration is of major importance, operating exposure market is determined primarily by market characteristics, not by the currency in which prices are quoted.

Exhibit 5.10 Operating impact of real exchange rate shift: Case 2 (sales and costs expressed in Swiss francs)

| Firm descriptor: | Case 2: 20% real appreciation of the local currency Nominal exchange rate: SF 1.20 = LC 1 | | | |
	Exporter	Local market	Importer	World market
Sales	100(world	120(local)	120(local)	100(world)
Costs	96(local)	96(local)	80(world)	80(world)
Contribution margin	4	24	40	20
% change from base case	−80	+20	+100	0

A Simple Taxonomy of Operating Exposure

To assess a firm's operating exposure to changes in exchange rates, it is useful to unbundle the problem into two parts. First, examine the structure of the markets in which the company sells its products. And, second, examine the structure of the markets in which the company and its competitors purchase their inputs.

Imagine four possible source/sell configurations describing the firm (or subsidiary) for which the operating exposure audit is being conducted. The first type of firm purchases its inputs in segmented local markets, so its input prices will move like local prices. This firm sells its products in competitive world markets, so its output prices move like world prices. This type of firm will be called the *exporter firm*. This category could include, for example, a U.S. firm that sources and sells in U.S. domestic markets, but faces dominant Japanese competition. The second type of firm buys its inputs in segmented local markets and then sells its products in similar markets. Its input and output prices will move like local prices. This will be referred to as the *local market firm*. The third type of firm purchases its inputs in world markets and then sells its products into segmented local markets. This will be called the *importer firm*. Finally, the fourth type of firm purchases its inputs in competitive world markets and sells its products in similar markets. This is called the *world market firm*.

For the purposes of this example a few simplifying notions will be used. World prices will refer to prices of those goods for which the law of one price is a reasonably good approximation *and* whose currency habitat is the domestic currency of the person doing the analysis.[13] Local prices will refer to prices which are largely determined in the local economies and hence experience sharp deviations from the law of one price. These prices are fairly stable when expressed in the local currency (and, perhaps, deflated by a general price index if there is substantial local price inflation).

The entire analysis will be performed from the standpoint of a Swiss-

Exhibit 5.11 Operating impact of real exchange rate shift: Case 3 (sales and costs expressed in Swiss francs)

| Firm descriptor: | Case 3: Thin margins
Nominal exchange rate: $SF\ 1 = LC\ 1$ | | | World market |
	Exporter	Local market	Importer	
Sales	100(world)	100(local)	100(local)	100(world)
Costs	90(local)	90(local)	90(world)	90(world)
Contribution margin	10	10	10	10

Exhibit 5.12 Operating impact of real exchange rate shift: Case 4 (sales and costs expressed in Swiss francs)

| Firm descriptor: | Case 4: 20% real appreciation of the local currency Nominal exchange rate: SF 1.20 = LC 1 | | | |
	Exporter	Local market	Importer	World market
Sales	100(world)	120(local)	120(local)	100(world)
Costs	108(local)	108(local)	90(world)	90(world)
Contribution margin	−8	12	30	20
% change from base case	−180	+20	+200	0

based parent of a multinational. The purpose is to estimate the impact on contribution margin of a change in the real exchange rate. All sales and costs will be expressed in Swiss francs (SF). The local currency will be referred to as LC. Before the exchange rate changes, the exchange rate is SF 1 = LC 1. Sales are SF 100 and costs are SF 80. See Exhibit 5.9.

Now consider what happens to margins when the local currency appreciates by 20% to SF 1.20 = LC 1.[14] In the case of the exporter firm, sales remain at SF 100 because they are made at world prices, but costs increase by 20% to SF 96 because they are fixed in the local currency. Consequently, the exporter's margins drop by 80% to SF 4. In this example, the exporter is the biggest loser when the local currency experiences a real appreciation. In the case of the local market firm, sales and costs increase by 20% because they are both fixed in the local currency, so margins also increase by 20%. In the case of the importer, sales are local prices so they increase by 20% to SF 120, but costs are incurred at world prices so they remained fixed at SF 80; as a result, margins increase by 100% to SF 40 with a 20% real appreciation of the local currency. Since prices and costs are world prices for the world market firm, there is no change for its margins. See Exhibit 5.10.

As an additional note, consider the impact on margins of a real appreciation of the local currency if costs for all four firms were, say, 50% local and 50% world, and assume for simplicity that, because of the production technology, there can be no substitutions of one input factor for another when their relative prices change. Then costs for all four firms would increase by 10% to SF 88.

Now suppose margins were smaller at the start, say SF 10 instead of SF 20, as shown in Exhibit 5.11. In this case, a 20% real appreciation of the local currency pushes the exporter into a negative margin position while the importer's margins triple. These effects are summarized in Exhibit 5.12.

Notice that in both cases it is only the world market firm that has no operating exposure. The exchange rate elasticity of its margin is zero. The margin of the local market firm has a unit exchange rate elasticity. These two are the only simple cases for computing operating exposure. Notice also that the real exchange rate change has opposite impacts on the importer and the exporter. So knowing that the real exchange rate has, say, appreciated, does not signal whether the business conditions have improved or deteriorated for a firm; one must know something about the nature of the business.

Summary

There are four fundamental differences between operating exposure and contractual exposure:

(i) It is not the currency of invoice that determines the operating exposure for a firm, but the market structure in which the firm operates.
(ii) Operating exposure may bear little relationship to the location of the firm's physical assets.
(iii) Operating exposure is a response to changing real exchange rates as opposed to the nominal exchange rates that drive contractual exposure.
(iv) Understanding the firm's accounting statements is not sufficient to assess its operating exposure; a competitive analysis must be done.

These differences have important implications for strategic and tactical operating choices, such as siting, sourcing, and market positioning, for the measurement of management performance, and for the management of foreign exchange risk. Consider the case of hedging for a well-known high-tech manufacturer in the U.S.[15] This particular company is a U.S.-based firm that does business in France, but its primary competition in France is the Japanese. Consequently, it is a U.S. firm with French franc denominated revenues that move with the yen. Imagine what would happen if this firm decided to hedge its foreign currency exposure based on a traditional accounting exposure analysis. It would see French franc receivables on the books so it would conclude that it was "long" (*i.e.*, had a positive exposed position) in French francs. To offset that it would "go short" francs either by selling francs forward or by borrowing francs. From the standpoint of the firm's operating exposure, this would be a very incomplete hedge (and, perhaps, entirely wrong). By understanding the competitive structure of the market, the firm realized that it was actually long not only in francs but also substantially in yen. Thus, to hedge its exposure over time, it would need to short a combination of francs and yen. One has to be quite careful to note that operating exposure is largely driven by the *real* exchange rate, while the short positions previously described are tied to the nominal exchange rate. Hedging operating exposure with contractual positions in debt or forwards may be very imperfect.

Notes

[†] We would like to thank Thomas Piper, Alan C. Shapiro and Robert Taggart for their helpful suggestions. Financial support was provided by the Graduate School of Business of Stanford University, the Stanford Program in Finance, the Hoover Institution, the Center for Economic Policy Research, and the Sloan School of Management of the Massachusetts Institute of Technology.

1 See, for example, Adler and Dumas [2]

2 The concept that is referred to here as "operating exposure" is referred to by many authors and practitioners as "economic exposure" (see, *e.g.*, Levi [21] and Cornell and Shapiro [6], and Srinivasulu [27]). This usage is misleading since the exposure of foreign currency denominated (contractual) assets and liabilities, typically resulting in either transaction or translation gains or losses in the firm's financial statements, also is an economic exposure in that the dollar value of the assets in question does change in response to exchange rate shifts. See Lessard [18] for a consistent classification of exposures along the accounting and economic dimensions.

The concept of operating exposure has long been implicit in economists' discussions of exchange rate impacts on industries and on the macroeconomy. It has become known as "pass-through" analysis since it focuses on the extent to which exchange rate changes are "passed through" by firms. Early work by Kindleberger [16] studied this phenomenon using comparative statics at an industry level. Others who have studied this phenomenon at the industry level include Dunn [10] and Kalter [15]. Branson [5] used it in examining the effect on the 1971 dollar devaluation on the U.S. trade balance, while Magee [22] focused on the time dimension of the pass through.

Two early references to this concept in the managerial literature are Dufey [8] and Heckerman [13]. In the subsequent years it has been clarified and refined by various authors including Shapiro [23], Levi [21], and Shapiro [24].

Finally, note that there is no firm valuation model or intertemporal price and exchange rate adjustment mechanism proposed here. Both would be necessary to have a complete discussion on the implications of exchange rate changes on firm value. This point is stressed by Adler and Dumas [2]. Hekman [14], using some simplifying assumptions, proposes a model of the effect of exchange rate changes on firm value.

3 An early discussion of the distinction between contractual and noncontractual exposures and their sensitivity to the nominal and real exchange rates, respectively, appeared in Lessard [17]. However, it clearly is implicit in many earlier works on the subject. It also is very similar to the monetary/nonmonetary distinction in international accounting, except it refers to future cash flows rather than balance sheet assets.

4 See Adler and Dumas [1].

5 The terms "conversion effect" and "competitive effect" are referred to as the "translation effect" and "dependence effect" by Lessard and Sharp [20].

6 Changes in relative prices do not tell the entire story for changes in competitiveness internationally, especially in the short run. However, they do capture a large proportion of the impact. A measure of productivity changes is needed to complete the story.

132 United Nations Library on Transnational Corporations

7 The German firm, on the other hand, will see West German prices and costs up by 5% and effective U.K. prices and costs up by 17% (10% in pounds plus a 7% increase in the cost of the pound in terms of DM). Note that the German firm sees the same shift in the relative attractiveness of the markets in the two countries as the U.K.-based firm.

8 It is, of course, also possible for relative prices to change within a country. Because of the manner in which price indexes are constructed this can cause apparent deviations from PPP when there are none in actuality. See, for example, Feiger and Jacquillat, Ch. 5 [11], and Shapiro [25].

9 The exact formula used here for the real exchange rate is the nominal exchange rate expressed as pounds per DM multiplied by the German price index divided by the U.K. price index.

10 There is an ongoing debate among economists about whether shifts in the real exchange rate merely reflect shifts in relative prices among goods and services within countries (see, for example, Shapiro [25], Barro [4]) or whether movements in exchange rates themselves cause such shifts in relative prices (see, for example, Dornbusch [7]). What is important in the analysis of operating exposure is not the direction of causation, but the correlation between prices and exchange rates.

11. The law of one price states that, aside from transportation costs, the price of a commodity is the same in two countries once the exchange rate is taken into account.

12 See Flood [12] for a formal derivation of these statements.

13 For example, if the parent firm is a Swiss-based multinational corporation and it is analyzing a foreign subsidiary, a world price is one for which the law of one price holds and one that is fairly stable in Swiss francs. This would be the case for a relatively competitive industry in which the elasticity of supply is high and firms with largely Swiss-based costs are the marginal suppliers.

14 Note that this is also a 20% change in the real exchange rate, because local prices remain fixed in the local currency.

15 An important issue directly related to this point (but not addressed here) is whether or not firms should hedge, that is, whether the management should be willing to pay to reduce diversifiable or non-diversifiable risk. Dufey and Srinivasulu [9], Cornell and Shapiro [6], Shapiro and Titman [26], and Barnea, Haugen, and Senbet [3] discuss this issue. Moreover, in the case of operating exposure, since many groups within the firm are involved, the question of who should take responsibility for offsetting the risks arises.

References

[1] M. Adler and B. Dumas, "The Exposure of Long-Term Foreign Currency Bonds," *Journal of Financial and Quantitative Analysis* (November 1980), pp. 973–995.

[2] —— "Exposure to Currency Risk: Definition and Measurement," *Financial Management* (Summer 1984), pp. 41–50.

[3] A. Barnea, R. A. Haugen, and L. W. Senbet, "Management of Corporate Risk," in *Advances in Financial Planning and Forecasting*, Volume 1, JAI Press, 1985, pp. 1–27.

[4] R.J. Barro, *Macroeconomics*, New York, John Wiley, and sons, 1985.

[5] W. H. Branson, "The Effects of the 1972 Currency Realignments," *Brookings Papers on Economic Activity*, Vol. 1 (1972), pp. 15–18.

[6] B. Cornell and A. C. Shapiro, "Managing Foreign Exchange Risk," *Midland*

Corporate Finance Journal (Fall 1983).

[7] R. Dornbusch, "Expectations and Exchange Rate Dynamics," *Journal of Political Economy* (December 1976), pp. 1161–1176.

[8] G. Dufey, "Corporate Finance and Exchange Variations," *Financial Management* (Summer 1972), pp. 51–57.

[9] G. Dufey and S. L. Srinivasulu, "The Case for Corporate Management of Foreign Exchange Risk," *Financial Management* (Winter 1983), pp. 54–62.

[10] R. M. Dunn, "Flexible Exchange Rates and the Price of Traded Goods: A Study of Canadian Markets," Unpublished Ph.D. dissertation, Stanford University, 1967.

[11] G. Feiger and B. Jacquillat, *International Finance*, Boston, Allyn and Bacon, 1981.

[12] E. Flood, *Global Competition and Exchange Rate Exposure*, Stanford University Graduate School of Business Working Paper #837, September 1985.

[13] D. Heckerman, "The Exchange Risk of Foreign Operations," *Journal of Business* (January 1972), pp. 42–48.

[14] C. R. Hekman, "A Financial Model of Foreign Exchange Exposure," *Journal of International Business Studies* (Summer 1985), pp. 83–99.

[15] E. R. J. Kalter, "The Effect of Exchange Rate Changes on Matched Domestic and Export Prices," Unpublished Ph.D. dissertation, University of Pennsylvania, 1978.

[16] C. P. Kindleberger, *International Economics*, fifth edition, Homewood, IL, R.D. Irwin, 1978.

[17] D. R. Lessard, ed., *International Financial Management*. Boston and New York, Warren, Gorham, & Lamont, 1979, pp. 354–357.

[18] —— "Finance and Global Competition," in *Competition in Global Industries*, Michael Porter, ed., Harvard Business School Press, 1986 (forthcoming).

[19] D. R. Lessard and J. B. Lightstone, "Coping With Exchange Rate Volatility: Operating and Financial Responses," *Harvard Business Review*, March/April 1986.

[20] D. R. Lessard and D. Sharp, "Measuring the Performance of Operations Subject to Fluctuating Exchange Rates," *Midland Corporate Finance Journal* (Fall 1984). pp. 18–30.

[21] M. Levi, *International Finance*, New York, McGraw-Hill, 1983.

[22] S. P. Magee, "Currency Contracts, Pass Through and Devaluation, *Brookings Papers on Economic Activity*, Vol. 1., 1973.

[23] A. C. Shapiro, "Exchange Rate Changes, Inflation, and the Value of the Multinational Corporation," *Journal of Finance* (May 1975), pp. 485–501.

[24] —— *Multinational Financial Management*, Boston, Allyn and Bacon, 1982.

[25] —— "What Does Purchasing Power Parity mean?," *Journal of International Money and Finance* (1983), pp. 295–318.

[26] A. C. Shapiro and S. Titman, "Why Total Risk Matters," *Midland Corporate Finance Journal* (Summer 1985).

[27] S. L. Srinivasulu, "Classifying Foreign Exchange Exposure," *Financial Executive* (February 1983), pp. 36–44.

6

Hedging foreign exchange risk: selecting the optimal tool*

Sarkis J. Khoury and K. Hung Chan†

*Source: *Midland Corporate Finance Journal,* 1 (Winter 1988), pp. 40–52.

The various tools which have emerged to deal with foreign exchange risk have been treated extensively in the finance literature.[1] The nature, uses, and efficiency of their markets are quite well understood today. What has been ignored, however, are the factors a finance officer should consider when choosing from among the various available hedging tools to reduce the risk resulting from a certain type of exposure to foreign exchange risk.

Our study relies on a questionnaire survey to gauge the preferences of finance officers in terms of the specific characteristics of a hedging tool. Besides enabling us to determine why some hedging instruments are used more often than others, it also may suggest useful modifications of existing contracts or the introduction of new ones.

This study is organized as follows: the first section offers a brief review of the existing literature on foreign exchange risk management; the second summarizes three distinct ways of measuring risk exposure; the third summarizes the history, nature, and characteristics of the currently available hedging tools; and the fourth describes our survey and its findings.

The Literature Survey

The literature on foreign exchange has thus far concentrated on the following issues: (1) the decision to hedge or not to hedge and its implications for corporate value;[2] (2) the merits of the various approaches to exposure measurement and their implications on international accounting and the valuation models;[3] (3) discussion of individual hedging tools;[4] (4) surveys on how seriously corporations look at the various exposures and how they deal with them;[5] (5) the sequential nature of foreign exchange risk management;[6] (6) the efficiency of the various foreign exchange markets and their impact on each other;[7] the implications of foreign exchange markets on the financing decision in an international context;[8] and (8) the hedging, speculative, and arbitrage opportunities within and across the various foreign exchange markets.[9]

Of all the research summarized above, however, no study has provided the corporate decision maker with fundamental reasons why one specific hedging instrument should be used more extensively than another. One survey conducted in the early 1970s raised more questions in this regard than it answered.[10] This survey focused on how corporations measured their foreign exchange risk exposure and on their preferred method for hedging it; but the reasons for their preference were never explored. The only other study to deal with the choice among foreign exchange hedging tools does not include consideration of futures contracts, option contracts and currency swaps.[11] At the time of this study, options and swaps were not available and futures contracts were still struggling for acceptance. The results of this survey, presented in Table 6.1, clearly demonstrate that the most useful tools were the borrowing hedge and the forward contract, in that order.

Our study expands the horizon of this earlier survey and provides a systematic and comprehensive analysis of available tools and of the reasons for preferring one over the other.

Measuring Foreign Exchange Risk Exposure

Three forms of exposure are clearly identified in the literature on foreign exchange management. The first is designated "transaction exposure." This exposure results from having an asset or liability position requiring settlement in a foreign currency during the accounting period. In this regard, transaction exposure is a "flow" concept. For example, a company may purchase four million Taiwan dollars of merchandise, which requires payment in Taiwan dollars. At the time the transaction took place, the exchange rate was US $1 to T $40. If the rate goes up to US $1 to T $30 at the time of payment, the company will have to pay US $333,333 more as a result of the rate change. This kind of financial risk is called transaction exposure. The exposure results from the uncertainty regarding the value of the foreign currency in terms of the domestic currency.

Translation exposure, on the other hand, results mainly from an accounting requirement to consolidate the records of a multinational corporation. It is a "stock" concept because it looks at the net accounting position of a MNC at a point in time in terms of the domestic currency.

The method for measuring translation exposure is set forth in FASB statement No. 52. This statement requires that "the assets, liabilities, and operations of a foreign entity shall be measured using the functional currency of that entity. An entity's functional currency is the currency of the primary economic environment in which the entity operates; normally, that is the currency of environment in which the entity primarily generates and expends cash [FASB, para. 5]."

Once the functional currency for a foreign entity is determined, its accounts must be denominated in terms of the functional currency. If its accounts are not maintained in the functional currency, remeasurement in the functional currency is required.

All elements of financial statements shall be translated using the current exchange rate. This means that balance sheet accounts shall be translated using the rate as of the balance sheet date. Income statement accounts may be translated using an appropriately weighted average exchange rate for the period covered by the income statement. Translation adjustments should then be reported in the consolidated financial statements.

The last type of exposure, of particular concern to finance theorists and participants in the financial markets, is economic exposure. This exposure results from changes in the value of the firm resulting from foreign exchange-induced changes in the projected future cash flows of a business entity. For example, a change in foreign exchange rates may affect not only the value of the company's assets, but also the company's ability to compete both in the domestic and the foreign markets. Exchange rate changes could affect both the revenue and the expense items in the income statements and consequently the cash flows. This could have negative effects on the value of the firm (the market price of the stock). The effects, moreover, can be either direct in nature or indirect. The direct effects are immediately reflected in the value of assets, liabilities, revenues and expenses which are sensitive to exchange rate changes. The indirect effects are felt through the competitive effects as prices adjust (not always fully) to reflect exchange rate changes.

As one earlier survey found, the amount of attention paid to these exposures varies among companies and appears to have changed during the 1970s. "During 1974 interviews," the survey concludes,

> translation exposure for the current reporting period was used almost exclusively as the measure of exposure to exchange risk and as the basis for hedging this risk in these companies. By 1977, transaction exposure was followed simultaneously in most of the companies. And, when the decision was whether to hedge an exposure, only 20 percent of the companies interviewed in 1977 based their hedging decision solely on translation exposure.[12]

The same survey found that economic exposure was largely ignored by financial executives. They concentrated largely on transaction exposure. The decision to hedge or not was found to depend on the type of exposure (asset or liability) and on the expectations regarding the direction of

Table 6.1 How finance executives rate exchange risk management techniques

As part of the study conducted for the FASB, the financial executives responding to the questionnaire were asked to rate exchange-risk management techniques. Each executive was asked whether or not he used a specific technique, and how useful the technique proved to be when implemented (1 = low usefulness, 3 = high usefulness). Using-rates and average-usefulness ratings for firms using the various techniques are:

Techniques	Usage rate (%)	Usefulness rating
(1) Increase borrowing levels in currency	83.3	2.462
(2) Use forward exchange contracts	82.1	2.297
(3) Decrease borrowing levels in currency	71.8	2.286
(4) Lead/lag intracompany receivables/payables	71.2	2.243
(5) Adjust product price in local markets	67.9	2.075
(6) Lead/lag local currency external receivables/payables	51.3	2.050
(7) Reschedule intracompany debt payments	55.8	2.000
(8) Accelerate/decelerate subsidiary dividend payments	82.7	1.979
(9) Adjust transfer prices	28.8	1.867
(10) Adjust product price levels in export markets	48.7	1.855
(11) Finance fund requirements or invest excess cash of third country subsidiaries in currency	36.5	1.789
(12) Net exposure with exposure in other currencies	41.7	1.753
(13) Adjust inventory levels	41.7	1.723
(14) Use contractual clauses calling for assumption of exchange risk by supplier's customers	40.4	1.716
(15) Vary currency of billing to external parties	39.1	1.705
(16) Seek different credit terms from suppliers	32.1	1.540
(17) Formally alter credit terms to customers	25.0	1.513
(18) Lease rather than buy from suppliers	10.3	1.438
(19) Utilize government exchange risk guarantee programs	24.4	1.395
(20) Lease rather than sell to customers	7.1	1.272
(21) Factor receivables	28.8	1.244

Source: Evans, Thomas G., William R. Folks Jr., and Michael Jilling, *the Impact of Statement of Financial Accounting Standards No. 6 in the Foreign Exchange Risk Management Practices of American Multinationals: An Economic Impact Study*, Stamford, Conn.: Financial Accounting Standards Board, November 1978, Table S2, pp. 149–175.

exchange rates. Managers were careful to avoid reporting foreign exchange losses whenever possible. Their decision to hedge, however, was influenced by the actual and expected value of the currency.

The measurement of foreign exchange risk exposure, especially economic exposure, remains incomplete to date. There does not exist an effective model to gauge the overall exposure of the firm to changes in exchange rates. The true nature of economic exposure and its impact on the value of the firm remains largely a mystery to accountants and financial executives alike. The positive and negative effects it has on the perform-

Table 6.2 The characteristics of the various currency hedging techniques

IMM futures market	Forward interbank market	Options market (listed)	Option market (over the counter)	Money market hedge	Matching maturity and duration of exchange sensitive assets and liabilities	Currency swap	No hedge
Trading is conducted in a competitive area by "open outcry."	Trading is done by telephone or telex.	Competitive, auction-like pricing mechanism.	Trading is done by telephone or telex.	No trading.	Internal market.	Telephone and telex.	No market.
Participants are either buyers or sellers of a contract at a single, specified price at any given point in time.	Participants usually make two-sided markets.	Participants are on one side of the market.	Two-sided markets are made by participants.	—	Two-sided markets.	Two-sided markets.	No market.
Non-member participants deal through brokers (Exchange members), who represent them on the IMM floor. Exchange contracts are available to anyone.	Participants deal on a principal-to-principal basis. Access to market is restricted.	Brokered market. Access to everyone.	Principal market.	Participants deal on a principal-to-principal basis.	Principal market.	Principal market.	—

Market participants usually are unknown to one another.	Participants in each transaction always know who is on the other side of the trade.	Market participants are unknown to one another.	Participants do not necessarily know each other.	Participants in each transaction always know who is on the other side of the trade.	Participants do not necessarily know each other.	—
The Exchange's Clearing House become the opposite side to each cleared transaction: the credit risk for a futures market participant is always the same and there is no need to analyze the credit of other market participants.	Each counter party, with whom a dealer does business, must be examined individually as to a credit risk and credit limits must be set for each. As such, there may be a wide range of credit capabilities of participants.	Exchange clearing house is used.	Bank is the guarantor.	No direct external guarantee. Borrower is assessed individually as to credit risk and credit limits.	—	—
Price movements have a maximum (adjustable by the Exchange) daily limit.	No daily price limit.	No daily price limit.	No daily price limit.	Price (interest rates) may be adjusted (with or without limits) at regular time intervals if rates are pegged.	Prices fluctuate without limit.	—

Table 6.2 The characteristics of the various currency hedging techniques

	IMM futures market	Forward interbank market	Options market (listed)	Option market (over the counter)	Money market hedge	Matching maturity and duration of exchange sensitive assets and liabilities	Currency swap	No hedge
	Margins are required for all participants for both long and short positions. – Initial – Maintenance Variation = one day's change in value of futures position	Margins are not required by banks dealing with other banks, although for smaller, non-bank customers, margins may be required on certain occasions.	100% of the value of the option is paid the second day after the order is executed. No leverage is possible as compared with forward and futures contract.	Full cost of option paid at the time of transaction.	—	All fees paid up front.	All fees paid up front.	—
	Daily marketing to market.	No daily marking to market.	No daily marking to market.	No daily marking to market.	Marking to market ie rates are floating rates.	No daily marking to market.	Possible daily marking to market.	—
	No loss on position if prices remain constant.	Prices are "locked in." Any loss is an opportunity loss.	The entire premium is lost if prices remain constant.	The entire premium is lost if prices remain constant.	The cost of the hedge is "locked in" $C = a(1 \times f_{us}) - a(1 + f_f)$ where a = PV of foreign currency	No loss if there are major price changes.	Results known in advance.	Cost is unknown.

Represents an obligation. Settlements are made daily via the Exchange's Clearing House. Gains on position values may be withdrawn and losses are collected daily.	Represents an obligation. Settlement takes place two days after the spot transaction (one day for the Canadian dollar and Mexican peso). For forward transactions, settlement occurs on the date agreed upon between the bank and its customer.	It is an *option* to do. Settlements are made daily.	Option. Bank arranges the settlement.	Represents a debt obligation. Settlement takes place on the date agreed upon between the bank and its customer.	An obligation.	An obligation. Bank arranges settlement.
				exposure in $ (home currency) terms.	—	—
						—
Regulated by the Commodities Futures Trading Commission (CFTC).	Self-regulated market.	Regulated by CFTC	Regulated by SEC.	Largely self-regulated. The Federal Reserve System's regulations must be observed across clients.	No direct regulation.	No regulation.

ance of a corporation over time may well cancel each other, and perhaps for this reason, corporate executives have traditionally ignored it.

For this reason, our survey concentrates only on transaction and translation exposures and ignores economic exposure.[13]

The Alternative Hedging Tools

For the purpose of statistical analysis, this discussion of various hedging tools treats each instrument or strategy as if it were completely independent of the other. In fact, the various hedging tools are interrelated and if the relationships among them are violated, arbitrage opportunities will present themselves. The reader should note that the forward contract can be reproduced in the money market. Borrowing in one market and lending in another creates a synthetic forward contract which should have the same hedging effects as a regular forward contract purchased from a bank. This relationship between a money market hedge and the forward market is established through an equation referred to as interest rate parity. The forward contract can also be synthetically produced in the option market.[14] A short put and a long call make up the equivalent of a forward contract.

The equivalence of forward contracts to futures contracts is strictly dependent on the behavior of interest rates. This is so because of the marking-to-market feature of futures contracts on a daily basis. If the futures position is profitable, funds are released to the position holder. These funds should earn the prevailing interest rate. If the position is losing money, funds will be required of the position holder by the next business day. The funds have an actual, or opportunity, cost equal to the then prevailing interest rate. Thus, if interest rates are expected to be constant throughout the life of the futures contract, the futures contract reduces to the forward contract which does not have an initial margin requirement nor daily marking to market.[15]

Table 6.2 defines eight hedging tools (or strategies) in terms of twelve different characteristics.[16] The entries in each column in Table 6.2 represent factual descriptive aspects of each contract, such as when and how the contract is traded. The opinion of the authors regarding the characteristics of the contracts appear in the body of the survey.

The Survey

Our survey was designed mainly to measure the strength of finance executives' preferences among the various characteristics of specific hedging tools.[17] The strength of the executives' preferences are registered in a numerical ranking system in which the number one registered the weakest and the number seven the strongest possible preference for a given aspect of a hedging instrument.

The survey was also designed to find out whether a financial manager's choice of hedging tools is influenced by the type of exposure, by the size of the firm, and whether there is an industry effect. We also assess the risk profile of the manager and his familiarity with the hedging tool.

The original survey and a follow-up survey were conducted between June and September 1985 using 500 systematically selected industrial and service (including financial) companies from the 1985 Fortune Directories. A total of 73 companies replied to the questionnaire. A surprisingly large number of companies (48) said they did no or minimal hedging.[18] Many of these companies indicated that they are beginning to establish or expand their hedging programs, but their hedging volume is minimal at this time. This suggests that hedging may become a much more important activity for these companies in the near future. There were eight companies that completed only part of the questionnaire. Seventeen companies completed the entire comprehensive questionnaire. (Given the length of the questionnaire, the complexity of the issue, and the sensitivity of the hedging operation for many companies, these response rates are not surprising.)

The seventeen respondents who completed the entire questionnaire indicated that forward contracts, matching, futures contracts, and the over-the-counter type option contracts are, in that order, the most often used hedging instruments. Tables 6.3 and 6.6 provide the managers' average ratings of each of these four contracts.

In the case of forward contracts (as shown in Table 6.3), the cost of hedging and the high degree of flexibility are the two most important aspects recommending its use. Compared with the futures contract, the "fixity" of the cost of a forward contract makes it much more attractive. Furthermore, the lack of any initial financial commitment also appears to be an important inducement for choosing forwards.

In the case of the second most popular strategy—matching exchange rate sensitive assets and liabilities—Table 6.4 indicates that flexibility in terms of size and maturity, together with the effectiveness and liquidity of the hedge, are the more important characteristics. Because matching does not involve any hedging contract involving a third party, it is considered the most flexible hedging instrument. In fact, many companies view matching as a "self-reliant" approach to hedging. Skillful matching, however, requires considerations not only of the size and maturity of the exposure, but also dealing effectively with considerable uncertainty with respect to future cash receipts and disbursements.

In the case of futures contracts (see Table 6.5), the liquidity, the cost, and the profit potential of the hedge were considered the more important inducements. This is true in managing either transaction or accounting exposures. The preference ratings for futures, however, were considerably

Table 6.3 Hedging instrument: forward contract

Characteristics of the hedging contract	Importance weights											
	If used to hedge transaction exposure					If used to hedge accounting exposure						
	Currency is expected to appreciate		Currency is expected to depreciate			Currency is expected to appreciate			Currency is expected to depreciate			
	When net cash outlay/cash is expected receipt is expected	When net cash receipt is expected	When net cash outlay/cash is expected	When net cash receipt is expected	W/net current asset exposure	W/net long-term asset exposure	W/net current liability exposure	W/net long-term liability exposure	W/net current asset exposure	W/net long-term asset exposure	W/net current liability exposure	W/net long-term liability exposure
Cost of the hedge is known and fixed at the beginning of the contract	6.21	6.20	6.21	6.20	5.78	5.70	5.70	5.70	5.70	5.70	5.63	5.70
No initial financial commitment is required	5.30	5.42	5.38	5.43	5.0	4.89	4.89	4.89	4.89	4.89	4.80	4.89
No daily marking to market	4.31	4.43	4.31	4.43	4.13	4.11	4.11	4.11	4.11	4.11	4.20	4.11
Low liquidity for the contract	4.0	4.17	4.0	4.0	3.71	3.63	3.63	3.63	3.63	3.63	3.78	3.63

Contract eliminates upside potential (profit from hedge)	3.62	3.57	3.62	3.57	3.63	3.67	3.67	3.67	3.67	3.67	3.70	3.67
The contract is an obligation (as opposed to an option)	3.85	3.79	3.85	3.79	3.36	3.44	3.67	3.67	3.67	3.67	3.50	3.44
High degree of flexibility (in terms of contract size, maturity, strike price, etc.)	6.21	6.60	6.21	6.07	5.56	5.7	5.7	5.7	5.7		5.64	5.70
There are no price limits	4.08	4.08	4.08	4.08	3.89	3.89	3.89	3.89	3.89	3.89	3.90	3.89

Table 6.4 Hedging instrument: matching exchange rate sensitive assets and liabilities by amount, maturity, or duration

	Importance weights											
	If used to hedge transaction exposure					If used to hedge accounting exposure						
	Currency is expected to appreciate		Currency is expected to depreciate			Currency is expected to appreciate				Currency is expected to depreciate		
Characteristics of the hedging contract	When net cash outlay is expected	When net cash receipt is expected	When net cash outlay is expected	When net cash receipt is expected	W/net current asset exposure	W/net long-term asset exposure	W/net current liability exposure	W/net long-term liability exposure	W/net current asset exposure	W/net long-term asset exposure	W/net current liability exposure	W/net long-term liability exposure
Cost of the hedge is not known with certainty at the beginning of the contract	4.36	4.55	4.55	4.36	4.33	4.0	4.0	4.0	4.0	4.0	4.0	4.0
Initial financial commitment is 100% of the cost of raising funds or disposing of assets	4.45	4.45	4.45	4.45	4.45	4.50	4.50	4.50	4.50	4.50	4.50	4.50

There is no daily marking to market	4.64	4.64	4.64	4.64	4.64	4.78	4.80	4.80	4.80	4.80	4.80	4.80	4.80	4.80
The liquidity of the hedge is average to high	5.27	5.27	5.27	5.27	5.27	5.44	5.50	5.50	5.50	5.50	5.50	5.50	5.50	5.50
The effectiveness of the hedge against foreign exchange rate risk is medium to high	5.55	5.55	5.55	5.55	5.55	5.33	5.40	5.40	5.40	5.40	5.40	5.40	5.40	5.40
The hedge is an obligation	4.09	4.09	4.09	4.09	4.09	4.11	4.10	4.10	4.10	4.10	4.10	4.10	4.10	4.10
The hedging arrangement is flexible in terms of the size of the hedge maturity, etc.	5.55	5.55	5.55	5.55	5.55	5.55	5.60	5.60	5.60	5.60	5.60	5.60	5.60	5.60
There are no price limit	4.55	4.55	4.55	4.55	4.55	4.40	4.60	4.60	4.60	4.60	4.60	4.60	4.60	4.60

Table 6.5 Futures contract

Characteristics of the hedging contract	Importance weights											
	If used to hedge transaction exposure				If used to hedge accounting exposure							
	Currency is expected to appreciate		Currency is expected to depreciate			Currency is expected to appreciate			Currency is expected to depreciate			
	When net cash outlay/cash receipt is expected	When net cash receipt is expected	When net cash outlay/cash receipt is expected	When net cash receipt is expected	W/net current asset exposure	W/net long-term asset exposure	W/net current liability exposure	W/net long-term liability exposure	W/net current asset exposure	W/net long-term asset exposure	W/net current liability exposure	W/net long-term liability exposure
Cost of the hedge (depends on the behavior of the basis)	4.44	4.30	4.44	4.30	4.57	4.57	4.57	4.57	4.47	4.47	4.63	4.57
Margin requirement on contract	2.90	3.09	3.00	3.09	3.13	3.13	3.13	3.13	3.13	3.13	3.22	3.13
Daily marking to market	3.22	3.20	3.11	3.20	3.0	3.0	3.0	3.0	3.0	3.0	3.125	3.0
Liquidity	4.89	4.90	5.0	4.90	4.71	4.71	4.71	4.71	4.71	4.71	4.75	4.71

Hedging allows the hedger the possibility of realizing a profit on the hedge	4.77	4.40	4.67	4.70	4.43	4.43	4.43	4.43	4.43	4.43	4.50	4.43
The contract is an obligation (as opposed to an option)	3.67	3.50	3.67	3.80	3.71	3.71	3.71	3.71	3.71	3.71	3.88	3.71
Flexibility of the contract is limited (e.g., with respect to contract size, maturity, strike price, etc.)	2.70	2.63	2.70	2.73	3.13	3.13	3.13	3.13	3.13	3.13	3.22	3.13
There exists price limits (e.g., maximum loss on a given day or maximum daily price movement)	4.22	4.10	4.22	4.0	4.29	4.29	4.29	4.29	4.29	4.29	4.25	4.29

lower than the corresponding ratings for forward contracts. Therefore, it appears that forward contracts are generally preferred over futures contracts.

Finally, in the case of options contracts (over-the-counter type), Table 6.6 shows that the cost, the effectiveness, the flexibility, and the "optional" nature of the hedge were all considered moderate to strong inducements. The comparative ratings across all hedging contracts confirm, moreover, that the characteristic of having an "option" is a very attractive feature.

Forward contracts were rated the most familiar and often used hedging instruments for both of our financial and non-financial respondents. For financial companies, this is followed by money market hedge and matching. For non-financial companies, matching and currency swaps were ranked second and third. In the cases of both forward contracts and matching, the ratings of the characteristics by both financial and non-financial companies are generally compatible with the overall ratings.

Respondents were also classified into large (over $10 billion of sales in 1984), medium (between $1 and $10 billion) and small (below $1 billion) companies. For both large and medium companies, the most often used hedging instruments are (in this order): forward contract, matching, and futures contract; for small companies the most often used hedging instruments were forward contracts, matching, and options (over-the-counter type). Small companies placed more emphasis on the option characteristic and ranked option contracts higher than larger companies, possibly because flexibility and the known cost of the contract are very strong inducements for them.

It is interesting to note that forward contracts were given the top ranking by all groupings. It appears that the fixity of cost and flexibility of forward contracts appeal to all companies. Another popular hedging tool for all companies is matching. The flexibility, effectiveness, and liquidity of matching, together with the perceived no-cost, self-reliant nature of the hedge, make it attractive to a wide variety of companies.

Overall, the ratings do not appear significantly different whether the currency is expected to appreciate or depreciate, whether net cash receipt or outlay is expected, and whether long-term or short-term asset or liability exposure is expected. We do find, however, that companies generally placed more emphasis on transaction exposure than accounting exposure and are more likely to hedge transaction exposure. The change in foreign exchange accounting methods by FASB in the past few years may be partly responsible for shifting the emphasis more onto transaction exposure. In fact, seven of our respondents reported that they hedged more often against transaction exposure, three said they hedged more often against accounting exposure, and seven companies hedged against both exposures with equal frequency. All of the seven respondents that hedged more often against transaction exposure are non-financial companies. This finding seems quite predictable, given that the transactions of non-financial companies are trade-related and, in such cases, the objective is to lock in the sale price and avoid speculation on the direction and level of foreign exchange rates.

Out of the seventeen respondents, nine characterized themselves as "risk neutral" and eight saw themselves as "risk averse." None classified itself as a "risk seeking." This suggests that respondents are on the conservative side in their use of hedging instruments (which can also, of course, be used to take speculative positions). In addition, seven of the eight risk-averse executives are from non-financial companies. It appears that non-financial companies are more conservative than financial companies in terms of hedging. Financial companies, which may have a better understanding of the money market, appear willing to take more risk.

The seventeen respondents rated the Japanese yen, the Canadian dollar, and the British pound, in this order, as the three currencies they most often hedge. The Japanese yen was given top ranking by both financial and non-financial companies. However, the larger companies in our sample gave the Canadian dollar top ranking. The huge U.S. investment in Canada, as well as the recent fluctuation of the Canadian dollar, probably explain this result.

Finally, our analysis indicates that, on the whole, liquidity, flexibility, and certainty about cost are the three most important considerations in choosing a hedging contract. In formulating new hedging instruments or in revising existing instruments, these factors should be given particular attention. For example, the attractiveness of futures contract may be increased by setting a ceiling not only on daily price movement, but also on the maximum price change of a contract during its life. This feature would be analogous to the maximum rate "cap" in variable rate home mortgages. Such a cap would be much more reassuring than the best method available for arriving at the optimal hedge ratio. The flexibility of futures contracts may also be improved by having a larger variety of size and maturity so that the contract will be more closely "tailored" to the needs of market participants. A similar recommendation with regard to flexibility can be made for options contracts.

One qualification, however. The changes in the hedging instruments must be more than marginal to be worth making. On the other hand, too radical a change can alter the entire character of the foreign exchange markets, a consequence which may not be desirable. Furthermore, banks and exchanges contemplating changes must keep in mind that the demand curves of hedgers and speculators are not homogeneous. This requires the availability of a variety of hedging instruments. Making all available hedging tools perfect substitutes in terms of liquidity, flexibility, and cost leads inevitably to all but one hedging tool becoming redundant.

Table 6.6 Hedging instrument: options contract (over-the-counter type)

	Importance weights											
	If used to hedge transaction exposure				If used to hedge accounting exposure							
	Currency is expected to appreciate		Currency is expected to depreciate		Currency is expected to appreciate				Currency is expected to depreciate			
Characteristics of the hedging contract	When net cash outlay/cash receipt is expected	When net cash outlay/cash receipt is expected	When net cash outlay is expected	When net cash receipt is expected	W/net current asset exposure	W/net long-term asset exposure	W/net current liability exposure	W/net long-term liability exposure	W/net current asset exposure	W/net long-term asset exposure	W/net current liability exposure	W/net long-term liability exposure
Cost of the hedge is known and fixed at the beginning of the contract	6.13	6.13	6.13	6.13	6.0	6.0	6.0	6.0	6.0	6.0	5.86	6.0
Initial financial commitment is 100% of the value of the option	3.25	3.25	3.25	3.25	3.0	3.0	3.0	3.0	3.0	3.0	3.29	3.0
There is no daily marking to market	4.67	4.67	4.67	4.67	4.43	4.43	4.43	4.43	4.43	4.43	4.38	4.43

The liquidity of the contract is medium to low relative to other hedging instruments	3.33	3.33	3.33	3.33	3.33	3.43	3.43	3.43	3.43	3.43	3.43	3.63	3.43
Highly effective in hedging exchange rate risk (while preserving the upside potential of the hedge)	5.75	5.75	5.75	5.75	5.75	6.14	6.14	6.14	6.14	6.14	6.14	5.88	6.14
The contract is an option	5.0	5.0	5.0	5.0	5.0	5.17	5.17	5.17	5.17	5.17	5.17	5.0	5.17
The contract is highly flexible in terms of contract size, maturity, strike price, etc.	5.56	5.56	5.56	5.56	5.56	5.57	5.57	5.57	5.57	5.57	5.57	5.50	5.57
There are no price limits	4.50	4.50	4.50	4.50	4.50	4.50	4.50	4.50	4.50	4.50	4.50	4.43	4.50

Concluding Remarks

Our survey of hedging strategies by the U.S. corporations with foreign exchange exposure yielded interesting results. Although the findings would be more reliable if we had a larger sample of respondents, they offer a nonetheless suggestive picture of the hedging practices and concerns of financial managers. Corporate finance executives appear to be quite aware of the differing characteristics of the various contracts and how they match their own preferences and risk aversion. The problem, however, lies in the fact that a hedging tool that is optimal at a point in time for a given company may not be the best choice under all circumstances for all companies. The apparent consistency of choice by the executives in our survey leaves us with the impression that they do not necessarily attempt to "optimize" (that is, find the minimum cost strategy) when setting up hedges, but instead allow nonquantifiable aspects of the contract (such as familiarity and flexibility) to guide their decisions.

Notes

† The authors wish to acknowledge the valuable assistance of Apichart Karoonkornsakul.

1. See Gunter Dufey and S.L. Srinivasulu. "The Case for Corporate Management of Foreign Exchange Risk", *Financial Management*, Winter 1983, pp. 54–62, and Laurent Jacque, "Management of Foreign Exchange Risk: A Review Article", *Journal of International Business Studies*, Spring/Summer 1981, pp. 81–100. The first paper argues that a hedgings strategy is always superior to a non-hedge strategy and the second reviews some of the hedging methods generally utilized to reduce, if not eliminate foreign exchange risk.

2. See Robert Aliber, *Exchange Risk and International Finance*, New York, John Wiley and Sons, 1979; and Gunter Dufey and S.L. Srinivasulu, op. cit. The first argues for market efficiency. Dufey & Srinivasulu consider the various market inefficiencies which necessitate a hedging strategy.

3. See Helen Gernon, "The Effect of Translation on Multinational Corporations Internal Performance Evaluation," *Journal of International Business Studies*, Spring/Summer 1983, pp. 103–112; and Hans-Martin Schoenfeld, "International Accounting: Development, Issues, and Future Directions," *Journal of International Business Studies*, Fall 1981, pp. 83–100.

4. See Sarkis Khoury and Animesh Ghoshal, *International Finance. A Focused Analysis*, Mossberg and Co., South Bend, Indiana, 1984.

5. Rita Rodriguez, "Corporate Exchange Risk Management: Theme and Aberrations,", *The Journal of Finance*, Vol. XXXVI No. 2, May 1981, pp. 427–444.

6. Alan C. Shapiro and David Rutenberg, "Exchange Rate Change, 'When to Hedge'," *Management Science*, August 1974, pp. 1514–1530.

7. Richard Levich, "The Efficiency of Markets for Foreign Exchange: A Review and Extension," in Donald Lessard, Editor, *International Financial Management: Theory and Application*, Warren, Gorham, and Lamont, Boston, MA. pp. 243–276.

8. Alan C. Shapiro, "The Impact of Taxation on the Currency of Denomination Decision of Long-Term Borrowing and Lending," *Journal of International Business Studies*," Spring/Summer, (1984), pp. 115–126.

9. Sarkis Khoury, *Speculative Markets*, Macmillan Publishing Co., NY, 1984.

10. Rita Rodriguez, "Corporate Exchange Risk Management: Theme and Aberrations,", *The Journal of Finance*, Vol. XXXVI, No. 2, May 1981, pp. 427–444.

11. Thomas G. Evans, William R. Folks, Jr., and Michael Jilling, *The Impact of Statement of Financial Accounting Standards No. 8 in the Foreign Exchange Management Practices of American Multinations: An Economic Impact Study.* Stamford, Connecticut: Financial Accounting Standards Board, November 1978.

12. Rodriquez, cited earlier, p. 428.

13. For excellent discussions of economic exposure, the reader is referred to Donald R. Lessard, "Finance and Global Competition," *Midland Corporate Finance Journal*, Fall 1987; see also Brad Cornell and Alan Shapiro, "Managing Foreign Exchange Risk," *Midland Corporate Finance Journal*, Fall 1983.

14. Op cit. S. Khoury.

15. See John Cox, Jonathan E. Ingersoll, Jr. and Stephen A. Ross "The Relation Between Forward Prices and Future Prices," *Journal of Financial Economics*, 9, 1981, pp. 321–346, and Bradford Cornell and Marc R. Reinganum, "Forward and Futures Prices, Evidence from the Foreign Exchange Markets," The *Journal of Finance*, 1981, pp. 1035–1045.

16. The hedging tools studied are by no means exhaustive. Leads and lags, parallel loans, black market-type operations, adjustment to transfer pricing, etc., are not examined. The reasons are that the survey became quite bulky and extensive with only eight tools, and the marginal benefit from adding other tools was not thought to be significant.

17. The survey method of analysis was one of many methods with which the authors experimented. We believe the survey method is most appropriate in this study because we must have direct contact with "consumers" (in this case, finance managers) in order to assess their preferences and the justification for them.

18. This supports the results obtained by Rodriguez, cited earlier, who found that a percentage of companies do not hedge at all.

PART TWO: Cost of Capital

7

Internationally diversified portfolios: welfare gains and capital flows*

Herbert G. Grubel[†]

*Source: *American Economic Review*, 58 (December 1968), pp. 1299–1314.

The models of portfolio balance developed by Markowitz [5] and Tobin [8] explain the real world phenomenon of diversified asset holdings elegantly and properly. The models have been criticized, extended, and empirically tested; by now their basic content has become economic orthodoxy. Strangely, however, the analysis has not yet been applied explicitly to the explanation of long-term asset holdings that include claims denominated in foreign currency.[1]

The present paper fills this gap and yields some interesting results. First, the international diversification of portfolios is the source of an entirely new kind of world welfare gains from international economic relations, different from both the traditional "gains from trade" and increased productivity flowing from the migration of the factors of production. This specific theoretical proposition is illustrated with some calculations based on empirical data drawing on *ex post* realized rates of return from investment in 11 major stock markets of the world.

Second, the theoretical model shows that international capital movements are a function not only of interest rate differentials but also of rates of growth in total asset holdings in two countries. As a result, capital may flow between countries when interest rate differentials are zero or negative and may not flow when a positive interest differential exists. Third, the analysis has some important policy implications in a growing world where monetary and fiscal policies are mixed to achieve internal and external balance.

The Static Model

Consider a world consisting of two countries, A and B, each with independent monetary and fiscal authorities and initially economically isolated from each other. Populations, income, and wealth are constant through time. There are only three forms of holding wealth: real assets, money, and bonds. The latter are issued by the government to provide investors with an interest-bearing instrument that allows bridging individuals' periods of net savings and dissavings over their lifetimes. In addition, the quantity of bonds in the market and the interest rate they fetch are regulated by the government in such a manner as to maintain full employment. For example, if there is unemployment, the government purchases bonds, paying for them with newly issued money. As a result of the increased money holdings and the lower yield of bonds, real assets are relatively more attractive than money and bonds and individuals try to adjust their portfolio imbalance through the purchase of more real assets, which has the desired upward effect on employment.

Assume that initially domestic portfolio balance exists at interest rates on bonds of R_A and R_B, and variances and covariances of returns of σ_A^2, σ_B^2, $\sigma_{A,B}$, where the subscripts A and B refer to the two countries and are measured from the point of view of Country A. That is R_B, σ_B^2, and $\sigma_{A,B}$ include an adjustment for exchange risk stemming from past variations in some shadow price of foreign exchange. Furthermore, assume for analytical convenience that when economic relations between the two countries are opened up only bonds and consumer goods can be exchanged so that the opening of trade does not affect the return and variance from holding real assets and money. Consequently, attention can be focused on the changes in bond holdings resulting from the opening of trade.

Before trade the expected rate of return $E(R_A)$ and risk $V(R_A)$ on the "average" investor's bond portfolio in Country A and B are:

$$(1) \qquad E(R_A) = R_A$$

$$(2) \qquad V(R_A) = \sigma_A^2$$

$$(3) \qquad E(R_B) = R_B$$

$$(4) \qquad V(R_B) = \sigma_B^2$$

After diversification a portfolio containing bonds of both Countries A and B has the following expected rate of return:

$$(5) \qquad E(R_{A,B}) = P_A R_A + P_B R_B$$

Where P_A and P_B are the proportions of bonds of country A and B respectively held in the average portfolio of Country A, P_A plus P_B must sum to one and neither may be negative. The variance of the diversified portfolio is

$$(6) \qquad V(R_{A,B}) = P_A^2 \sigma_A^2 + 2P_A P_B \sigma_{A,B} + P_B^2 \sigma_B^2$$

As the two equations show, investors have the opportunity to choose from a whole range of combinations of expected rates of return and variance by picking the appropriate sizes of P_A and P_B. Which specific combinations of risk and return they choose depends on their personal preferences, as has been demonstrated by Markowitz [5] and Tobin [8].

While the exact diversification is not important for the present purposes of analysis, it is useful to demonstrate with the help of a numerical example that diversification results in portfolios superior to one-asset portfolios of either kind of bonds.[2] Assume that $R_A = R_B = 5$ per cent. Therefore, before trade, $E(R_A) = E(R_B) = 5$. Diversification of the nature $P_A = P_B = .5$ yields an expected rate of return:

$$(7) \qquad E(R_{A,B}) = E(R_{B,A}) = 5$$

Assume that the variances of expected returns on Country A and B's properly adjusted for exchange rate fluctuations are $\sigma_A^2 = \sigma_B^2 = 10$, with a correlation between the two rates of return of $r = .3$. The variances on undiversified portfolios are $V(R_A) = V(R_B) = 10$ but the variance on the portfolio containing both assets is

$$(8) \qquad V(R_{A,B}) = 6.5$$

Thus, holding both assets does not change the expected rate of return but does reduce the riskiness of the portfolio as compared with the one-asset portfolio. By similar calculations and data it can be shown that the exchange of financial assets can lead to higher expected rates of return with equal risks and other combinations of returns and risks, all of which are superior to those from undiversified portfolios and, therefore, make the holders of wealth better off than they were without the opportunity for international diversification. The same principles apply to the residents of Country A and Country B.

The quantity of foreign bonds demanded by the residents of Country A and Country B after the opening of trade in this model depends on five primary factors. First, the size of total wealth assets held by the public: Since the variables P_A and P_B represent proportions, the absolute size of bond holdings is greater the greater the stock to which these proportions are applied.

Second, the size of the interest rate differential: Given the variances and covariance of the two-asset returns for any risk avoider, the trade-off between return and risk is more favorable the greater the foreign interest rate and, therefore, the more of the foreign asset will be held in the portfolio. Third, the size of the risk differential: For a given earnings differential and covariance of returns the foreign asset is more attractive the smaller the risk attached to it, given the riskiness of the domestic asset.

Fourth, the degree of correlation of returns on domestic and foreign assets: As can be seen from equation (6) the variance of a diversified portfolio is smaller the smaller the correlation of returns. Thus, given the earnings differential and variance of each asset independently, diversification reduces portfolio variance more and, therefore, is more desirable the smaller the covariance. Fifth, the tastes of the public: The combination of risk and return actually chosen from among the combinations made possible by diversification depends on wealth holders' preferences with respect to risk and return and current vs. future consumption.

Given the magnitudes of the five determinants of the demand for foreign bonds, the opening up of economic relations between the two countries is assumed to lead to a mutual exchange of bonds by the private wealth holders. Only if tastes, returns, variances and relative sizes of total wealth holdings are equal are the demands generated by each country equal. In the following analysis the empirically most relevant and theoretically most interesting assumption is made that the potential demand for foreign bonds by the residents of Country A exceeds that by the residents of Country B. The real effects of such a net excess demand are analysed first, under the assumption of rigidly pegged exchange rates, and second, under the assumption of perfectly flexible exchange rates.

First, at pegged rates Country A's excess demand for bonds tends to depress its exchange rate and official sales of B's currency are required to keep it stable. We assume that the government of A obtains this foreign exchange from the government of B in return for its official IOUs.

When international relations are open, the private residents of A sell off some of the bonds issued by their own government and acquire those of Country B. Some of A's bonds thus offered are purchased by residents of Country B, but under the present assumption of an excess demand for bonds by Country A, that government must purchase some of its old obligations to maintain aggregate portfolio balance and full employment. At the same time B's government issues a net supply of new bonds to the residents of A.

All of these changes in the balance sheets of governments and private wealth holders are completed a certain time after opening of international relations. The length of the adjustment depends on institutional arrangements in the bond markets and is not important for the present analysis. In the new equilibrium the excess demand for foreign exchange ceases and along with it the need for official intervention.[3] The excess demand by Country A's residents has caused the government of A to be indebted to the government of B rather than to its own citizens. B's government finds its obligation to A's private citizens matched by claims on A's government.

At no time between the two points of asset equilibrium did the exchange rate move and since full employment in both countries has been maintained there have been no income or price effects on the balance of trade and no real resources transferred between the two countries. The new pattern of asset holdings involves a net transfer of resources only if the interest rate on the official IOUs issued by government A and held by government B is different from that paid on the bonds issued by government B and held by the public in A, assuming equal liquidity and other service yields on each type and assuming equal taxation rates.

Second, under flexible exchange rates the net demand for B's bonds causes a lowering of A's exchange rate, the appearance of a balance of trade surplus for A, which persists until real resources equal in value to A's excess demand for bonds is realized. Then the exchange rate returns to its previous level under the present assumptions of a static world.

Assuming that neither government changes the quantity of its bonds outstanding, the net demand for B's bonds from the residents of A tends to raise the prices and lower the yields on B's bonds, inducing the residents of B to substitute real assets transferred from A for these bonds in their portfolios. There is a tendency for the return on real capital to fall in B and rise in A, reducing what *ceteris paribus* would have been the net excess demand for bonds in A. However, given the other determinants of this demand, total asset holdings and tastes, there is no necessity for this net asset demand to be moved to zero.

As long as the interest rate paid by Country B on the bonds held by the residents of A is equal to the marginal productivity of the resources transferred to B, the real income in both countries is the same as before the opening of international relations, except for the welfare gains accruing to the wealth holders from the diversification of their portfolios.

The model just presented gives rise to the possibility that real capital flows away from the country with the higher to the one with lower physical productivity of capital. Such an event occurs if the size of total asset portfolios in Country A is greater than that in Country B so that even at the initial interest rate differential in favor of A a net demand for B's bonds is created. Under flexible exchange rates these conditions result in a transfer of real resources to Country B through the process described in the preceding paragraphs.

It is clear that the welfare gains accruing to wealth holders through international diversification of their portfolios are different in nature from those known from the traditional literature in international economics, i.e., the Ricardo–Heckscher–Ohlin gains from trade and the classical gains from factors moving to higher productivity employment.

Some Empirical Estimates of Potential Gains From Diversification

In order to demonstrate the range of possible gains to American investors from international diversification of their portfolios, information on rates

Table 7.1 Rates of return and standard deviation from investing in foreign capital market averages 1959–1966

	Per cent Per Annum (1)	Value of $100 at End of Period (2)	Standard Deviation (3)	Correlation (R) with USA (4)
USA	7.54	178.92	47.26	1.000
Canada	5.95	158.82	41.19	0.7025[a]
United Kingdom	9.59	208.00	65.28	0.2414[a]
West Germany	7.32	175.95	94.69	0.3008[a]
France	4.27	139.69	49.60	0.1938[a]
Italy	8.12	186.74	103.33	0.1465
Belgium	1.09	109.02	37.56	0.1080
Netherlands	5.14	149.33	86.34	0.2107[a]
Japan	16.54	340.21	92.52	0.1149
Australia	9.44	205.75	34.87	0.0585
South Africa	8.47	191.60	61.92	−0.1620

[a]Statistically significant at the 5 per cent level.

Note: For computational methods see text.

Sources: The share price index for the United States is Moody's industrial average of common stocks from *Moody's Indus. Manual*, June 1967. The share price index for Canada is the industrial series from the Toronto Stock Exchange Supplement Booklet No. 2, the Toronto Stock Exchange, Jan. 15, 1966.

The share price indices for the United Kingdom, West Germany, France, Italy, Belgium, and the Netherlands are from the industrial series of the *Allgemeines Stat. Bull.*, European Economic Communities, various issues. The share price indices for Japan and Australia are industrial series from *Internal. Fin. Stat.*, International Monetary Fund, various issues. The price index for South Africa is a gold mining shares index from the *Quart. Bull.*, South Africa Reserve Bank, various issues.

The industrial dividend yields for the United States are from *Moody's Indus. Manual*, June 1967. The dividend yield on industrials series for the United Kingdom, West Germany, France, Italy, and the Netherlands are from *Allgemeines Stat. Bull.*, European Economic Communities, various issues; for Belgium, from personal correspondence with the Drediet-bank; for Japan, from *The Oriental Economist*, various issues; for Australia, from personal correspondence with the Reserve Bank of Australia; for Canada, from one published by Moss Lawson and adapted to the Toronto Stock Exchange Industrial Index, from personal correspondence with the Toronto Stock Exchange.

The dividend yield on gold mining shares series for South Africa is from personal correspondence with the South Africa Reserve Bank.

The exchange rates for all countries are taken from *Internal. Fin. Stat.*, International Monetary Fund, various issues.

of return from portfolio-investment in common stock market averages of 11 major countries (see Table 7.1) was collected, covering the period from January 1959 to December 1966.[4] For each of these eleven markets the following monthly observations were obtained: Indexes of common share prices (P), dividend yields on the shares in the index (Y) expressed as per cent per year, and the dollar exchange rate (X), defined as the price of one dollar. Subscripts 0 and 1 used below refer to the beginning and end of each monthly investment period; the share price index and exchange rate at the end of the current month is considered to be the price at which the next month's investment is made.

The monthly rates of return were calculated on the basis of the following considerations. The dollar price of one foreign stock market index unit is $PE_0 = P_0/X_0$. The dollar value of the investment at the end of the first month, (VE_1), is equal to the foreign currency value of dividends received $DP_1 = P_0 Y_0/12$ plus the foreign currency value of one unit of the index at the end of the month (P_1) converted to dollars at the exchange rate (X_1), i.e.,

(9) $$VE_1 = [(P_0 Y_0)/12 + P_1]/X_1$$

The problem then becomes to find the solution value for r_1 in the equation

(10) $$VE_1 = PE_0(1 + r)^{1/12}$$

which after some manipulation and substitution becomes

(11) $$r_1 = \left[\left(Y_0/12 + \frac{P_1}{P_0} \right) \left(\frac{X_0}{X_1} \right) \right]^{12} - 1.0$$

A matrix of correlation among the eleven countries' monthly returns was computed and the variances and covariances were used in the subsequent calculations. Average rates of return were computed by taking the geometric mean of 95 monthly rates.[5]

(12) $$R = \left[\prod_{t=1}^{95} (1 + r_i) \right]^{1/12} - 1.0$$

This formula, thus, computes the annual rate of return from capital gains due to common stock price and exchange rate changes, under the assumption that dividends are reinvested each month in fractional shares at current prices and that interest is compounded annually. No adjustments were made for withholding taxes on income or transactions costs. It should also be noted that exchange rate variations are assumed to be the only risks attached to foreign investment. Risks on foreign investment stemming from war, confiscation and exchange restrictions could not be quantified and were disregarded. Consequently the variances used in the subsequent calculations understate foreign risk and the estimates of gains from diversification are biased upward.

The empirical calculations are unrealistic in one other important respect.

Due to indivisibilities, transactions costs, and limited portfolio sizes, it is virtually impossible for anyone to hold portfolios containing all of the shares making up the indices used in the calculations. Because the portfolio variance decreases with the number of individual stocks held, the underestimate of variance available to investors implicit in the calculation procedure is smaller the more diversified portfolios are in the real world. In general, the bias may not be too large in view of the availability of mutual funds in most of the foreign markets, though more empirical information on the investment patterns, transactions costs, etc., of these funds is needed.

In Table 7.1, column (1) shows average rates of return calculated in the manner just discussed while column (2) shows the capital value in December of 1966 of $100 invested in January of 1959. Columns (3) and (4) report the standard deviation of monthly returns and the correlation of these fluctuations with those of Moody's industrial average of common stocks. As can be seen, the U.S. yield has been the sixth lowest, but the riskiness of the investment as measured by variance has been the fourth lowest.

Given these historic rates of return and interdependencies of the national stock markets, it is possible to compute rates of return and variances of portfolios which would have accrued to investors who had purchased foreign assets in various combinations. The most interesting of these combinations are those which for any given variance maximize the return. Portfolios which have these characteristics and are attainable with the available set of assets can be found through methods of quadratic programming, for which standard computer algorithms are available.[6]

Table 7.2 presents the results of two different calculations for efficient sets of internationally diversified portfolios. Part A is based on rates of return and variances of the eleven industrialized countries mentioned before, while Part B is restricted to the data of the eight countries of the Atlantic Community. The eight portfolios shown for each case are socalled corner portfolios, i.e., those at which further reduction in variance can be achieved only through the inclusion or omission of additional assets. The rates of returns and standard deviations for the corner portfolios are shown in the last two rows of Parts A and B of Table 7.2 and are plotted in Figure 7.1.[7] Other attainable combinations of return and standard deviations can be found by interpolation between corner portfolios, as is done by the lines drawn between the points in Figure 7.1.

As can be seen, diversification among the assets from the eleven countries in general would have permitted investors to attain higher rates of return or lower variance of their portfolios than they could have by purchasing a portfolio consisting of Moody's industrial average of common stocks. Which combination of assets given investors would in fact have chosen cannot be known since it depends on their individual marginal rate

Table 7.2 Efficient internationally diversified portfolios

	Percentage of portfolio invested in country portfolio number							
	Part A: Eleven industrial countries							
Country:	1	2	3	4	5	6	7	8
United States						12.3	12.8	12.5
Canada							14.0	15.9
United Kingdom		2.4	6.3	11.9	12.0	10.7	8.4	7.6
West Germany								
France								2.7
Italy					0.2	1.7	1.7	1.5
Belgium								
Netherlands								
Japan	100.0	97.6	74.9	32.1	30.8	17.0	8.5	7.0
Australia			18.9	42.6	43.1	42.6	39.0	37.3
South Africa				13.4	13.8	15.7	15.6	15.4
Portfolio Return	16.54	16.37	14.76	11.61	11.50	10.25	9.15	8.84
Portfolio Stand. Dev.	92.62	90.55	71.02	37.12	36.26	27.37	22.82	22.09
	Part B: Atlantic Community Countries							
Country:	1	2	3	4	5	6	7	8
United States			26.6	42.9	35.7	32.1	29.5	16.4
Canada					21.3	24.9	27.3	25.4
United Kingdom	100.0	90.8	63.4	43.3	31.0	26.0	22.4	8.5
West Germany				4.7	5.0	4.3	3.6	
France						6.8	11.1	12.9
Italy		9.2	9.9	9.2	7.1	5.8	5.0	1.3
Belgium								34.4
Netherlands							1.1	1.2
Portfolio Return	9.59	9.45	8.90	8.47	7.87	7.48	7.20	4.65
Portfolio Stand. Dev.	65.28	60.63	46.67	39.76	34.49	32.23	30.96	25.10

Notes: For computational method see text.
Sources: Same as Table 7.1.

of substitution between risk and return. It can be said unambiguously, however, that if an investor had wanted to maintain the same variability in return found in the New York investment, international diversification would have permitted him to earn 12.6 per cent as against 7.5 per cent, a gain of 68.0 per cent in the annual rate of return. When the opportunities for investment in Japan, South Africa, and Australia are excluded from consideration, the opportunity for gains from diversification are reduced considerably, as can be seen from Part B of Table 7.2, and the appropriate efficiency frontier in Figure 7.1. However, the increase in return attainable at the New York variance is from 7.5 per cent to 8.9 per cent, a gain of

Figure 7.1 Efficient portfolios

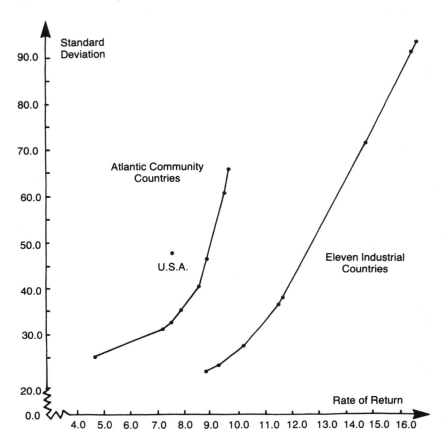

18.7 per cent. As can be seen from Table 7.2, Part B, Column 3, such a portfolio would consist of the following approximate investments: 26.6 per cent in New York, 63.4 per cent in London and 9.9 per cent in Italy.

Analogous calculations can be carried out to demonstrate the reduction in variance attainable by investing in internationally diversified portfolios with the same expected rate of return as that from investment in New York alone. Such calculations are not shown here; rough estimates can be made by inspection of Figure 7.1.

In general, the preceding analysis and calculations suggest that recent experience with foreign investment returns would have given rise to substantial gains in welfare to wealth holders. If past experiences are considered to be indicative of future developments, then these data suggest that future international diversification of portfolios is profitable and that more of it will take place.[8]

The Dynamic Model

Some interesting conclusions from the model of internationally diversified portfolios result from the assumption that assets in both countries are growing through time. To simplify the analysis it is assumed that growth occurs in perfect balance, i.e., that income and assets in various forms grow at the same rate r_a and r_b for countries A and B respectively, and that exchange rates are pegged rigidly. If $Q^0_{A,B}$ and $Q^0_{B,A}$ are the initial stocks of foreign assets held in static equilibrium in Countries A and B respectively, then the gross flows ($\dot{Q}^t$) at any point in time t are :

$$(13) \qquad \dot{Q}^t_{A,B} = r_a e^{r_a t} Q^0_{A,B}$$

$$(14) \qquad \dot{Q}^t_{B,A} = r_b e^{r_b t} Q^0_{B,A}$$

and the net flow from A to B ($\dot{N}^t_{A,B}$) is

$$(15) \qquad \dot{N}^t_{A,B} = r_a e^{r_a t} Q^0_{A,B} - r_b e^{r_b t} Q^0_{B,A}$$

Thus, it can be seen that the net flows of bonds between the two countries is a function of the growth rates and the size of the initial stocks in both countries. It is recalled that the initial stocks are determined primarily by the relative sizes of the two countries' wealth holdings and the existing interest rate differential.

Because of these determinants of bond flows, we have the following interesting possibilities. First, *gross* capital flows can occur between countries even if interest rates differentials are zero at all times. This is true whenever initial stocks of foreign bonds and growth rates are positive. Second, net capital flows into the low interest country (assumed to be Country A) can take place when first, $r_a > r_b$ and $Q^0_{A,B} = Q^0_{B,A}$; second, $Q^0_{A,B} > Q^0_{B,A}$ and $r_a = r_b$; third, $r_a > r_b$ and $Q^0_{A,B} > Q^0_{B,A}$; fourth, $r_a < r_b$ and $Q^0_{A,B} > Q^0_{B,A}$. In the last two cases, however, the net flow to Country A occurs only if the growth effect outweighs the stock effect or vice versa.

Under the assumed system of fixed exchange rates there are no equilibrating forces set into motion by *net* bond flows as long as the government of the country selling the private bonds is willing to accept the other country's official IOUs in the manner described in the first section of this chapter. In the long run, however, these stocks of official IOU's can become very large and it is doubtful that any governments are willing to accumulate them indefinitely. Pressures for a real transfer of resources will be generated and these will bring into being equilibrating forces.

The nature of these forces can be discerned most readily in the world of perfectly flexible exchange rates, where the net demand for bonds by residents of Country A results in the transfer of real resources to Country B through the generation of a trade surplus for A. This transfer has two effects. First, the rate of real economic growth in B increases while that in A decreases. Second, the marginal productivity of capital falls in B and rises in A. Both the real growth and interest rate effects tend to reduce the gross demand for bonds in A and raise the gross demand for bonds in B. The effects persist until gross bond flows have become equalized. However, such equality does not necessarily occur when the interest rate differential is zero. The differential can be either positive or negative and gross flows can remain equal as long as the products of growth rates times stocks of foreign assets are equal for both countries.

Interest Elasticity of Capital Flows

In this part special attention is given to the role of interest rates in the preceding models, primarily because of some interesting policy conclusions following from the analysis.

In the static model after stock equilibrium has been established bonds cease to flow between the two countries. However, the potential for flows in response to interest rate changes is always present. Thus, if for some domestic policy purpose Country A decides to lower its interest rate, foreigners will decrease their holdings of Country A's bonds and domestic wealth holders will increase their holdings of foreign bonds. The result is a net demand for bonds by Country A which leads to a transfer of IOUs to the government of B or to the transfer of real resources in the manner discussed above. However, it is important to note that in this static model the flow of capital following the interest rate change is a once-and-for-all stock adjustment, which is accomplished within a certain time period, the length of which depends on institutional characteristics of the bond market.

In the dynamic version of the model the change in the interest rate differential calls forth the equivalent of a stock adjustment flow which is superimposed on the flow due to portfolio growth. The duration of this stock-adjustment flow component depends on the institutional characteristics of the bond market, as in the static model. After completion of the stock adjustment flow, the regular transfer of bonds continues to grow at the same rate as before, but the level is different. These points can also be made with the help of the accompanying Figure 7.2.

Figure 7.2

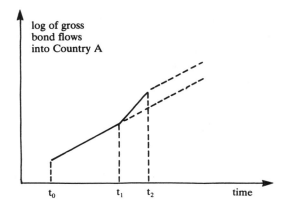

On the horizontal axis we plot time, on the vertical axis the log of gross capital flows from B to A. The line segment t_0t_1 has a slope r_a, equal to the rate of growth of wealth portfolios in Country A. At period t_1, Country A lowers its interest rate and the growth rate of foreign bond holdings in A increases, as is shown by the steeper slope of the line segment t_1t_2. After the completion of the stock-adjustment process, the rate of growth in foreign bond holdings returns to its old level r_a but the *level* of bond holdings is raised at any given moment in time by the vertical distance between the solid and broken growth lines as a result of the increased rate differential.

Some Implications of the Model

First, the classical theory of factor movements considers rates of return alone as the determinants of international capital flows. In its basic form, therefore, it cannot explain the real world phenomenon of simultaneous European investments in the United States and U.S. investments in Europe. Direct investment of this nature has been explained as resulting from the cost conditions in oligopolistic industries [2]. The present model provides an additional explanation that is especially applicable to the purchase of foreign bonds and other noncontrol conferring assets.

Second, the present model suggests that the empirical measurement of the interest elasticity of international capital movements can be improved by the inclusion of independent variables representing the growth in total asset portfolios and by studying gross flows of capital from each country. Consider, for example, the case where the interest rate differential is zero, gross flows are positive and large but net flows are zero. In our model it is possible that an increase in the rate of economic growth of one country causes the rise of that country's gross purchases of foreign assets and causes the appearance of a net flow even though the interest rate differential remained at zero.[9] A measurement of the interest elasticity of net flows would yield nonsensical results, but the measurement of gross flows and inclusion of total portfolio growth can explain the phenomenon.

Third, the model leads to the hypothesis that the large scale U.S. investments in Europe during the last decade are part of a stock adjustment phenomenon that started when European currencies became convertible *de jure* in 1958 after having been convertible *de facto* a few years earlier. If this hypothesis is correct, then there may eventually take place a slowdown in the rate of U.S. capital outflows to Western Europe.[10] However, because of the proportionately larger size of U.S. portfolios, normal growth in both continents leads to the expectation of a continued net demand for European assets. If this is so, European governments must either be willing to accept more of the U.S. government's IOUs or permit a greater trade surplus to occur if the free convertibility of the major Western currencies is to be maintained. Equalization of interest rates will be insufficient to equalize gross flows, because of the different sizes of total asset holdings in Europe and the United States.

Fourth, the portfolio model suggests that a once-and-for-all change in international interest rate differentials leads to only a once-and-for-all stock adjustment, after which gross flows return to their old levels. This implication of the portfolio model leads to an empirically important extension of the arguments over the proper mix of monetary and fiscal policy for the achievement of internal and external balance.

In Mundell's formulation of this argument [6] the domestic interest rate is set at such a level as to attract a quantity of foreign capital sufficient to fill the current account gap in international payments while fiscal policy is set at a level of restrictiveness sufficient to attain domestic full employment. Our model suggests that at the international interest rate differential initially chosen, there will be a stock-adjustment flow of a size that cannot be sustained beyond the attainment of the new stock equilibrium. If the external deficit on current account persists beyond this point of new stock equilibrium, then the interest rate differential has to be raised again to finance the deficit in the next period and so on until it is eliminated by some other policies. If foreign wealth holders run into diminishing returns to international diversification, then the subsequent increments to the interest differential have to be increasingly larger.[11]

Fifth, the model can be used to explain holding of foreign short-term assets as well as bonds, corporate securities, and direct investment. Continuous and growing international diversification demand for short-term assets has some interesting implications for U.S. balance of payments "deficits" under the liquidity definition. Even if the growing exchange of short-term assets between the United States and the rest of the world is perfectly balanced, the United States would show a continuous and growing balance of payments deficit since the foreign holdings of short-term dollar assets are considered to be a potential claim on U.S. reserves which the balance of payments statistics are designed to reflect. Yet, the model presented suggests that these potential liabilities are counter-balanced by U.S. holdings of foreign short-term assets and that the foreign asset demand is normal and permanent because of the continued welfare gains from holding internationally diversified portfolios. The model thus strengthens the arguments made against the use of the liquidity concept and in favor of the official-reserve-transactions concept.[12]

Notes

[†] The members of the University of Pennsylvania Finance Workshop have made valuable comments on an earlier draft of this paper. K. Fadner, a fellow in the University of Pennsylvania Work-Study Program, collected the data and helped with the calculations in the section on pp. 163–9. While writing this paper the author was supported by the National Science Foundation under grant GS 1678.

1 The importance of the real world phenomenon is exemplified by the recent report in [10].

2 The discussion of circumstances under which diversification does not take place, i.e., investors are risk lovers, domination of assets, perfect correlation of returns, etc., go beyond the scope of this paper and it is assumed that investors and assets in both countries meet the necessary requirements for diversification to take place.

3 The lower the risk or higher the return on bond holdings in both countries, the more likely an increase in the total demand for assets. Under these circumstances, savings will increase, causing a fall in the interest rate and requiring changes in employment policy. We neglect these effects by assuming that they are likely to be small. On the same grounds we disregard balance of payments and income problems arising from net interest payments.

4 January 1959 was chosen as a starting point because in December 1958 European currencies became convertible *de jure*. Common stocks rather than bonds were analyzed because of the greater variance around the average returns and across countries found in the former. The theoretical analysis can easily be modified to account for foreign stock purchases.

5 Taking the simple arithmetic mean of the monthly rates vastly overstates the value of the capital gains between the beginning and the end of the period plus the value of the dividends. For a discussion of the biases inherent in the calculation of indices and averages see [1].

6 The program used is available in SHARE program under the code RSQPE4. It has been developed by the RAND Corporation. Finding the efficient set for 11 assets required 124 seconds on the IBM 7040. For the 8 assets the time requirement was 65 seconds.

7 In the plotting of the data it was more efficient to use standard deviations rather than variances. Throughout this section the two terms are used interchange-

ably since this leaves substantive conclusions unaffected but facilitates exposition.

8 The validity of this statement depends on the interpretation of the results. One could argue that U.S. investors are in equilibrium and that the measures of risk used in the calculations represent an underestimate, which if properly accounted for would show little advantage to be gained from diversification. On the other hand, one could also argue that the calculations show the existance of a disequilibrium, that in fact U.S. investors are in the process of making stock adjustments which are taking time to accomplish. See the section on pp. 171–3 and footnote 10 for more comments on this possibility.

9 Harry G. Johnson has suggested a similar dependence of international capital flows on rates of economic growth in his [4].

10 This point has also been made by J. Tobin [9, p. 168].

11 I have proved the existence of such diminishing returns to diversification in the traditional quadratic utility function [3, p. 20].

12 These issues have been analyzed in [7].

References

[1] L. Fisher, "Some New Stock Market Indexes," *Jour. Bus.*, Jan. 1966, *39* (1), Part II, 191–225.

[2] H.G. Grubel, "Intra-Industry Specialization and the Pattern of Trade," *Can. Jour. Econ.*, Aug. 1967, *33* (3), 374–88.

[3] —— *Forward Exchange, Speculation and the International Flow of Capital.* Standford, Calif. 1966.

[4] H. G. Johnson, "Some Aspects of the Theory of Economic Policy in a World of Capital Mobility," *Essays in Honour of Marco Fanno*. Padova 1966.

[5] H. Markowitz, *Portfolio Selection: Efficient Diversification of Investments.* New York 1959.

[6] R. A. Mundell, "The Appropriate Use of Monetary and Fiscal Policy for Internal and External Stability," *Internat. Mon. Fund Staff Papers*, March 1962, *9*, 70–77.

[7] Review Committee for Balance of Payments Statistics, Bureau of the Budget=, *The Balance of Payments Statistics of the United States, Review and Appraisal,* April 1965.

[8] J. Tobin, "Liquidity Preference as Behavior Towards Risk," *Rev. Econ. Stud.*, Feb. 1958, *25* (2), 65–86.

[9] —— *National Economic Policy.* New Haven 1966.

[10] "European Investors Step Up Their Purchases of American Corporate Securities," *Wall Street Journal,* Oct. 12, 1967.

8

Market Imperfections, Capital Market Equilibrium and Corporation Finance*

R. C. Stapleton and M. G Subrahmanyam[†]

*Source: *Journal of Finance*, 32 (May 1977), pp. 307–319.

This paper is concerned with two types of market segmentation and their implications for corporate financial decisions. The first type is caused by restrictions on certain individuals investing in certain securities and is exemplified by segmentation in international capital markets. The second type is induced by the simultaneous existance of differential personal tax rates and a fixed element of transactions costs. Segmentation of the former type produces incentives for firms to merge and affects the cost of capital, while the latter type raises questions about the tax effect of dividend policy. The framework of the analysis is the single period capital asset pricing model (CAPM).

The derivation of equilibrium security prices given these market imperfections and the comparative statics of the corporate policy changes is analytically intractable. For example, if fixed transactions costs exist investors face complicated maximization problems for which no neat analytical results are possible. However, numerical solutions for equilibrium can be obtained by modelling the tâtonnement process towards equilibrium. A Walrasian auctioneer presents a set of prices, investor demands are calculated, prices changed according to a function whose argument is excess demand across all investors and demands recalculated. Equilibrium prices are found when excess demands reach zero. The same technique allows us to compute prices of stocks for cases of partial market segmentation where prices cannot be stated analytically in closed form.

The paper will be built around an eight firm, twenty investor example. The standard results of corporate finance given perfect capital markets are illustrated using this example in the second section. In the third section, the market is segmented by placing various restrictions on investors and the effect of mergers and dual listings analysed. The fourth section introduces personal taxes and derives the effect of dividend policy and the last section introduces fixed transactions costs, illustrates the segmentation induced, and derives analogous conclusions regarding the effect of dividend policy.

Table 8.1 8 Firm economy: data

			No. of shares	1,000,	$j = 1,\dots,8$		
			μ_j	100,000,	$j = 1,\dots,8$		

Correlation Matrix

			1	.7	.1	.1	.9	.7	.1	.1
			.7	1	.1	.1	.7	.9	.1	.1
	= 25,000	$j = 1,5$	.1	.1	1	.7	.1	.1	.9	.7
	= 30,000	$j = 2,6$	.1	.1	.7	1	.1	.1	.7	.9
$\sigma_j =$	= 18,000	$j = 3,7$	.9	.7	.1	.1	1	.7	.1	.1
	= 22,000	$j = 4,8$	.7	.9	.1	.1	.7	1	.1	.1
			.1	.1	.9	.7	.1	.1	1	.7
			.1	.1	.7	.9	.1	.1	.7	1

rate of interest $(r-1) = .08$

CARA utility function parameter i/a_i, 000's

i		i		i		i	
1	6	6	6.8	11	7.6	16	8.5
2	6.2	7	7.0	12	7.8	17	8.8
3	6.4	8	7.2	13	8.0	18	9.0
4	6.5	9	7.4	14	8.2	19	9.5
5	6.6	10	7.5	15	8.4	20	10.0

Corporate Financial Policy in a Perfect Capital Market

Throughout the paper, propositions regarding the effect of corporate financial policies will be illustrated by reference to an eight firm, twenty investor economy, the basic data about which is contained in Table 8.1. The firms generate returns at the end of a single period with expected values μ_j of $100,000 and standard deviations σ_j ranging from $18,000 to $30,000, and a correlation matrix as shown. All the standard assumptions of the CAPM are assumed to hold.

The returns can either be regarded as cash flows in a strictly single period world or, assuming the single period CAPM holds in each period, as exogenously given market values plus dividends at the end of the period. This latter interpretation is required for the discussion of dividend policy in the fourth section. The correlation matrix and the σ_j have been chosen so that the firms fall into "risk classes". Firms (1, 5), (2, 6), (3, 7) and (4, 8) are each in the same industry (correlated 0.9) and (1, 2, 5, 6) and (3, 4, 7, 8) can be viewed as being in the same sector of the economy.

The investors, who each have constant absolute risk aversion (CARA) utility functions, have coefficients of absolute risk aversion (a_i) indicated in

Table 8.1. Investor 1, for example, will maximize a utility function of form

$$U_1(E_1, V_1) = E_1 - (1/6,000)V_1$$

where E_1 and V_1 are the expected value and variance of his end of period wealth. Initial wealth is $17,000 for each investor and the market rate of interest (specified exogenously) is 8%.

Corporate Financial Decisions

We will first illustrate some well-known propositions regarding the effect of corporate financial policy in perfect capital markets. In all cases, the security prices were found by converging a model of the tâtonnement process by which equilibrium is achieved.[1] The results are presented in Table 8.2.

The implications of the CAPM for optimal corporate investment decisions can best be seen by first considering equilibrium in a seven firm economy (excluding firm 1) and then the comparative statics involved in moving to an eight firm economy. Case (1) is a seven firm economy with firm 1 of the eight firms in Table 8.1 deleted. Equilibrium prices reflect the covariance structure and the β's indicate the relative riskiness of the firms. The expected rates of return on the stocks vary from 18% to 29% and are linearly related to the β's. The portfolios of the twenty investors are simply the market portfolio, and as an example, investor 10 holds 49 shares of each stock.

Wealth Maximizing Investment Decisions

As noted by Jensen and Long (1972) and Merton and Subrahmanyam (1974), the investment decision may be dependent on the number of firms in the market, which firm is considering the project, and more fundamentally, whether the firm has monopoly control of the project. The simplest decision scenario is that where firm 1 has the chance of undertaking a project. If it undertakes the project, it will have a value (Case (2)) of $77,890. If it does not, it will have a zero value whether or not it has monopoly control over the project. The investment criterion is clear: invest if the cost is less than $77,890, i.e. if the return is greater than 28%, the cost of capital for firm 1.

Now, consider the decision of firm 2 if it has the chance to invest in the same project. If it invests in the project after issuing 1,000 new shares to do so, it has a price per share (Case (3)) of $76.18 or a total value of $152,360, which is the value it would have if firm 1 took the investment and then firms 1 and 2 are merged. If it does not have monopoly control and does not invest in the project, and instead firm 1 takes it, firm 2 has a value (Case (2)) of $74,500. Hence, given this scenario, firm 2 invests if the cost is less than $152,360–$74,500 = $77,860. In the absence of

Table 8.2 No tax model: corporate finance results

Firm	1	2	3	4	5	6	7	8
7 Firm Economy:								
Price		77.66	84.61	82.57	81.28	77.66	84.61	82.57
β		1.42	.70	.90	1.03	1.42	.70	.90
Rate of return %		29	18	21	23	29	18	21
Portfolio ($i=10$)		49	49	49	49	49	49	49
8 Firm Economy:								
Price	77.89	74.50	84.34	82.23	77.89	74.50	84.34	82.24
β	1.17	1.51	.61	.78	1.17	1.51	.61	.78
Rate of return %	28	34	19	22	28	34	19	22
Portfolio ($i=10$)	49	49	49	49	49	49	49	49
Firm 2 and 1 Merged:								
Price		76.18	84.34	82.24	77.88	74.48	84.34	82.24
β		1.34	0.61	0.78	1.17	1.51	0.61	0.78
Rate of return %		31	19	22	28	34	19	22
Portfolio ($i=10$)		98	49	49	49	49	49	49
Firm 1 Levered:								
Price	59.37	74.50	84.34	82.24	77.89	74.50	84.34	82.24
β	1.49	1.46	.59	.76	1.14	1.46	.59	.76
Rate of return %	35	34	19	22	28	34	19	22
DEBT + EQUITY* VALUE	77,890	74,500	84,340	82,240	77,890	74,500	84,340	82,240
Portfolio ($i=10$)	49	49	49	49	49	49	49	49

*For Firm 1, Debt is valued at $(20,000/1 + 0.8) = 18,520$.

monopoly control, the investment decision is the same whichever firm takes it (the difference of $30 is a rounding error). However, if firm 2 has monopoly control, its no investment alternative leaves it with a value (Case (1)) of $77,660 and it will undertake the project if and only if the cost is less than $152,390–$77,660 = $74,730. The difference is due to the fact that it takes into account the effect on the value of its existing investment.

The Neutrality of Conglomerate Mergers

The proposition that a pure conglomerate merger would be neutral in its effect on the value of the firms involved, first mooted by Alberts and Segall (1966), can be illustrated by the merger of firms 1 and 2 in Case (3). After the merger, the firms are worth $152,360. In the absence of the merger, they are worth Case (2) $77,890 and $74,500 respectively, which sums to the merged value (except for the $30 rounding error). Note also that the β and the rate of return after the merger are simple weighted averages of their pre-merger values and that investors hold the merged firm in the same proportion as in the pre-merger equilibrium.

Capital Structure and the Value of the Firm

As Hamada (1969) noted, it is possible to establish the MM propositions from the CAPM. An illustration is provided by Case (4) in Table 8.2 where firm 1 has been given debt valued at $18,250 yielding the market rate of interest of 8%, a total repayment at the end of the period of $20,000. The number of shares of firm 1 is assumed to be 1,000 but the expected equity payoff is now $80,000. The debt is assumed also to be non-risky and hence the variance of the total equity return remains unchanged at $(25,000)^2$. The effect of the leverage is to lift the β of firm 1 to 1.49 and the expected rate of return on its stock to 35%. However, if the debt and equity values of firm 1 are added, they total $77,890, the same as in the unlevered Case (2). This illustrates the Modigliani and Miller proposition I. Proposition II also follows since the expected rate of return to equity is a rising linear function of leverage.

Market Segmentation due to Investment Restrictions

In this section, we will first look at the effect on prices of various types of segmentation of the eight firm twenty investor market assuming that 4 of our firms and 10 investors are in one country and the remaining firms and investors in another. We will then show how segmentation produces incentives for international mergers and multiple listing of securities to take place.[2]

The first case to be considered, case (1), is the one studied by Adler and Dumas (1975), complete segmentation of the market where investors in one country are unable to invest in the other and vice versa.

Case (1) is simple to analyse but suffers from lack of realism. While markets are not completely integrated, they are not rigidly segmented either. In practice, markets are reasonably integrated with some restrictions on capital movement across national boundaries. The precise form of most of these restrictions can be modelled as one of the following cases.

Case (2) A restriction on the amount of investment in foreign securities allowed for each individual.[3]

Case (3) A percentage premium or tax levied on investment in foreign securities, the premium being specified exogenously.[4]

Case (4) A restriction on the aggregate amount of investment by one country's nationals in the other country. This aggregate restriction gives rise to a "dollar premium" of the type which U.K. investors have to pay on foreign portfolio investments. In this case, the "dollar premium" is determined endogenously.

In Table 8.3, we present the results of the four different types of market segmentation. In each case, firms (1, 2, 5, 6) and investors 1–10 are in one market (the U.K.) and firms (3, 4, 7, 8) and investors 11–20 are in the other (the U.S.). The effect of total segmentation in case (1) is to decrease all prices and, in particular, those in the U.K. which has both the riskiest stocks and the most risk averse investors. The cost of capital rises dramatically, although the β's within each market are not radically affected. Finally, portfolios within each market are simply proportions of the (four stock) market portfolio. The effect of segmentation on investment decisions is obvious and reflected in the rate of return figures.

The first type of partial segmentation, case (2a), is produced by a $5,000 restriction on foreign investment by U.K. investors. Each U.K. investor is restricted to a $5,000 total investment in stocks 3, 4, 7, 8. U.S. investors (11–20) are unrestricted. The restriction turns out to be binding for each U.K. investor and the shadow price of the constraint varies from 0.107 for investor 1 to 0.114 for investor 10. The prices of the restricted stocks are down (stock 3 for example is priced at $80.67 per share, down from $84.34), while other prices (U.K. stocks) are unaffected. U.K. investors (10 for example) keep to their restriction by shorting 3 and 7 and holding a considerable number of shares in 4 and 8. U.S. investors (11 for example) take up the spare shares in 3 and 7.

Case (2b) shows the effect of tightening the restriction. The shadow prices of the constraint rise to 0.140 for investor 1 and to 0.144 for investor 10; the stock prices of the U.K. stocks are correspondingly lower due to the reduced demand. The shadow prices of the foreign investment constraints are the equivalent of taxes on foreign investment. Case (3) directly models the affect of a 10% tax on foreign investment by U.K. investors, a special case of the Black model discussed above. The results are very similar to the $5,000 restriction case as they must be, since in that case the effective tax on investors ranged only from 10.7% to 11.4%. The 10% tax is a slightly less stringent condition and this is reflected in prices and the portfolios of U.K. investors.

A straight tax across investors is produced effectively also by a total restriction on dollar investment (Case (4)). We call this the dollar premium case since it closely models the case of U.K. foreign exchange restrictions on overseas investment which produces the dollar premium. A $15,000 total restriction on foreign investment for investors 1–10 causes a premium or effective tax of 14.40%. The effect on prices is just a more extreme case of the price effect in case (3).

Corporate Financial Policy in Segmented Markets

In most cases, the effect of segmenting capital markets is to depress security prices and also to produce an incentive for corporations to increase the diversification opportunities available to investors. Three corporate financial policies that effectively reduce the effects of segmented markets are

a. Foreign portfolio/direct investment by firms.
b. Mergers with foreign firms.
c. Dual listing of the securities of the firm on foreign capital markets.

Cases a and b are similar in nature and it is sufficient to analyse the merger as an example.

Mergers in totally segmented markets have been analysed by Adler and Dumas (1975). We will provide an example of the effect and then show the effect of mergers in a partially segmented market. We will also discuss in this section the effect of dual listing of securities in a totally segmented market.

The incentive to merge with a foreign firm is illustrated by case (1) in Table 8.4, where firm 2 has taken over firm 3 in a pure conglomerate merger and the joint firm quoted on the U.K. exchange. The value of the new firm is 69.77 × 2,000 = 139,540 which exceeds the sum of the values of the separate firms (54,800 + 79,970 = 134,770). In our small scale example there are also significant side effects of pulling firm 3 out of the U.S. market and into the U.K. The summed covariances of the remaining firms 4, 7, and 8 fall, causing increased prices, and the covariance of 1, 5, and 6 increase, causing lower prices. These effects would be insignificant in a larger scale example and should be regarded as second order.

Case 2 illustrates the similar effect of a merger of 2 and 3 in a partially segmented market. Again, there is an incentive to merge since the value of 2 and 3 after the merger (158,840) is greater than the sum of their pre-merger values (74,820 + 80,670). The effective relaxation of the 5000 restrictions on investors 1–10, resulting in a reduction in the shadow prices of the constraints, is reflected in the increased prices also of stocks 4, 7, and 8.

Table 8.3 Equilibrium in segmented markets*

	U.K.				U.S.			
	1	2	5	6	3	4	7	8
(1) Total Segmentation:*								
Prices	61.96	54.80	61.96	54.80	79.97	76.69	79.97	76.69
β	.84	1.18	.84	1.18	.87	1.14	.87	1.14
Rate of Return %	61	82	61	82	25	30	25	30
Portfolio (Investor 10)	111	111	111	111	0	0	0	0
Portfolio (11)	0	0	0	0	89	89	89	89
(2a) Partial Segmentation								
$5,000 restriction:								
Prices	77.88	74.82	77.88	74.48	80.67	78.67	80.68	78.67
Portfolio (10)	52	51	52	52	−10	42	−9	41
Portfolio (11)	47	47	47	48	94	55	94	55
Effective tax: Investor (1)	.107							
Investor (10)	.114							
(2b) $2,500 restriction:								
Prices	77.90	74.51	77.90	74.51	79.73	77.75	79.73	77.75
Portfolio (10)	52	52	52	52	−23	40	−23	40
Portfolio (11)	47	47	47	47	105	57	105	57
Effective tax: Investor (1)	.140							
Investor (10)	.144							
(3) 10% Tax on Foreign								
Investment:								
Prices	77.89	74.50	77.89	74.50	80.78	78.77	80.78	78.77
Portfolio (10)	52	51	52	51	−5	42	−5	42
Portfolio (11)	47	48	47	48	93	55	93	55

(4) **Dollar Premium:**

Prices	77.90	74.51	77.90	74.50	79.31	77.34	79.31	77.34
Portfolio (10)	53	52	53	52	-28	39	-28	39
Portfolio (11)	46	47	46	47	110	57	111	57
$ Premium	.144							

---

*Firms 1, 2, 5, 6 and investors 1–10 comprise the U.K. market. Firms 3, 4, 7, 8 and investors 11–20 comprise the U.S. market. In the partial segmentation cases U.K. investors are restricted in their investment in U.S. stocks. US investors are unrestricted. All prices are in one common currency, dollars.

Table 8.4 Mergers and dual listings in segmented markets

	U.K.				U.S.			
	1	2	5	6	3	4	7	8
(1) Acquisition of 3 by 2								
Total Segmentation								
Prices	61.36	69.77	61.36	54.08	—	79.68	83.12	79.68
Portfolio (10)	111	222	111	111	—	0	0	0
Portfolio (11)	0	0	0	0	—	89	89	89
(2) Acquisition of 3 by 2								
Partial Segmentation (5,000 restriction)								
Prices	77.88	79.42	77.88	74.49	—	81.21	83.28	81.21
Portfolio (10)	45	197	45	11	—	42	−22	42
Portfolio (11)	52	25	52	78	—	54	102	54
Effective tax:								
Investor (1)	.029							
Investor (2)	.033							
(3) Dual listing of 3,								
Total Segmentation								
Prices	61.19	53.89	61.19	53.89	84.33	80.42	83.89	80.42
Portfolio (10)	111	111	111	111	139	0	0	0
Portfolio (11)	0	0	0	0	−22	89	89	89

The effect of listing stock 3 on both exchanges with complete segmentation is shown in case (3). The demand for 3 is now always the sum of the demand from the 2 markets. In equilibrium U.K. investors demand a great deal of 3's shares and U.S. investors tend to short it. The price of 3 is substantially above its previous value. The prices of the other U.K. stocks are depressed because of the covariance effect in the expanded market and those of the U.S. stocks raised.

Dividend Policy and Clientele Effects with Personal Taxes in Otherwise Perfect Markets

Differential personal income and capital gains taxes can be introduced into the model and the effect of dividend policy analysed in the manner of Brennan (1970) by assuming (1) a personal income tax rate τ_i for investor i (2) a capital gains tax rate $\tau_i/2$, (3) a dividend component D_j of the cash flow and (4) the certainty of D_j. With these assumptions Brennan (1970) has shown that the extent of dependence of prices on dividend policy is a function of the weighted average of tax rates.

In Table 8.5, we show the results of simulating the tâtonnement in the case of the Brennan model. We analyse four different sets of dividend policies, assuming investors tax rates $\tau_1 = 0.02, \tau_2 = 0.04, \ldots, \ldots, \tau_{20} = 0.40$. Case (1) is one where there is maximum heterogeneity of dividend policies within each of the four industry risk classes. (1, 5) for example, are closely related (correlation 0.9) and 1 pays no dividend while 5 pays $30 per share. Case (2) represents maximum heterogeneity within the particular sector of the economy (for example 1, 2, 5, 6). Case (3) represents homogeneity within each of the four industry groups but heterogeneity within each sector. Finally, case (4) represents homogeneity both within the industry and within the sector.

The portfolio of a low tax-bracket investor, and those of a medium and high tax payer are shown in Table 8.5. Portfolio selection basically involves a balance of the diversification and tax characteristics of the stocks and, as noted by Black and Scholes (1974), it is not always clear which will dominate. In case (1), the investors can gain the advantages of diversification by holding stocks in each industry and the advantages of the tax characteristics of the stocks by going long in those that suit his tax bracket and short in those that do not. Investor 1, for example, the low tax payer, has a net holding of 62 shares in the firm (4, 8) made up of a long holding of 277 of the high dividend paying firm 8, and a 205 short holding of the low dividend paying firm 4. However, if as in Case (4), dividend policies are homogeneous within the risk classes, it is necessary for investors to hold stocks which do not suit their tax brackets in order to benefit from diversification.[5]

The Effect of Dividend Policy

The four cases in Table 8.5 amply illustrate the Brennan (1970) result regarding dividend policy, by comparing across equilibria. Whatever the clientele of the firm, a reduction in dividends leads unambiguously to an increase in price. Also, the price of a firm's stock depends on its dividend policy and not on its particular clientele. The price of firm 8 is the same in all four cases, although its clientele changes considerably. A reduction of dividends by firm 2, Case (1) rather than Case (2), or Case (4) rather than Case (3), leads to a rise in price ($76.10 per share to $77.38).

The effect of dividend policy can also be observed within a given equilibrium since we have pairs of firms which are identical except for their dividend policies. Comparison of the prices of firms 1 and 5 can be used to show the effect of dividend policy. In cases (3) and (4), these firms have the same dividend policy and, since the covariances of 1 and 5 with the market are identical, the same price. In Cases (1) and (2), firm 5 pays more dividends and its price is in each case less than that of firm 1. In all cases, whether the comparisons are across equilibria or within an equilibrium, a reduction of $10 per share in the dividend component leads to a price rise of $1.28.

Dividends and Tax Effects with Fixed Transactions Costs

Fixed transactions costs on the purchase of securities have the effect of limiting the optimal number of stocks in the portfolio (see Brennan (1975)) to a small number out of the set of available securities. We will examine the implications for market equilibrium and investment and dividend policies of firms, of limiting the number of stocks in the portfolio by restricting investors in our eight firm economy to any four stocks (representing one level of fixed transactions costs) and any two stocks (representing a higher level of fixed transactions costs) out of the eight.

At any given set of prices, the investor's portfolio problem can be solved by trying all the combinations of four out of eight stocks, for example, calculating the utility from an optimal portfolio for each case, and selecting the overall maximum. This 'brute force' method is a substitute in the small scale example for solving the mixed integer-programming problem that the investor faces or assuming a simplified variance–covariance matrix.

Following this procedure for the first dividend policy case, where the first four firms have zero dividends and the others have $30 per share dividends, changing prices according to excess demand as in the previous tâtonnement models leads to the following expected result. If limited to four stocks, most investors who previously held long and short positions in the eight stocks now hold just long positions in four stocks. To obtain optimal diversification, they also tend to choose one stock from each

Table 8.5 Dividend policy and clientele effects*

Stock	1	2	3	4	5	6	7	8
Case 1								
Dividend	0	0	0	0	30	30	30	30
Prices	80.41	77.38	86.19	84.31	76.57	73.54	82.34	80.48
Portfolio (1).02	-147	-94	-317	-205	226	165	403	277
Portfolio (10).20	-3	12	-51	-20	102	85	151	116
Portfolio (20).40	407	308	717	511	-288	-167	-604	-373
Case 2								
Dividend	0	10	0	10	20	30	20	30
Prices	80.41	76.10	86.17	83.00	77.85	73.54	83.60	80.45
Portfolio (1).02	97	-41	-219	-107	152	131	261	215
Portfolio (10).20	11	27	-23	8	81	75	111	98
Portfolio (20).40	314	212	538	332	-143	-105	-343	-258
Case 3								
Dividend	0	10	20	30	0	10	20	30
Prices	80.43	76.12	83.61	80.45	80.43	76.12	83.61	80.45
Portfolio (1).02	21	43	33	56	21	43	33	56
Portfolio (10).20	44	50	47	54	44	50	47	54
Portfolio (20).40	97	56	76	33	97	56	76	33
Case 4								
Dividend	0	0	30	30	0	0	30	30
Prices	80.42	77.39	82.32	80.45	80.42	77.39	82.32	80.45
Portfolio (1).02	30	33	61	40	30	33	61	40
Portfolio (10).20	46	47	55	49	47	47	55	49
Portfolio (20).40	81	75	25	63	81	75	25	63

* *Tax rates*. Investor i has an income tax rate $\tau_i = .02i$, and a capital gains tax of $\tau_i/2$.

Table 8.6 Equilibrium with taxes and fixed transactions costs

	1	2	3	4	5	6	7	8
(1) Dividend Policy 1, 4 out of 8:								
Dividends	0	0	0	0	30	30	30	30
Prices	80.96	77.87	86.42	84.55	76.92	73.57	83.23	81.35
Portfolio (1)					84	76	98	73
Portfolio (10)					93	100	87	91
Portfolio (20)	143	139	160	141				
(2) Dividend Policy 2, 4 out of 8:								
Dividends	0	10	0	10	20	30	20	30
Prices	80.80	75.85	86.67	82.95	77.56	73.56	83.84	81.14
Portfolio (10)					73	83	72	91
Portfolio (20)	158	126	175	112	103	93	102	85
(3) Dividend Policy 1, 2 out of 8:								
Dividends	0	0	0	0	30	30	30	30
Prices	79.28	76.33	85.15	83.18	75.63	72.51	81.81	79.71
Portfolio (1)							191	171
Portfolio (10)				206	162	163		
Portfolio (15)		190	335					
Portfolio (20)	295							
(4) Dividend Policy 2, 2 out of 8:								
Dividends	0	10	0	10	20	30	20	30
Prices	78.86	73.90	85.44	81.61	75.76	71.89	82.38	79.60
Portfolio (1)							217	154
Portfolio (10)				203	206	138		
Portfolio (15)		199	322					
Portfolio (20)	305							

industry group—(1,5), (2, 6), (3, 7), (4, 8). In fact, at most price iterations, the first few individuals, those with low tax rates, choose a portfolio of (5, 6, 7, 8) and the last few a portfolio of (1, 2, 3, 4).

The tendency to hold only long positions was confirmed by the two out of eight cases tried later. In those cases, investors invariably choose one stock from each sector of the economy, (1, 2, 5, 6) and (3, 4, 7, 8). We conclude that fixed transactions costs and the consequent reduction in the number of stocks in the portfolio reduces the need for short selling. Short selling restrictions *per se* may hence be of little significance when fixed transactions costs exist. Also, it seems that the level of fixed transactions costs has the effect of placing stocks into groupings (risk classes) from each of which the investors choose one stock which best suits their tax status.

Equilibrium prices for dividend policies (1) and (2) of the previous section, assuming investors are restricted to first four, and then two, stocks, are reported in Table 8.6. Prices in the four out of eight cases are approximately the same as in the no fixed transactions costs case. This is to be expected, since in this case the restrictions of investors to four stocks does not significantly limit the diversification possibilities open to investors. Neither do investors have to choose stocks outside their tax preference in order to diversify. However, in the two out of eight cases, prices are on average significantly lower since here diversification is effectively restricted. In all cases, the dividend policy effect remains strong, relative prices being approximately the same as in the no fixed transactions costs case.

Table 8.6 summarizes the optimal portfolios, at the equilibrium prices for various investors. In both the four out of eight cases, the low tax paying investors, as expected, choose stocks (1, 2, 3, 4) and the high tax payers stocks (5, 6, 7, 8). Investor II is on the borderline, being almost indifferent between the two portfolios.

A more spectacular example of the strengthened clientele effect is provided by the two out of eight securities cases. For example, in the case of dividend policy 2, investors 1 to 7 hold the high dividend stocks 6 and 8, investors 8 to 12 hold stocks 5 and 7, investors 13–17 hold 2 and 4, and finally 18–20 hold the zero dividend stocks 1 and 3. However, in spite of the generally strengthened clienteles, the price effect of dividend policy remains virtually the same as in the no fixed transactions costs case.

Conclusions

The analysis of equilibrium prices given fixed transactions costs and the associated restriction of the number of stocks in the portfolio has confirmed the Brennan (1970) results regarding the effect of dividend policy. While more extensive sensitivity tests are required to prove this proposition, our examples reveal no radical effect on the relative prices of dividend and non-dividend paying stocks. Even with restrictions on the number of stocks in the portfolio, a strong negative tax effect of dividend policy is produced, in spite of the strengthened clientele effect. The dividend policy effect still depends on the weighted average of all investors' tax rates, although only a few investors hold each stock. Our analysis adds no support to the contention of Black and Scholes (1974) and the original conjecture of Miller and Modigliani that clientele effects negate the tax influence of dividend policy.

Many of the problems associated with transaction costs have been ignored in this paper. However, the technique of modelling in tâtonnement could be used to further analyse some of the analytically difficult problems of short run equilibrium with transactions costs, i.e. the effect of investors being locked into stocks when dividend policies change. Investors then hold portfolios of stocks which are effectively "non-marketable" assets.

The general method of analysis has been fruitful also in illustrating well-known perfect markets conclusions regarding corporate financial policy and in analysing the effect of total and partial segmentation on equilibrium prices and corporate financial policy. Two types of market segmentation have been analysed, that due to explicit restrictions and that induced by the combined effect of taxes and fixed transactions costs. The general technique of simulating the tâtonnement applied to these cases would be capable also of analysing other market equilibrium scenarios.

Notes

† We would like to thank Biplab Das for computer programming assistance and the Salomon Brothers Center for the Study of Financial Institutions, New York University, for financial support.

1 Details of the tâtonnement model are contained in Stapleton and Subrahmanyam (1976) and will be discussed in detail in Stapleton and Subrahmanyam (1978). Although it is not necessary to use such a model for the present examples (since the numerical data could be put directly into the reduced form price equation) it does provide a useful test of the price change mechanism which is necessary for the non-analytically solvable cases, discussed later on.

2 We ignore the problems caused due to the risk of foreign exchange rate fluctuations. These are considered in Adler and Dumas (1975). As far as this paper is concerned, we will assume that the two countries have the same currency, dollars.

3 Investor demand in this case can be modelled by using Lagrange multipliers. In equilibrium, prices depend on the weighted sum of the shadow prices of the constraints. The tâtonnement model solves for these shadow prices and the equilibrium stock prices.

4 This case, in which the shadow prices are given exogenously, has been analysed by Black (1974).

5 The degree of homogeneity within risk classes and hence the strength of the clientele effect (shown most dramatically in case (1)) is an empirical issue which has not yet been resolved. For one point of view, see Black and Scholes (1974).

References

[1] W. W. Alberts and Joel E. Segall. *The Corporate Merger,* University of Chicago Press, 1966.

[2] Michael Adler and Bernard Dumas. "Optimal International Acquisitions," *Journal of Finance,* 30, (March 1975), pp. 1–20.

[3] Fisher Black. "International Capital Market Equilibrium with Investment Barriers," *Journal of Financial Economics,* 1 (December 1974), pp. 337–352.

[4] —— and Myron Scholes. "Dividend Yields and Common Stock Returns: A New Methodology," *Journal of Financial Economics,* 1 (June 1974), pp. 1–22.

[5] Michael J. Brennan. "Taxes, Market Valuation and Corporate Financial Policy," *National Tax Journal,* 23 (December 1970), pp. 417–427.

[6] —— "The Optimal Number of Securities in a Risky Asset Portfolio When There are Fixed Costs of Transacting: Theory and Some Empirical Results," *Journal of Financial and Quantitative Analysis,* 10 (September 1975), pp. 483–496.

[7] Robert S. Hamada. "Portfolio Analysis, Market Equilibrium and Corporation Finance," *Journal of Finance,* 24 (March 1969), pp. 13–31.

[8] M. C. Jensen and J. Long Jr. "Corporate Investment under Uncertainty and Pareto Optimality in the Capital Markets," *The Bell Journal of Economics and Management Science,* 3 (Spring 1972), pp. 151–174.

[9] R. C. Merton and M. G. Subrahmanyam. "The Optimality of a Competitive Stock market," *The Bell Journal of Economics and Management Science,* 5 (Spring 1974), pp. 145–170.

[10] Richard C. Stapleton and Marti G. Subrahmanyam. "Market Imperfections and Capital Market Equilibrium," Working Paper, Salomon Brothers Center for the Study of Financial Institutions, New York University, 1976.

[11] —— and —— *Capital Market Equilibrium and Corporation Finance,* JAI Press, forthcoming, 1978.

9

The role of the multinational firm in the integration of segmented capital markets*

Wayne Y. Lee and Kanwal S. Sachdeva[†]

*Source: *Journal of Finance*, 32 (May 1977), pp. 479–492.

Introduction

A capital market for asset claims is integrated when the opportunity set of investments available to each and every investor is the universe of all possible asset claims. In contrast, a capital market is segmented when certain groups of investors limit their investments to a subset of the universe of all possible asset claims. Such market segmentation can occur because of ignorance about the universe of possible asset claims, or because of transactions costs (brokerage costs, taxes, or information acquisition costs), or because of legal impediments. From an international perspective market segmentation typically occurs along national borders, a condition wherein investors in each country acquire only domestic asset claims.

Early literature on segmented capital markets—Grubel [9], Levy-Sarnat [15], Lessard [14], employing a mean-variance portfolio theoretic framework, have stressed the benefits of diversifying investments across national borders, namely the pooling of risks that results from investing in projects that are less than perfectly correlated. More recently, Subrahmanyam [21] points out, however, that when segmented capital markets are integrated, in addition to the diversification effect (always positive), there is a wealth effect (possibly negative) which arises out of changes in the macro-parameters of the risk–return relationship. Hence, in general, no statement can be made regarding the welfare implications of capital market integration without specification of the investors' utility functions. For the special cases of quadratic, exponential, and logarithmic utility functions, it can be shown[1] that international capital market integration is Pareto-optimal, that is, the welfare of individuals in the integrated economies will not decline, and will generally improve. The positive effect of an expansion in the opportunity set offsets any negative wealth effect.

The literature cited above, however, is concerned primarily with the complete and direct integration of segmented capital markets, a situation in which the opportunity to invest directly in foreign asset claims is available to individual investors of different countries. But in some important cases, especially when the segmented capital markets are associated with developed and underdeveloped economies, integration may be at best, partial and indirect. That is to say, only individuals in one country may be able to invest in foreign securities, and then only indirectly through ownership of multinational corporations (MNCs). In this context, the issues of valuation, cost of capital, and optimal foreign acquisition for a single value maximizing MNC have been the subjects of recent articles by Adler [1] and Adler–Dumas [2]. This paper reflects a continuation of the latter inquiries into the basic nature of the partial and indirect integration of segmented capital markets. Specifically, two broad questions can be raised: (i) to what extent can the MNC's foreign acquisition decisions substitute for direct foreign portfolio diversification decisions by home country individual investors to result in a welfare optimal allocation; and (ii) does a partial and indirect capital markets integration also unambiguously benefit the local investors in the foreign host countries in which the MNCs make investments.

In the subsequent discussion these questions will be addressed in the context of the mean–variance theoretic framework to permit ready comparison with the existing literature. The second section presents the assumptions and notations underlying the analysis. It is shown in the third section that indirect investment through market value maximizing MNCs can substitute for foreign portfolio diversification decisions by individual investors only under conditions of perfect competition. The resulting suboptimal welfare implication for home country investors, of foreign investment decisions by market value maximizing MNCs, under conditions of imperfect competition and restrictions on the number of MNCs, are examined in the fourth section. The fifth section considers the welfare implications of partial integration for local investors of host countries, and it is noted that these investors would generally prefer complete segmentation to partial integration. Some concluding remarks are contained in the final section.

A Model of the Partial Integration of Segmented Capital Markets

The formal analysis of the partial integration of segmented capital markets will systematically treat the two countries—two capital markets case. For this purpose the following assumptions are made.

A1 Each capital market is frictionless in the sense that asset claims (risky and riskfree) are infinitely divisible, and transactions costs (taxes included) are zero.

A2 Individual investors in each country are free to acquire domestic asset claims. But, in addition, country 1 investors can invest in country 2's asset claims either directly, or indirectly, through ownership of country 1 MNCs. A similar foreign investment opportunity is, however, not available to country 2 investors.

A3 The exchange rate between the two countries is deterministic and set equal to one.

A4 The after-tax dollar returns on the risky asset claims of both countries are normally distributed, and investors hold identical beliefs regarding the relevant security returns available to them.

A5 Individual investors of both countries have negative exponential utility functions which exhibit constant absolute risk aversion.

The first two assumptions describe the essential nature of the problem to be discussed. Assumption A3 in conjunction with A2 ensures that a one-way arbitrage process by country 1 investors or MNCs will force the equality of the riskfree rates of interest between the two countries. As will become clear later, this is in the nature of a simplifying assumption and the results obtained in the subsequent analysis will be unaffected by allowing for two different riskfree rates of interest. The normality of security returns assumption in A4 provides a sufficient justification for investors taking an expected utility approach to investment portfolio decisions, to make these decisions on the basis of expected portfolio return and variance of portfolio return, and implies that the portfolio separation property will continue to hold for each individual investor within each capital market. The homogeneity of beliefs assumption of A4 simply assures then that within each capital market, each individual investor will invest in the same two mutual funds, one of which will be the riskfree asset, and the other, in equilibrium, will be the appropriate (i.e., country 1 or country 2) "market" portfolio. Hence, there will be a unanimity or consensus of opinion among individual investors within each country, on what constitutes the welfare optimal foreign investment policy from their respective points of view. Country 1 investors may however, differ from country 2 investors on what that policy should be. Finally, assumption A5 together with the normality of security returns assumption, insures that the aggregate market price of risk for each country will be a constant. This condition will turn out to be the most crucial element of the analysis.

The variable notations that will be used in the analysis are listed below.

k = (1,2) denotes the index for a country or capital market.

ki, kj = denotes the ith investor and j^{th} firm in country k, respectively.

$\tilde{D}_k$ = denotes a column vector of uncertain after-tax dollar returns (dividends plus ending price) on country k firms arising from domestic investments.

$\overline{D}_k$ = denotes a column vector of expected after-tax dollar returns on country k firms arising from domestic investments.

Z_{lk} = is the covariance matrix of the after-tax dollar return vector of country l firms with the after-tax dollar return vector of country k firms.

Y_{lk} = is a matrix denoting the fraction of country l firms acquired by country k firms (MNCs).

$W_k, \tilde{W}_k$ = denotes a column vector of initial wealth and uncertain terminal wealth of individual investors in country k, respectively.

V_k = denotes a column vector of current market values of country k firms.

r = is one plus the riskfree rate of interest in both countries.

Additionally, the following matrix–vector operators will be defined. 1 is a column vector of ones; 0 is a column vector of zeros; e_{ki} is a column vector relating to country k with a one in the ith position and zeros elsewhere; I is an identity matrix; and $'$ together with subscript switching denotes transposition.

From the above variable definitions and the preceding assumptions, the ki^{th} investor's utility of terminal wealth can be expressed as $\tilde{u}_{ki} = -\exp[-\theta_{ki} e'_{ik} \tilde{W}_k]$, where θ_{ki} denotes the ki^{th} investor's risk aversion index. Concomitantly, since the after-tax dollar returns are normally distributed, the ki^{th} expected utility of terminal wealth is given by the relation.

$$U_{ki} = \left[-\exp \ - \theta_{ki} \left\{ e'_{ik} \overline{W}_k - (\theta_{ki}/2) e'_{ik} \overline{\overline{W}}_{kk} e_{ki} \right\} \right] \quad (2.1)$$

where $\overline{W}_k$ is the vector of country k investors' expected terminal wealth, and $\overline{W}_{kk}$ is the covariance matrix of country k investors' terminal wealth. Moreover from (2.1), it is clear that θ_{ki} simply represents the ki^{th} investor's marginal rate of substitution in expected utility terms, between risk and return—i.e., $\theta_{ki} = - [1/2][(\partial U_{ik}/\partial e'_{ik} \overline{W}_{kk} e_{ik})/(\partial U_{ik}/\partial e'_{ik} \overline{W}_k)]$.

Home Country Investor Welfare Under Perfectly Competitive Conditions

In this section, the welfare comparisons under two forms of indirect investment will be treated, namely the welfare of country one investors when they exercise control over foreign investments decisions, and their welfare when investment takes place indirectly through value maximizing MNCs under conditions perfect competition.

In both cases of indirect foreign investment, if country one MNCs financed their purchases of country 2 firms through additional home country borrowings, then the dollar returns net of interest costs on the foreign acquisitions is $\tilde{D}_1 + Y'_{12}(\tilde{D}_2 - rV_2)$. Additionally, since for each country 1 investor, the budget constraint will be binding, the $1i^{th}$ investor's uncertain terminal wealth can be written as

$$e'_{i1}\tilde{W}_1 = e'_{i1}X'_{11}[\tilde{D}_1 - rV_1 + Y'_{12}(\tilde{D}_2 - rV_2)] + re'_{i1}W_1 \quad (3.1)$$

Then, from (3.1), the $1i^{th}$ investor's mean and variance of terminal wealth are given by the relations,

$$e'_{i1}\overline{W}_1 = e'_{i1}X'_{11}[\overline{D}_1 - rV_1 + Y'_{12}(\overline{D}_2 - rV_2)] + re'_{i1}W_1 \quad (3.2)$$

$$e'_{i1}\overline{\overline{W}}_{11}e_{1i} = e'_{i1}X'_{11}[Z_{11} + Z_{12}Y_{21} + Y'_{12}Z_{21} + Y'_{12}Z_{22}Y_{21}]X_{11}e_{1i}$$

First-order conditions for maximizing the $1i^{th}$ investor's expected utility with respect to his domestic acquisition vector, by setting $\partial U_{1i}/\partial e'_{i1}X'_{11} = 0$, yields

$$0 = \theta_{1i}^{-1}[\overline{D}_1 - rV_1 + Y'_{12}(\overline{D}_2 - rV_2)] - [Z_{11} + Z_{12}Y_{21} + Y'_{12}Z_{21} + Y'_{12}Z_{22}Y_{21}]X_{11}e_{1i} \quad (3.3)$$

Since equilibrium in capital market one requires that the total demand for country 1 MNCs sum to one, we have, by summing (3.3) over all i investors in country one the $1i^{th}$ investor's holdings of country one securities as

$$X_{11}e_{1i} = \theta_{1i}^{-1}\theta_1 1 \quad (3.4)$$

while firm values in country one as

$$V_1 = r^{-1}[\overline{D}_1 + Y'_{12}(\overline{D}_2 - rV_2) - \theta_1(Z_{11} + Z_{12}Y_{21} + Y'_{12}Z_{21} + Y'_{12}Z_{22}Y_{21})1] \quad (3.5)$$

Further, the mean and variance of the $1i^{th}$ investor's final wealth can be written as

$$e'_{i1}\overline{W}_1 = \theta_{i1}^{-1}\theta_1[1'(\overline{D}_1 - rV_1) + 1'Y'_{12}(\overline{D}_2 - rV_2)] + re'_{21}W_1 \quad (3.6)$$

$$e'_{i1}\overline{\overline{W}}_{11}e_{i1} = \theta_{i1}^{-2}\theta_1^2[1'Z_{11}1 + 21'Y'_{12}Z_{21}1 + 1'Y'_{12}Z_{11}Y_{21}1]$$

Hence from (3.6), if country one investors act as price-takers with regard to the market values of country 1 and 2 firms, the firm-order conditions for expected utility maximization with respect to the foreign acquisition vector, i.e. by setting $\partial U_{12}/\partial e'_{i1}Y'_{12} = 0$, results in a consensus aggregate foreign acquisition vector given by the relation

$$Y_{21}1 = \theta_1^{-1}Z_{22}^{-1}[\overline{D}_2 - rV_2 - \theta_1 Z_{21}1] \tag{3.7}$$

Concomitantly, equations (3.5), (3.6), (3.7), determine country one investor welfare in the indirect foreign investment situation where country one investors exercise control over the foreign investment decision. The question now is, will foreign investments decisions made by market value maximizing MNCs achieve the same level of country one investor welfare.[2]

Observe that from (3.5), the market value of the $1j^{\text{th}}$ MNC is,

$$V_{1j} = e'_{j1}V_1 = [r^{-1}][e'_{j1}\{\overline{D}_1 + Y'_{12}(\overline{D}_2 - rV_2) - \theta_1(1Z_{11} + Z_{12}Y_{21} +$$

$$Y'_{12}Z_{21} + Y'_{12}Z_{22}Y_{21})1\}] \tag{3.8}$$

Writing the covariance matrix in (3.8) in more familiar looking notation

$$(Z_{11} + Z_{12}Y_{21} + Y'_{12}Z_{21} + Y'_{12}Z_{22}Y_{21})1 = \text{Cov}(\tilde{D}_{1j}, \sum_j \tilde{D}_{1j}) +$$

$$\text{Cov}(\tilde{D}_{1j}, \sum_n \sum_j Y_{nj}\tilde{D}_{2n}) + \text{Cov}(\sum_n Y_{nj}\tilde{D}_{2n}, \sum_j \tilde{D}_{1j}) +$$

$$\text{Cov}(\sum_n Y_{nj}\tilde{D}_{2n}, \sum_n \sum_j Y_{nj}\tilde{D}_{2n}) \tag{3.9}$$

where (j,n) are the indices for country 1 MNCs and country 2 firms, respectively, we see that the foreign investment decision of the $1j^{\text{th}}$ MNC will depend on what impact the $1j^{\text{th}}$ MNC perceives its foreign investment decision will have on the foreign investment decisions of the other MNCs, or alternatively, on the aggregate foreign investment level. A behavioral specification of the reactions of the other MNCs is necessary. For now, perfectly competitive behavior will be treated, with other behavioral situations considered in a subsequent section.

In the perfect competitive situation, the $1j^{\text{th}}$ MNC believes that it is unable to affect the aggregate foreign investment level by its own foreign investment decision. Alternatively stated, in the spirit of the Fama–Laffer [7] reaction principle, the $1j^{\text{th}}$ MNC perceives that the other MNCs will react in a direct counter to its own foreign investment decision. Consequently, the $1j^{\text{th}}$ MNC takes the aggregate foreign investment vector $Y_{21}1 (\equiv \sum_j Y_{nj}$ for all $n)$, to be fixed and constant. From (3.8), the first-order conditions for maximizing the $1j^{\text{th}}$ MNCs market value; i.e., by setting $\partial V_{1j}/\partial e'_{j1}Y'_{12} = 0$, yields the optimal aggregate foreign investment vector as

$$Y_{21}1 = \theta_1^{-1}Z_{22}^{-1}[\overline{D}_2 - rV_2 - \theta_1 Z_{21}1] \tag{3.10}$$

Notice that in this perfect competitive situation, the manner in which the optimal aggregate foreign investment is to be shared amongst the country 1

MNCs is indeterminate. This result is as it should be, since in a perfect competitive situation, no single MNC has an advantage over other MNCs with regard to foreign investments. More importantly, since market value maximizing MNCs under perfect competition choose the same aggregate foreign acquisition vector that country one investors would themselves make, it is clear that investor welfare in country one will be the same in the cases of indirect investments by country one investors, and indirect investments by perfectly competitive market value-maximizing MNCs.

Home Country Investor Welfare Under Imperfectly Competitive Conditions

The impact on home country investor welfare when the foreign investment decisions are made by market value maximizing MNCs under non-perfectly competitive situations, is the subject matter of this section. Specifically, the analysis will consider the following behavioral specifications: (i) Cournot behavior, (ii) Stackelberg (leader–follower) behavior and (iii) collusive behavior; first, when all country 1 firms are permitted to act as MNCs, and next, when the number of country 1 MNCs is restricted.

Contrasting the perfect competitive situation, in a Cournot environment, the $1j^{th}$ MNC perceives that the other MNC's foreign investment decisions will not change in reaction to its own foreign investment decision; i.e., that $\partial[Y_{21}1 - Y_{21}e_{1j}]/\partial[Y_{21}e_{1j}] = 0$. Hence, from (3.15) we have the first-order condition for maximizing the $1j^{th}$ MNC's market value as

$$Y_{21}e_{1j} = \theta_1^{-1}Z_{22}^{-1}[\bar{D}_2 - rV_2 - \theta_1 Z_{21}(1 + e_{1j})] - y_{21}1 \qquad (4.1)$$

Equation (4.1) is a Cournot reaction function, indicating the manner in which the $1j^{th}$ MNC's foreign investment decision will depend on the other MNC's foreign investment decisions contained in the aggregate foreign acquisition vector, $Y_{21}1$. Because of this interdependence in the foreign investment decisions by country 1 MNCs, the basic behavior assumption of the Cournot environment is rather naive. Each country 1 MNC acting as a Cournot firm behaves as if the other MNC's foreign acquisition decisions were fixed. But this is not the case, except when equilibrium has been attained following a sequence of instantaneous adjustments. It can be shown however, given the reaction function (4.1), that there will be a convergence to a stable equilibrium solution provided the number of adjustments is arbitrarily large.[3] The optimal aggregate foreign acquisition vector in equilibrium will be given as

$$Y_{21}1 = \theta_1^{-1}Z_{22}^{-1}\left[\left(\frac{n}{n+1}\right)(\bar{D}_2 - rV_2) - \theta_1 Z_{21}1\right] \qquad (4.2)$$

which not surprisingly, is the summation of (4.1) over all country 1 MNCs.

Another form of oligopolistic competition, suggested by Stackelberg, is a situation wherein one firm, say the $1j^{th}$ MNC, because of size or superior management skills, acts as a leader and all other MNCs, as followers. Thus, the $1j^{th}$ MNC, as the leader firm, maximizes its market value taking into explicit account the reactions of the other MNCs to its own foreign investment decision. The other MNCs, as the follower firms are assumed to behave in a Cournot fashion, and thereby have reaction functions of the form expressed in (4.1). Summing (4.1) over all country 1 MNCs except for $1j^{th}$, and noting that

$$\sum_{\substack{1k \\ 1k \neq 1j}} Z_{21}e_{1k} = Z_{21}1 - Z_{21}e_{1j} \tag{4.3}$$

$$\sum_{\substack{1k \\ 1k \neq 1j}} Y_{21}e_{1k} = Y_{21}1 - Y_{21}e_{1j}$$

we can rewrite $Y_{21}1$ in the market value expression of the $1j^{th}$ MNC, (3.8), as

$$Y_{21} = \frac{n-1}{n}\theta_1^{-1}Z_{22}^{-1}\left[\overline{D}_2 - rV_2 - \frac{n}{n-1}\theta_1 Z_{21}1 - \frac{1}{n-1}\theta_1 Z_{21}e_{1j}\right]$$
$$+ \frac{1}{n}Y_{21}e_{1j} \tag{4.4}$$

First-order condition for maximizing the $1j^{th}$ MNC's market value, yields the $1j^{th}$ MNC's optimal foreign acquisition decision as

$$Y_{21}e_{1j} = \tfrac{1}{2}\theta_1^{-1}Z_{22}^{-1}[\overline{D}_2 - rV_2 - 2\theta_1 Z_{21}e_{1j}] \tag{4.5}$$

Substituting (4.5) into (4.4), the optimal aggregate foreign acquisition vector can be derived as

$$Y_{21}1 = \left(\frac{2n-1}{2n}\right)\theta_1^{-1}Z_{22}^{-1}\left[\overline{D}_2 - rV_2 - \left(\frac{2n}{2n-1}\right)\theta_1 Z_{21}1\right] \tag{4.6}$$

Lastly, let us consider the situation wherein all country 1 MNCs collude and jointly act to maximize aggregate market value. Utilizing the aggregate market value of all country 1 MNCs, V_1, from (3.5), the first-order condition for maximizing the aggregate market value of all country 1 MNCs, by setting $\partial V_1/\partial 1'Y'_{12} = 0$, yields the optimal foreign aggregate acquisition vector as

$$Y_{21}1 = (\tfrac{1}{2})\theta_1^{-1}Z_{22}^{-1}[\overline{D}_2 - rV_2 - 2\theta_1 Z_{21}1] \tag{4.7}$$

Table 9.1 Optimal foreign aggregate acquisition vectors when all Country 1 firms are MNCs

$$Y_{21} 1 = K\theta_1^{-1} Z_{22}^{-1} (\overline{D}_2 - rV_2) - Z_{22}^{-1} Z_{21} 1$$

$$K = \begin{cases} 1 & \text{Perfect Competition} \\ n/(n+1) & \text{Cournot} \\ (2n-1)/2n & \text{Stackelberg (Leader-Follower)} \\ 1/2 & \text{Collusion} \end{cases}$$

For convenience, the optimal foreign aggregate acquisition vectors for the alternative competitive environments, when all country 1 firms are permitted to act as MNCs, are summarized in Table 9.1.

The optimal foreign acquisition vectors, for the same imperfect competitive environments considered previously, can be developed in a similar manner for the case when the number of country 1 MNCs is restricted.[4] The results are presented in Table 9.2, where $1j = 1,2, \ldots, p$ are the country 1 firms that are allowed to act as MNCs. Note from Table 9.2 that when the number of country 1 MNCs is limited to one; i.e., $p = 1$, then $Z_{21}^* 1 = Z_{21} e_{1j}$ and the optimal foreign acquisition vectors is given as: $Y_{21} 1 = Y_{21} e_{1j} = (1/2)\theta_1^{-1} Z_{22}^{-1} [\overline{D}_2 - rV_2 - \theta_1 Z_{21}(1 + e_{1j})]$, which is the Adler–Dumas [2] result.[5] Assuming the same market price of risk in both countries, Adler–Dumas interpret the factor, $(1/2)$, as implying a greater risk-aversion on the part of the MNC with regard to country 2 investments, compared to local country 2 investors whose aggregate demand[6] is given as: $X_{21} 1 = \theta_2^{-1} [\overline{D}_2 - rV_2]$. It is clear from our analysis, however, that the factor, $(1/2)$ arises not because the MNC is a foreign entity in contrast to local country 2 investors, but rather, as a consequence of restrictions on the number of MNCs. Moreover, supposing that the dollar returns on country 1 and 2 firms are sufficiently positively correlated so that $Z_{21} 1 - Z_{21}^* 1$ is positive, then a comparison of the optimal foreign aggregate acquisition vectors contained in Tables 9.1 and 9.2 indicates that the effect of a restric-

Table 9.2 Optimal foreign aggregate acquisition vectors when the number of Country 1 MNCs is restricted

$$Y_{21} 1 = K^0 \theta_1^{-1} Z_{22}^{-1} (\overline{D}_2 - rV_2) - Z_{22}^{-1} Z_{21} 1 + K^1 Z_{22}^{-1} (Z_{21}^* 1 - Z_{21} 1)$$

	K^0	K^1
Cournot	$p/(p+1)$	$1/(p+1)$
Stackelberg (Leader-Follower)	$(2p-1)/2p$	$1/2p$
Collusion	$1/2$	$1/2$

Note: $Z_{21}^* 1 \equiv \Sigma_{1j=1}^p Z_{21} e_{1j}$

tion on the number of MNCs is to make the MNCs behave less risk-adversely than they otherwise would.

To properly assess, however, the impact on country 1 investor welfare of foreign investment decisions made by market value maximizing MNCs under imperfectly competitive conditions, we need to derive the market value of country 2 firms. Since country 2 investors invest in domestic securities exclusively, the mean and variance of the $2i^{th}$ investor's terminal wealth are

$$e'_{i2} \overline{W}_2 = e'_{i2} X'_{22} [\overline{D}_2 - rV_2] + e'_{i2} rW_2 \tag{4.8}$$

$$e'_{i2} \overline{\overline{W}}_{22} e_{2i} = e'_{i2} X'_{22} [Z_{22}] X_{22} e_{2i}$$

First-order conditions for maximizing the $2i^{th}$ investor's expected utility with respect to the acquisition vector for domestic securities, obtained by setting $\partial U_{2i} / \partial e'_{i2} X'_{22} = 0$, yields the portfolio conditions

$$0 = \theta_{2i}^{-1} \theta_2 [\overline{D}_2 - rV_2] - Z_{22} X_{22} e_{2i} \tag{4.9}$$

Since equilibrium in the country two capital market requires that the aggregate demand for country two securities by investors in both countries must sum to unity, i.e., $X_{22}1 + Y_{21}1 = 1$, it follows from (4.9) that the market value of country 2 firms is

$$V_2 = [r^{-1}][\overline{D}_2 - \theta_2 Z_{22}(1 - Y_{21}1)] \tag{4.10}$$

Moreover substituting (3.10) into (3.5) we obtain the equilibrium market value of country 1 firms as

$$V_1 = [r^{-1}][\overline{D}_1 - \theta_1(Z_{11}1 + Z_{12} Y_{21}1)] \tag{4.11}$$

Utilizing (4.7), (4.10), and (3.5), the country 1 investor's mean and variance of final wealth in market equilibrium are

$$e'_{i1} \overline{W}_1 = \theta_{i1}^{-1} \theta_1 [\theta_1(1'Z_{11}1 + 1'Z_{12} Y_{21}1) + \theta_1 1' Y'_{12} Z_{21}1 + \theta_1 1' Y'_{12} Z_{22}$$
$$Y_{21}1] + re'_{21} W_1 \tag{4.12}$$

$$e'_{i1} \overline{\overline{W}}_1 e_{12} = \theta_{i1}^{-2} \theta_1^2 [1'Z_{11}1 + 21' Y'_{12} Z_{21}1 + 1' Y'_{12} Z_{22} Y_{21}1]$$

where

$$Y_{21}1 = (\theta_1 + K\theta_2)^{-1}(K\theta_2 1 - \theta_1 Z_{22}^{-1} Z_{21}1). \tag{4.13}$$

Hence, recalling the expression for the ki^{th} individual's expected utility given by (2.1), it can be easily shown that the $1i^{th}$ investor's expected utility

Figure 9.1 $1i^{th}$ investor's expected utility under alternative competitive environments

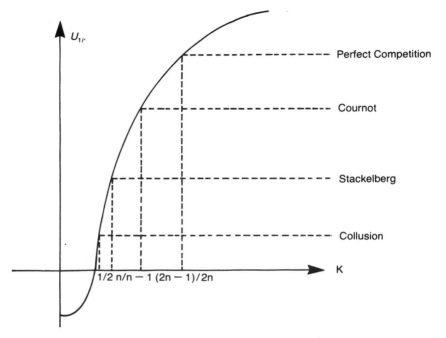

is non-linear in K. But, provided $Y_{21}1$ is monotone increasing in K,[7] the $1i^{th}$ investor's expected utility will be quasi-concave in K as depicted in Figure 9.1.

Consequently it is clear that country 1 investor welfare, is least when country 1 MNCs collude, and is higher under a Cournot compared to a Stackelberg situation. In the Cournot and Stackelberg environments, however, the divergence from the welfare optimal situation will be small, the larger the number of MNCs permitted. It should be noted also that country 1 investor welfare under perfect competition is not an interior maximum, but rather one which saturates the resource availability constraint, $1'V_1 = $ constant, concomitant with price-taking behavior with respect to country 2 firm market values.

Similarly, the foreign investment decisions by market value maximizing MNC's under imperfect competitive conditions and restrictions on the number of MNCs permitted, will in general, result in suboptimal welfare for country 1 investors. Direct welfare comparisons to the imperfectly competitive but unrestricted case is not possible, however, because as pointed out earlier, the MNCs in the restricted case, to some extent compensate by behaving less risk adversely, when dollar returns between country 1 and 2 firms are sufficiently positively correlated.

Host Country Investor Welfare

The effect of partial integration on investor welfare in country two will now be evaluated. In order to do this, first observe that by summing over all $2i$ in equation (4.9), and utilizing equation (4.10), we have the country two investor's portfolio holdings to be

$$Y_{22}e_{2i} = \theta_{2i}^{-1}\theta_2[1 - Y_{21}1] \qquad (5.1)$$

Substitution of (5.1) in (4.8) provides expressions for the mean and variance of final wealth as a function of the aggregate foreign acquisition vector.

$$e_{i2}'\overline{W}_2 = \theta_{2i}^{-1}\theta_2[1' - 1'Y_{12}'][\overline{D}_2 - rV_2] + e_{i2}'rW_2 \qquad (5.2)$$

$$e_{i2}'\overline{\overline{W}}_{22}e_{2i} = \theta_{2i}^{-2}\theta_2^2[1' - 1'Y_{12}'][Z_{22}][1 - Y_{21}1]$$

We can now address the following question. If country two investors could decide on whether to permit foreign investors into the country or not, would they favor partial integration or complete segmentation of capital markets?

First-order conditions for expected utility maximization or minimization with respect to the aggregate foreign acquisition vector are given by setting $\partial U_{2i}/\partial 1'Y_{12}' = 0$.

$$0 = \theta_2^{-1}[\overline{D}_2 - rV_2] - Z_{22}[1 - Y_{21}1] \qquad (5.3)$$

Equation (5.3) is always satisfied in equilibrium by virtue of the nature of market clearing conditions when capital markets are partially integrated.[8] However, we note that the Hessian matrix of second derivatives is Z_{22}, the variance–covariance matrix of dividends from country two securities, which is positive–definite, so long as no two securities have returns that are perfectly correlated. Consequently, (5.3) represents a minimization rather than maximization expected utility.

Since partial integration leads to expected utility minimization for country two investors, complete segmentation will generally bé preferred over partial integration of capital markets. Exceptions to this rule occurs only when (i) foreign investment is permitted but country one investors choose not to make any foreign investments or (ii) investments in country 2 are characterized by constant returns to scale. Both situations have the effect of insuring that the market value of country 2 firms to country 2 investors is independent of country 1 MNCs foreign investment decisions, thereby mitigating the effect of such decisions on country 2 investor welfare. In the first situation, by setting $Y_{21}1 = 0$, in (4.12) we obtain the general condition under which no foreign investment to take place as

$$K\theta_2 Z_{21}1 = \theta_1 Z_{21}1 \qquad (5.4)$$

But, since $K = 1$ in (5.4) corresponds to partial integration with foreign investment that is welfare optimal for country one investors, the condition simplifies to

$$\theta_2 Z_{22}1 = \theta_1 Z_{21}1 \qquad (5.5)$$

Namely, that if the risk premium for each country two security is evaluated identically in both capital markets, then no foreign investment will take place. In contrast, in the second situation, we note that under stochastic constant returns to scale, the total dividends of a country 2 firm are not fixed but rather, will vary in direct proportion to the amount of invested capital. That is to say, the dividends accruing to country 2 investors on the $2j^{th}$ firm, $\tilde{D}_{2j}$, is equal to $e'_{j2}(1 - 1'Y'_{12})\tilde{D}_{2j}$, and the market value to country 2 investors of the $2j^{th}$ firm, $\hat{V}_{2j}$, is equal to $e'_{j2}(1 - 1'Y'_{12})V_{2j}$, are such that $\tilde{D}_{2j}/\hat{V}_{2j} = \tilde{D}_{2j}/V_{2j} = \tilde{\rho}_{2j}$. Then resolving the country 2 investor's portfolio problem in terms of the mean and variance of their own dividend receipts from country 2 firms, i.e. $(\tilde{D}_{2i}\hat{Z}_{22})$, it can be verified that the market value of country 2 firms to country 2 investors, i.e. $\hat{V}_2$, are unaffected by country 1 MNCs foreign investment decisions. Hence, country 1 MNCs foreign investment decisions will have no impact on country 2 investor welfare. The intuitive explanation for this result is simply that if the total dividends of country 2 firms are fixed, the more the fractional ownership by country 1 MNCs of country 2 firms, the less is available from these dividends as a return to invested capital to local country 2 residents.[9] This reduction in the opportunity set available to country 2 investors is removed under the assumption of stochastic constant returns to scale.

Conclusions

The level of welfare, achieved by investors in country one when exercising direct control over foreign investment decisions, is also attained through indirect foreign investment by value-maximizing MNCs under conditions of perfect competition. Thus, the MNC performs the useful function of making welfare-optimal investment decisions on behalf of investors, and in this role provides a purely *financial* rationale for the MNC. In conditions, other than perfect competition, however, value-maximizing MNCs do not make welfare-optimal foreign investment decisions. Further, while the welfare of country one investors generally improves when completely segmented capital markets are partially integrated, the welfare of country two investors is reduced. But if the risk premium on each country two security is evaluated identically in both countries, or investments in country 2 are characterized by stochastic constant returns to scale, then country two investors will be indifferent between complete segmentation and partial integration of international capital markets.

The usefulness of the results obtained in this paper must be qualified by the fairly restrictive assumptions on which the analysis is based. In addition to the usual assumptions of the CAPM, we have assumed equal risk-free rates in both countries, a non-stochastic foreign exchange rate and a constant market price of risk. The assumption of equal risk-free rates simplifies the equations. If we begin with unequal risk-free rates in each country, the final equilibrium solutions will contain a weighted average of the initial risk-free rates. Apart from making our equations more complex, there is no reason for unequal risk-free rates to make any difference in our analysis. The assumption of a non-stochastic exchange rate, however, is necessary because a stochastic exchange rate introduces multiplicative risk on foreign investments of country one investors. With multiplicative risk, the assumption of normally distributed dividends, for investors in both countries, is no longer tenable because the product of two random variables is not necessarily normally distributed even if both random variables are normally distributed individually. Finally, the assumption of a constant market price of risk is crucial to our analysis. Firm values are a function of the market price of risk and, in order to maximize their value, firms must take into account possible changes in the market price of risk, as a result of their investment decisions. For general utility functions, the market price of risk is a function of the mean and variance of final wealth of each investor. Therefore, the MNC would need to have detailed knowledge of investor preferences as well as each investor's initial wealth, in order to make welfare-optimal investment decisions. With exponential utility functions, this problem does not arise because the market price of risk can be treated as a constant which is known to every firm.

Notes

[†] Comments by Michael Adler and Bernard Dumas on an earlier draft of this paper are gratefully acknowledged.

1 See Subrahmanyam [21].

2 Country 2 security prices are arrived at in the same manner for both indirect investment situations and hence are irrelevant provided the aggregate foreign acquisition vectors are identical.

3 For proof, see Lee-Sachdeva, [12], Appendix I.

4 See Lee-Sachdeva [12], Appendix II.

5 See their equation (8).

6 Obtained by summing (2.14) over all country 2 investors.

7 Assuming that the demand for country 2 securities by country 2 investors is positive, i.e. $X_{22}1 = 1 - Y_{21}1 > 0$.

8 I.e., by summing (4.9) over all $2i$ and imposing market clearing conditions (4.10).

9 See Goldberg and Lee [8].

References

[1]   M. Adler. "The Cost of Capital and Valuation of a Two-Country Firm" *Journal of Finance*, Vol. 29, No. 1, (March 1974).

[2]   M. Adler and B. Dumas. "Optimal International Acquisitions," *Journal of Finance*, Vol. 30, No. 1 (March 1975).

[3]   K. J. Arrow and F. H. Hahn. *General Competitive Analysis*, (San Francisco: Holden-Day, 1971).

[4]   F. Black. "International Capital Market Equilibrium with Investment Barriers," *Journal of Financial Economics*, Vol. 1, No. 4 (1974).

[5]   R. A. Cohn and J. J. Pringle. "Imperfections in International Financial Markets: Implications for Risk Premia and the Cost of Capital to Firms," *Journal of Finance*, Vol. 28 (1975).

[6]   E. Fama. "Perfect Competition and Optimal Production Decisions under Uncertainty," *The Bell Journal of Economics and Management Science*, Vol. 3, No. 2 (Autumn 1972).

[7]   E. Fama and A. Laffer. "The Number of Firms and Competition," *American Economic Review*, Vol. 62 (September 1972).

[8]   M. Goldberg and W. Y. Lee. "The Cost of Capital and Valuation of a Two-Country Firm: Comment," *Journal of Finance*, forthcoming.

[9]   H. G. Grubel. "Internationally Diversified Portfolios: Welfare Gains and Capital Flows," *American Economic Review*, Vol. 58, No. 5 (1968).

[10] M. C. Jensen and J. B. Long Jr. "Corporate Investment under Uncertainty and Pareto Optimality in the Capital Markets," *The Bell Journal of Economics and Management Science*, Vol. 3, No. 1 (Spring 1972).

[11] W. Y. Lee. "Oligopoly and Entry," *Journal of Economic Theory*, Vol. II, No. 1 (August 1975).

[12] W. Y. Lee and K. S. Sachdeva. "The Role of the Multinational Firm in the Integration of Segmented Capital Markets," Indiana University, Discussion Paper No. 57 (July 1976).

[13] H. E. Leland. "Production Theory and the Stock Market," *The Bell Journal of Economics and Management Science*, Vol. 5, No. 1 (Spring 1974).

[14] D.R. Lessard. "International Portfolio Diversification: Multivariate Analyses for a ses for a of Latin-American Countries," *Journal of Finance*, Vol. 28, No. 3 (June 1973).

[15] H. Levy and M. Sarnat. "International Diversification of Investment Portfolios," *American Economic Review*, Vol. 60, No. 4 (1970).

[16] J. B. Long Jr. "Wealth, Welfare and the Price of Risk," *Journal of Finance*, Vol. 27, No. 2 (May 1972).

[17] R. C. Merton and M. G. Subrahmanyam. "The Optimality of a Competitive Stock Market," *The Bell Journal of Economics and Management Science*, Vol. 5, No. 1 (Spring 1974).

[18] R. Radner, "A Note on Unanimity of Stockholders' Preferences Among Alternative Production Plans: A Reformulation of the Ekern--Wilson Model," *The Bell Journal of Economics and Management Science*, Vol. 5, No. 1 (Spring 1974).

[19] B. H. Solnik. "An Equilibrium Model of the International Capital Market," Research Paper No. 129, Graduate School of Business, Stanford University (1972).

[20] ——— "International Pricing of Risk: An Empirical Investigation of the World Capital Market Structure," *Journal of Finance*, Vol. 29, No. 2, (May 1974). 1974).

[21] M. G. Subrahmanyam. "On the Optimality of International Capital Market Integration," *Journal of Financial Economics*, Vol. 2, pp. 3–28 (1975).

10

Investor Recognition of Corporate International Diversification*

Tamir Agmon and Donald R. Lessard[†]

*Source: *Journal of Finance*, 32 (September 1977), pp. 1049–1055.

In the presence of barriers to portfolio capital flows, multinational firms (MNCs) have an advantage relative to single-country firms because of their ability to diversify internationally. This financial advantage—the result of financial market imperfections–complements the advantages MNCs derive from imperfections in real goods and factor markets and represents an additional motive for multinational expansion.[1] This paper argues that such barriers do exist and provides empirical support for the diversification motive by showing that investors appear to recognize the extent of multinational diversification of a sample of U.S. firms listed on the New York Stock Exchange.

Relevance of International Diversification at the Corporate Level

The benefits of international diversification at the investor level are well documented (e.g., [3], [8], and [16]). However, the mere presence of less than perfect correlations among company earnings and/or asset values in various countries is insufficient to establish that international diversification is relevant at the corporate level. Two further conditions must be satisfied: 1) there must exist greater barriers or costs to portfolio capital flows than to capital flows forming part of the direct investment package; and 2) investors must recognize that MNCs provide a diversification opportunity which otherwise is not available.

If there were no barriers to international capital flows, and if capital markets were uniformly well developed, investors would diversify their portfolio holdings internationally and required rates of return on securities (projects) would reflect only their contributions to the risk of a fully diversified world portfolio. Under such circumstances, diversification at the firm level would be of no consequence and the required rate of return on a particular project would be the same whether it was undertaken by an MNC or a local firm.[2]

Verifying the Diversification Motive

In order to verify the existence of a diversification motive for multinational expansion by corporations, we seek to determine if the two conditions cited above are true. In the case of the first condition, we observe that there are numerous examples of barriers to portfolio flows which are or have been more stringent than those applying to direct investment flows.[3] Further, the flexibility of the MNC in shifting revenue-producing resources among its operating units suggests that even when barriers are nominally the same, direct investment flows will be freer than portfolio flows.[4] Although these observations are not conclusive, they lend substantial support to the first condition. We concentrate on the second condition, whether investors appear to recognize the diversification opportunities provided by MNC shares. We do this by investigating the share price behavior of a sample of U.S.-based MNCs.

Direct measures of the existence and magnitude of the diversification motive based on the pattern of MNC expansion are avoided since the diversification motive coexists with motives resulting from imperfections in product and real factor markets. As a result, in many cases it is consistent with the same patterns of expansion explained by alternative hypotheses and cannot be isolated empirically.[5] For example, the foreign investment "balance sheet" of the United States, characterized by a preponderance of outward FDI and inward foreign portfolio investment (FPI), has been explained in terms of real goods and factor market relationships, but the same pattern is consistent with the argument outlined above. The U.S. investor, seeking diversification but facing relatively less efficient capital markets abroad and barriers imposed by legal restrictions as well as by a lack of previous foreign investment experience, would prefer to diversify by purchasing shares of U.S.-based MNCs which include claims on foreign operations while non-U.S. investors, to whom the U.S. market appears quite open and efficient, would diversify by purchasing shares in U.S. firms. Direct measures based on the risk adjusted performance of the shares of multinational firms relative to single-country firms suffer from similar drawbacks.[6]

Investor Recognition of MNC Diversification

Since the shares of U.S.-based MNCs represent claims on foreign as well as domestic activities, one would expect share price movements to reflect this fact. If prices behave as if the market does not distinguish between firms with different degrees of international involvement, one would have to conclude that as far as the American equity market is concerned, international diversification of activities does not matter. On the other hand, if the movements of share prices indicate that the market perceives international corporations as different than those less internationally inclined, this evidence, in combination with evidence of barriers to capital flows, lends support to the view that the MNC's ability to diversify internationally is an advantage.

The Relationship Between Share-Price Behavior and the Extent of International Involvement

Fluctuations in share prices reflect events (i.e., new information) which change expectations of the future cash flows of corporations or the mechanism by which these future cash flows are capitalized by investors in the market. For purposes of exposition, it is useful to classify fluctuations within a single economy as those resulting from three arbitrarily defined types of effects—those which affect virtually all stocks (although perhaps to a different degree), those which affect certain groups of stocks such as industries, and those specific to single stocks. The first type of effect is the main component of the systematic risk which cannot be eliminated by diversification. Thus the most important relationships between returns on securities can be described in terms of a "market model":

$$\tilde{R}_{jt} = \alpha_j + \beta_j \tilde{R}_{mt} + \tilde{\epsilon}_{jt} \tag{1}$$

where $\tilde{R}_{jt}$ is the return on security j (a random variable) in period t. $\tilde{R}_{mt}$ is the return on the market index, α_j and β_j are parameters for security j, and $\tilde{\epsilon}_{jt}$ is a random variable with a zero mean, and $\text{Cov}(\tilde{\epsilon}_i, \tilde{\epsilon}_j) = 0$, $\text{Cov}(\tilde{R}_j, \tilde{\epsilon}_j) = 0$.

Internationally, the structure of returns appears to be more complex. Returns on securities within each domestic market appear to be reasonably well described by the market model, but they are related internationally through a world factor.[7] In this case the interdependence of changes in the prices of securities in the international market can be summarized in terms of an "international market model";

$$\tilde{R}_{jk} = \alpha_j + \beta_{jk} \tilde{R}_k + \gamma_j \tilde{R}_w + \tilde{\epsilon}_j \tag{2}$$

where $\tilde{R}_{jk}$ is the return on security j from country k, and where time subscripts were dropped for simplicity, $\tilde{R}_k$ is the return on the country k market factor, and $\tilde{R}_w$ is the return on the world market excluding country k (i.e. the rest of the world).

If we view an international firm as a collection of activities in different countries, then the return on its traded shares can be described as:

$$\tilde{R}_j = \alpha_j + \sum_{i=1}^{N} w_{jr}\beta_{ji}\tilde{R}_i + \gamma_j\tilde{R}_w + \tilde{\epsilon}_j \tag{3}$$

where the $\tilde{R}_i$ represent the market factors for each of the N countries in which firm j generates proportion w_{ji} of its revenues ($\Sigma_i w_i = 1$). Equation (3) implies a direct relationship between the international composition of the firm's activities and the pattern of the price changes of its shares. Unfortunately such a complex relationship would be difficult to test due to the lack of necessary data and the need for a more specific and explicit international valuation model.

In this section we take a more modest and preliminary step. We test the proposition that securities of firms with relatively large international operations are more closely related to the rest of the world market factor and less to their home country factor than shares of firms which are essentially domestic. We expect this since non-U.S. activities should be reflected by a dependence on the rest of the world factor and the appropriate country factors, but not by dependence on the U.S. country factor. Therefore, the higher the proportion of non-U.S. activities, the lower the dependence on the U.S. country factor. Further, since the rest of the world factor by construction does not reflect U.S. activities, it should become more important as non-U.S. activities increase. Thus an examination of the relationship between security price changes and the domestic and the rest of the world factors, controlling for the degree of international involvement, provides a partial and indirect test of whether the international composition of a firm's operations is reflected in the market behavior of its securities.[8] Thus the return on the shares of a U.S.-based MNC may be thought of as arising from the following relationship:

$$\tilde{R}_{js} = \alpha_j + \beta_{js}\tilde{R}_{us} + \gamma_{js}\tilde{R}_w + \tilde{\epsilon}_j \tag{4}$$

where $\tilde{R}_{js}$ = return on the share of the jth corporation with a proportion s of non-U.S. sales, $\tilde{R}_{us}$ the return of the NYSE index, and $\tilde{R}_w$ the return of the rest of the world index, defined to be orthogonal to $\tilde{R}_{us}$.

We test the hypothesis that β_{js} is a decreasing function of s, and that γ_{js} is an increasing function of s.

Empirical Results

In order to test the hypothesis that security returns reflect the international composition of a firm's activities, monthly returns (ending stock price plus cash dividend, divided by the previous price) for 168 months from January 1959 to October 1972, and an estimate of the proportion of a firm's revenue from non-U.S. sources were obtained for a sample of 217 U.S. firms. The firms were then ranked according to the degree of international

Table 10.1 Dependence of monthly returns on U.S. and world indexes
$R_j = \alpha_j + \beta_j \tilde{R}_{us} + \gamma_j \tilde{R}_w + \tilde{\epsilon}_j$

Portfolio no.	Proportion of sales outside the U.S. (%)	β (U.S.)	Std. er. of β	γ (world)	Std. er. of γ	R^2 of regression
1	1–7	1.04	.03	.16	.09	.898
2	7–10	1.06	.03	−.11	.10	.884
3	10–13	.98	.03	.13	.08	.894
4	13–17	.82	.03	.56	.08	.861
5	17–21	.98	.03	.18	.10	.866
6	21–25	.98	.03	.20	.10	.856
7	25–28	.82	.03	.50	.09	.853
8	29–35	.99	.03	.30	.10	.872
9	35–42	.86	.03	.59	.10	.820
10	43–62	.88	.03	.60	.09	.864

activity and grouped in deciles in order to reduce the influence of differences other than the extent of international activity. The composite return series for the resultant portfolios (about 20 stocks were included in each one) were regressed on the indexes for the U.S. stock market and the rest of the world.[9] To obtain the latter, the Capital International world index was regressed on to the New York Stock Exchange index and the residuals of this regression were defined as the "rest of the world" stock market index. The results of this regression are presented in Table 10.1 above.

The data presented in Table 10.1 shows that those portfolios with a high degree of international involvement, measured by proportion of sales outside the U.S., have relatively high γ's, the coefficient relating the changes in the share price to the rest of the world index (not including the U.S.). Moreover, the higher the level of international involvement, the more statistically significant is the γ coefficient. Similarly, the β coefficient relating the returns on each of the portfolios to the U.S. index are much higher for those portfolios with little international involvement.[10] This evidence supports the hypothesis that the market recognizes the geographically diversified nature of the U.S.-based international corporations as well as the extent of their international involvement.

These results, however, are only indicative since they do not show whether the observed differences in β's and γ's are statistically significant. Further, although the grouping of stocks into portfolios is useful for isolating the impact of the extent of international activity, it does not lend itself easily to such a test. Therefore, we performed a two-stage regression on individual stock data to test the relationship between a firm's national dependence (β_j) and international dependence (γ_j) on its degree of international involvement.

In the first stage, β_j and γ_j were determined for each of the 217 securities using equation (4). In the second stage the β_j's and γ_j's were related to IS, the international sales ratio, in two separate equations:

$$\beta_j = a_j + b_j\text{IS} + u_j \qquad\qquad (5\,a)$$

$$\gamma_j = a'_j + b'_j\text{IS} + u'_j \qquad\qquad (5\,b)$$

The evidence presented in Table 10.1 suggests that b_j will be negative and that b'_j will be positive.[11] A summary of the two-stage regression is presented in Table 10.2 below.

Table 10.2 U.S. and world dependence as a function of international involvement

b_j *(U.S. dependence)*	b'_j *(world dependence)*
−.010	.012
T statistic	*T* statistic
−3.98	4.42
F statistic (1,215)	*F* statistic (1,215)
15.91	19.52
R-squared	*R*-squared
.069	.083

Both b_j and b'_j have the expected sign and are statistically significant at a 5 percent level.

Conclusions

The results support the hypothesis that U.S. investors recognize the international composition of the activities of U.S.-based corporations. This is only a first step towards a specification of the relationship between real corporate variables, such as the international distribution of operations, and capital market variables, such as changes in share prices. However, when coupled with the observation that MNCs often can diversify internationally at a lower cost than portfolio investors, it suggests that the diversification motive should be given more serious consideration than has been the case to date.

Notes

[†] This paper was written while Dr. Agmon was a Visiting Professor at the Sloan School of Management, M.I.T. We would like to thank Michael Adler, Fischer

Black, Dennis Logue, James Paddock, Robert Pindyck, Alan Rugman and Marshall Blume, a reviewer for the *Journal of Finance*, for helpful comments and Alex Henry for computational assistance.

1. It is generally acknowledged that in order to justify foreign investment, the multinational corporation must have some advantage relative to local firms in the countries in which it invests which allows it to overcome the costs imposed by cultural and geographical distance not borne by local firms. Most economists have argued that the primary sources of advantages of MNCs relative to local firms are imperfections in markets for products and factors of production, generally excluding capital. Reviews of the theory of foreign investment are provided by Dunning [2], Kindleberger [7], Ragazzi [13], and Stevens [17]. The benefits of international diversification were introduced into the literature by Grubel [3]. Ragazzi [13] and Rugman [14] extend them to FDI.

2. Myers [12] provides a clear argument for this case in reference to the domestic conglomerates. Others, including Lewellyn [10] and Hughes, Logue and Sweeney [5], have argued that diversification at the corporate level is advantageous since it increases a firm's debt capacity. However, this conclusion has been questioned on the grounds that when a firm which has outstanding debt diversifies, it increases the value of the debt and thus reduces the value of equity. See for example Higgins and Schall [4].

3. These may include formal "border" barriers such as the U.S. IET, formal internal barriers such as SEC registration requirements, informal border barriers resulting from investor tradition and/or lack of information, and informal internal barriers which would include relatively undeveloped or inefficient domestic capital markets.

4. Foreign direct investment often involves transfers of intangible factors of production such as technology or managerial skills. To the extent that these real transfers are not paid for in cash, they are accompanied by financial transfers, usually of a risk-bearing nature since the eventual payment for the factors involved is contingent on future outcomes. Clearly, such inward transfers are not captured by controls over financial flows. Remittances of profits from these transferred resources often will not be restricted and even if they are, the MNC has a number of options for bypassing such restrictions, especially transfer pricing of goods and factors of production.

5. This problem has plagued most empirical research on the motivation for multinational expansion. For a critical review of these studies, see Stevens [17].

6. This approach faces the same empirical difficulties as tests of the capital asset pricing model in the domestic context as well as the yet unresolved issue of specifying an appropriate international capital asset pricing model. For a review of the first set of issues, see Jensen [6], for the second Agmon [1], and Solnik [15]. Hughes, Logue, and Sweeney [5] raise a series of interesting issues in this regard.

7. Agmon [1], Lessard [8], and Solnik [15] explore the international structure of returns. All conclude that country elements are very strong and industry elements of little importance. However, they do not accept a common definition of the world market factor nor do they resolve whether price changes of individual stocks are directly related to the world factor or are related only indirectly through the respective domestic market factors.

8. It should be emphasized that our analysis is restricted to determining the impact of degree of a firm's international involvement on the relationship of its stock's movements with general ᛌdomestic and world market effects. It does not encompass tests of the relationship between the stock's riskiness and average return over time. Hughes, Logue, and Sweeney [5] interpret similar results as showing that

stocks are priced internationally rather than domestically. While this is an attractive hypothesis, this interpretation can be questioned on several grounds.

9. The monthly holding period returns for individual stocks are from the CRSP monthly file, the U.S. index is a market-value weighted index for the New York Stock Exchange also from the CRSP file, and the world market index is the Capital International World index, a market-value weighted index of the major securities listed on the 18 most important national stock markets. The foreign activity measures, proportion of sales generated outside of the U.S., were taken from Standard and Poor's *The Outlook* (August 13, 1973). The ideal measure of foreign activity would be proportion of total market value represented by non-U.S. operations, sales, etc. However, for obvious reasons this number is not available— nor is it known by the firms in question. Other measures such as assets, employees, or profits appear to be even further from the ideal than sales. The international distribution of profits, for example, is arbitrary since it depends on transfer prices, overhead allocations, and various accounting conventions regarding recognition of foreign activities. However, the grouping procedure employed should alleviate some of the problems associated with the foreign activity measure.

10. Similar relationships hold when the 14-year period was split into two seven-year periods.

11. β_j and γ_j are regression coefficients themselves and hence are measured with error. However, to the extent that this error is uncorrelated with IS, it will not bias the estimates of b and b' but will reduce the t-statistics.

References

[1]   T. Agmon. "The Relations Among Equity Markets: A Study of Share Price Co-Movements in the U.S., U.K., Germany and Japan," *The Journal of Finance* (September 1972).

[2]   J. H. Dunning. "The Determinants of International Production", *Oxford Economic Papers* (January 1973).

[3]   H. G. Grubel. "Internationally Diversified Portfolios", *The American Economic Review* (December 1968).

[4]   R. C. Higgins and L. D. Schall. "Corporate Bankruptcy and Conglomerate Merger", *Journal of Finance* (March 1975).

[5]   J. S. Hughes, D. E. Logue, and R. J. Sweeney. "Corporate International Diversification and Market Assigned Measures of Risk and Diversification", *Journal of Financial and Quantitative Analysis* (November 1975).

[6]   M. J. Jensen. "The Foundations and Current State of Capital Market Theory", in M. J. Jensen, ed., *Studies in the Theory of Capital Markets* (Praeger, 1972).

[7]   C. P. Kindleberger. *American Business Abroad; Six Lectures on Direct Investment* (Yale University Press, 1969).

[8]   D. R. Lessard. "World, Country and Industry Relationships in Equity Returns: Implications for Risk Reduction Through International Diversification", *Financial Analysts Journal* (Jan./Feb. 1976).

[9]   ———. "The Structure of Returns and Gains from International Diversification", in Elton and Gruber, eds., *International Capital Markets* (North-Holland, 1976).

[10] W. G. Lewellyn. "A Pure Financial Rationale for the Conglomerate Merger", *Journal of Finance* (May 1971).

[11] H. M. Markowitz. "Portfolio Selection", *The Journal of Finance* (March 1952).

[12] S. C. Myers. "Procedures for Capital Budgeting Under Uncertainty", *Industrial Management Review* (Spring 1968).

[13] G. Ragazzi. "Theories of the Determinants of Direct Foreign Investment", *IMF Staff Papers* (July 1973).

[14] A. R. Rugman. "Motives for Foreign Investment: The Market Imperfections and Risk Diversification Hypothesis", *Journal of World Trade Law* (September/October 1975).

[15] B. H. Solnik. *European Capital Markets* (Heath Lexington Books, 1973).

[16] —— "Why Not Diversify Internationally?" *Financial Analysts Journal* (July 1974).

[17] G. V. G. Stevens. "The Determinants of Investment", from J. H. Dunning, *Economic Analysis and the Multinational Enterprise* (Allen and Unwin, 1974).

11

Exchange Rate Uncertainty, Forward Contracts, and International Portfolio Selection*

Cheol S. Eun and Bruce G. Resnick[†]

*Source: *Journal of Finance*, 43 (March 1988), pp. 197–215.

Abstract. In this paper, ex ante efficient portfolio selection strategies are developed to realize potential gains from international diversification under flexible exchange rates. It is shown that exchange rate uncertainty is a largely nondiversifiable factor adversely affecting the performance of international portfolios. Therefore, it is essential to effectively control exchange rate volatility. For that purpose, two methods of exchange risk reduction are simultaneously employed, multicurrency diversification and hedging via forward exchange contracts. The empirical findings show that international portfolio selection strategies designed to control both estimation and exchange risks almost consistently outperform the U.S. domestic portfolio in out-of-sample periods.

Since Grubel [11] applied modern portfolio theory (MPT) to international investment, various authors, such as Levy and Sarnat [17], Solnik [20], and Lessard [16], have examined the gains from international diversification of investment portfolios. For the purpose of establishing the gains from international diversification, these studies constructed international portfolios using historical risk and return data from a period of fixed or relatively stable exchange rates and showed that internationally diversified portfolios dominated purely domestic portfolios in terms of mean-variance efficiency. From the standpoint of today's investors, however, the previous studies fail to offer operational guidance for international diversification for two important reasons. First, it is now questionable whether the past findings are still relevant under the current flexible exchange rate regime. Second, by being "ex post" in nature, the past studies ignored the issue of estimation risk, or parameter uncertainty, and therefore may have overstated the realizable portion of the potential gains from international diversification.

Fluctuating exchange rates are likely to mitigate the potential gains from international diversification by making investment in foreign securities more risky. As will be shown later, a fluctuating exchange rate contributes to the risk of foreign investment not only through its own variance but also through its "positive" covariances with the local stock market returns. During our sample period of 1980 through 1985, for example, exchange rate volatility is found to account for about fifty percent of the volatility of dollar returns from investment in the stock markets of such major countries as Germany, Japan, and the U.K. Furthermore, the exchange rate changes vis-à-vis the U.S. dollar are found to be highly correlated across currencies. This, of course, implies that a large portion of exchange risk would remain nondiversifiable in a multicurrency portfolio.[1]

In addition, fluctuating exchange rates are likely to compound the problem of estimation risk. As is well known, investors must estimate the risk-return characteristics of securities in order to construct ex ante optimal portfolios according to MPT. Gyrating exchange rates will make this task more difficult, possibly leading to suboptimal portfolio selection. Underscoring the problem of estimation risk, the simulation analysis of Jorion [14] suggests that the classical international tangency portfolio constructed using "historical" mean returns and covariance matrix will often fail to outperform the U.S. domestic portfolio in out-of-sample periods. However, Jorion's results also suggest that, when estimation risk is controlled, it is possible by some strategies for the U.S. investor to realize a sufficient portion of the potential gains available from international diversification to warrant making international investment. Eun and Resnick [8] also show that certain ex ante international strategies controlling estimation risk outperform the purely domestic portfolios for most of fifteen national investors over their out-of-sample holding period, but not for the U.S. investor. They point out, however, that the actual gains would have been greater for most national investors in the absence of exchange rate fluctuations.

Considering the adverse effect of fluctuating exchange rates, it is highly desirable to develop an "ex ante" efficient international portfolio strategy that is capable of capturing the potential gains from international diversification as much as possible. Of central importance to such a strategy is the design of the effective mechanism for offsetting exchange rate volatility. In this study, we simultaneously employ two methods of exchange risk reduction, i.e., multicurrency diversification and hedging via forward exchange contracts. Specifically, the main objectives of this study are to

(i)   examine the effect of exchange rate changes on the risk of international portfolios,

(ii) investigate how the negative effects of exchange rate volatility can be mitigated in a portfolio context by the judicious use of forward exchange contracts, and

(iii) develop an ex ante efficient international diversification strategy that can effectively control exchange and estimation risks.

In fulfilling these objectives, we take the viewpoint of the U.S. investor using the U.S. dollar as the numeraire currency.

Though much of the exchange risk may remain nondiversifiable in a multicurrency portfolio due to the high correlations among exchange rate changes, U.S. investors can conceivably eliminate much of the exchange risk by selling the "expected" foreign currency proceeds forward on a currency-by-currency basis. Since the forward exchange premium is known to be a nearly unbiased predictor of the future change of the exchange rate, the U.S. investor might be able to eliminate much of the exchange risk without having to lower the expected dollar returns from foreign investment.[2] From a portfolio standpoint, the size of the hedge position will depend upon the ex ante portfolio weights selected. The effectiveness of the hedge will depend upon the investor's ability to estimate accurately the expected foreign currency proceeds. Both of these factors pertain to the estimation-risk problem of implementing MPT in an international setting. If MPT can be implemented efficaciously using forward contracts, any "residual" exchange risk arising from unexpected foreign currency proceeds (due to misestimates of the expected proceeds) should be small in magnitude and conceivably diversifiable in an international portfolio. Overall, the investor should be able to realize a larger portion of the potential gains from international diversification.

The organization of the paper is as follows. The first section analyzes the effect of fluctuating exchange rates on the international investment opportunity set and discusses the rationale for international diversification using a forward hedge strategy. The second section discusses alternative ex ante portfolio strategies in the presence of estimation risk and extends these strategies to incorporate forward hedging. The third section presents out-of-sample performance results from empirically testing these strategies. The final section offers a summary and concluding remarks.

Exchange Rate Volatility and the Hedging Strategy

In this section, we examine the effect of fluctuating exchange rates on the risk of foreign stock market investment and compare the hedging strategy with the unhedged strategy. In doing so, we take the viewpoint of the U.S. investor investing in the U.S. and six major foreign stock markets, i.e., Canada (CA), France (FR), Germany (GE), Japan (JP), Switzerland (SW), and the U.K. (UK). It is in the currencies of these countries that the U.S. investor can readily hedge exchange risk via the well-developed forward exchange market.

The Effect of Fluctuating Exchange Rates

The dollar rate of return, $\tilde{R}_{i\$}$, from an unhedged investment in the ith foreign market is

$$\tilde{R}_{i\$} = (1 + \tilde{R}_i)(1 + \tilde{e}_i) - 1, \tag{1a}$$

$$\tilde{R}_{i\$} = \tilde{R}_i + \tilde{e}_i + \tilde{R}_i\tilde{e}_i, \tag{1b}$$

where $\tilde{R}_i$ is the local currency rate of return, $\tilde{e}_i$, is the rate of appreciation of the local currency against the dollar, and the symbol " $\sim$ " denotes a random variable. Since the cross-product in equation (1b) is small in magnitude, $\tilde{R}_{i\$}$ is well approximated by

$$\tilde{R}_{i\$} \approx \tilde{R}_i + \tilde{e}_i. \tag{2}$$

Based on equation (2), the variance of the dollar rate of return can be approximated as

$$\text{var}(\tilde{R}_{i\$}) \approx \text{var}(\tilde{R}_i) + \text{var}(\tilde{e}_i) + 2\,\text{cov}(\tilde{R}_i, \tilde{e}_i). \tag{3}$$

As can be seen from equation (3), the exchange rate change contributes to the variance of dollar returns through not only its own variance but also its covariance with the local stock market returns.

Table 11.1 presents the breakdown of the volatility of dollar returns into different components. Contrary to the conventional belief that the exchange market should be substantially less volatile than the stock market, the dollar exchange rates of such major currencies as the German mark and the Japanese yen exhibit nearly as much volatility as their respective stock markets during the sample period of 1980 through 1985. In the case of Switzerland, the exchange market turns out to be even more volatile than the stock market. For other countries, i.e., France, the U.K., and especially Canada, the stock market remains more volatile relative to the exchange market counterpart. It is also noteworthy that the covariance between the local stock market returns and the exchange rate changes is positive for each of the six foreign countries. In fact, the correlation coefficient between the two variables is significantly different from zero at least at the ten percent level in each country. The exchange rate movements are thus found to reinforce rather than offset, the stock market movements. Table 11.1 also shows that, through its own variance as well as its covariance with the local stock market returns the exchange rate changes account for a significant fraction of the volatility of dollar returns in each country except Canada. For example, the fraction is 52.35 percent for Japan, 58.49 percent for Germany, 69.99 for Switzerland, and 48.77 percent for the U.K.

Table 11.1 Decomposition of the volatility of stock market returns in U.S. dollars (weekly data: January 1980 through December 1985)[a]

Stock market	(1) $\mathrm{var}(\tilde{R}_i)$	(2) $\mathrm{var}(\tilde{e}_i)$	(3) $\mathrm{cov}(\tilde{R}_i, \tilde{e}_i)$	(4) $\mathrm{cor}(\tilde{R}_i, \tilde{e}_i)$	(5) $\mathrm{var}(\tilde{R}_{iS})$	(6) $\frac{(1)}{(5)} \times 100\%$	(7) $\frac{(2)}{(5)} \times 100\%$	(8) $\frac{2 \times (3)}{(5)} \times 100\%$
Canada	7.37	0.37	0.47	0.281*	8.68	84.91	4.26	10.83
France	7.52	3.61	0.52	0.100**	12.17	61.79	29.66	8.55
Germany	3.69	3.46	0.87	0.244*	8.89	41.51	38.92	19.57
Japan	3.86	2.58	0.83	0.264*	8.10	47.65	31.85	20.50
Switzerland	2.35	4.32	0.58	0.180*	7.83	30.01	55.17	14.81
U.K.	5.21	3.28	0.84	0.205*	10.17	51.23	32.25	16.52
U.S.	5.42	—	—	—	5.42	100.00	—	—

[a]The variances and covariances of columns (1), (2), (3), and (5) are stated in terms of squared percentages.
*Correlation coefficient is significantly different from zero at the five percent level.
**Correlation coefficient is significantly different from zero at the ten percent level.

The preceding analysis can be extended into a portfolio context. The variance of dollar portfolio returns, $\check{R}_{pS}$, can be written as

$$\text{var}(\check{R}_{pS}) = \Sigma_i X_i^2 \text{var}(\check{R}_{iS}) + \Sigma_i \Sigma_{j \neq i} X_i X_j \text{cov}(\check{R}_{iS}, \check{R}_{jS}), \qquad (4)$$

Where X_i denotes the fraction of wealth invested in the ith market. Noting from equation (2) that

$$\text{cov}(\check{R}_{iS}, \check{R}_{jS}) \approx \text{cov}(\check{R}_i, \check{R}_j) + \text{cov}(\tilde{e}_i, \tilde{e}_j)$$
$$+ \text{cov}(\check{R}_i, \tilde{e}_j) + \text{cov}(\check{R}_j, \tilde{e}_i)$$

and using equation (3), equation (4) can be approximated as

$$\text{var}(\check{R}_{pS}) \approx \Sigma_i \Sigma_j X_i X_j \text{cov}(\check{R}_i, \check{R}_j) + \Sigma_i \Sigma_j X_i X_j \text{cov}(\tilde{e}_i, \tilde{e}_j)$$
$$+ 2 \Sigma_i \Sigma_j X_i X_j \text{cov}(\check{R}_i, \tilde{e}_j). \qquad (5)$$

It is clear from equation (5) that the overall portfolio risk depends on (a) the covariances among the local stock market returns, (b) the covariances among the exchange rate changes, and (c) the cross-covariances among the local stock market returns and the exchange rate changes. Fluctuating exchange rates contribute to the portfolio risk via the second and third terms of equation (5). If the exchange rate correlations and the stock/exchange market cross-correlations are largely positive (negative), then fluctuating exchange rates will increase (decrease) the portfolio risk.

Table 11.2 provides the stock market correlations, the exchange market correlations, and the stock/exchange market cross-correlations calculated using weekly data from the period of January 1980 through December 1985. It can be seen from comparing Panel A with Panel B that the correlations are much higher among the exchange rate changes than among the local stock market returns. In fact, the average correlation is 0.669 for the exchange rate changes, compared with 0.319 for the local stock market returns. This implies that, while the local stock market risk can be diversified away to a large extent, much of the exchange risk is nondiversifiable.[3]

It is noted from Panel C of Table 11.2 that the cross-correlations among the stock and exchange markets are relatively low, with an average value of 0.189. Remarkably, however, every entry in panel C is positive. Furthermore, thirty-nine out of forty-two of the entries in Panel C are statistically significantly different from zero at the five percent level.[4] This result implies that the exchange rate changes in a given country reinforce the stock market movements in the same country as well as in the other countries examined. This reinforcement will, as shown by equation (5), further increase the overall portfolio risk.

The effect of exchange rate volatility can be clearly demonstrated by

Table 11.2 Correlation matrices of seven major countries (weekly data: January 1980 through December 1985)

	CA	FR	GE	JP	SW	UK	US
A: Stock market returns in local currencies							
Canada		0.247	0.274	0.267	0.326	0.472	0.722
France			0.132	0.167	0.203	0.266	0.205
Germany				0.363	0.393	0.341	0.300
Japan					0.294	0.390	0.337
Switzerland						0.266	0.297
U.K.							0.429
B: Exchange rate changes against dollar							
Canada		0.508	0.528	0.397	0.517	0.518	0.000
France			0.941	0.626	0.884	0.774	0.000
Germany				0.656	0.937	0.795	0.000
Japan					0.661	0.516	0.000
Switzerland						0.772	0.000
C: Stock exchange markets cross-correlations[a]							
Canada	0.281	0.191	0.213	0.223	0.239	0.256	0.000
France	0.039	0.100	0.121	0.122	0.111	0.118	0.000
Germany	0.217	0.210	0.244	0.209	0.226	0.133	0.000
Japan	0.099	0.158	0.209	0.264	0.212	0.193	0.000
Switzerland	0.165	0.189	0.187	0.157	0.180	0.198	0.000
U.K.	0.191	0.155	0.174	0.186	0.199	0.205	0.000
U.S.	0.183	0.205	0.244	0.240	0.276	0.220	0.000

[a]Each entry in Panel C denotes the correlation between the row stock market returns in the local currency and the column exchange rate changes. All nonzero entries are statistically significant at least at the ten percent level, except for the correlation between the French stock market and the Canadian exchange market.

constructing an equally weighted portfolio from the seven stock markets previously mentioned. Doing so results in an overall portfolio risk, var($\tilde{R}_{pS}$, of 4.804 squared percent, using the weekly data from the 1980 through 1985 period. The var($\tilde{R}_{pS}$) decomposition according to equation (5) is shown in Table 11.3. As shown in the table, fluctuating exchange rates account for 32.20 percent of the risk of the equally weighted portfolio through its own covariances and an additional 24.92 percent through its cross-covariances with the stock market returns. In the absence of exchange rate volatility, the portfolio variance would have been 2,060 squared percent, as opposed to 4.804 squared percent.

The Hedging Strategy

The preceding analysis shows that exchange risk may be nondiversifiable to a large extent and, as a result, substantially contributes to the overall risk of

Table 11.3 Decomposition of portfolio risk

Component	Absolute contribution	Relative contribution
1. $\sum_i \sum_j (1/n)^2 \operatorname{cov}(R_i, R_j)$	2.060	42.88%
2. $\sum_i \sum_j (1/n)^2 \operatorname{cov}(\tilde{e}_i, \tilde{e}_j)$	1.547	32.20%
3. $2 \sum_i \sum_j (1/n)^2 \operatorname{cov}(R_i, \tilde{e}_j)$	1.197	24.92%
	$\operatorname{var}(R_{pS}) \approx 4.804$	100.00%

the portfolio. This observation leads one to consider the use of foreign exchange forward contracts as a tool for exchange risk management.

Assume that the U.S. investor sells the *expected* foreign currency proceeds forward. In dollar terms, it amounts to exchanging the uncertain dollar return $(1 + E(\tilde{R}_i))(1 + \tilde{e}_i) - 1$ for the certain dollar return $(1 + E(\tilde{R}_i))(1 + f_i) - 1$, where $E(\tilde{R}_i)$ is the expected rate of return on the ith foreign stock market in terms of the foreign currency and f_i is the forward exchange premium. The unexpected foreign currency proceeds, however, will have to be converted into U.S. dollars at the uncertain future spot exchange rate. The dollar rate of return under the hedging strategy is thus given by[5]

$$\tilde{R}_{iS}^H = [1 + E(\tilde{R}_i)](1 + f_i) + [\tilde{R}_i - E(\tilde{R}_i)](1 + \tilde{e}_i) - 1, \qquad (6a)$$

$$\tilde{R}_{iS}^H = \tilde{R}_i + f_i + \tilde{R}_i \tilde{e}_i + E(\tilde{R}_i)(f_i - \tilde{e}_i). \qquad (6b)$$

Because the third and fourth terms of equation (6b) will be small in magnitude, the following approximation results:[6]

$$\tilde{R}_{iS}^H \approx \tilde{R}_i + f_i. \qquad (7)$$

Equation (7) suggests that much of the effect of exchange rate changes on the risk of the foreign stock market investment can be offset by means of the forward exchange contract.[7] Table 11.4 provides a comparison between the hedged and unhedged strategies with regard to the risk-return characteristics of foreign investment. In light of the empirical results presented in the subsection on pp. 219–222, it is clear that the hedging strategy results in a lower variance and covariance i.e.,

$$\operatorname{var}(\tilde{R}_{iS}^H) < \operatorname{var}(\tilde{R}_{iS})$$

$$\text{and } \operatorname{cov}(\tilde{R}_{iS}^H, \tilde{R}_{jS}^H) < \operatorname{cov}(\tilde{R}_{iS}, \tilde{R}_{jS}).$$

Since the forward exchange premium is known to be a nearly unbiased

Table 11.4 Risk and return from foreign stock market investment: hedged versus unhedged strategy[a]

	Hedged strategy	Unhedged strategy
Expected return	$E(R_{iS}^H) = (1 + E(R_i))(1 + f_i) - 1$	$E(R_{iS}) = (1 + E(R_i))(1 + E(\tilde{e}_i)) - 1$
Actual return	$R_{iS}^H = (1 + E(R_i))(1 + f_i)$ $+ (R_i - E(R_i))(1 + \hat{e}_i) - 1$ $\approx R_i + f_i$	$R_{iS} = (1 + R_i)(1 + \tilde{e}_i) - 1$ $\approx R_i + \tilde{e}_i$
Variance of returns	$var(R_{iS}^H) \approx var(R_i)$	$var(R_{iS}) \approx var(R_i) + var(\tilde{e}_i)$ $+ 2 cov(R_i, \hat{e}_i)$
Covariance of returns	$cov(R_{iS}^H, R_{iS}^H) \approx cov(R_i, R_j)$	$cov(R_{iS}, R_{jS}) \approx cov(R_i, R_j) + cov(\tilde{e}_i, \tilde{e}_j)$ $+ cov(R_i, \tilde{e}_j) + cov(R_j, \tilde{e}_i)$

[a] The forward premium, f_i, is equal to $f_i/S_i - 1$, where F_i and S_i are, respectively, the forward and spot exchange rates in U.S. dollar equivalents.

predictor of the future change of the exchange rate, i.e., $f_i \approx E(\tilde{e}_i)$, this is indeed one of the rare occasions where risk can be reduced without adversely affecting return.

Although we are going to test the forward hedging strategy in this paper, it is pointed out that investors can hedge exchange risk alternatively via borrowing in the international money market. Suppose a U.S. investor borrows, in terms of foreign currency, the present value of the expected foreign currency proceeds, i.e., $[1 + E(\tilde{R}_i)]/(1 + r_i)$, where r_i denotes the risk-free interest rate in the foreign country, and then immediately converts this borrowing into dollars and invests at the U.S. risk-free interest rate, r_S. Then, at maturity, the U.S. investor will have to repay the maturity value of the borrowing, i.e., $1 + E(\tilde{R}_i)$, which can be met by using the expected (foreign currency) proceeds from the foreign stock market investment. As was the case with the forward hedging strategy, any unexpected foreign currency proceeds would remain exposed to exchange risk.

Based on the preceding analysis, it can be shown that the dollar rate of return from the foreign stock market investment with the money market hedging is equal to

$$\tilde{R}_{iS}^H = [1 + E(\tilde{R}_i)] \; \frac{1 + r_S}{1 + r_i} \; + [\tilde{R}_i - \hat{E}(\tilde{R}_i)](1 + \tilde{e}_i) - 1. \qquad (8)$$

Equation (8) is, in fact, the analog of money market hedging to equation (6a). Note that both equations (6a) and (8) consist of a hedged component and an unhedged component, and also that the unhedged component is identical. Furthermore, the apparent difference in the hedged component can be shown to disappear if interest rate parity (IRP) holds, i.e.

$$\frac{1 + r_S}{1 + r_i} = 1 + f_i, \qquad (9)$$

where f_i is, as previously defined, the forward exchange premium. (That is, $f_i = (F_i - S_i)/S_i$, where F_i (S_i) is the forward (spot) rate.) From equations (6a), (8), and (9), it can be seen that, if IRP holds, the two hedging methods will yield the identical investment results in dollar terms. As is well known, IRP is a pure arbitrage condition that must hold to preclude arbitrage opportunities in the absence of investment barriers. Previous empirical studies, most notably Frenkel and Levich [10], confirmed the empirical validity of IRP.

Alternative Ex Ante Strategies

Preliminary Discussion

In this section, alternative "ex ante" international diversification strategies, both with and without forward exchange hedging, are presented. The objective is to develop an effective strategy for controlling both estimation risk and exchange rate uncertainty. To lay the foundation for the discussion, the intertemporal stability of two "ex post" portfolios, i.e., the optimal international (tangency) portfolio and the minimum-variance portfolio, is first examined. As is well known, the entire efficient set can be constructed by combining these two portfolios.[8] Using 310 weeks of weekly stock index return data commencing with the first week of January 1980, we construct these two portfolios for a variety of six-month (twenty-six-week) holding periods using the ex post parameter values. Table 11.5 presents the portfolio weights for ten (largely) nonoverlapping holding periods. In solving for the tangency portfolio, the risk-free rate was assumed to be zero and the returns were in the U.S. numeraire.

Examination of Table 11.5 shows that the composition of the ex post tangency portfolio is highly unstable over time. This point is further confirmed by the very high standard deviations of the intertemporal portfolio weights relative to the average portfolio weights. As was pointed out by Jorion [14], the instability of the tangency portfolio weights is mainly due to the intertemporal instability of the mean-return vector; the variance–covariance matrix of international stock index returns demonstrates greater stability through time. Jobson and Korkie [12, 13] reach the same conclusion in a purely domestic context. Unlike the tangency portfolio, the minimum-variance portfolio is much more stable through time. Table 11.5 shows that the minimum-variance portfolio standard deviations of intertemporal portfolio weights for the seven stock indices are often only one tenth of the size of the respective values for the tangency portfolio. This result is due to the fact that the solution of the minimum-variance portfolio does not use the mean-return vector as input; it further confirms the relative intertemporal stability of the variance–covariance matrix. Accurate estimation of the mean-return vector thus proves to be of critical importance to the formulation of efficacious ex ante portfolio strategies.

Recently, Jorion [14, 15] has formalized in an expected-utility-maximization framework a Bayes–Stein approach for estimating the ex ante expected-return vector to use in solving the portfolio problem. This approach will result in a uniform improvement on the ex post classical sample mean because it relies on a more general model that includes the ex post sample mean as a special case. Jorion shows that the optimal portfolio choice should be based on the predictive density function of the vector of future rates of return. With a suitable informative prior on expected returns, the conditional predictive distribution he derives is multivariate normal with expected return

$$\underline{R} = (1 - \hat{w})\underline{Y} + \hat{w}\underline{1}Y_0, \tag{10}$$

Table 11.5 Intertemporal stability of international portfolios

Holding Periods (Weeks)[a]	Tangency portfolio							Minimum-variance portfolio						
	CA	FR	GE	JP	SW	UK	US	CA	FR	GE	JP	SW	UK	US
1 (1–26)	0.3418	0.0763	-0.1356	1.5900	-1.4024	1.3880	-0.8580	-0.1165	0.1548	0.3417	0.5022	-0.3327	0.1327	0.3179
2 (21–46)	-0.4133	-0.2514	-1.3419	0.4148	0.4119	0.9851	1.1948	-0.2641	0.2872	0.2187	0.2977	0.2043	0.2224	0.0339
3 (49–74)	-0.0436	-0.5737	-1.1133	3.3265	-0.0074	-1.3699	0.7814	0.1686	0.0503	-0.1256	0.5046	0.0511	0.1158	0.2352
4 (97–122)	-6.5169	2.7039	-6.4784	-2.6742	2.2692	6.5914	5.1050	-0.2656	0.1503	-0.0743	0.0768	0.4386	-0.0216	0.6957
5 (145–170)	2.9439	0.3950	1.2933	0.2597	-0.1788	-3.3620	-0.3511	-0.2323	0.1587	-0.0220	0.0033	0.4790	0.3492	0.2642
6 (169–194)	1.4393	0.2070	-0.3202	0.0860	-0.7546	0.1446	0.1979	-0.0061	0.1322	-0.0469	-0.0446	0.5273	0.0403	0.3978
7 (193–218)	-0.5439	0.5255	-0.0078	0.5902	0.7834	0.0476	-0.3950	-0.1704	0.1299	-0.0512	-0.0022	0.5638	0.1275	0.4025
8 (241–266)	0.1923	0.5441	-0.0550	0.5587	-0.6588	-0.0347	0.4534	0.0848	0.1850	-0.2407	0.3526	0.1108	0.0906	0.4168
9 (265–290)	-0.4780	0.2974	0.3957	0.3058	0.3375	-0.4456	0.5870	0.2132	0.0042	-0.1559	0.4339	-0.0623	0.0420	0.5249
10 (285–310)	-1.2205	0.4092	0.8278	-0.3908	1.8520	-1.1438	0.6661	0.4266	-0.0432	-0.0272	0.2090	0.0039	0.0577	0.3731
Average	-0.4299	0.4333	-0.6935	0.4067	0.2652	0.2801	0.7382	-0.0162	0.1209	-0.0183	0.2333	0.1984	0.1157	0.3662
S.D.	2.4427	0.8730	2.1817	1.4998	1.1438	2.5878	1.6566	0.2351	0.0948	0.1735	0.2148	0.2973	0.1056	0.1761

[a] For reference purposes, week number one corresponds to the first week in January 1980.

where a bar under a variable symbol denotes a vector, $\underline{Y}$ is the $N \times 1$ ex post sample mean-return vector of the N assets, $\underline{1}$ is the vector of ones, Y_0 denotes the mean return from the ex post minimum-variance portfolio, and $\hat{w}$ represents the estimated shrinkage factor for shrinking the elements of $\underline{Y}$ toward Y_0. The shrinkage factor is estimated by

$$\hat{w} = \frac{(N+2)(T-1)}{(N+2)(T-1) + (\underline{Y} - Y_0\underline{1})' TS^{-1}(T-N-2)(\underline{Y} - Y_0\underline{1})},$$

where T represents the length of the time series of the sample observations and S is the usual $N \times N$ sample variance-covariance matrix. In related work, Jobson and Korkie [12, 13] have derived a variation of equation (10), where the grand mean of the $\underline{Y}$ elements is substituted for Y_0 and the shrinkage factor is estimated differently.

Using equation (10) and an estimate of the inverse of the variance-covariance matrix, the optimal ex ante portfolio can be determined. As previously mentioned, the sample variance–covariance matrix is relatively stable through time. Therefore, in this study, we use the conventional unbiased estimator (see Jobson and Korkie [12]),

$$\hat{\Sigma}^{-1} = \frac{(T-N-2)}{(T-1)} S^{-1}, \tag{11}$$

in estimating the inverse of the true variance–covariance matrix.[9]

The Ex Ante Strategies

Altogether, we examine eight ex ante investment strategies from the perspective of the U.S. investor confronted with making the optimal international investment decision in the presence of estimation risk and exchange rate uncertainty. The results from testing these strategies are compared with investment in solely the U.S. stock market. This latter strategy is denoted US. The eight international strategies are divided into four unhedged and four hedged strategies.

If the investor selects an unhedged strategy, realized returns are defined by equation (1). Implementation of the strategy requires obtaining a historical time-series sample of dollar returns, R_{iS} $(i = 1, \ldots, N)$, to calculate the $\underline{Y}$, Y_0, S, and $\hat{w}$ in equations (10) and (11). If the investor selects a hedged strategy, realized returns are defined by equation (6). Equation (7), which approximates equation (6), suggests that, when a hedged strategy is employed, the variability in $\tilde{R}_{iS}^H$ will be primarily due to the variability in the local currency return, $\tilde{R}_i$ $(i = 1, \ldots, N)$. This, in turn, suggests that the ex ante hedged expected-return vector be estimated as

$$E(\tilde{\underline{R}}_S^H) = \underline{R} + \underline{f}, \tag{12a}$$

$$E(\tilde{\underline{R}}_S^H) = (1 - \hat{w})\underline{Y} + \hat{w}\underline{1}Y_0 + \underline{f}, \tag{12b}$$

where $\underline{Y}$, Y_0, S, and $\hat{w}$, and thus $\underline{R}$, are calculated from a historical time series of local currency returns, $R_i(i = 1, \ldots, N)$. The vector f, on the other hand, is not estimated from historical data but rather contains as elements the current market-determined forward exchange premiums.

One unhedged strategy would be to construct an equally weighted (EQW) portfolio. This approach can be viewed as a naive diversification strategy in the attempt to capture some of the potential gains from international diversification. Alternatively, it can be viewed as an ad hoc method for controlling estimation risk, where the investor believes that the best ex ante estimate of the expected-return (standard deviation) vector is the grand mean of the ex post sample mean returns (standard deviations) and that the best estimate of the pairwise correlation coefficients is the grand mean from the ex post sample correlation matrix.[10] These inputs into the portfolio problem will result in an equally weighted portfolio being selected as the optimal portfolio. The second unhedged strategy is to identify the weights of the ex post (or historical) tangency portfolio and to invest accordingly. In terms of equation (10), this amounts to setting $\hat{w} = 0$. This method implicitly assumes no estimation risk and is labeled the certainty-equivalence-tangency (CET) portfolio strategy.[11] The third strategy, which is due to the simulation results of Jobson and Korkie [12, 13] in a purely domestic setting, is to arbitrarily set $\hat{w} = 1$ and estimate Σ^{-1} by equation (11). This strategy identifies as the optimal ex ante weights those of the ex post minimum-variance portfolio (MVP). The MVP strategy implicitly assumes that there is no useful asset-specific information in $\underline{Y}$ because it is not required as input to solve the portfolio problem.[12] The fourth strategy we consider is the Bayes–Stein (BST) strategy, which solves for the optimal ex ante tangency portfolio using equations (10) and (11).

Each of the four unhedged strategies has a hedged (H) counterpart. When a hedged strategy is employed, the realized returns are defined by equation (6). Examination of equation (6) shows that $\tilde{R}_{iS}^H$ ($i \neq US$) is dependent on how $\tilde{E}(R_i)$, is estimated. For the EQW(H) strategy, the $E(\tilde{R}_i)$ values are each estimated as the grand mean of the $\underline{Y}$ elements. This is also done for the MVP(H) strategy, following Jobson and Korkie [12, 13].[13] For the CET(H) strategy, the $E(\tilde{R}_i)$ values are the respective Y_i elements. In the BST(H) strategy, the $E(\tilde{R}_i)$ values are the respective elements from the vector $\underline{R}$ in equation (12a).

In the next section, we empirically test the four unhedged and hedged ex ante international diversification strategies and compare their performance results with one another and with the US strategy. It is noted that Jorion

[14, 15] and Eun and Resnick [8] have previously examined the unhedged strategies. These works, however, relied on simulation testing or covered only one out-of-sample holding period.[14] The empirical tests in this paper use actual data and multiple out-of-sample holding periods to draw inferences. Consequently, the results of the unhedged strategies are interesting in their own right as the current test results obtained under actual market conditions can be compared with the previous test results. Moreover, it is noted that actual market data were required because the hedged strategies rely on market-determined forward premiums. Hence, any differential investment performance detected from employing a hedged versus unhedged strategy represents a realizable gain from international diversification.[15]

Empirical Tests of the Ex Ante Strategies

The Data and Test Structure

The primary data used in this study are the Morgan Stanley Capital International Perspective daily stock index values for the U.S. and the six countries previously mentioned, for which forward contracts are readily available. Each of the stock indices is value weighted and is representative of a domestic stock index fund. The data series are provided in both the U.S. and the local currencies for the period from December 31, 1979, through December 10, 1985. From these data, a time series of 310 weekly returns is constructed for each index in both the U.S. and local currency. Using the U.S. and local currency returns, a corresponding time series of exchange rate changes versus the dollar is constructed for each country via solving equation (1) for e_i.

The weekly stock index return and exchange rate change data are used to test the performance of the ex ante investment strategies developed in the section on pp. 225–30. In conducting the tests, it is assumed that the investor has a twenty-six-week (six-month) investment holding period. For the strategies that require estimation of the "optimal" ex ante investment-weight vector, it is assumed that the investor has knowledge of the 156 weekly returns prior to the inception date of the holding period. The holding-period returns are calculated by starting with a one-day lag beyond the close of the estimation period so that investment is not being made at ex post values. For the hedging strategies, the six-month forward premiums are calculated as of the inception date of the holding period from the applicable spot and 180-day forward exchange rates obtained from *The Wall Street Journal.* The six-month forward premiums are then converted to weekly premiums to calculate the ex ante expected-return vector and the actual holding-period returns.

In total, the performance results form each strategy are examined for thirty-three out-of-sample (overlapping) holding periods using the 310 weeks of data. The sample periods are structured as follows. For the first holding period covering weeks 157 through 182, the estimation period covers weeks 1 through 156. For the second holding period of weeks 161 through 186, the estimation period covers weeks 5 through 160. Each subsequent pair of estimation and holding periods is shifted forward in time by four weeks.

Test Results

Table 11.6 presents the performance results from employing the various ex ante strategies in the thirty-three out-of-sample holding periods. For each strategy, the table shows the average portfolio mean return and standard deviation stated in percentage per week. The table also shows the average Sharpe (SHP) measure of portfolio performance, i.e., reward-to-variability ratio. In conducting the tests, the weekly risk-free rate was assumed to be zero.

From Table 11.6, first consider the performance of the unhedged strategies. The three international strategies that attempt to control estimation risk, i.e., EQW, MVP, and BST, clearly outperform the US strategy in terms of the average SHP value. Each of these three strategies registered an average SHP value of approximately 0.200, which is about twice as high as that of the US strategy (0.104). The CET strategy, which ignores the problem of estimation risk, however, failed to outperform the US strategy. On average, the CET strategy realized a somewhat higher mean return than the US but at a substantially high risk level, resulting in the lowest SHP value (0.084) among all strategies considered.[16] The performance results of the unhedged strategies indicate that, as long as the estimation risk is adequately controlled, investors can actually benefit from international diversification.

The international diversification strategies designed to control exchange risk as well as estimation risk, i.e., EQW(H), MVP(H), and BST(H), performed extremely well. As can be seen from Table 11.6, each of the three strategies realized an average SHP value in excess of 0.400. This is about twice the size of the unhedged counterpart and about four times the size of the US strategy. This result clearly shows that, when both estimation and exchange risks are controlled, investors can actually reap very substantial gains from international diversification.

Surprisingly, the CET(H) strategy, which makes no attempt to control estimation risk, performed nearly as well, with an average SHP of 0.399. The strong performance of the CET(H) strategy may, in fact, reflect not only the benefit of exchange risk hedging but also a reduction in the estimation risk "incidentally" achieved by the exchange risk hedging policy. Under the CET strategy, the expected return on the stock market is estimated as the historical sample mean of the dollar returns ($\bar{R}_{iS}$), which is

Table 11.6 Out-of-sample performance results of the ex ante investment strategies[a]

Strategy	Mean (%)	S.D. (%)	SHP
1. EQW	0.315	1.515	0.214
2. CET	0.198	3.862	0.084
3. MVP	0.336	1.545	0.210
4. BST	0.293	1.810	0.188
5. EQW(H)	0.393	1.054	0.423
6. CET(H)	0.466	1.266	0.399
7. MVP(H)	0.500	1.202	0.429
8. BST(H)	0.491	1.203	0.424
9. US	0.189	1.744	0.104

[a]For each ex ante investment strategy, the table shows the averages of the resulting mean portfolio returns, the portfolio standard derivations, and the reward-to-variability ratios (SHP) for the thirty-three out-of-sample test periods.

approximately equal to the sum of the sample mean of local currency stock market returns ($\bar{R}_i$) and the sample mean of exchange rate changes ($\bar{e}_i$). Under the CET(H) strategy, on the other hand, the expected return is estimated using the current market-determined forward exchange premium (f_i) instead of the historical sample mean of exchange rate changes. To the extent that the current forward exchange premium provides a more accurate estimate of the expected change in the exchange rate, which is likely to be the case in an efficient exchange market, the CET(H), which controls exchange risk, also controls estimation risk to a degree.[17]

The average performance results presented in Table 11.6 indicate that hedging exchange risk is beneficial, but they do not allow for clear discrimination among the various strategies. Table 11.7 facilitates discrimination by presenting a dominance analysis of the performance results.[18]. A number in the table denotes the number of times out of the thirty-three holding periods that the row strategy had a larger SHP value than the strategy at the top of the table. Examination of the table shows that the CET strategy was the worst-performing strategy; it did not dominate any of the others. By comparison, the US strategy had a larger SHP than the CET strategy in seventeen of the thirty-three out-of-sample holding periods, but it did not dominate any other international strategies. Table 11.7 also reveals that all of the hedging strategies clearly dominate any of the unhedged strategies. Among the hedging strategies, the MVP(H) and BST(H) emerge as the best-performing strategies, whereas the EQW(H) performs most poorly. It is noted that each of the former strategies outperformed the latter in twenty-two out of thirty-three periods. It is also noted that these two strategies outperformed the US strategies in over ninety percent of the holding periods.

It is clear from the performance results presented in Tables 11.6 and

Table 11.7 Dominance analysis of the out-of-sample performance of the ex ante investment strategies[a]

	EQW	CET	MVP	BST	EQW(H)	CET(H)	MVP(H)	BST(H)	US	Total
EQW		23	14	16	6	5	5	5	24	98
CET	10		11	8	3	2	3	2	16	55
MVP	19	22		16	5	7	4	6	23	102
BST	17	25	17		4	5	4	4	20	96
EQW(H)	27	30	28	29		15	11	11	31	182
CET(H)	28	31	26	28	18		15	14	27	187
MVP(H)	28	30	29	29	22	18		17	32	205
BST(H)	28	31	27	29	22	19	16		30	202
US	9	17	10	13	2	6	1	3		61

[a] A number in the table represents the number of times, out of thirty-three ex ante test periods, that the left-hand-side strategy had a larger out-of-sample reward-to-variability ratio than the strategy at the top. To facilitate multilateral comparison, the sum of these numbers is provided for each strategy in the "Total" column.

11.7 that, even in the presence of exchange rate uncertainty, the U.S. investor can realize a substantial gain from international diversification, as long as estimation risk is controlled by any method (EQW, MVP, or BST). Furthermore, the U.S. investor can substantially increase the gains from international diversification by employing a hedging strategy controlling both estimation and exchange risks, especially by the BST(H) or MVP(H) strategy.

Summary and Conclusion

It was shown in this paper that fluctuating exchange rates make foreign investment more risky and, at the same time, aggravate estimation risk, thereby diminishing the gains from international diversification. The purpose of this paper was to develop an ex ante international portfolio selection strategy that can effectively control both exchange and estimation risks and capture the gains from international diversification as much as possible.

Our analysis showed that exchange risk is nondiversifiable to a large extent due to the high correlations among the changes in the exchange rates and, as a result, substantially contributes to the overall risk of the international portfolio. We thus proposed to simultaneously use two methods of exchange risk reduction, i.e., multicurrency diversification and the forward exchange contract on a currency-by-currency basis. Since the size of the forward contract is dependent upon the ex ante portfolio weights selected, alternative ex ante portfolio strategies controlling estimation risk are extended to incorporate forward hedging.

Performance results of the alternative strategies in the out-of-sample periods reveal that the U.S. investor can actually capture a substantial gain from international diversification if estimation risk is controlled by any method considered, i.e., EQW, MVP, or BST. The CET strategy, which ignores estimation risk, produced out-of-sample performance that is inferior to the US strategy. More importantly, the U.S. investor can substantially increase the gains from international diversification by using a hedging strategy. All of the hedging strategies, designed to control both estimation and exchange risks, were found to outperform any of the unhedged strategies by far. It was noted that MVP(H), the best-performing strategy, registered an average SHP value that is more than four times the size of the corresponding value for the US strategy, and it had the higher SHP value in thirty-two out of thirty-three out-of-sample periods.

Notes

† The authors gratefully acknowledge helpful comments by an anonymous referee.

1 In an update examining the potential gains from international diversification, Eun and Resnick [7] estimated the potential gains using a decade of data characterized by flexible exchange rates. They found that large potential gains still existed but the fluctuating exchange rates mitigated the gains by making foreign investment more risky.

2 For the empirical evidence on the forward exchange premium as an unbiased predictor of the future change of the exchange rate, refer to Frenkel [9] and Agmon and Amihud [3].

3 Adler and Simon [2] present evidence consistent with this statement. They show that, in a pre-1979 period, portfolio diversification did serve to reduce currency risk exposure but that, in a post-1979 period, exposure reduction through diversification was diminished.

4 Two of the three remaining entries are statistically significant at the ten percent level. The only insignificant entry is the correlation between the French stock market and the Canadian exchange market.

5 The hedging strategy described by equation (6) hedges expected foreign currency proceeds on a unitary basis. Adler and Simon [2] present empirical evidence that each of the foreign stock indices used in the present study has approximately unitary exposure exclusively to its own currency and to no other. In related work, Eaker and Grant [4] analytically show that, for the case of quadratic utility, the optimal hedge is the expected value of the uncertain exposure.

6 To make sure that it is appropriate to use equation (7) as an approximation for equation (6b), we calculated the mean-return vector and variance-covariance matrix using both equations. The historical mean return was used for $E(\tilde{R}_i)$ in equation (6b). As expected, we found that the approximation error resulting from using equation (7) is indeed negligible. Specifically, the magnitude of absolute error relative to the precise value was found to be only about two percent for the mean returns and less than one percent for the variances–covariances, with the exception of a few entries. Thus, omission of $\tilde{R}_i \tilde{e}_i$, which is customary in the literature, together with $E(\tilde{R}_i)(f_i - \tilde{e}_i)$ was found to be justifiable on empirical grounds. This omission also simplifies the ensuing analysis, which is summarized in Table 11.4, by preventing proliferation of the variance–covariance terms.

7 Obviously, equation (7) ignores the existence of residual exchange risk arising from the unexpected foreign currency proceeds. To isolate the effect of residual exchange risk, equation (6b) can be written as follows:

$$\tilde{R}_{iS}^H = \tilde{R}_i + fi + E(\tilde{R}i)fi + [\tilde{R}_i - E(\tilde{R}_i)]\tilde{e}_i.$$

Clearly, only the last term of the equation, which must be very small in magnitude, is still subject to exchange risk, and this residual risk can be conceivably diversified away in an international portfolio. To see the effectiveness of our hedging strategy, we constructed an equally weighted hedged portfolio and found its variance to be about 2.06 squared percent. This is, of course, equal to the value that the variance of the equally weighted unhedged portfolio would have assumed in the absence of exchange rate volatility. This result implies that our hedging strategy is fully capable of eliminating the adverse effect of fluctuating exchange rates on the portfolio risk.

8 See Merton [19] for proof.

9 In addition to the expected-return vector stated as equation (10), Jorion [15] also derives the variance-covariance matrix for the conditional predictive multi-variate normal distribution. In our empirical testing, we considered strategies using Jorion's derivation as an alternative to Σ of equation (11) and found, as did Jobson and Korkie [12. 13], that more conventional estimators, such as (11), work as well as if not better than alternative estimators in obtaining good ex ante estimates of the investment weight vector. Hence, we decided to use equation (11) in this paper.

10 Elton and Gruber [5] first developed the grand (overall) mean approach for forecasting the dependence structure of domestic share prices. They found the grand mean estimate to be superior to conventional (full historical) estimation in out-of-sample periods. Eun and Resnick [6] show the grand (global) mean model to be a very poor method for forecasting the pairwise correlation structure of international share prices. They present evidence that the international correlation structure contains a strong country factor that can best be captured by a country mean model or conventional (full historical) estimation. When using national stock index data, as in the present study, conventional estimation of the variance-covariance matrix is consistent with using a country mean model.

11 It is noted that our CET strategy is consistent with Jobson and Korkie's [12, 13]. Jorion [15], however, uses the estimator S^{-1} instead of equation (11) for estimating the inverse of the variance–covariance matrix. The difference is minimal when T is large and N is small, as it is in the present study.

12 Interestingly, Adler and Dumas [1] show in the context of worldwide investments (and in the absence of parameter uncertainty) that the MVP computed in nominal returns is the optimal international portfolio choice for an investor with zero risk tolerance. They call this portfolio the investor's hedge portfolio and show that it is almost entirely made up of a nominal bank deposit denominated in the investor's home currency. This portfolio offers the very risk-averse investor the best hedge against home-country inflation (i.e., provides a stable real return) while minimizing exchange rate and stock price uncertainty. In the present study, we assume that the U.S. investor ignores his home-country inflation (or assumes it to be zero) and therefore considers security rates of return denominated in dollars as being real rates of return. Under this assumption, the U.S. bank deposit or Treasury bill is riskless in real terms. In this context and in the presence of parameter uncertainty, a worldwide MVP strategy assumes that the MVP is the best ex ante portfolio for all U.S. investors to combine with investment in the risk-free asset.

13 It is noted that the name "MVP(H) strategy" is actually a misnomer since the ex ante expected returns for all N securities will not be the same after the respective forward premiums are added according to equation (12). Consequently, the expected-return vector is required as input into the portfolio problem to find the ex ante solution weights. The name, however, is retained for simplicity.

14 To be more precise, the work of Jorion [14] is a simulation analysis using actual data.

15 Madura and Reiff [18] performed an ex post test of hedged portfolio returns. They document large potential gains versus an unhedged strategy. However, since their study assumed parameter certainty, it is not known to what extent the potential gains are realizable in out-of-sample periods. Moreover, they examine only a single time period.

16 This result is consistent with the previous findings of Jorion [14, 15] and Eun and Resnick [8]. This result is also consistent with the purely domestic simulation results of Jobson and Korkie [12, 13].

17 This explanation does indeed appear to be correct. As a test, we modified the (unhedged) CET strategy where in one case the expected returns were estimated as

$\bar{R}_i + f_i$ and in the other merely as $\bar{R}_i$, i.e., a martingale assumption with respect to the expected exchange rate change. The forward premium model resulted in an average SHP of 0.146, and the martingale model yielded 0.147, both higher than the CET strategy's average SHP value of 0.084. This implies that the forward premium or "no-change" extrapolation provides a more accurate estimate of the expected change in the exchange rate than the historical sample mean of exchange rate changes.

18 In this study, a strategy is said to dominate another strategy if the former has a higher SHP value than the latter in at least seventeen out of thirty-three holding periods.

References

[1] Michael Adler and Bernard Dumas. "International Portfolio Choice and Corporation Finance: A Synthesis," *Journal of Finance* 38 (June 1983), 925–84.

[2] Michael Adler and David Simon. "Exchange Risk Surprises in International Portfolios." *Journal of Portfolio Management* 12 (Winter 1986), 44–53.

[3] Tamir Agmon and Yakov Amihud. "The Forward Exchange Rate and the Prediction of the Future Spot Rate." *Journal of Banking and Finance* 5 (December 1981), 425–37.

[4] Mark Eaker and Dwight Grant. "Optimal Hedging of Uncertain and Long-Term Foreign Exchange Exposure." *Journal of Banking and Finance* 9 (June 1985), 221–321.

[5] Edwin Elton and Martin Gruber. "Estimating the Dependence Structure of Share Prices—Implications for Portfolio Selection." *Journal of Finance* 28 (December 1973), 1203–32.

[6] Cheol Eun and Bruce Resnick. "Estimating the Correlation Structure of International Share Prices." *Journal of Finance* 39 (December 1984), 1311–24.

[7] —— "Currency Factor in International Portfolio Diversification." *Columbia Journal of World Business* 20 (Summer 1985), 45–53.

[8] —— "International Diversification under Estimation Risk: Actual *vs* Potential Gains." In S. Khoury and A. Gosh (eds.), *Recent Developments in International Banking and Finance, Vol. 1.* Lexington, MA: D. C. Heath, 1987, 135–47.

[9] Jacob Frenkel. "Flexible Exchange Rates, Prices and the Role of News: Lessons from the 1970's." *Journal of Political Economy* 89 (August 1981), 665–706.

[10] —— and Richard Levich. "Transactions Costs and Interest Arbitrage: Tranquil versus Turbulent Periods." *Journal of Political Economy* 85 (November–December 1977), 1209–26.

[11] Herbert Grubel. "Internationally Diversified Portfolios: Welfare Gains and Capital Flows." *American Economic Review* 58 (December 1968), 1299–1314.

[12] J. D. Jobson and Bob Korkie. "Improved Estimation and Selection Rules for Markowitz Portfolios." Paper presented at the Western Finance Association meeting (June 1980).

[13] —— "Putting Markowitz Theory to Work." *Journal of Portfolio Management* 7 (Summer 1981), 70–74.

[14] Philippe Jorion. "International Portfolio Diversification with Estimation Risk." *Journal of Business* 58 (July 1985), 259–78.

[15] —— "Bayes–Stein Estimation for Portfolio Analysis." *Journal of Financial and Quantitative Analysis* 21 (September 1986), 279–92.

[16] Donald Lessard. "World, Country and Industry Relationships in Equity Returns: Implications for Risk Reduction through International Diversification." *Financial Analysts Journal* 32 (January/February 1976), 2–8.

[17] Haim Levy and Marshall Sarnat. "International Diversification of Investment Portfolios." *American Economic Review* 60 (September 1970), 668–75.

[18] Jeff Madura and Wallace Reiff. "A Hedge Strategy for International Portfolios." *Journal of Portfolio Management* 11 (Fall 1985), 70–74.

[19] Robert Merton. "An Analytic Derivation of the Efficient Portfolio Frontier." *Journal of Financial and Quantitative Analysis* 7 (September 1972), 1851–72.

[20] Bruno Solnik. "Why Not Diversify Internationally?" *Financial Analysts Journal* 20 (July/August 1974), 48–54.

PART THREE: Financial Structure

12

Financial Structure and Multinational Corporations*

Arthur Stonehill and Thomas Stitzel

The time has come for financial executives of multinational corporations, their bankers, and financial theorists to rethink domestically oriented concepts which have traditionally influenced the choice of corporate financial structures. Increased reliance by United States corporations on multinational operations, financed in part by foreign sources of funds, necessitates focusing on a new set of environmental variables which must be incorporated into the determination of an appropriate financial structure.

Given the current set of circumstances, multinational firms would like to finance their foreign subsidiaries with as much foreign borrowing as possible. Despite the likelihood of increasing their overall cost of debt, United States firms borrow abroad:

1   To comply with the United States balance of payments program.
2   to reduce the dollars exposed to foreign exchange and political risks.
3   To improve the dollar rate of return by minimizing the dollar investment base.

Increased foreign borrowing complicates the choice of an appropriate financial structure. The two major reasons for difficulties are that financial structure norms vary dramatically between countries, even if we hold constant such traditional determinants as industry, size, and variability of sales, and both the United States and foreign host governments are becoming more concerned about the way in which foreign subsidiaries of United States firms are financed.

Most multinational corporations report consolidated foreign and domestic balance sheet and income figures. Any change in foreign borrowing will automatically change the ratio of debt to total assets for the consolidated corporation, unless offset by a change in domestic borrowing.

One of the unresolved issues of finance theory is whether or not an optimal financial structure exists for a firm, and if so, how it can be determined.[1] Regardless of the theoretical argument, similarity of financial structures of firms in the same industry suggests that they act as if there is an optimal financial structure for an industry.[2] Furthermore, industry financial ratios published by Dun and Bradstreet, Robert Morris Associates, and the Securities Exchange Commission-Federal Trade Commission influence the lending organizations to expect similar ratios in their customer's financial structures. The burden of proof is on the borrowing firm to show that its financial structure should diverge significantly from the industry norms.

Despite the influence of industry norms on financial structure, there are still of course some intra-industry differences due to such variables as size, managerial risk preference, and credit standing. For example, small firms would find it too expensive to float bond issues because of the relatively heavy underwriting costs. Some managements are more sensitive to the risk of loss of control to the creditors than others, especially considering differences in overall level and variability of profits. Poor credit standing might limit a firm's ability to acquire as much debt as it desired.

The concept that industry norms influence financial structure does not hold true if firms in the same industry but domiciled in different countries are compared. Country norms are probably more important than industry norms. Results of a study of 463 corporate financial structures in nine selected industries of eleven developed countries provide empirical data to support this conclusion. Table 12.1 shows that the average proportion of debt to total assets of the sample corporations in each of the nine industries is consistently higher in Japan, Italy, Sweden, and West Germany than it is in the United States or France. Using the data in Table 12.1, an F ratio test of statistical significance was performed. The results, presented in the Appendix, give further support to the contention that financial structures of firms in the same industry do not adhere to any worldwide industry norm.

It is beyond the scope of this paper to explain definitively how country financial norms became established. However, the following environmental variables undoubtedly play a role.

Most of the capital markets outside of the United States and the United Kingdom have been unable to absorb major security flotations, although the situation is now improving in Europe as a result of the development of the Euro-dollar market. There has been both a lack of widespread interest by individuals in security ownership and a shortage of large institutional investors, such as mutual funds, insurance companies, and private pension funds. Government regulations have often given priority to placement of government debt issues with those financial intermediaries which do exist. As a result, most private security issues of both debt and equity have had to be placed directly with the banks and private lenders. Combining the

Table 12.1 Debt ratios in selected industries and countries*

	Alcoholic beverages	Automobiles	Chemicals	Electrical	Foods	Iron and steel	Non-ferrous metals	Paper	Textiles	Total
Benelux	45.7	–	44.6	37.5	56.2	50.0	59.2	35.9	54.2	47.9
France	35.8	36.0	34.3	59.1	24.7	33.7	55.0	35.5	20.9	37.2
W. Germany	59.2	55.1	54.8	67.5	42.5	63.8	68.1	71.8	44.9	58.6
Italy	64.9	77.3	68.2	73.6	66.4	77.9	67.5	–	66.6	70.3
Japan	60.9	70.3	73.2	71.1	78.3	74.5	74.5	77.7	72.2	72.5
Sweden	–	76.4	45.6	60.1	46.8	70.0	68.7	60.7	–	61.2
Switzerland	–	–	59.7	50.8	29.2	–	26.3	–	–	41.5
UK	43.8	56.5	38.7	46.9	47.6	44.9	41.7	46.6	42.4	45.5
US	31.1	39.2	43.3	50.3	34.2	35.8	36.7	33.9	44.2	38.7
Total	48.8	58.7	51.4	57.4	47.3	56.3	55.3	51.7	49.4	

Sources: US corporations are the 10 largest in each industry (4 only for automobiles), ranked by 1965 sales and reports in Moody's Industrial Manual (New York: Moody's Investor Service, Inc., June 1966). Japanese corporations are the largest publically owned corporations in each industry as reported in Kaisha Shikiho (Quarterly Reports on Corporations) (Tokyo: Toyo Keizai Shinpo Sha, June 1967). European corporations are all the publically owned corporations reported in Beerman's Financial Yearbook of Europe (London: R. Beerman Publishers, 1967).
*The number in the matrix represents average total debt as a percent of total assets based on book value. Each company is weighted equally, i.e., the individual company debt ratios are summed and divided by the number of companies in each sample. See the Appendix for supporting statistical data.

functions of stockholder and lender, which is particularly true of banks in Japan, West Germany, and Sweden, may reduce the perceived risk of default on loans to captive corporations and increase the perceived desirability of substantial leverage, thus explaining the high debt ratios of corporations in these countries.

Difference in tax regulations between countries have an influence on comparative financial structures. Tax treatment of interest on debt is not the same in all countries. Depreciation policy and the use of tax-free reserves varies greatly, which would affect the debt ratios calculated in Table 12.1, because the book value of total assets was used.

Finance theory suggests that lack of adequate corporate leverage can be offset by an individual's personal leverage, but such an option does not usually exist outside the United States.

National attitudes toward financial risk differ. For example, Japanese and Swedish bankers do not get upset if 90 per cent of their funds have been loaned. American bankers panic.

High debt ratios would be considered a good hedge in those countries where inflation is a problem. Inflation would also increase debt ratios based on book value, because the equity would typically be undervalued relative to market value.

Given the fact of different country financial structure norms, our contention is that wherever host countries permit, multinational corporations should require each subsidiary to adopt a financial structure which makes sense from the viewpoint of local norms and local cash flow patterns. In attempting to make this operational it would probably be useful to define debt as borrowing outside of the multinational corporation. This would include local currency loans as well as Euro-dollar loans, with or without parent company guarantees. The reason for this peculiar definition is that parent company loans to foreign subsidiaries are often regarded as equivalent to equity investment both by host countries and the investing corporations. A parent company loan is usually subordinated to all other kinds of debt and does not represent the same threat of insolvency as an external loan. Furthermore, the choice of debt or equity investment is often arbitrary and may even be determined by negotiation between the host country and the corporation.

The main advantages of a localized financial structure are: The environmental factors which influence local companies to adopt a particular financial structure would be taken into account by the foreign subsidiary. (It is unfortunate that we do not have a model which includes all possible environmental variables, but local financial executives would be aware of the ones which pertain to their own country.)

A localized financial structure would reduce criticism of foreign subsidiaries which have been operating with too high a proportion of debt (judged by local standards), often resulting in the accusation that they are not contributing a fair share of risk capital to the host country. At the other end of the spectrum, it would improve the image of foreign subsidiaries which have been operating with too little local debt and thus appear to be insensitive to local monetary policy.

It would enable management to evaluate their return on equity investment relative to local competitors in the same industry. In economies where interest rates are relatively high as an offset to inflation, the penalty paid would remind management of the need to consider price level changes when evaluating investment performances.

In economies where interest rates are relatively high due to the scarcity of capital, the penalty paid would remind management that unless return on assets is greater than the local price of capital, i.e., negative leverage, they are probably misallocating scarce domestic resources. This may not appear to be relevant to management decisions, but it will certainly be considered by the host country in making its decisions with respect to the firm.

In the case of United States multinational corporations, the transition to localized foreign financial structures would usually have a favorable impact on the balance of payments program. This is based on the assumption that since United States corporations appear to have a low debt-to-total assets ratio compared to other countries (Table 12.1), their natural tendency would have been to use relatively little local debt in foreign subsidiaries as well. The inadequacy of most foreign capital markets since World War II would have reinforced this tendency to use United States funds.[3]

As mentioned previously, increased local borrowing has the effect of reducing dollar exposure, while increasing the dollar rate of return on dollar investment by reducing the dollar investment base.

If each foreign subsidiary of a United States multinational corporation localizes its financial structure, the resulting consolidated balance sheet for the whole multinational corporation would show a financial structure, expressed in dollars, which would probably not conform to the norm for the industry in the United States. The debt-to-total-asset ratio would be a simple weighted average of the corresponding ratios of each country in which it happened to be operating.

Is there anything wrong with a consolidated balance sheet diverging from the industry financial structure norm in the United States? In our opinion, the answer is "No!" We are forced to agree with Gordon Donaldson's analysis of corporate debt capacity, which suggests that the financial structure of a firm should be analyzed from the internal viewpoint of the management rather than from the external viewpoint of the lender.[4] United States lenders, and even parent company management, are not in as good a position to analyze the cash flow positions of foreign subsidiaries as are their individual managements and are therefore not qualified to measure the risk of any specific debt to total asset ratio.

Localized debt structures may seem to be suboptimal from the viewpoint of financial theorists, who would like to build an analytical model of optimal financial structure which has general application. However, most of the work so far has been on devising a model which can be used to analyze the trade-off between debt and equity with respect to its effect on the market value of a firm's common stock and its cost of capital in its home market. The models generally consider such variables as interest, dividends, growth, perceived risk, and taxes.

On the other hand, some of the environmental and institutional factors which are considered to be parameters in existing finance models would actually be additional variables if these models were extended to include the multinational case. Furthermore, adoption of a financial structure which attempts to minimize the firm's cost of capital conflicts with the desirability of borrowing abroad for noncost reasons, because interest costs are typically higher abroad than in the United States.

Summary

Multinational operation complicates the choice of an appropriate corporate financial structure. Financial structure norms vary significantly among countries, even among companies in the same industry. Differences are caused by such environmental variables as inadequacy of national capital markets and financial intermediaries, difference in tax regulations, inability of individuals to obtain foreign financial leverage, varying national attitudes toward risk, and different rates of inflation.

In our opinion, wherever local authorities permit, multinational corporations should require each subsidiary to adopt a financial structure which makes sense from the viewpoint of local norms and local cash flow patterns. Of course if this were done, the consolidated balance sheet for the whole multinational corporation would show a financial structure, expressed in dollars, which would not conform to the United States industry norm. This should not be a critical factor if one considers that local management is in a far better position than either United States lenders or parent company management to evaluate local cash flows and, therefore, the risk of any specific debt-to-total asset ratio.

Localized debt structures may seem to be suboptimal from the viewpoint of financial theorists who would like to build an analytical model of financial structure which has general application. However, a general model should include the foreign environmental variables. Perhaps an even more serious problem arises when the desire to adopt a financial structure which minimizes the firm's cost of capital conflicts with the desire to borrow abroad for noncost reasons, because interest rates are usually higher abroad than in the United States.

References

We would like to acknowledge the assistance of our colleague Dr. Matsu-kichi Amano and our graduate assistant Robert Holm, as well as the service and funding support provided by the School of Business and Technology, Oregon State University.

1   The main elements of the theoretical argument can be found in Ezra Solomon, *The Theory of Financial Management* (New York: Columbia Univ. Press, 1963). An excellent managerial approach to the same problem can be found in Gordon Donaldson, "New Framework for Corporate Debt Policy," *Harvard Business Review*, XL:2 (March–April 1962).
2   Eli Schwartz and J. Richard Aronson, "Optimal Financial Structure," *Journal of Finance*, March 1967, pp. 10–18. The authors found similarity in the financial structures of firms classified into very broad industry groups. The results might not have been the same for narrower groups, because it is becoming increasingly difficult to classify companies into a single industry.
3   Proof of this hypothesis is difficult to find because separate balance sheets for foreign subsidiaries are not available either in annual reports prepared for stockholders or those submitted to the SEC.
4   Donaldson, "New Framework for Corporate Debt Policy."

Appendix

Table 12.A1 Supporting data for average debt ratios in selected industries and countries

	Alcoholic beverages		Automobiles		Chemicals		Electrical		Foods		Iron and steel		Nonferrous metals		Paper		Textiles		Total
	Sample size	Standard deviation	Sample size	Standard deviation	Sample size	Standard deviation	Sample size	Standard deviation	Sample size	Standard deviation	Sample size	Standard deviation	Sample size	Standard deviation	Sample size	Standard deviation	Sample size	Standard deviation	
Benelux	2	8.1	–	–	3	4.2	4	14.8	3	9.7	8	19.8	3	19.9	4	12.9	4	3.4	31
France	5	13.3	2	23.7	6	15.9	5	15.6	2	22.3	10	27.0	2	2.8	3	18.5	1	–	36
W. Germany	5	7.9	2	3.0	11	7.8	5	5.3	2	11.7	15	10.7	5	11.6	2	3.1	4	10.5	51
Italy	1	–	1	–	5	16.4	7	6.7	4	27.2	3	5.8	1	–	–	–	7	10.8	29
Japan	10	13.9	10	13.3	15	9.2	15	6.1	16	14.9	10	3.2	15	10.1	15	4.7	15	9.2	121
Sweden	–	–	2	1.1	1	–	3	7.3	2	6.5	2	0.7	1	7.1	4	–	–	–	15
Switzerland	–	–	–	–	4	20.0	4	15.8	3	8.8	–	–	1	–	–	–	–	–	12
UK	8	8.6	2	7.7	14	11.5	19	11.1	12	10.8	12	8.8	4	22.4	9	10.6	4	5.3	84
US	10	9.5	4	6.7	10	13.7	10	11.2	10	12.2	10	4.6	10	18.6	10	11.8	10	16.5	84
Total	41	–	23	–	69	–	72	–	54	–	70	–	42	–	47	–	45	–	463

Table 12.A2 F ratio test of statistical significance of differences among average industry debt ratios

| | F ratios | | |
	Calculated	95% confidence level	99% confidence level
Alcoholic beverages	7.70	2.38	3.38
Automobiles	3.53	2.74	4.20
Chemicals	10.14	2.10	2.82
Electrical	9.57	2.09	2.80
Foods	10.05	2.15	2.93
Iron and steel	11.24	2.16	2.94
Nonferrous metals	8.46	2.24	3.10
Pulp and paper	23.61	2.34	3.29
Textiles	13.32	2.35	3.32

Explanation of Table 12.A2

Based on data in Table 12.1 and Appendix Table 12.A1, an F-distribution was used to test the hypothesis that average debt ratios for the same industry in each country are statistically equivalent. (The F-distribution is used to test for the significance of differences among sample means. A description of the rationale and methodology involved can be found in most basic statistical textbooks, e.g., Samuel B. Richmond, *Statistical Analysis* [New York: Ronald Press, 1964], pp. 306–317.)

For example, to accept this hypothesis for the iron and steel industry at the 95 per cent confidence level, F must be less than 2.16. Since F is 11.24 for the iron and steel industry, we reject the hypothesis that the average ratio of debt-to-total assets in the iron and steel industry is statistically equivalent for the nine sample country groups tested. The same conclusion is true for each of the other industries at the 95 per cent confidence level and is even true for all industries except automobiles at the 99 per cent level. Results of the tests are summarized in Table 12.A2.

13

Financial Structure and Cost of Capital in the Multinational Corporation*

Alan C. Shapiro

*Source: *Journal of Financial and Quantitative Analysis*, 13 (June 1978), pp. 211–226.

Introduction

As the multinational corporation (MNC) becomes the norm rather than the exception, the need to internationalize the tools of domestic financial analysis is apparent. A key question is: What cost-of-capital figure should be used in appraising the profitability of foreign investments? This paper seeks to provide a comprehensive approach to analyze the cost-of-capital question. It begins by extending the weighted cost-of-capital concept to the multinational firm. It then builds on previous research to address the following related topics: national or multinational financial structure norms; the role of parent company guarantees; the costing of various fund sources particularly when exchange risk is present; the impact of tax and regulatory factors; risk and diversification; and joint ventures.

The Weighted Cost of Capital—The Domestic Firm

The average incremental cost of funds which the domestic firm seeks to minimize by choosing an appropriate capital structure equals:

$$k_e(1 - \lambda) + i_d\lambda$$

where k_e is the stockholders' risk-adjusted required return (the cost of new equity); i_d is the after-tax cost of new debt; and λ is the firm's target debt ratio (total debt/total assets). The target debt ratio, λ, is based on the financial structure which minimizes the average cost of new funds. If leverage is irrelevant in the absence of taxes, as Modigliani–Miller [13] argue, then λ would be based on institutional constraints. The general consensus today appears to be that an optimal capital structure does exist, particularly when taxes are considered, but that the "average cost of capital curve is relatively flat over a fairly wide range of leverage ratio" [28, p. 340]. Thus the cost of deviating from the optimum is likely to be minimal.

The cost-of-capital figure relevant for investment decisions is the marginal cost of capital. In this paper, the marginal cost of capital will be assumed constant and hence will equal the average cost of new funds k_e $(1 - \lambda) + i_d\lambda$.

The Multinational Firm

The multinational corporation is assumed to finance its foreign subsidiaries in such a way as to minimize its incremental weighted cost of capital. As in the domestic firm, this figure will be assumed to equal the MNC's marginal cost of capital.

Following Adler [1, p. 120], suppliers of capital to the MNC will be assumed to associate the risk of default with the MNC's consolidated worldwide debt ratio λ.[1] This is primarily because bankruptcy or other forms of financial distress in an overseas subsidiary could seriously impair the parent company's ability to operate domestically. Any deviations from the MNC's target capital structure will cause adjustments in the mix of debt and equity used to finance future investments. The required adjustments and their cost implications are elaborated below.

Costing Various Sources of Funds

Suppose a foreign subsidiary requires I dollars to finance a new investment, to be funded as follows:

P dollars by the parent; E_f dollars by the subsidiary's retained earnings, and D_f dollars by foreign debt with $P + E_f + D_f = I$.

In computing the subsidiary's weighted cost of capital, we will first examine the individual cost of each component as follows:

Parent Company Funds

The required rate of return on parent company funds (the rate used in capital budgeting) is the firm's marginal cost of capital. Hence, parent funds invested overseas should yield the parent's marginal cost of capital provided that the foreign investments undertaken do not change the overall riskiness of the MNC's operations. The effect of risk will be addressed in a later section.

Retained Earnings

The cost of retained earnings overseas is an issue of current concern (see Ness [15], for example). The existence of dividend withholding taxes, tax deferral, and transfer costs could yield specific benefits to retaining earnings abroad. With an effective foreign tax rate of t_f, each dollar of earnings abroad will provide $1 - t_f$ dollars of retained earnings. If these earnings are then remitted to parent headquarters in the form of dividends, though, only $\$.52 < 1 - t_f$ will get through if $t_f < .48$ and no excess foreign tax credits are available.[2] Therefore, if the parent has a required rate of return on equity of k_e, retained earnings need yield only $(.52k_e/1 - t_f) < k_e$ overseas to provide an equivalent return.[3] On the other hand, if the parent has an effective tax rate overseas in excess of 48 percent, then repatriated earnings will provide foreign tax credits. If these foreign tax credits can be used by the MNC, then the cost of retained earnings abroad, $.52k_e/1 - t_f$ will be greater than k_e.[4]

The question arises as to whether a company should incorporate these adjustments in computing its cost of retained earnings. The major argument against such an approach is that since MNCs typically have other, lower cost, means of shifting funds from one country to another, the use of a uniform cost of equity would be more appropriate. These transfer mechanisms include adjustments in transfer prices, dividend flows, fee and royalty charges, and intracompany loan and credit arrangements. Rutenberg [19] analyzes these methods and the costs associated with each. A firm which operates through joint ventures or which has few intercorporate trade linkages will find that its ability to shift funds by means other than dividend payments is probably limited. Thus, the answer for a given firm to the question as to whether these tax adjustments should be incorporated depends upon how significant these tax and transfer cost effects are (i.e., if the cost of sending funds to headquarters is minimal, then the subsidiary's cost of equity should equal k_e; if not the cost of retained earnings should be adjusted to reflect the minimum-cost means of transferring these funds).

Depreciation

As in a purely domestic corporation, the cost of depreciation-generated funds equals the firm's incremental average cost of capital.

Local Debt

Many firms borrow locally to provide offsetting liabilities for their exposed local currency assets. The after-tax dollar cost of borrowing locally equals the sum of the interest expense plus the exchange gain or loss. If e_0 is the current dollar/local currency (LC) exchange rate, $(LC1 = \$e_0)$, e_1 is the expected exchange rate at the end of one year, and r_L is the local currency interest rate, then the effective dollar interest rate equals $r_L(e_1/e_0)(1 - t_f)$

$- (e_0 - e_1/e_0)$ where, as before, t_f is the foreign tax rate. The first term is the after-tax dollar interest cost on $LC(1/e_0) = \$1$ (paid at year-end when the exchange rate is e_1) while the second term is the gain or loss involved in repaying a local currency loan of one dollar with local currency valued at year-end at e_1/e_0 dollars. The gain or loss has no tax implications since $LC(1/e_0)$ was borrowed and $LC(1/e_0)$ repaid.[5] (See [21] and [24] for additional details on how to compute the cost of debt when exchange rate changes are likely.)

Computing with Weighted Cost of Capital

With no change in risk characteristics, the parent's cost of debt and equity remains at i_d and k_e respectively. Let the subsidiary's cost of retained earnings equal k_s and its after-tax dollar cost of foreign debt equal i_f.

Since the debt ratio for parent funds P already equals λ, an additional amount of equity, E, is required to bring the corporate debt ratio back to λ where E is the solution to:

$$\frac{D_f}{D_f + E_f + E} = \lambda.$$

Then $E = (D_f/\lambda) - D_f - E_f$. The opportunity cost associated with this additional equity is the difference between the cost of this equity $k_e E$ and the parent's weighted cost of capital $[k_e(1-\lambda)+i_d\lambda]E$. By substituting and rearranging terms, this cost is seen to equal

$$[D_f(1 - \lambda) - E_f\lambda](k_e - i_d).$$

If $E = 0$ [i.e., $(D_f/D_f + E_f) = \lambda$], then this term also equals 0. The incremental weighted cost of capital is then equal to

$$k_1 = \frac{P}{I}[k_e(1 - \lambda) + i_d\lambda] + k_s \frac{E_f}{I} + \frac{i_f D_f}{I} + (k_e - i_d)[D_f(1 - \lambda) - E_f\lambda].$$

The last term is the penalty (reward) for over- (under-)leveraging abroad. If this investment changes the parent company risk characteristics, then the parent's cost of equity capital must be adjusted.[6]

A simplified version of this formula is possible by redefining and reorganizing terms. If we set $k_o = k_e(1-\lambda)+i_d\lambda$, then k_1 reduces to:

$$k_0 - \alpha(k_e - k_s) - \beta(i_d - i_f)$$

where

$$\alpha = \frac{E_f}{I} \text{ and } \beta = \frac{D_f}{I}.$$

This formula ignores the possibility that the optimal D/E ratio may itself be dependent on the relative costs of debts and equity. It, therefore, provides an upper bound for estimating a subsidiary's cost of capital. Furthermore, this formula is appropriate whether or not an optimal capital structure exists. If it does exist, then λ should equal the optimal debt ratio. If not, then the cost of capital measured at λ remains constant over the entire range of leverage and the leverage penalty is exactly defined.

Using this formula, it is possible to settle one controversy in the literature. Zenoff and Zwick [29] argue for the use of the company-wide marginal cost-of-capital estimate as the discount factor to be used in evaluating foreign investments. On the other hand, Stonehill and Stitzel [26] claim that a firm should use the cost of capital appropriate to local firms operating in the same industry. Both these approaches are incorrect since they ignore the factor of multinationality. As the formula above indicates, in countries where the local cost of capital is high relative to an MNC's cost of funds, using the local cost of capital to evaluate investments will cause profitable ventures to be foregone. At the same time, it would be suboptimal for a multinational corporation to ignore the possibility that some of its subsidiaries may have access to lower cost funds than does the parent.

A related issue is the choice of subsidiary capital structure.

Subsidiary Financial Structure

The question has been raised as to whether subsidiary financial structures should:

(a) conform to parent company norms;
(b) conform to the capitalization norms established in each country; or
(c) vary, so as to take advantage of opportunities to minimize the cost of capital.

The third alternative appears to be the appropriate choice. As Adler [1, p. 122] points out, "Any accounting rendition of a separate capital structure for the subsidiary is therefore wholly illusory and should be ignored in planning foreign investments." Thus, within the constraints set by foreign statutory or minimum equity requirements and the need to maintain a worldwide financial structure, a multinational corporation should finance its requirements in such a manner as to minimize its incremental average cost of capital.

A subsidiary with a capital structure similar to its parent may miss out on profitable opportunities to lower its cost of funds. For example, rigid adherence to a fixed debt/equity ratio may not allow a subsidiary to take advantage of government-subsidized debt or low-cost loans for international agencies. On the other hand, forcing a subsidiary to borrow funds locally to meet parent norms may be quite expensive in a country with a high-cost capital market. The cost-minimising approach would be to allow subsidiaries in low-cost countries to exceed the parent company capitalization norm while subsidiaries in high-cost nations would have lower target debt/equity ratios. This assumes that capital markets are at least partially segmented. While there are no definite conclusions on this issue at present, the variety and degree of governmental restrictions on capital market access lend credence to the segmentation hypothesis.[7] In addition, the behavior of MNCs in lobbying against regulations such as the OFDI restrictions indicates that they believe capital costs vary significantly among countries.

A counterargument by Stonehill and Stitzel [26] is that a subsidiary's financial structure should conform to local norms. Hence, subsidiaries based in Japan or West Germany should have much higher debt/equity ratios than the U.S. parent or a French subsidiary. As Naumann-Etienne [14, p. 867] points out, the problem with this argument is that it ignores the strong linkage between U.S.-based multinationals and the U.S. capital market. Since most of its stock is owned and traded in the United States, it follows that that firm's target debt/equity ratio is dependent on U.S. shareholders' risk perceptions. Furthermore, the level of foreign debt/equity ratios is usually determined by institutional factors which have no bearing on U.S. multinationals. For example, Japanese and German banks own much of the equity as well as the debt issues of local corporations. Combining the functions of stockholder and lender may reduce the perceived risk of default on loans to captive corporations and increase the desirability of substantial leverage. This would not apply to a wholly-owned subsidiary. However, a joint venture with a corporation tied into the local banking system may enable an MNC to lower its local cost of capital by leveraging itself, without a proportional increase in risk, to a degree that would be impossible otherwise.

The basic hypothesis that underlies this paper thus far is that a subsidiary's capital structure is relevant only insofar as it affects the parent's consolidated worldwide debt ratio. The related issues of consolidation and parent company guarantees appear to indicate that at least some MNCs believe otherwise. The next section explores these issues at greater length.

Parent Company Guarantees and Consolidation

Multinational firms are often thought to be reluctant to explicitly guarantee the debt of their subsidiaries even when a more advantageous interest rate can be negotiated. Their assumption appears to be that nonguaranteed debt would not be included in the parent company's worldwide debt ratio whereas guaranteed debt, as a contingent liability, would affect the parent's debt-raising capacity.

This assumption ignores certain realities. It is very unlikely that a parent company would allow a subsidiary to default on its debt, even if that debt were not guaranteed. In fact, a survey by Stobaugh [25] showed that not one of a sample of 20 medium and large multinationals (average foreign sales of $200 million and $1 billion annually, respectively) would allow their subsidiaries to default on debt which did not have a parent company guarantee. Of the small multinationals interviewed (average annual sales of $50 million), only one out of 17 indicated that it would allow a subsidiary to default on its obligations under some circumstances. It is reasonable, therefore, to assume that the multinationals feel a "moral" obligation, for very practical reasons, to implicitly, if not explicitly, guarantee their subsidiaries' debt. Since an explicit guarantee will generally lower subsidiary borrowing costs, it will usually be in the parent's best interest to issue such a guarantee provided that the parent is actually committed to making good on its subsidiaries' debt.[8]

Related to this issue of parent guaranteed debt is the belief, among some firms which do not consolidate their foreign affiliates, that unconsolidated (and nonguaranteed) overseas debt need not affect the MNC's debt ratio. Unless investors and analysts can be fooled permanently, though, unconsolidated overseas leveraging would not allow a firm to lower its cost of capital below the cost of capital for an identical firm which consolidated its foreign affiliates. Any overseas debt offering large enough to materially affect a firm's degree of leverage would very quickly come to the attention of financial analysts.[9]

The effects of tax and regulatory factors on subsidiary capital structures will now be examined.

Tax and Regulatory Factors

Parent company funds, whether called equity or debt, require the same rate of return. However, the appropriate ratio of parent company loans to parent equity may be a crucial decision. Loans are generally preferred to equity by MNCs for a number of reasons. First of all, parent company loans to foreign subsidiaries are often regarded as equivalent to equity investments both by host countries and local creditors. A parent company loan is generally subordinated to all other kinds of debt and does not represent the same threat of insolvency as an external loan. Given this equivalence in the eyes of potential creditors and host governments, the tax and flexibility advantages of debt could become dominant considerations. A firm typically has wider latitude in repatriating funds in the form of interest and loan repayments than as dividends or reductions in equity, since the latter fund flows are usually more closely controlled by governments.

Another reason for the use of parent company loans as opposed to equity investments is the possibility of reducing taxes. If foreign tax rates are below U.S. rates, dividends will typically lead to increased taxes whereas loan repayments will not. If foreign tax rates are above 48 percent, and a withholding tax is assessed on dividends, paying out dividends will lead to higher taxes unless the excess foreign tax credits can be used elsewhere.

Firms do not have complete latitude in choosing their debt/equity ratios abroad. This is frequently a subject for negotiation with the host governments. In addition, dividends are often restricted to a fixed percentage of equity. A small equity base could also lead to a high return on equity, opening up a company to charges of exploitation.

It should be reiterated here that a firm's cost of capital is not affected by whether it calls its overseas investments debt or equity. However, the cash flow from foreign investments could very well be affected by the form of this investment. According to Robbins and Stobaugh [17, p. 58], U.S. multinationals usually use more equity than is required to meet government regulations. As a result, total foreign plus U.S. taxes are greater than they need be.

Thus far, we have assumed that international investments will not affect a firm's risk characteristics. The next section examines this assumption both theoretically and empirically.

Riskiness of Foreign Operations

The traditional approach to international investment considers foreign operations as adding to overall firm riskiness. Foreign exchange risk, the risks of expropriation and continued governmental intervention are pointed out as increasing the political and economic risks facing any firms operating abroad. However, this view is quite limited.

According to modern capital asset pricing theory, investors must be compensated only for their securities' systematic risk since nonsystematic risk can be diversified away by holding a market portfolio. Based on the pioneering work of Grubel [8] and Grubel and Fadnor [9] on international portfolios, this concept of systematic versus nonsystematic risk has been extended to the analysis of the riskiness of foreign operations. Although individual foreign investments may be riskier than comparable investments in the United States, the diversification effect due to operating in a number of countries whose economic cycles are not perfectly in phase could reduce the variation in a firm's earnings. We will now examine each of these sources of risk, concluding with evidence on the actual risk perceptions of investors.

Political Risk

Political risk is relevant to the MNC insofar as it results in a deprivation of wealth.[10] Empirical evidence by Truitt [27] on the expropriation experiences of U.S. and British MNCs since World War II indicates that industries can be ranked in terms of their susceptibilities to political risk. Expropriation or creeping expropriation is much more likely to happen in the extractive, utility, or financial service sectors of an economy than in the manufacturing sector although there is a trend toward increasing takeovers of manufacturing firms [11].

In general, the greater the benefits to the local economy provided by a given subsidiary, the lesser the degree of risk. Thus, political risk appears to be inversely related to a subsidiary's exports, the amount of local labor employed, the extent of capital and technology supplied by the firm, and the difficulty of replacement by local firms. In addition, joint ventures are less susceptible to political interference than are wholly-owned subsidiaries [6], perhaps because of the reduced perception of foreign control. Therefore, any arbitrary increase in a firm's cost of capital for political risk is likely to neglect the degree to which the firm can influence this risk. Furthermore, increasing a firm's discount rate to compensate for political risk will ignore the time pattern as well as the magnitude of this risk.

Inflation and Exchange Risks

Foreign inflation will not affect the MNC's dollar cost of borrowing abroad [4]. However, exchange rate changes will affect these costs. To the extent that capital markets overseas are segmented, though, the cost of borrowing abroad may not fully reflect these exchange rate expectations.

Inflation and exchange rate changes will affect the future cash flows of a project. In fact, there are systematic and predictable changes to foreign currency cost and revenue streams, predictable both as to direction and magnitude. Recent studies have shown that the sector of the economy a firm operates in (export, import—competing, or purely domestic) and the sources of its inputs (imports, domestic traded, or nontraded goods) are the major determinants of a firm's exchange risk (for example, see [22]).

This means that the incremental effects of changes in currency values on the parent's risk characteristics and, hence, the parent's cost of capital, can only be determined by examining the impact of variations in foreign earnings on variations in the firm's worldwide consolidated earnings [23]. However, variations due to exchange rate changes will be difficult, if not empirically impossible, to separate out from variations due to other events such as changes in government policies, competitors' actions, etc. Nor need these exchange effects be isolated. The important factor to analyze is the simultaneous impact on firm earnings of the myriad of events to which a multinational firm is prone.

Diversification

As we mentioned above, the greater riskiness of individual projects overseas could well be offset by beneficial portfolio effects. Supporting evidence is provided by Cohen [3] whose work indicates that there is little correlation between the earnings of the various national components of MNCs. To the extent that foreign cash flows are not perfectly correlated with those of domestic investments, the overall risk associated with variations in cash flows which confronts a stockholder might be reduced. Thus, the greater riskiness of individual projects overseas could well be offset by beneficial portfolio effects. However, international diversification by firms will benefit their stockholders only if there are barriers to direct international portfolio diversification by individual investors.[11] According to Agmon and Lessard [2] these barriers do exist. "Available evidence suggests that neither individual nor mutual funds are broadly diversified internationally, presumably at least in part due to institutional barriers to foreign investment" [2, p. 2]. Thus, the extent to which these portfolio effects are beneficial to an MNC is an empirical question.

Some tentative evidence is available. Severn [20] has found that the greater the foreign involvement of a firm, the lower the covariance of its earnings per share with the earnings per share of Standard and Poor's Composite Index. Gordon and Halpern [7] have demonstrated the close positive correlation between the systematic risk of a firm's earnings and its stock price β. Thus, Severn's conclusion that the higher the percentage of foreign to total earnings the lower the capitalization rate on its earnings appears reasonable. However, since multinationals are larger, on average, than are nonmultinationals, the reduction in earnings variability may be due to size, and a consequent increase in product diversification, rather than to the influence of foreign-source earnings. In fact, Haegele [10] has shown that while the stock price βs are slightly lower for MNCs, when corrected for size, there is no significant difference between the βs of MNCs and non-MNCs.

Rugman [18] does show that earning variability is a decreasing function of foreign-source earnings even when corrected for size. The relationship between this reduction in earnings variability and a reduction in the systematic risk of an MNC's earnings, however, is not demonstrated. This is an important distinction because there is no empirical evidence to suggest a correlation between a firm's stock price β and its degree of earnings variability. The only evidence available relates to a firm's systematic earnings risk. However, the risk of bankruptcy for a firm is dependent on total as opposed to only systematic earnings variability. Thus, a reduction in the total earnings variability could allow an MNC to leverage itself more highly leading to a reduction in its marginal cost of capital.

Investor Perceptions

Agmon and Lessard [2] have tested the proposition that investors recognize and reward the geographical diversification of U.S. multinationals by using a two-factor capital asset pricing model with the second factor being the percentage of foreign sales. According to the authors, "The results reported above support the hypothesis that the market (NYSE) behaves as if it recognizes the international composition of the activities of U.S. based corporations" [2, p. 12]. Taking a different approach, Kohers [12] has used the dividend valuation model (see [28] for an explanation of this model) to measure the cost of equity capital for MNCs. He found no statistically significant differences in the cost of equity capital for six of the seven industries studied including the oil and nonferrous metals industries.

Thus, while the evidence is scant, the available empirical research indicates that if multinationality alters a firm's perceived riskiness, the effect is slight for most firms and may well be beneficial.

Joint Ventures

Since many MNCs participate in joint ventures, either by choice or necessity, establishing the required rate of return for this form of investment is particularly important. Several problems arise. The most troublesome is the case where the MNC's required rate of return in a joint venture differs from its partner's cost of capital. Adler [1] suggests using a complex compensation principle whereby each partner is compensated on the basis of its opportunity cost of money. This will lead to a situation where each partner tries to declare as high a cost of capital as possible. Agreement on a joint venture cost of capital using this principle will then be even less likely. One solution is to set the required rate of return for the joint venture equal to the maximum cost of capital among the participants.

The firm can use the formula presented earlier to establish its marginal cost of capital in a joint venture. There is one caveat. A joint venture partner may have access to local sources of capital which enable the joint venture to be leveraged beyond what the subsidiary would be able to do on its own. The formula presented earlier penalized a subsidiary which leverages itself more than the parent itself is leveraged. This is due to the increased risk of financial distress associated with more highly leveraged firms. However, in countries such as Japan and Germany, increased leverage will not necessarily lead to increased financial risks due to the close relationship between the local banks and corporation. Thus, increased leverage in a joint venture in Japan, for example, may not require application of the leverage penalty. The assessment of the impact of leverage in a joint venture is a judgmental factor which requires an analysis of the partner's ties with the local financial community, particularly with the local banks.

Summary and Conclusions

This paper has analyzed a number of factors related to an MNC's cost of capital. If capital markets are segmented or a subsidiary's risk characteristics are different from those of the parent, then the subsidiary's cost of capital must be adjusted to reflect these differences. It was decided that the issues of consolidation and parent-guaranteed debt are largely false ones— that the parent cannot significantly change its cost of capital by choosing whether to consolidate foreign earnings or guarantee local debt.

Analysis of the available evidence on the impact of foreign operations on firm riskiness suggests that, if there is an effect, it is generally to reduce both actual and perceived riskiness. However, some investments are more risk-prone than others and this must be accounted for. Much work remains to be done in empirically testing the proposition of international capital market segmentation. In addition, further empirical testing of investor perceptions of the riskiness of MNCs is required. These perceptions are likely to be affected by the location as well as the percentage of foreign-source earnings.

Notes

1. If the perceived risk of default is affected by the sources of funds in addition to the ratio of total debt to assets, then the multinational firm has a more complex optimization problem which may allow it to discriminate monopsonistically among lenders in different markets.

2. These calculations only hold for subsidiaries in developed countries. The relevant tax rules for subsidiaries in less developed countries are reported in [16].

3. For example, if $k_e = 16$ percent and $t_f = .4$, then the cost of retained earnings abroad would equal only 13.9 percent.

4. These formulas also hold if there are dividend withholding taxes.

5. For example, if the annual cruzeiro cost of debt in Brazil is 35 percent, the Brazilian tax rate is 30 percent, and the cruzeiro is expected to depreciate 10 percent per annum, then the effective after-tax dollar cost of borrowing cruzeiros equals .7 (.90) 35 percent − 10 percent = 12.05 percent. This expression arises as follows: suppose $100 worth of cruzeiros are borrowed today. The cost of repaying the principal, at the end of one year, equals $90 since the exchange gain is not recog-

nized by the Brazilian government (X cruzeiros were borrowed and X cruzeiros were repaid). In addition, the interest expense equals $35 (.90) (.07). The total cost then equals $12.05 for an effective dollar interest rate of 12.05 percent.

6. A numerical example will illustrate some of the concepts presented here. Assume that a new investment requires $100 million. Of this total, $20 million will be provided by parent company funds, $25 million by retained earnings in the subsidiary, and $55 million through the issue of new long-term debt by the subsidiary. The parent's cost of equity equals 14 percent and its after-tax cost of long-term debt equals 5 percent. However, this investment is expected to increase the systematic risk of the firm, thereby requiring a rate of return of 16 percent on new parent equity and 6 percent after-tax on new long-term debt. With a foreign tax rate of 40 percent and no excess foreign tax credit available, the cost of retained earnings will be set equal to 13.9 percent. Let the nominal rate of interest on the subsidiary's debt be 16 percent with an anticipated average annual devaluation of 5 percent over the life of the loan. Then the effective after-tax dollar cost of this foreign debt equals 4 percent. Assume further that the MNC's current debt/equity ratio, which is considered to be optimal, equals 3/7 with present debt equal to $300 million and equity equal to $700 million. Then the new corporate D/E ratio equals 355/725. To return to a D/E ratio of 3/7, additional equity in the amount of $103 million must be raised. Ordinarily, $31 million of this $103 million would be in the form of debt. Thus, an opportunity cost equal to $31,000,000 (.16 − .06) or $3,100,000 is paid for the additional overseas leverage. The total annual risk-adjusted cost of the parent company funds equals $20,000,000 (.16 × .7 + .06 × .3) = $2,600,000. The annual cost of the retained earnings equals $25,000,000 (.139) = $3,500,000 and the total annual expected cost of the foreign debt issued is $55,000,000 (.04) = $2,200,000. Including the annual opportunity cost involved in over-leveraging abroad, the average incremental cost of capital (and the marginal cost) equals (2.6 + 3.5 + 2.2 + 3.1/100) = 11.4 percent. This compares with the parent company's cost of capital for this investment of 13 percent.

7. A recent study by Dufey [5] for the U.S. Treasury classifies the rich variety of international constraints on international capital market efficiency.

8. It is likely that the market has already incorporated this practical commitment in its parent's worldwide debt capacity. An overseas creditor, on the other hand, may not be as certain regarding the firm's intentions. The fact that the parent doesn't guarantee its subsidiaries' debt may then convey some information, i.e., commitment to subsidiary debt is not that strong.

9. Some evidence of market efficiency was provided through talks with bond raters at Moody's and Standard and Poor's. Individuals from both agencies stated that they would closely examine situations where nonguaranteed debt issued by unconsolidated foreign affiliates would noticeably affect a firm's worldwide debt equity ratio. In addition parent company guaranteed debt is included in bond rater analyses of a firm's contingent liabilities, whether this debt is consolidated or not. Thus, it appears that the growing financial sophistication of MNCs has been paralleled by increased sophistication among rating agencies and investors.

10. Any definition of political risk is arbitrary but in this paper it refers to expropriation, nationalization, and any other government interference with a subsidiary's operations which results in a loss of wealth to the MNC.

11. Even if there are no barriers to individual diversification internationally, the reduced risk of bankruptcy associated with a more stable cash flow could lower an MNC's cost of capital.

References

[1] Adler, M. "The Cost of Capital and Valuation of a Two-Country Firm." *Journal of Finance* (March 1974), p. 119.

[2] Agmon, T., and D. Lessard. "International Diversification and the Multinational Corporation: An Investigation of Price Behavior of the Shares of U.S. Based Multinational Corporations on the N.Y.S.E." Working Paper 1804–75, Sloan School of Management, Massachusetts Institute of Technology (1975).

[3] Cohen, B. I. *Multinational Firms and Asian Exports.* New Haven, Conn.: Yale University Press (1975).

[4] de Faro, C., and J. V. Jucker. "The Impact of Inflation and Devaluation on the Selection of an International Borrowing Source." *Journal of International Business Studies* (Fall 1973), p. 97.

[5] Dufey, G. "The Structure of Private Foreign Investment with Specific Reference to Portfolio Investment." Report prepared for U.S. Dept. of Treasury, OASIA/Research (January 31, 1976), cited with permission of author.

[6] Friedman; Dalmonoff; and Wolfgang. *Joint International Business Ventures.* New York: Columbia University Press (1961).

[7] Gordon, M. J., and P. J. Halpern. "Cost of Capital for the Division of a Firm." *Journal of Finance* (September 1974), p. 1153.

[8] Grubel, H. G. "Internationally Diversified Portfolios: Welfare Gains and Capital Flows." *American Economic Review* (December 1968), p. 1299.

[9] Grubel, H. G., and K. Fadner. "The Interdependence of International Equity Markets." *Journal of Finance* (March 1971), p. 89.

[10] Haegele, M. J. "Exchange Rate Expectations and Security Returns." Unpublished Ph.D. dissertation, The University of Pennsylvania (1974).

[11] Hawkins, R. G., and N. Mintz. "Government Takeovers of U.S. Foreign Affiliates." *Journal of International Business Studies* (Spring 1976), p. 3.

[12] Kohers, T. "The Effect of Multinational Corporations on the Cost of Equity of U.S. Corporations: An Empirical Study." *Management International Review* (2–3/1974), p. 121.

[13] Modigliani, F., and M. H. Miller. "The Cost of Capital, Corporation Finance, and the Theory of Investment." *American Economic Review* (June 1958), p. 261.

[14] Naumann-Etienne, R. "A Framework for Financial Decisions in Multinational Corporation-Summary of Recent Research." *Journal of Financial and Quantitative Analysis* (November 1974), p. 859.

[15] Ness, W. L., Jr. "U.S. Corporate Income Taxation and the Dividend Remittance Policy of Multinational Corporations." *Journal of International Business Studies* (Spring 1975), p. 67.

[16] Price-Waterhouse. "Information Guide on U.S. Corporations Doing Business Abroad." (January 1972).

[17] Robbins, S. M., and R. S. Stobaugh. "Financing Foreign Affiliates." *Financial Management* (Winter 1972), p. 56.

[18] Rugman, A. M. "Risk Reduction by International Diversification." Paper presented at the Academy of International Business – INSEAD Conference, Fountainbleau, Paris (July 7, 1975).

[19] Rutenberg, D. P. "Maneuvering Liquid Assets in a Multinational Corporation." *Management Science* (June 1970), p. 671.

[20] Severn, A. K. "Investor Evaluation of Foreign and Domestic Risk." *Journal of Finance* (May 1974), p. 545.

[21] Shapiro, A. C. "Evaluating Financing Costs for Multinational Subsidiaries." *Journal of International Business Studies* (Fall 1975), p. 25.

[22] ——— . "Exchange Rate Changes Inflation and the Value of the Multinational Corporation." *Journal of Finance* (May 1975), p. 485.

[23] ——— . "Defining Exchange Risk." *Journal of Business* (forthcoming).

[24] Solnick, B. H., and J. Grall. "Eurobonds; Determinants of the Demand for Capital and the International Interest Rate Structure." *Journal of Bank Research* (Winter 1975), p. 218.

[25] Stobaugh, R. S. "Financing Foreign Subsidiaries of U.S.-Controlled Multinational Enterprises." *Journal of International Business Studies* (Summer 1970), p. 43.

[26] Stonehill, A., and T. Stitzel. "Financial Structure and Multinational Corporations." *California Management Review* (Fall 1969), p. 91.

[27] Truitt, J. F. "Expropriation of Foreign Investment: Summary of the Post World War II Experience of American and British Investors in Less Developed Countries." *Journal of International Business Studies* (Fall 1970), p. 21.

[28] Weston, J. F., and E. G. Brigham. *Managerial Finance*, 4th ed. New York: Holt, Rinehart and Winston (1972).

[29] Zenoff, D. B., and J. Zwick. *International Financial Management.* Englewood Cliffs, N. J.: Prentice-Hall (1969).

14

Multinational corporations vs. domestic corporations: international environmental factors and determinants of capital structure*

Kwang Chul Lee and Chuck C.Y. Kwok[†]

*Source: *Journal of International Business Studies*, 19 (SUmmer 1988), pp. 195–217.

Abstract. This paper examines whether or not U.S.-based multinational corporations (MNCs) have different capital structures than U.S. domestic corporations (DCs), and if so, what causes the differences. In explaining the difference between the capital structures of MNCs and DCs, previous studies tended to directly discuss the relationships between international environmental factors (e.g., political risk, foreign exchange risk) and the capital structure. A framework of analysis is proposed in this paper that examines the influence of environmental factors on the firm-related capital structure determinants (e.g., agency costs, bankruptcy costs) that in turn affect the capital structure of the MNC. Among the determinants that are examined, more emphasis is placed on the discussion of agency costs since no previous studies have applied this concept in the international arena. Empirical tests were conducted to investigate whether MNCs are significantly different from DCs regarding agency costs of debt, bankruptcy costs, and capital structure. Contrary to conventional wisdom, the empirical findings show that MNCs do not have lower bankruptcy costs and that they tend to have lower debt ratios than DCs.

Ever since the article of Modigliani and Miller [1958] was published, there has been a long debate in the domestic finance area as to whether or not an optimal capital structure exists. While some finance theories argue that capital structure decision is irrelevant to the value of the firm, corporations in the real world persist in following certain debt-equity ratios when capital is raised. In recent years, several theories have been developed with the intention of bridging the gap between the academic field and the actual practice. New concepts such as agency costs, bankruptcy costs, non-debt tax shields, liquidation costs, collateral value, market power, size and asymmetric information are suggested to explain why an optimal capital structure may exist for a firm.

The issue of capital structure also attracts the attention of international finance scholars. Among those who believe that optimal capital structure exists, many think that multinational corporations (MNCs) tend to be more highly leveraged than domestic corporations (DCs). It is thought that since the cash flows of MNCs are internationally diversified, they are in a better position than DCs to support higher debt ratios. This paper will empirically examine if MNCs are indeed more highly levered than DCs. It will also apply some of the recently developed concepts in the domestic finance area (e.g., agency costs, bankruptcy costs) in explaining the difference between the capital structures of MNCs and DCs.

The paper is divided into five sections. The first section reviews previous studies of capital structures in both the domestic and the international finance literature. The second section suggests a rudimentary framework of analysis which attempts to incorporate some of the new concepts in domestic finance to the international finance area. This section discusses how international environmental factors affect some firm-related characteristics (e.g., agency costs, bankruptcy costs and affiliates' capital structures) which in turn lead to the differences between the capital structures of MNCs and DCs. In the third section the research methodology is explained and some of the above-mentioned concepts are empirically tested. Empirical findings are present in section four followed by a summary and conclusions section at the end.

Literature Review

Domestic Finance Literature

Since the publication of Modigliani and Miller's (M&M) path-breaking article in 1958, the issue of whether an optimal capital structure exists has generated considerable interest within academic circles. Though some theoreticians argue that the leverage decision of a firm is irrelevant to its value, many corporations in the real world still follow certain debt-equity ratios in financing investments. To bridge the gap between theory and practice, new theories have been suggested to explain the possible existence of an optimal capital structure. For instance, Jensen & Meckling [1976] put forward the concept of agency costs. The existence of monitoring, bonding and other agency costs of debt counteract the tax advantages of debt financing; these trade-offs may then lead to the existence of an optimal capital structure. Following this line of thought, Myers [1977] points to another type of agency cost of debt which arises from the under-investment problem. When a firm has debt which matures after an investment option expires, shareholders have the incentive to reject projects that have positive net present values because the benefits from accepting the projects accrues to the bondholders without increasing the shareholders' wealth. The issuance of debt therefore leads to suboptimal investment for the firm, requiring this type of agency cost to be traded off against the tax savings of debt financing to determine the optimal capital structure.

Besides the agency cost arguments, the existence of bankruptcy costs has also been suggested. Bankruptcy costs can be direct (e.g., legal, trustee and accounting fees plus other administrative costs associated with legal proceedings) or indirect (e.g., loss of sales, loss of key employees and so forth). Expected bankruptcy costs depends on the cost of bankruptcy and the probability that bankruptcy will occur. Therefore, Baxter [1967] and Kraus & Litzenberger [1973] argue that there is a trade-off between the tax advantages of debt financing and expected bankruptcy costs. The optimal debt ratio is reached when marginal tax savings from debt financing is equal to the marginal expected loss from bankruptcy costs.

In addition to agency and bankruptcy costs, other concepts have been suggested to explain the existence of an optimal capital structure. These include non-debt tax shields in DeAngelo & Masulis [1980], liquidation costs in Titman [1983], collateral value in Scott [1977], market power in Sullivan [1974] and Lyn & Papaioannou [1985], firm size effect in Scott & Martin [1975], and asymmetric information in Ross [1977] among others.

International Finance Literature

Studies in international finance have focused on the capital structure of MNCs. Some scholars examine whether or not Modigliani and Miller's theorems can be applied in an international setting. Others study the effects of international environmental factors on MNCs' capital structures from the perspective of the International Capital Asset Pricing Model. Still others compare the capital structures of MNCs and DCs. The following brief review groups these studies under the different international environmental factors which are examined:

Foreign Exchange Risk. Krainer [1972], examining the applicability of Modigliani and Miller's propositions to a bi-national firm, argues that the existence of foreign exchange risk is sufficient to cause two otherwise identical firms to belong to different risk classes. Since Modigliani and Miller's principles assume firms of similar risk class, Krainer concludes that such principles cannot be applied in the international case. Nevertheless, Adler [1974] and Adler & Dumas [1975] find fault with Krainer's definition of foreign exchange risk. By using an explicit behavioral model of mean-variance expected-utility maximization, these authors demonstrate that exchange risk is irrelevant to the financial leverage decision. This thesis is confirmed by later works of Mehra [1978], Senbet [1979] and Lachenmayer [1984].

Political Risk. The significance of political risk in affecting the MNC's capital structure has a wider support. Krainer [1972] refers to the "repatriation risk" as another factor which renders Modigliani and Miller's principles inapplicable to a bi-national firm. Adler & Dumas [1975] also discuss the default risk of foreign bonds which may arise from the inconvertibility of currency, a political risk factor relevant to the MNC's financing decision. Beside the MNC as a whole, the capital structure of a foreign subsidiary is also thought to be affected by political risks. Stonehill & Stitzel [1969] discuss how foreign affiliates tend to borrow heavily in the local market to reduce asset exposure to political risks.

International Tax Differentials. Robbins & Stobaugh [1972] mention that MNCs operate in countries with a variety of tax structures. The complicated tax differences may violate the assumptions of Modigliani and Miller's principles. Senbet [1979] derives a bi-national firm valuation model in which both domestic and foreign corporate income tax variables are incorporated into Modigliani and Miller's tax-adjusted domestic valuation model. It is shown that international tax differentials interact with the financing mix and affect firm value. Such findings suggest that international tax differentials may be a relevant factor in determining the capital structure of the subsidiary and that of the MNC as a whole.

International Market Imperfections (Barriers to International Investment). Hirshleifer [1970] demonstrates that Modigliani and Miller's principles rely on the assumption of complete markets, requiring the absence of taxes, bankruptcy and transaction costs so that market discrepancies can be corrected by arbitrage actions. Nevertheless, in the international environment various barriers exist which hinder investment. According to Black [1975], these barriers include the possibility of expropriation of foreign holdings, direct controls on inflows and outflows of capital, reserve requirements on bank deposits and other assets held by foreigners, and restrictions on the percentage of a business that can be foreign owned. Given these barriers, arbitrage actions that can correct the discrepancy between the sum of the market value of security issues and the present value of the income stream may not be possible. Discussions along this line are found in Errunza & Senbet [1981] and Lee & Zechner [1984].

Corporate International Diversification. Shapiro [1978] points to corporate international diversification as a factor which may be relevant in establishing worldwide capital structures. With subsidiaries in different countries, MNCs are able to diversify cash flows internationally. Such diversification reduces overall bankruptcy risk which, in turn, enables MNCs to be more highly leveraged than DCs.

International Availability of Capital. Stonehill et al. [1975] contend that given more financing channels and better availability of capital in international markets, it is easier for the MNC to maintain a target debt ratio than the DC. Small domestic companies of U.S. or non-U.S. MNCs, which do not have access to liquid national equity markets, can only maintain their optimal debt ratio up to a moderate level of financing. As capital requirements increase while equity capital is limited, those companies may have to borrow more and exceed the optimal debt ratio.

Influence of Local Factors on a Foreign Affiliate's Capital Structure. Conflicting views have been raised regarding how the financial structure of foreign subsidiaries should be designed. The options available to the foreign subsidiary are: a) to follow the norm of local companies, b) to conform to the capital structure of the parent company, or c) to vary the capital structure in order to take advantage of local opportunities. Naumann-Etienne [1974] argues that since most of the stocks of U.S. MNCs are traded in the U.S., the firms' target debt ratios should depend on U.S. shareholders' risk perception and on criteria established by U.S. rating agencies. The affiliate should follow the parent's capital structure in order to meet the expectation and criteria of investors in the parent country. Alternatively, Stonehill & Stitzel [1969] and Shapiro [1978] argue for variation of the subsidiary's capital structure to reflect local conditions. In following a strict, uniform capital structure, subsidiaries may not be able to fully utilize local opportunities to enhance or maintain a competitive advantage over other firms.

International Environmental Factors and Determinants of MNCs' Capital Structures: A Suggested Analytical Framework

After reviewing the domestic and the international finance literature on the study of capital structures, this section suggests an analytical framework that may introduce some of the recently developed domestic finance concepts into the international area. These concepts (such as agency costs, bankruptcy costs and so forth) are more related to the firm's characteristics. On the other hand, when the capital structure of the MNC was discussed, previous studies usually dealt directly with the influence of international environmental factors on the capital structure instead of going through the firm's characteristics. The framework suggested here attempts to integrate the environmental factors with the firm-related characteristics.

As shown in Exhibit 14.1, the framework of analysis consists of three levels of variables. The first level contains factors that represent the particular nature of the international business environment. These include political risk, international market imperfections, opportunities for international diversification, complexity of international operations, foreign

Exhibit 14.1   A suggested framework of analysis

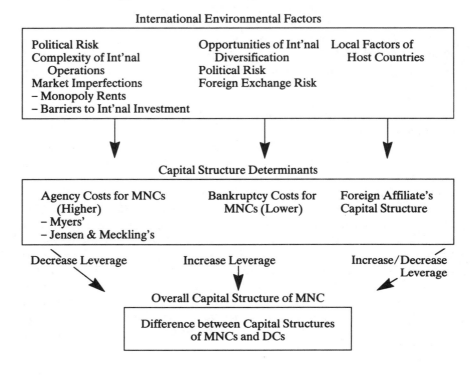

exchange risk and local factors of host countries. These factors have been mentioned in previous literature as salient to the operations of the MNC. The list is certainly not exhaustive; more factors need to be identified and added by future research.

The second level of variables, which we call capital structure determinants, are more related to the firm than to the environment in which it operates. These variables fall into two groups: one group is concerned with the MNC as a whole (e.g., agency costs, bankruptcy costs) while the other deals with the capital structures of foreign affiliates. The international environmental factors above effect these capital structures determinants which in turn lead to the difference between the capital structures of MNCs and DCs (variable of the third level). It is obvious that the suggested framework is still in its rudimentary stages. There may exist other determinants not yet included here.

In the following discussion, agency costs, bankruptcy costs and foreign affiliates' capital structures are used as examples to illustrate the relationships among these three levels of variables. Of these three determinants, more emphasis is placed on the discussion of agency costs since no previous studies of which we are aware have applied this concept in the international arena.

Agency Costs

Since the publication of Jensen & Meckling [1976], the study of agency costs has been an important research topic in the domestic finance area. The underinvestment problem (Myers [1977]) and the substitution problem (Jensen & Meckling [1976]) are the two major sources of agency costs of debt cited in the literature.

Agency Costs of Debt According to Myers: The Underinvestment Problem.
Myers [1977] suggests that the value of a firm consists of two parts. The first part is derived from its real assets, the market values of which are independent of the firms' future investment strategy. These assets are called "assets in place". The second part of the value is derived from the firm's "real options"; these are intangible assets, the value of which depends on future discretionary investments. Because of the existence of "real options" and the conflict of interest between shareholders and bond-holders, an underinvestment problem may arise. When a firm has outstanding debt which matures after an investment option expires, share-holders would prefer to reject projects that have positive net present values. This is because benefits from accepting these projects accrue mainly to the bondholders while shareholders' wealth is not increased. Nevertheless, the underinvestment problem is taken into consideration by bondholders who will demand a lower bond price when they buy the bonds. This reduction of bond value is an agency cost to the firm.

When the asset structure of an MNC is analyzed, it is expected that MNCs will have a higher proportion of "real options" than DCs. This hypothesis is based on the theoretical arguments of previous studies:

(a) Political Risk

MNCs tend to have more intangible assets which are less vulnerable to expropriation by host governments. Phillips-Patrick [1985] describes the relationship between political risk and these types of assets. Unlike intangible assets, "assets in place" are more politically appropriable. Firms whose values depend more on "real options" are less politically appropriable and are therefore subject to lower political risk.

(b) International Market Imperfections (Monopoly Rents)

In his pioneering work, Stephen Hymer [1976] considers the multinational operations of firms as the result of imperfections in product and factor markets. Given imperfect markets, MNCs possess monopolistic advantages which enable them to outperform local companies in host countries. Using Tobin's q ratio, Kim & Lyn [1986] find the MNCs indeed have excess market values, values that indicate the existence of monopoly rents. As remarked by Myers [1977], these monopoly rents ae reflected by the value of "real options" of the company. Hence, MNCs are expected to have higher proportions of "real options" than their domestic counterparts. Given the higher proportion of real options in the case of MNCs, the agency cost of debt due to the underinvestment problem will be higher.

Agency Costs of Debt According to Jensen & Meckling: The Substitution Problem. Prior to Myers [1977], Jensen & Meckling [1976] suggest the existence of an agency cost of debt due to the substitution problem. Jensen & Meckling contend that debt financing gives shareholders the incentive to accept high-risk projects which tend to transfer wealth from bondholders to shareholders. Knowing that their interests may be substituted by those of shareholders, bondholders demand a lower bond price when they purchase bonds issued by the company. This reduction of bond value is another kind of agency cost of debt financing. To increase the confidence of bond-holders in order to maintain the value of the bonds, the firm may write bond covenants which prevent wealth expropriation. The firm may also allow monitoring and bonding activities of its behavior. Nevertheless, the costs of monitoring and bonding activities are also agency costs.

With regard to Jensen-Meckling's substitution problem, MNCs are also expected to incur higher agency costs of debt than DCs because of several international environmental factors:

(a) Complexity of International Operations

Because of the complexity of international operations, agency costs due to the monitoring and bonding activities of MNCs are expected to be higher than those of DCs. These activities may include auditing activities and the preparation of multiple financial statements for each country in which the firm has operations. Since the subsidiaries of MNCs are located in different countries, different national accounting standards make it more difficult and costly to prepare a consolidated financial statement. Alternatively, geographical dispersion also increases auditing costs substantially. According to Eichenseher [1985], CPA firms can use three approaches to serve a client with subsidiaries in different parts of the world: i) temporarily transporting personnel from one office to the client's various overseas locations, ii) entering into contracts with other CPA firms to audit the client's overseas operations, or iii) having offices in each of the client's localities and utilizing its own local personnel for the audit. The first alternative incurs substantial travel costs. The second alternative involves high subcontracting costs. And the third alternative incurs additional fixed costs since operating an overseas office is usually more costly than operating a domestic office. All of these approaches mean higher auditing costs accrue to the MNCs. This argument is supported by Simunic [1980] who finds a positive relationship between auditing fees and the degree of foreign involvement of the company.

(b) International Market Imperfections (Barriers to International Investments)

Barnea, Haugen & Senbet [1985] indicate that a well-functioning capital market has several mechanisms by which agency problems can be costlessly reduced or eliminated. These mechanisms can work even between national markets provided that there are no barriers to international investment. In actuality, however, barriers to international investment abound. These barriers may be restrictions on the degree of foreign ownership of firms, direct controls on the export and import of capital, reserve requirements on bank deposits held by foreigners, and the possibility of expropriation of foreign holdings. Arbitrage processes which help to reduce agency problems are therefore more limited in international markets than in domestic markets. Because of this, the agency costs of MNCs are expected to be higher than those of DCs.

Owing to the influence of international environmental factors, MNCs are expected to have higher agency costs than DCs. Thus, the following hypothesis is formulated:

H1: MNCs have higher agency costs of debt than DCs
Null Hypothesis: MNCs have the same level of agency costs of debt as DCs

Empirical tests of these hypotheses will be presented in later sections of this paper. Before the discussion is switched to bankruptcy costs, the implications of agency costs of debt on the capital structure of the MNC needs to be drawn. Though increased debt financing brings greater tax advantages, marginal agency costs of debt will rise. Therefore, a trade-off relationship exists which leads to an optimal leverage point for the firm. Since the MNC is expected to incur higher agency costs of debt than the DC, other things being equal, the optimal leverage point of the MNC will be lower than that of the DC.

Bankruptcy Costs

Baxter [1967] and Kraus & Litzenberger [1973] use the concept of bankruptcy costs to argue for the existence of an optimal capital structure. Expected bankruptcy costs depend on the cost of bankruptcy (e.g., legal fees, loss of sales, employees and suppliers) and the probability of occurrence. Increased debt financing will increase the probability of bankruptcy and will in turn increase expected bankruptcy costs. The optimal debt ratio is reached when the marginal tax savings from debt financing is equal to the marginal loss from expected bankruptcy costs.

In the international environment, there are several factors which may lead to the difference between the bankruptcy costs of MNCs and DCs:

(a) Opportunities for International Diversification

Compared with DCs which operate in only one economy, MNCs may have affiliates located in multiple economies. The performance of these economies are not perfectly correlated, giving rise to diversification opportunities for the MNC. Given this opportunity, the overall cash flows of an MNC can be more stable. Reduction of cash flow variability reduces the probability of bankruptcy and therefore the expected bankruptcy costs. These arguments are expressed in Shapiro [1978].

(b) Foreign Exchange Risk and Political Risk

The effect of foreign exchange risk and political risk on bankruptcy costs is unclear. It can be argued that foreign exchange rate fluctuations and political risk will increase the variability of cash flows of an MNC. Nevertheless, some scholars counter that even foreign exchange and political risks specific to MNCs may be eliminated through international diversification.

Based on the above analysis, scholars of international finance tend to give more weight to the benefits of international diversification. As a result, the following hypothesis concerning the MNC's bankruptcy costs is formulated:

H2: MNCs have lower bankruptcy costs than DCs
Null Hypothesis: MNCs have the same level of bankruptcy costs as DCs

These hypotheses will be tested in later sections. Following the argument of Baxter [1967] and Kraus & Litzenberger [1973], the optimal debt ratio of a firm is reached when the marginal tax savings from debt financing is equal to the marginal loss from expected bankruptcy costs. With lower expected bankruptcy costs than DCs, MNCs can raise more debt and sustain a higher optimal debt ratio. The effects of bankruptcy costs on the MNCs' capital structure is therefore opposite to that of agency costs.

Foreign Affiliates' Capital Structures

In addition to the firm-related characteristics above, another major variable affecting the overall capital structure of an MNC is the capital structures of its foreign affiliates. Operating under different political, social, and economic circumstances, foreign affiliates of the MNC may vary their capital structures in response to local conditions. Since the consolidated capital structure of the MNC includes the financial structures of foreign affiliates, the latter can be viewed as another important determinant of the MNC's capital structure.

Local factors such as political risks, foreign exchange and inflation risks in the host country induce foreign affiliates to be more highly leveraged. Political risks can range from mild governmental interference to blocked funds or even outright expropriation. To reduce political risk, a foreign affiliate may borrow from the local market. When debt is borrowed from the local market, losses due to expropriation or inconvertibility of local currency may be partly offset by a corresponding reduction in local debt liability. By the same token, when the inflation rate is high in the host country and a devaluation of the local currency is expected, the affiliate may borrow more from the local market to reduce its net asset exposure. When devaluation finally occurs, exchange rate losses due to exposed assets may be partly offset by the exchange rate gains due to exposed liabilities.

In most countries, interests paid on debt are deductible from the affiliate's taxable income while dividend payments to the parent are not. As remarked by Shapiro [1978], this may be another reason for the affiliate to rely more on debt financing.

The local affiliate may also incur more debt because of encouragement from the host government. To attract foreign investment in an effort to strengthen local economic development, host governments may provide subsidized or guaranteed loans to foreign subsidiaries as incentives. Conversely, under other circumstances, local affiliates may incur lower debt because of pressure from the host government. With a view to reducing the balance of payments deficit, the government may restrict the amount of local borrowing by the affiliate. It may require that a certain minimum percentage of the foreign subsidiary's capital must be in the form of equity investment. Sometimes, the pressure may not be directly from the government; it may arise form local norms. Affiliates with too high a proportion of debt relative to that of local norm may be accused of not contributing a fair share of capital to the host country. To keep a low profile and to avoid potential conflicts, the affiliate of an MNC may reduce the proportion of debt financing.

Capital markets in many of the host countries are not as well-developed as those in the United States. Capital markets are often too shallow to absorb a large amount of financing. Medium- and long-term borrowings may be unavailable to foreign affiliates without the support of the host government. This shortage of local capital may prompt the foregoing affiliate to borrow more from foreign banks or resort to debt or equity investment from the parent company.

Based on the above analysis, the influence of local factors on the capital structure of a foreign affiliate can go both ways — some factors tend to push the debt ratio upward while others tend to push it downward.

Although the influence of affiliates' financial structures on the overall MNC's capital structure is stressed, it should be noticed that when the financial structures of foreign subsidiaries are consolidated to the parent's financial statements, intracorporate loans will be cancelled. In other words, even when a foreign subsidiary may appear to be highly leveraged, it does not necessarily increase the overall debt ratio of the MNC if most of its debts are provided by the parent company or sister affiliates.[1]

Implications for the MNC's Capital Structure

The discussion above utilized the framework introduced earlier to examine how international environmental factors affect some firm-related capital structure determinants, which in turn lead to the difference between the capital structures of MNCs and DCs. Agency costs and bankruptcy costs, together with the affiliate's capital structure, have been chosen as illustrations. There may be other variables, yet to be explored by future research, which will further refine the analytical framework. Nevertheless, by considering the influence of the three determinants discussed so far, it is difficult to draw a conclusion as to whether MNCs are more leveraged than DCs. It would be interesting to examine the empirical findings. To formulate a tentative hypothesis for empirical tests, the conventional wisdom is followed:

H3: MNCs have higher debt ratios than DCs
Null Hypothesis: MNCs have the same debt ratios as DCs

Empirical tests are presented in the following sections. Because of data availability problems, the tests are limited to the comparisons between MNCs and DCs regarding agency costs, bankruptcy costs and debt ratios. The testing of foreign affiliates' capital structures was not conducted because it would require detailed financial statements for each of the MNCs in the sample.

Research Methodology

Sample Selection

The empirical tests intend to determine whether or not MNCs and DCs have the same levels of agency costs, bankruptcy costs, and debt ratios. The population of this study are U.S.-based multinational and domestic corporations. Two samples were formed for these two groups from companies listed on the COMPUSTAT tapes.

Various criteria for defining MNCs have been used in previous studies, yet there is no one single definition that is generally accepted. Some definitions emphasize structural characteristics (e.g., the number of countries in which a firm is doing business or the nationality of top management) while others stress performance characteristics (e.g., sales or earnings). Because other data are less easily available, many of the previous studies used foreign sales ratio (foreign sales/total sales) as a measure of multinationality. Foreign sales figures, however, include both sales by foreign subsidiaries and sales due to exports from the parent company.

Exhibit 14.2 Number of firms by asset sizes

Asset sizes	MNC		DC	Total
	MNC–10	MNC–25		
– 5,000	18	15	1	19
5,000 – 2,500	28	19	5	33
2,500 – 1,000	71	40	8	79
1,000 – 500	57	28	18	75
500 – 250	57	35	25	82
250 – 100	60	30	83	143
100 – 50	63	34	86	149
50 – 25	35	20	92	127
25 – 10	24	9	103	127
Total	413	231	421	834

Using this measure may lead to the disadvantage of mixing international trade with international investment. To avoid this shortcoming, this study used the foreign tax ratio as an alternative measure of multinationality. There are several advantages with this measure: 1) By using this measure, most of the companies listed in the COMPUSTAT tapes can be used. Consequently, larger samples can be obtained for both MNCs and DCs. 2) Previous measures were based on data available only for a small number of years (usually one) while data of foreign tax ratios are available for a period of twenty years (1964–1983). 3) Foreign taxes which are imposed on income made by foreign subsidiaries seem to be a more appropriate proxy for measuring the level of foreign investment than foreign sales.[2]

Using the foreign tax ratio as the criterion, companies were separated into samples of MNCs and DCs. In order to minimize potential bias due to size differences, only companies with total assets more than $10 million were included in the samples. The DC sample consisted of companies which had an average foreign tax ratio of less than 1% over the period 1964–1983. There were 421 firms which belonged to this category. The MNC sample included companies with foreign tax ratios greater than 25%. To confirm that these companies were, in fact, engaged in overseas operations, Moody's Directory of Corporate Affiliation was consulted. As a result, 231 companies were included in this sample. Since the MNC sample was much smaller than the DC sample, another MNC sample was prepared in order to reduce potential bias due to sample size differences. The second MNC sample was prepared using companies with foreign tax ratios greater than 10% and was comprised of 413 companies. Two MNC samples would therefore be compared with the DC sample in later empirical tests.

Exhibit 14.2 shows the asset sizes of sample companies. The figures indicate that firms of large asset sizes are mostly MNCs (i.e., corporations with relatively high levels of international investment). In addition, a breakdown of the sample companies by industry indicates that MNCs are concentrated more in technology-intensive industries (such as chemicals, machinery, pharmaceuticals, petroleum refining and transportation equipment) and industries with extensive marketing skills (e.g., convenience foods and cosmetics). Regulated firms (SIC Code 4000–5000) are excluded from the samples since there may exist a systematic relation between the regulations and the firms' financial leverage. In the empirical tests, the size and the industry factors would be controlled to ensure that the differences between MNCs and DCs are not due to size or industry effects.

Operationalization

Agency Costs. As mentioned above, the two major types of agency costs of debt arise from the substitution incentive and the underinvestment problem. At the present stage, the substitution incentive is a concept too general to be tested with available data: micro information on the magnitude of monitoring and bonding costs is required at the very least. Because of this, the present study tests only Myers' agency cost. Myers himself suggested that this type of agency cost can be proxied by the amount of expenditure that the company incurs in advertising or other marketing skills, research and development and so forth. These expenses are discretionary investments, creating intangible assets which may or may not be utilized by the firm in the future. The higher the proportion of company resources expended in these discretionary investments, the higher is the agency costs of debt due to the underinvestment motive. Several studies have followed this approach (Bradley, Jarrel & Kim [1984], Titman [1983] and Krishnaswamy & Shrieves [1984]). This study adopted the same approach and proxied the agency costs of debt with the sum of annual advertising and research and development expenses divided by the amount of annual sales:[3]

Myers' Agency Cost of Debt = (Advertising
+ R&D Expenses)/Annual Sales.

Bankruptcy Costs. Expected bankruptcy costs are equal to the bankruptcy costs times probability of bankruptcy. If actual bankruptcy costs are assumed constant and positive, then the variation of expected bankruptcy costs depends mainly on the probability of bankruptcy. Baxter [1967], who was the first to suggest a bankruptcy model, used the variance of cash flows as a proxy of bankruptcy costs. This argument has been widely followed and applied in later studies on bankruptcy (Lewellen [1971], Gordon & Malkiel [1981] and Bradley, Jarrel & Kim [1984]). Following this approach, the present study used the variance of cash flows to proxy bankruptcy costs. This was measured by the standard deviation of the first difference in annual operating earnings (earnings before the deductions of interest, depreciation and taxes). To adjust for firm size, the standard deviation was divided by the average value of the firm's total assets over the period 1964–83.

Capital Structure (Debt Ratios). The capital structure of a firm is usually represented by its debt ratio. The operational definition of the debt ratio used in this study is:

Debt Ratio = Long-Term Debt/(Market Value of Equity
           + Long-Term Debt).

This definition has frequently been seen in previous literature. Since market value instead of book value is used for equity, this measure better represents the theory of optimal capital structure.[4]

Statistical Tests

To test whether MNCs and DCs differ with respect to agency costs, bankruptcy costs and overall capital structures, the Kolmogorov-Smirnov test was first used to test the normality of the distributions. The results indicated that the distributions were not normal. Therefore, Kruskal-Wallis test, a nonparametric test which does not assume any population characteristics except continuity, was applied.

To ensure that the differences between MNCs and DCs were not simply due to size or industry differences, a two-way ANOVA test was employed to control the industry and size effects separately. In controlling the size factor, the MNC and DC samples were ranked by asset size and seven subgroups were formed before two-way ANOVA was applied.

Empirical Findings

Agency Costs

The means of agency costs of the MNC-10 (companies with foreign tax ratio higher than 10%) and the MNC-25 samples (foreign tax ratio higher than 25%) are respectively 3.90 and 4.17 while that of DC sample is 1.69. The Kruskal-Wallis test statistics indicate that the means of the MNC samples are significantly higher than that of the DC sample at the .01 level.

Two-way ANOVA was then applied to control for the size effect. Exhibit 14.3.a shows the agency costs of MNCs and DCs at various size levels. The results show that MNCs clearly have higher means of agency costs than DCs even after the size effect is controlled. The two-way ANOVA statistics show that both the multinationality effect and the size

Exhibit 14.3a   Agency costs: MNC vs. DC tests by asset size

Size portfolio	Agency costs		
	MNC–10	DC	Total
1	3.90	2.31	3.74
	(107)	(12)	(119)
2	4.47	.67	3.58
	(91)	(28)	(119)
3	3.62	1.12	2.45
	(63)	(55)	(119)
4	3.90	1.39	2.43
	(49)	(69)	(119)
5	3.83	1.71	2.60
	(50)	(69)	(119)
6	3.51	2.05	2.42
	(30)	(89)	(119)
7 (smallest)	3.18	2.09	2.29
	(22)	(98)	(120)
Total	3.91	1.69	

Note: The figures in parentheses indicate the numbers of firms.

	ANOVA Results	
	F-value	PR> F
Multinationality Effect	58.53	.0001
Size Effect	3.17	.0044

effect are significant at the .01 level. Similar conclusions can be drawn when the industry effect is controlled (Exhibit 14.3.b). The means for MNCs are higher than those of DCs in all industries. Again, both the multinationality and industry effects are significant at the .01 level.

The empirical findings therefore reject the null hypothesis, confirming the hypothesis that MNCs tend to have higher agency costs than DCs. As argued above, this is probably due to the international environmental factors such as political risk and market imperfection. Higher political risk will lead MNCs to use more "real options," which are less politically appropriable, in forming their asset structrues. Alternatively, market imperfections provide MNCs with firm-specific advantages and therefore monopoly rents, which are also reflected by a higher proportion of "real options" in the asset structure. These casual relationships are, however, not tested in this paper; further research is needed to ensure that higher agency costs do indeed arise from these environmental factors.

Bankruptcy Costs

The means of bankruptcy costs of the MNC-10 and the MNC-25 samples

Exhibit 14.3b Agency costs: MNC vs. DC tests by industry

Industries	MNC		DC
	MNC–10	MNC–25	
10, 1200 Mining	.43 (.40)	.78 (.75)	.03
1300 Oil Gas Extraction	.69 (.58)	.75 (.64)	.11
1400 Nonmetallic Mineral	.00 (.00)	.00 (.00)	.00
15, 16, 1700 Construction	.12 (−.05)	.12 (−.05)	.17
2000 Food and Kindred Products	3.68 (1.51)	3.00 (.83)	2.17
2100 Tobacco	5.33 (2.16)	–	3.17
2200 Textile	2.03 (1.23)	1.64 (.84)	.80
2300 Apparel	2.54 (1.80)	2.32 (1.46)	.84
2400 Lumber and Wood	.64 (.05)	–	.59
2500 Furniture	–	–	–
2600 Paper	1.68 (1.22)	1.96 (1.50)	.46
2700 Publishing and Printing	3.24 (2.10)	6.02 (4.88)	1.14
2800 Chemical	7.13 (.35)	8.40 (1.62)	6.78
2900 Petroleum Refining	.58 (.54)	.50 (.46)	.04
3000 Rubber	2.84 (2.18)	3.94 (2.28)	.66
3100 Leather	–	–	–
3200 Glass, Stone and Clay	1.97 (1.67)	1.19 (.89)	.30
3300 Primary Metals	.63 (.15)	.78 (.30)	.48
3400 Fabricated Metal Products	2.27 (1.00)	2.06 (.79)	1.27
3500 Machinery	2.50 (1.22)	2.50 (1.22)	1.28
3600 Electronics	6.01 (1.43)	6.29 (1.71)	4.58
3700 Transportation Equipments	2.31 (.56)	2.75 (1.00)	1.75
3800 Scientific Instruments	6.26 (2.52)	6.37 (2.63)	3.74
3900 Other Manufacturing Products	6.02 (3.47)	5.86 (3.31)	2.55

Note: The figures in parentheses indicate the differences from the means of the corresponding DC groups.

	ANOVA Results	
	F-value	PR> F
Multinationality Effect	16.98	.00001
Industry Effect	22.42	.00001

are respectively 5.13 and 486 while that of the DC sample is 7.69. Both MNC-10 and MNC-25 have means significantly lower than that of DC at the .01 level. This finding remains valid even when the industry factor is controlled. Exhibit 14.4.b shows that both the multinationality and industry effects are significant at the .01 level when two-way ANOVA is applied.

Nevertheless, surprising results are observed when the size effect is controlled. The companies, both multinational and domestic, are ranked

Exhibit 14.4a   Bankruptcy costs: MNC vs. DC tests by asset size

| | Bankruptcy costs | | |
Size portfolio	MNC–10	DC	Total
1	3.04	2.73	3.00
	(107)	(12)	(119)
2	3.93	3.53	3.83
	(91)	(28)	(119)
3	4.67	5.80	5.20
	(63)	(55)	(119)
4	6.20	5.74	5.93
	(49)	(69)	(119)
5	7.48	7.38	7.42
	(50)	(69)	(119)
6	6.60	10.42	9.45
	(30)	(89)	(119)
7 (smallest)	11.60	9.48	9.88
	(22)	(98)	(120)
Total	5.12	7.65	

Note: The figures in parentheses indicate the numbers of firms.

| ANOVA Results | | |
	F-value	PR> F
Multinationality Effect	.39	.5325
Size Effect	19.55	.0001

under seven levels according to asset sizes. Exhibit 14.4.a shows the effect of the size factor. The means of bankruptcy costs of the smaller companies are substantially higher than those of the larger companies. The size effect is significant at the .01 level. Within each size group, however, the difference between MNCs and DCs is not significant. These results show that MNCs have lower means of bankruptcy costs than DCs not because of their international involvement but simply because of their large sizes. This finding, therefore, does not support the conventional thinking that corporate international diversification reduces bankruptcy risk.[5]

The reason that international involvement does not seem to reduce bankruptcy risks may be explained by an increase in the unsystematic risks which MNCs encountered over the past decade. Overseas operations are confronted with special risk elements: economic risk (including foreign exchange risk) and political risk. The slowdown of foreign economies in the 1970s, caused partly by high inflation and increased energy costs, has suppressed the performance of MNCs. To ameliorate their economic problems, foreign governments have increased the practice of protectionism. This, in turn, has hurt the profitability of international operations. The

Exhibit 14.4b   Bankruptcy costs: MNC vs. DC tests by industry

Industries	MNC		DC
	MNC–10	MNC–25	
10, 1200 Mining	4.5 (−8.2)	4.0 (−8.7)	12.7
1300 Oil Gas Extraction	10.9 (−3.0)	9.4 (−4.5)	13.9
1400 Nonmetallic Mineral	3.5 (−3.7)	3.5 (−3.7)	7.2
15, 16, 1700 Construction	4.7 (−2.4)	4.7 (−2.4)	7.1
2000 Food and Kindred Products	3.5 (−2.7)	4.5 (−1.7)	6.2
2100 Tobacco	1.7 (−2.5)	–	4.2
2200 Textile	5.0 (.0)	3.6 (−1.4)	5.0
2300 Apparel	3.6 (−1.7)	2.7 (−2.6)	5.3
2400 Lumber and Wood	4.4 (−2.8)	5.1 (−2.5)	7.6
2500 Furniture	–	–	3.4
2600 Paper	2.3 (−8.2)	2.0 (−8.5)	10.5
2700 Publishing and Printing	7.0 (−1.6)	4.3 (−1.1)	5.4
2800 Chemical	2.8 (−4.3)	3.1 (−4.0)	7.1
2900 Petroleum Refining	3.9 (−3.0)	4.0 (−2.9)	6.9
3000 Rubber	4.2 (−1.8)	2.3 (−3.7)	6.0
3100 Leather	–	–	5.7
3200 Glass, Stone and Clay	2.4 (−4.8)	2.5 (−4.7)	7.2
3300 Primary Metals	5.6 (−1.2)	3.8 (−3.0)	6.8
3400 Fabricated Metal Products	4.3 (−1.2)	4.8 (− .7)	5.5
3500 Machinery	6.7 (.3)	5.4 (−1.0)	6.4
3600 Electronics	6.1 (−3.5)	5.6 (−4.0)	9.6
3700 Transportation Equipments	4.8 (−3.7)	7.3 (−1.2)	8.5
3800 Scientific Instruments	4.6 (−6.0)	4.5 (−6.1)	10.6
3900 Other Manufacturing Products	11.9 (−5.0)	9.8 (−2.9)	6.9

Note: The figures in parentheses indicate the differences from the means of the corresponding DC groups.

	ANOVA Results	
	F-value	PR> F
Multinationality Effect	28.76	.0001
Industry Effect	3.49	.0001

1970s also witnessed dramatic changes in the international monetary system contributing to instability in the foreign exchange markets. Political risks, in terms of outright expropriation or abrupt policy changes of host governments, have also played a part in increasing the overall risks of international operation. These additional risk factors may have offset the benefits of corporate international diversification; as a result, the volatility of cash flows remains unchanged and the bankruptcy risk is not reduced.

Exhibit 14.5a Debt ratios: MNC vs. DC tests by asset size

| Size portfolio | Debt ratios | | Total |
	MNC-10	DC	
1 (largest)	25.0	30.9	25.6
	(107)	(12)	(119)
2	22.7	30.8	23.6
	(91)	(28)	(119)
3	25.4	28.4	26.8
	(63)	(55)	(119)
4	25.6	29.2	27.7
	(49)	(69)	(119)
5	26.1	27.7	27.0
	(50)	(69)	(119)
6	26.3	30.6	29.5
	(30)	(89)	(119)
7 (smallest)	24.9	23.9	24.1
	(22)	(98)	(120)
Total	24.9	28.1	

Note: The figures in parentheses indicate the numbers of firms.

| ANOVA Results | | |
	F-value	PR> F
Multinationality Effect	7.85	.0052
Size Effect	1.71	.1156

Nevertheless, the validity of these explanations needs to be examined by future empirical tests.

The empirical findings thus far indicate that MNCs indeed tend to have higher agency costs than DCs. If only the agency costs and the bankruptcy costs are considered, the overall effect is that MNCs should be less leveraged than DCs. It is, therefore, interesting to examine whether MNCs show higher or lower debt ratios than DCs in reality. However, it should be noticed that there exist other capital structure determinants which have not been examined here and may also play a significant role in causing the difference between the capital structures of MNCs and DCs.

Capital Structure (Debt Ratios)

The capital structure of MNcs and DCs were compared and the results indicate that in general MNCs have significantly lower debt ratios than DCs at the .05 level. The means of debt ratios of the MNC-10 and the MNC-25 samples are respectively 24.9 and 25.0 while that of DC is 28.1. Such results are consistent with that of Shaked [1986] who also found that MNCs have an higher average of capitalization ratios (equity/asset) than

Exhibit 14.5b Debt ratios: MNC vs. DC tests by industry

Industries	MNC		DC
	MNC-10	MNC-25	
10, 1200 Mining	29.1 (8.5)	39.1 (18.4)	20.6
1300 Oil Gas Extraction	32.9 (− 6.3)	35.6 (− 3.6)	39.2
1400 Nonmetallic Mineral	2.6 (− 3.0)	2.6 (− 3.0)	5.6
15, 16, 1700 Construction	25.1 (− 3.2)	25.3 (− 3.0)	28.3
2000 Food and Kindred Products	23.3 (− 6.7)*	26.7 (− 3.3)	30.0
2100 Tobacco	−	−	−
2200 Textile	53.5 (15.8)*	56.7 (19.0)*	37.7
2300 Apparel	41.4 (10.8)*	46.3 (15.7)*	30.6
2400 Lumber and Wood	26.3 (.9)	24.6 (− .8)	25.4
2500 Furniture	−	−	32.1
2600 Paper	30.5 (− 3.2)	25.4 (− 8.3)	33.7
2700 Publishing and Printing	27.2 (11.8)*	18.2 (2.8)	15.4
2800 Chemical	17.3 (− 6.0)*	15.4 (− 7.9)*	23.3
2900 Petroleum Refining	30.0 (.2)	27.4 (− 2.4)	29.8
3000 Rubber	33.2 (− .9)	33.7 (− .4)	34.1
3100 Leather	−	−	22.6
3200 Glass, Stone and Clay	32.2 (−11.6)*	33.7 (−10.1)*	43.8
3300 Primary Metals	37.4 (4.4)	44.7 (11.7)*	33.0
3400 Fabricated Metal Products	22.3 (− 5.8)*	22.9 (− 5.2)	28.1
3500 Machinery	25.2 (− 2.2)	24.1 (− 3.3)	27.4
3600 Electronics	21.5 (2.5)	21.7 (2.7)	19.0
3700 Transportation Equipments	25.3 (− 2.2)	22.7 (− 4.8)	27.5
3800 Scientific Instruments	21.2 (− .3)	21.3 (− .2)	21.5
3900 Other Manufacturing Products	35.1 (2.7)	34.5 (2.1)	32.4

Note: The figures in parentheses indicate the differences from the means of the corresponding DC groups.
*Significant at the .10 level.

DCs. This finding, is however, contrary to the hypothesis that MNCs are more highly leveraged than DCs, a hypothesis that is shared by most of the previous studies. Previous studies base the high-leverage hypothesis on three major arguments: i) the international diversification effect, ii) the reduction of bankruptcy risk as a result of diversification (Shapiro [1978]), and iii) higher debt ratios of affiliates due to local political risks. Nevertheless, results in Exhibit 14.4.b have already shown that international involvement (multinationality) does not lead to the reduction of bankruptcy risk. On the other hand, agency costs of debt financing increase with multinationality (Exhibits 14.3.a & 14.3.b). The finding here shows that, in general, debt-decreasing factors (such as agency costs) seem to have stronger influence than debt-increasing factors (such as bankruptcy costs, local factors) in determining the MNC's capital structure.

Exhibit 14.5.a shows that the conclusion remains intact when size effect is controlled; MNCs have lower means of debt ratios than DCs in most of the size groups. The multionationality effect is significant at the .01 level while the size effect is not.

Alternatively, Exhibit 14.5.b presents the estimates of the debt ratio under various industrial groups. It can be seen that the results vary significantly across industries. The industries in which MNCs have significantly lower debt ratios than DCs include food and kindred products (2000), chemical (2800), glasses (3200), and metal working (3400). The industries in which MNCs have significantly higher debt ratios include mining (1000), textile and apparel (2200, 2300), publishing (2700), and primary metals (3300).

MNCs which have high technology (e.g., chemical and metal working) tend to have lower debt ratios. This may be due to the higher agency costs of debt financing on the one hand and the lower influence of local factors on the other. With high technology, MNCs possess firm-specific advantages and therefore monopoly rents. The monopoly rents are reflected by the higher proportions of real options in their asset structures. According to Myers [1977], this would lead to higher agency costs and therefore lower leverage. On the other hand, equipped with the technological advantage, MNCs have strong bargaining power when they deal with the host government. Governmental restrictions are comparatively less so that the MNCs have more freedom in structuring the affiliates' capital structures. Since the assets are less politically appropriable, the foreign subsidiary may not need to resort to high leverage policy to reduce political risk exposure.

Alternatively, MNCs which belong to industries such as textile and apparel do not have a strong technological base. These companies go overseas mainly to explore new markets or to seek higher production efficiency. Without a technological edge, their bargaining power with the host government is relatively weak. As a result, the MNCs may adopt a high leverage policy, borrowing more from domestic and international markets to cover their political risk exposures.

It should be noted that the earlier results in Exhibit 14.3.b showed that the difference between the agency costs of MNCs and DCs are still statistically significant when the industry effect is controlled. Here in Exhibit 14.5.b, controlling the industry effect renders the difference between debt ratios of MNCs and DCs insignificant. Nevertheless, these two separate findings do *not* lead to the conclusion that agency cost has no influence on a corporation's capital structure. In fact, when the results of Exhibit 14.3.b are examined more closely, it can be seen that the significance of the industry effect is recognized and that the F-ratio of the industry effect (22.42) is stronger than that of the multionationality effect (16.98).

Summary and Conclusions

This paper has focused on the study of MNCs' capital structure, discussing whether MNCs have different capital structures than DCs, and if so, what causes such differences. Unlike previous studies which discussed the relationships between international environmental factors and MNCs' capital structure directly, this paper suggested an alternative analytical framework: examining the impact of international environmental factors on some firm-related capital structure determinants which in turn affect the MNC's overall capital structure.

A list of international environmental variables — political risk, international market imperfections, complexity of operations, opportunities for international diversification, foreign exchange risk and local factors of host countries — were considered. While there may be a few capital structure determinants, this paper selectively tested only two of them: agency costs and bankruptcy costs. The major findings included:

1) MNCs tended to have higher agency costs of debt (according to Myers' definition) than DCs. This finding remained unchanged even when size and industry effects were controlled.
2) Though MNCs appeared to have lower bankruptcy costs than DCs, the difference largely disappeared when the size effect was controlled.
3) Quite contrary to the conventional wisdom, the empirical findings showed that MNCs tended to be less leveraged than DCs. This finding remained even when the size effect was controlled. However, when companies were separated under different industry groups, the results varied significantly.

Although this study proposed an analytical framework for the study of MNCs' capital structure, a number of areas need to be refined with future empirical research:

- In discussing agency costs, only political risks, market imperfections and complexity of international operations were selected. The influence of the other unselected variables on capital structure determinant warrants further investigation.
- In discussing the capital structure determinants, only agency costs, bankruptcy costs and affiliates' capital structures were selected as examples. Other domestic concepts such as non-debt tax shields, liquidation costs, collateral value, market power, and others may play a part in determining the MNC's capital structure.

- Because of the data availability problem and the exploratory nature of this study, the empirical tests were confined to Myers' agency costs of debt, bankruptcy costs and debt ratios. The tests examined whether there existed significant differences between MNCs and DCs regarding these variables. Nevertheless, causal relationships that were suggested to explain these differences were not tested.

- It was interesting to find that industrial differences played an important part in explaining the differences in capital structures between MNCs and DCs. Further research is needed to examine the interaction between the industrial effects and the variables mentioned above (i.e., the international environmental factors and capital structure determinants).

Notes

†The authors would like to thank Professors Leroy Brooks and David Ricks at the University of South Carolina for their valuable suggestions and three anonymous referees for their useful comments.

1. Previous empirical results show that a foreign subsidiary tends to be more leveraged than its parent company. Such findings are found in Brooke & Remmers [1970] and Leftwich [1970]. Nevertheless, evidence which contradicts the above results is not unknown. Wilson [1979] concludes that the equity/asset ratios of subsidiaries in LDCs do not display a higher percentage of debt capital.

2. To examine how the foreign tax ratio is related to other proxies of multinationality, Spearman rank correlations were computed. Data for companies' foreign tax ratios were obtained from the COMPUSTAT tapes while figures of foreign sales, income and assets were collected from *Business International* [1974]. The following exhibit shows that all of the correlations were significant at the 1% confidence level:

	Foreign sales ratio	*Foreign income ratio*	*Foreign assets ratio*
Correlation with foreign taxes ratio	.31*	.56*	.29*

*Significant at .01 level.

As remarked by one of the reviewers, the sample size of 231 firms for the MNC group is unusually large and may consist of companies which do not have high percentages of assets placed abroad. An alternative approach is to have a smaller but 'cleaner' sample of MNCs with which the DC sample is compared. This latter approach, however, runs into the problem of comparing samples of very different sizes. Both approaches, therefore, have strengths and weaknesses. This study has chosen the first approach.

3. Owing to the limitations of the COMPUSTAT tapes regarding these data, the

sums were computed only over the last ten years of the sample period.

4. The debt ratio was averaged over the sample period of twenty years (1964–1983).

5. Similar results were obtained by using semi-variance as another definition of bankruptcy risk.

References

Adler, Michael. 1974. The cost of capital and valuation of a two country firm. *Journal of Finance*, March: 119–32.

—— & Bernard Dumas. 1975. Optimal international acquisitions. *Journal of Finance*, March: 1–19.

Baxter, N. 1967. Leverage, risk of ruin and the cost of capital. *Journal of Finance*, August: 663–81.

Barnea, A., R.A. Haugen, & L.W. Senbet. 1985. *Agency problems and financial contracting*. Englewood Cliffs, N.J.: Prentice-Hall.

Black, F. 1975. International capital market equilibrium investment barriers. *Journal of Financial Economics*, October: 337–52.

Bradley, M., G.A. Jarrel, & E.H. Kim. 1984. On the existence of an optimal capital structure: Theory and evidence. *Journal of Finance*, July: 857–80.

Brooke, M.Z. & H. Lee. Lemmers. 1970. *The strategies of multinationals enterprises: Organization and finance*. New York: American Elsevier Publishing Co.

Business International. 1974. *Foreign profit performance*.

DeAngelo, H. & R. Masulis 1980. Optimal capital structure under corporate and personal taxation. *Journal of Financial Economics*, March: 3–29.

Eichenseher, John W. 1985. The effect of foreign operations on domestic auditor selection. *Journal of Accounting, Auditing, and Finance*, Spring: 195–209.

Errunza, V. & L. Senbet. 1981. The effects of international operations on the market value of the firm: Theory and evidence. *Journal of Finance*, May: 401–17.

Ferri, M. & W. Jones. 1979. Determinants of financial structure: A new methodological approach. *Journal of Finance*, June: 631–44.

Gorden, R. & B. Malkiel. 1981. How taxes affect economic behavior. In Aaron and Pechaman, eds., *Corporate finance*. Washington: Brookings Institute: 131–97.

Hirshleifer, J. 1970. *Investment and capital*. Englewood Cliffs, N.J.: Prentice-Hall, Inc..

Hymer, Stephen H. 1976. *The international operations of national firms: A study of direct foreign investment*. Cambridge, Mass.: MIT Press.

Jensen, M.C. & W.H. Meckling. 1976. Theory of firm managerial behavior, agency costs and ownership structure. *Journal of Financial Economics*, October: 305–60.

Kim, Wi S. & Esmeralda O. Lyn. 1986. Excess market value, the multinational corporation, and Tobin's q ratio: A note. *Journal of International Business Studies*, Spring: 119–25.

Krainer, Robert E. 1972. The valuation and financing of the multinational firm: Reply. *Kyklos*, 25:553–73.

Kraus, A. & R. Litzenberger. 1973. A state preference model of optimal financial leverage. *Journal of Finance*, 28:911–21.

Krishnaswamy, C.R. & R.E. Shrieves. 1984. Agency costs and informational asymmetry as determinants of capital structure: A discriminant analysis approach. A paper presented at the Annual Meeting of Eastern Finance Association.

Lachenmayer, H. 1984. The effect of currency exchange risks on the cost of equity capital of the international and multinational firms. *Management International Review*, 2:28–37.

Lasman, D.A. & R.L. Weil. 1978. Adjusting the debt equity ratio. *Financial Analyst Journal*, Sept.–Oct.: 49–58.

Lee, K.C. 1986. The capital structure of the multinational corporation: International factors and multinationality. Unpublished dissertation, University of South Carolina.

Lee, M.H. & J. Zechner. 1984. Debt, taxes, and international equilibrium. *Journal of International Money and Finance*, 3:343–55.

Leftwich, R.B. 1970. US MNCs, financial leverage and effective income tax rates. *Special Survey of US MNCs*. US Department of Commerce.

Lewellen, W. 1971. A pure financial rationale for the conglomerate merger. *Journal of Finance*, May: 521–37.

Lyn, Esmeralda & G. Papaioannou. 1985. The empirical relationship between capital structure and market power. A paper presented at Financial Management Association Meeting.

Mehra, Rajnish. 1978. On the financing and investment decision of multinational firms in the presence of exchange risk. *Journal of Finance and Quantitative Analysis*, June: 227–44.

Modigliani, F. & Merton Miller. 1958. The cost of capital, corporate finance, and the theory of investment. *American Economic Review*, June: 261–97.

Myers, S.C. 1977. Determinants of corporate borrowing. *Journal of Financial Economics*, November: 147–75.

Nauman-Etienne, Rudiger. 1974. A framework for financial decision in multinational corporations: A summary of recent research. *Journal of Financial and Quantitative Analysis*, November: 859–74.

Neter, John & Wasserman W. 1974. *Applied linear statistical models*. Homewood, Il.: Richard D. Irwin.

Phillips-Patrick, Frederick J. 1985. Asset structure, political risk and the multinational firm: Evidence from Mitterand's election. Paper presented at the Annual Meeting of Eastern Finance Association, Dallas, Texas.

Remmers, L., A. Stonehill, R. Wright & T. Beckhuiser, 1974, Industry and Size as Debt Ratio Determinants in Manufacturing Internationally. *Financial Management*, Summer: 24–32.

Robbins, Sidney & R.B. Stobaugh. 1972. Comments. In Flitz Machlup, Walter Salant, & Lorie Tarshis, eds., *International mobility and movements of capital*, 354–57. Columbia University Press for National Bureau of Economic Research.

Ross, Stephen. 1977. The determinants of financial structure: The incentive signalling approach. *Bell Journal of Economics*, Spring: 23–40.

Scott, D.F. 1977. Bankruptcy, secured debt, and optimal capital structure. *Journal of Finance*, March: 1–19.

——— & J.D. Martin. 1975. Industry influence on financial structure. *Financial Management*, Spring: 67–73.

Senbet, L. 1979. International capital market equilibrium and the multinational firm financing and investment policies. *Journal of Financial and Quantitative Analysis*, September: 455–80.

Shaked, Israel. 1986. Are multinational corporations safer? *Journal of International Business Studies*, Spring: 83–106.

Shapiro, Allen C. 1978. Financial structure and the cost of capital in the multinational corporation. *Journal of Financial and Quantitative Analysis*, June: 211–66.

Simunic, Dan A. 1980. The pricing of audit services: Theory and evidence. *Journal of Accounting Research*, 18: 161–90.

Smith, Clifford W., Jr & Jerold B. Warner. 1979. On financial contracting: An analysis of bond covenants. *Journal of Financial Economics*, June: 117–61.

Stonehill, Arthur & Thomas Stitzel. 1969. Financial structure and multinational corporations. *California Management Review*, Fall: 91–96.

Stonehill, Arthur, Theo Beekhisen, Richard Wright, Lee Remmers, Norman Toy, Antonio Pares, Alan Shapiro, Douglas Egan & Tom Bates. 1975. Financial goals and debt ratio determinants: A survey of practices in five countries. *Financial Management*, Autumn: 27–41.

Sullivan, Timothy G. 1974. Market power, profitability, and financial leverage. *Journal of Finance*, December: 1407–14.

Titman, Sheridan. 1983. Determinants of capital structure. An empirical analysis. Working paper, UCLA, January.

Wilson, B.D. 1979. An examination of the capital structure of the foreign subsidiaries of MNCs. Working Paper 79–25, University of Virginia.

15

Cultural Influences on International Capital Structure*

William S. Sekely and J. Markham Collins

*Source: *Journal of International Business Studies,* 19 (Spring 1988), pp. 87–100.

Abstract. Many studies have been conducted on the impact of various factors on international capital structure. The literature still reveals disagreement on the significance of the industry and country effects in determining capital structure, and the basis of country differences. This paper presents the results of a study of the debt structure of 677 firms in 9 industries headquartered in 23 countries. The results of this study tend to agree with the hypothesis that cultural differences are correlated with the significant country and minimal industry influences which are found. Further, there appear to be some intercountry influences caused by underlying cultural patterns among groups of countries.

Probably no topic in financial management has received more interest than that of capital structure. Indeed, if an optimal capital structure exists, management need only finance the firm using these optimal proportions and the objective of maximization of the value of the firm is assured. In fact, any movement toward that optimal capital structure reduces the cost of capital and increases the value of the firm.

The topic becomes more complex when one moves from consideration of domestic to multinational firms. Here one must consider the capital structure of foreign subsidiaries as well as that of the consolidated parent organization. Does one establish a target capital structure at the parent level and require subsidiaries to employ that structure? Or does one find an optimal capital structure for each subsidiary, letting the consolidated parent's structure reflect the sum of the parts? Multinational managers would be better armed to make such choices if they understood why capital structure differs internationally.

A number of studies on international capital structure have been published, many addressing various factors which might be determinants of it. In a review article in this journal, Stanley cited 102 references [Stanley

1981]. The two variables most often examined as capital structure determinants are industry and country. However, the literature reveals disagreement on the significnce of the industry and country effects in determining capital structure.

One of the earliest examinations of the impact of industry and country found no significant industry effect for firms that are in the same industry but headquartered in different countries [Stonehill and Stitzel 1969]. Other studies (notably Remmers, et al. 1974, Toy et al. 1974, Aggarwal 1981, and Errunza 1979) have found both industry and country effects to be significant, although not in every case examined.

In a more recent and comprehensive study, Collins and Sekely examined 411 companies in 9 countries and 9 industries [Collins and Sekely 1983]. They found significant differences in the capital structures for firms headquartered in different countries, but less evidence was found for the impact of industry.

For the most part, the studies cited above found country influence to be significant. However, none explains the reason(s) behind the country effect. Stonehill and Stitzel suggested country-specific economic variables and cultural variables. Collins and Sekely examined several economic variables (size, tax rate, inflation) but found no significant relationships to capital structure. These authors suggested cultural factors influenced the capital structure decision, but did not attempt to measure or document the cultural influence.

Most other disciplines acknowledge cultural factors as playing a significant role in multinational business; however, finance tends to minimize the significance of cultural differences. This may be a serious mistake, for as Ball and McCulloch point out, "the study of foreign cultures is of primary importance to those in international business because cultural differences exert a pervasive influence on all of the business functions" [Ball and McCulloch 1982].

The authors of this paper recognize capital structure differences result from firm-specific policy decisions. They also recognize these decisions are based, in part, on the firm's managerial perceptions of the risk relative to the benefit of using fixed-cost debt financing. Prior studies, support the contention that firms within an industry have more similar capital structures than firms across industries [Scott 1972] and firms headquartered in the same country have more similar capital structures than those firms headquartered across countries [Collins and Sekely 1983]. Thus, firm-specific decisions may result in different capital structures for firms in the same industry and/or country, but these differences are less than the differences one finds across all industries or all countries.

Given that no prior study has established a significant relationship between an economic variable and international differences in capital structure, and given the conclusions of some earlier works that cultural factors must play a role, this research attempts to discover whether cultural factors are important determinants of capital structure. If some underlying relationship among countries can be shown to influence capital structure, future research should include more variables than simply economic ones in attempting to explain capital structure differences.

One of the major difficulties in this analysis is determining what is meant by cultural variables. Cultural factors cover a wide spectrum and include the whole set of social norms and responses that condition a population's behavior. It is these that make one social environment different from another and give each a shape of its own. While there is a great deal of discussion and debate over exactly wheat constitutes culture, most definitions include the following elements: social institutions, belief systems, aesthetics, language, and material culture. It is this last element, which includes a society's economic structure and technological capabilities, that probably is most closely related to the capital structure tendencies of a society. Specific areas most likely to influence capital structure include the different legal and tax systems, which give rise to differences in property rights across cultures. However, the potential impact on capital structure is not limited to the material portion of culture. There are a number of other aspects of a society's culture which also could impact on the financial structure of a firm.

It is not the purpose of this paper to determine which cultural elements play the most critical role in influencing multinational capital structure. This paper is limited in its purpose to determining if some broad cultural influence on capital structure can be found, beyond the more traditional industry and country influences. If this cultural influence exists, it should be reflected in the similarities of capital structure in organizations situated in countries having similar cultural backgrounds. if such similarities are found, it suggests further research on international capital structure can be enhanced by including variables such as the social and legal structures of countries in addition to the more traditional economic variables.

Scope of the Study

This present study extends the existing literature dealing with capital structure of firms headquartered in different countries in two ways:

1. More comprehensive conclusions are drawn from the analyses that were conducted. This is because the database was expanded significantly from that used in previous studies, both in terms of numbers of countries and also in terms of geographic coverage.
2. An analysis is conducted that goes beyond the statistical analysis of differences in debt ratios between companies. By disclosure of specific

industry-country patterns of these ratios, it allows more direct evaluation of the impact of culture on capital structure.

In order to test the various aspects of the preceding two objectives, extensive examinations were made of the differences in capital structure between multinational companies in different industries and headquartered in various countries. Aspects of this have been the primary questions of a number of previous studies. After discussion of the differences mentioned above, two formal hypotheses were developed to test differences between and within various cultural groupings of countries. These have not been addressed directly in previous literature.

Methodology

This study employs data for 677 firms in 9 industries headquartered in 23 countries. These are the same industries and countries examined by Stonehill & Stitzel and Collins & Sekely plus firms from 14 other countries. Following these previous studies, the 10 firms in each industry/country cell with the highest level of sales were selected for the sample, with all firms included when less than ten. Data were obtained from *Moody's Industrial Manual* for the United States and *Moody's International Manual* for all foreign firms. By using a single source, the problem of inconsistent accounting treatments should be reduced, although not eliminated.

One-way and two-way analyses of variance were used in earlier studies to examine the impact that industries and countries have on the capital structure of the multinational firms being studied. However, several recent studies have shown that the distributions of debt ratios have not met the necessary conditions for use of parametric procedures. In the most recent of these, Martin and Henderson found that both major conditions for use of parametric procedures in the analysis of capital structure, normality of distributions of ratios within industries and equal variances across industries, did not occur [Martin and Henderson 1984].

The nonparametric analysis discussed below used the same data from 1979–1980 as the previously cited Collins and Sekely study and included data from the same time period for the additional countries. The debt ratio was defined as total debt to total assets at book value and calculated as one minus the rate of stockholders' equity to total assets.

The analysis utilized the Kruskal-Wallis test[1] to examine the 165 industry/country aggregate cells for consistency of country rankings among industries and industry rankings among countries.[2] To the extent that patterns can be found in these analyses, conclusions can be made as to the consistency of capital structure approaches taken by corporations in various countries, industries, or cultural groupings.

Table 15.1 Debt ratios for selected industries and countries (arranged in order of increasing use of debt)

	Alcoholic beverages	Auto-mobiles	Chemicals	Electrical	Foods	Iron & steel	Nonferrous metals	Paper	Textiles	Country mean
Singapore	.20	.22		.57	.28	.28	.38			.34
Malaysia		.60	.41		.30	.38	.30	.77	.69	.37
Argentina	.29	.42		.44	.35	.32				.38
Australia		.50	.52	.51	.45	.53	.34	.48		.46
Chile			.33	.28	.70	.48	.50	.47	.54	.46
Mexico	.18		.47	.57	.59	.53	.47	.47		.47
South Africa	.59	.50	.51		.46	.53	.32	.42	.69	.50
Brazil		.66	.48	.53	.57	.61		.37		.54
United Kingdom	.45	.73	.50	.60	.55	.51	.57	.56	.52	.55
United States	.51	.58	.55	.54	.56	.54	.58	.58	.50	.55
Benelux	.41	.62	.60	.51	.64	.61	.49	.65	.54	.56
Canada	.55		.45	.52		.69	.61	.68		.58
India	.08	.75	.55			.49	.69	.74	.48	.60
Switzerland				.63	.54	.64				.60
West Germany	.66	.57	.56	.66	.49	.60	.70	.70	.65	.62
Denmark			.47	.74	.69	.52	.61	.74		.63
Spain	.79	.59	.64	.45	.66	.82	.70	.85	.43	.64
Sweden	.56	.75	.67	.67	.63	.67	.64	.61	.60	.68
France	.40	.67	.72	.72	.78	.73	.67	.74	.74	.71
Finland		.82	.71	.73	.77	.73	.72	.76	.82	.72
Pakistan		.87	.87				.71	.66	.70	.72
Norway			.76	.67	.79	.62		.82	.75	.74
Italy	.49	.49	.65	.79	.85	.87	.86	.77	.83	.76
Industry mean	.49	.58	.56	.59	.62	.61	.58	.63	.70	

Table 15.2 Debt ratios ranks for selected industries and countries (arranged in order of increasing use of debt)

	Alcoholic beverages	Auto-mobiles	Chemicals	Electrical	Foods	Iron & steel	Nonferrous metals	Paper	Textiles	Country median mean
Singapore	3.0	6.0		77.0	6.0	6.0	17.5			6.00
Malaysia		88.0	20.5		9.5	17.5	9.5		120.0	17.50
Argentina	2.0	22.5		25.0	15.0	11.5				18.75
Mexico			33.0	77.0	84.0	59.5	33.0	33.0		33.00
Chile			13.0	6.0	125.5	37.5	46.0	33.0		35.25
Australia	8.0	46.0	55.5	51.0	27.5	59.5	14.0	37.5	64.0	46.00
South Africa	84.0	46.0	51.0		30.0	59.5	11.5	22.5	120.0	48.50
Brazil		109.0	37.5	59.5	77.0	93.0		17.0		68.25
United Kingdom	27.5	135.0	46.0	88.0	68.5	51.0	77.0	72.5	55.5	68.50
United States	51.0	81.0	68.5	64.0	72.5	64.0	81.0	81.0	46.0	68.50
Canada	68.5		27.5	55.5		120.0	93.0	117.0		80.75
Benelux	20.5	96.5	88.0	51.0	101.5	93.0	41.5	104.0	64.0	88.00
India	1.0	143.5	68.5	125.5		41.5	120.0	139.0	37.5	94.25
West Germany		77.0	72.5	109.0	41.5	88.0	125.5	125.5	104.0	96.00
Switzerland				98.5	64.0	101.5				98.50
Spain		84.0	101.5	27.5	109.0	156.5	125.5	160.5	24.0	102.75
Denmark	109.0		33.0	139.0	120.0	55.5	93.0	139.0		109.00
Sweden	153.0	143.5	113.0	149.0	98.5	113.0	101.5	93.0	88.0	113.00
Pakistan		164.0	164.0				129.5	109.0	125.5	129.50
France	72.5	113.0	131.0	131.0	151.0	143.5	113.0	139.0	139.0	131.00
Finland	19.0	156.5	129.5	135.0	149.0	135.0	131.0	146.5	156.5	135.00
Norway			146.5	113.0	153.0	96.5		156.5	143.5	145.00
Italy		41.5	104.0	153.0	160.5	164.0	162.0	149.0	159.0	156.00
Industry median rank	27.5	88.0	68.5	82.5	80.5	61.8	81.0	109.0	104.0	

Results of Study

Debt ratios were calculated for all 677 companies in 9 industries and 23 countries. Averages for the 165 industry/country cells were then computed. Table 15.1 shows the results of these computations. These figures were then used as the basis of further analysis.

Given the significant interaction between the industry and country factors found in most previous studies, separate analyses for each factor were indicated (holding the other factor constant). Due to the differences in size of the 165 industry/country cells and the uncertainty of the underlying distributions which has been previously mentioned, a nonparametric test was used to examine the individual differences. The Kruskal-Wallis test for differences of ranks between multiple samples was used for the test. It uses the median ranks of the various country and industry debt ratios to test for differences between the samples.

Differences between Industries

The median ranks for the nine industries were computed. All the industries except alcoholic beverages had median ranks in the middle third of the total sample (i.e., median ranks between 56 and 110). Table 15.2 shows the ranks of all the industries among the test countries and the median rank for each industry. The Kruskal-Wallis test was conducted on the industry data. As might have been expected from observation, the differences in median rank were not found to be significant, even at the 0.1 significance

Table 15.3 Results of Kruskal-Wallis test differences between industries

Industry	$\sum\limits_{i=1}^{K}$	$\dfrac{[R-(1/2)n^*(N+1)]}{n}$
Alcoholic beverages		16276.9
Automobiles		1186.1
Chemicals		1216.8
Electrical		277.5
Foods		.4
Iron & Steel		158.2
Nonferrous Metals		142.3
Paper		4658.2
Textiles		2706.8
Total		26623.2

Kruskal-Wallis Test Statistic = 11.66
Level of significance – Not significant at the .1 level.

level. Table 15.3 shows the results of this test. Thus, the influence of industry grouping appears to be minimal in the extended data set used in this study.

Differences in Countries

The same analysis was performed on the 23 countries among the various industries. Unlike the industry analysis, the country results showed clear groupings of differences. Seven countries had overall median rankings in the bottom third of all 165 country-industry cell rankings, 10 countries had overall median rankings in the middle third of all rankings, and 6 countries had overall median rankings in the top third of all rankings. There was a fairly strong pattern of economic development and the degree of debt used in the various countries. All the countries using little debt, with the excep-

Table 15.4 Results of Kruskal-Wallis test differences between countries

Country	$\sum\limits_{i=1}^{K}$	$\dfrac{[R-(1/2)n^*(N+1)]}{n}$
Argentina		16641
Australia		16384
Benelux		841
Brazil		1837.5
Canada		45.4
Chile		9361.5
Denmark		1650.9
Finland		18769
France		16555.1
India		19.5
Italy		23005.1
Malaysia		13995.6
Mexico		9620.0
Norway		16120.2
Pakistan		15345.8
Singapore		18301.2
South Africa		7170.0
Spain		1937.5
Sweden		10370.0
Switzerland		75
United Kingdom		1764
United States		2116
West Germany		780.1
Total		202705.4

Kruskal-Wallis Test Statistic = 88.81
Level of significance – Significant at the .001 level.

tion of Australia and to a lesser degree South Africa, were less developed nations. All the countries using a great deal of debt, except Pakistan, were industrialized nations. The Kruskal-Wallis test was conducted on the country differences. It was found to be significant at greater than the 0.001 level. Thus, there appears to be a very definite relationship between country and use of debt in the extended data set that was examined. This influence is at least somewhat related to the economic development level of the country. Table 15.4 shows the results of this analysis.

Influence of Culture

The aspects just examined were very similar to a number of earlier studies. The following analyses are different in that they are looking for groups of countries with similar cultural attributes to help explain some of the differences in capital structure between multinational companies headquartered in different parts of the world. The first step in accomplishing this was to determine the appropriate groupings of countries.

One frequently used methodology for classification is the use of simple but meaningful groups of countries known as "cultural realms." These are groupings that have "fundamental unity of composition, arrangement, and integration of significant traits which distinguish them from other realms" [Broek and Webb 1973]. Broek, James, and several others have developed cultural models for dividing the world into homogeneous groupings [Broek and Webb 1973; James 1976]. While the specific terminology differs from model to model, the basic groupings are very similar. The model used in the present study utilizes the relevant parts of the Broek and James models. Seven cultural realms were identified for the 23 countries used in the study. The realms and countries grouped in each one are:

ANGLO-AMERICAN: Australia, Canada, South Africa, United Kingdom, and United States
LATIN AMERICAN: Argentina, Brazil, Chile, and Mexico
WEST CENTRAL
EUROPE: Benelux, Switzerland, and West Germany
MEDITERRANEAN
EUROPE: France, Italy, and Spain
SCANDINAVIA: Denmark, Finland, Norway, and Sweden
INDIAN PENINSULA: India and Pakistan
SOUTHEAST ASIA: Malaysia and Singapore

Table 15.5 shows the groupings that were established. Also shown are the median ranks for the industries, countries, and cultural groups examined.

Analyses were conducted on the country industry cells in these groupings to determine if there were patterns of differences that could be determined. More specifically, the hypotheses tested in this study can be formally summarized as follows:

(1) H^1_0: Multinational companies located in different cultural realms have the same financial structures.

   H^1_1: Multinational companies located in different cultural realms have significantly different financial structures.

(2) H^2_0: Multinational companies located in the same cultural realms but possibly different countries, have the same financial structures.

   H^2_1: Multinational companies located in the same cultural realms, but possibly different countries, have significantly different financial structures.

Differences between Cultural Groupings

Table 15.5 shows the median ranks that were computed for the various cultural groups preiously described. Using these divisions, the Kruskal-Wallis test for differences of rank was run on the median ranks of the various cultural groups. The results of the test indicate differences between the groups that are significant beyond the .001 level. Thus, the null hypothesis of no significant differences between the cultural groups must be rejected. Table 15.6 shows the calculations for this test. Table 15.6 also shows that the variance between cultural groups is very widespread. That is, the significant results come about because of wide variation between expected values and those found in four of the six cultural groups, not just a large deviation between one group and all the rest.

Low debt ratios are found in the Southeast Asian group, the Latin American group, and the Anglo-American group of countries. High debt ratios are found in the Scandinavian countries, Mediterranean countries, and the Indian Peninsula. The West Central European countries appear in the middle of the rankings. Thus, while there is a relationship between level of economic development and use of debt, it is not a very strong relationship. The Anglo-American group, with some of the most developed and industrialized countries in the world, are only very moderate users of debt compared to the average. The Indian Peninsula countries, on the other hand, with very low levels of development and industrialization, are very heavy users of debt. Also, while proximity is surely a contributing factor in simlarities of country capital structure patterns, it is by no means sufficient, as the differences between Mediterranean Europe, West Central Europe, and Scandinavia show.

Differences within Cultural Groupings

In addition to testing for significant differences of debt ratios between the cultural groupings, each cultural group was tested for differences between the median ranks of the specific country-industry cells that made up the group. The null hypothesis of no differences in ranks could not be rejected at the 0.05 level for any of the cultural groupings. There were differences at

Table 15.5 Debt-equity ranks for selected cultural groupings and industries

Cultural group	Alcoholic beverages	Automobiles	Chemicals	Electrical	Foods	Iron & steel	Nonferrous metals	Paper	Textiles	Country median rank	Group median rank
Anglo-American											59.5
Australia	8.0	46.0	55.5	51.0	27.5	59.5	14.0	37.5	64.0	46.00	
Canada	68.5		27.5	55.5		120.0	93.0	117.0		80.75	
South Africa	84.0	46.0	51.0	88.0	30.0	59.5	11.5	22.5	120.0	48.50	
United Kingdom	27.5	135.0	46.0	64.0	68.5	51.0	77.0	72.5	55.5	68.50	
United States	51.0	81.0	68.5		72.5	64.0	81.0	81.0	46.0	68.50	
Latin-American											33.0
Argentina		22.5	37.5	25.0	15.0	11.5				11.75	
Brazil		109.0		59.5	77.0	93.0		17.0		68.25	
Chile			13.0	6.0	125.5	37.5	46.0	33.0		33.25	
Mexico	2.0		33.0	77.0	84.0	59.5	33.0	33.0		33.00	
Mediterranean Europe											130.5
France	72.5	113.0	131.0	131.0	151.0	143.5	113.0	139.0	139.0	131.00	
Italy		41.5	104.0	153.0	160.5	164.0	162.0	149.0	159.0	156.00	
Spain		84.0	101.5	27.5	109.0	156.5	125.5	160.5	24.0	102.75	
Central Europe											90.0
Benelux	20.5	96.5	88.0	51.0	101.5	93.0	41.5	104.0	64.0	88.00	
Switzerland				98.5	64.0	101.5				98.50	
West Germany		77.0	72.5	109.0	41.5	88.0	125.5	125.5	104.0	96.00	
Scandinavia											131.0
Denmark	109.0		33.0	139.0	120.0	55.5	93.0	139.0		109.00	
Finland	19.0	156.5	129.5	135.0	149.0	135.0	131.0	146.5	156.5	135.00	
Norway			146.5	113.0	153.0	96.5		156.5	143.5	145.00	
Sweden	153.0	143.5	113.0	149.0	98.5	113.0	101.5	93.0	88.0	113.00	

Indian Peninsula											
India	1.0	143.5	68.5	125.5		41.5	120.0	139.0	37.5	94.25	125.5
Pakistan		164.0	164.0				129.5	109.0	125.5	129.50	
Southeast Asia											
Malaysia	3.0	88.0	20.5		9.5	17.5	9.5		120.00	17.50	13.5
Singapore		6.0		77.0	6.0	6.0	17.5			6.00	
Industry median rank	27.5	88.0	68.5	82.5	80.5	61.8	81.0	109.0	104.0		

Table 15.6 Results of Kruskal-Wallis test differences between cultural groups

Cultural group	$\sum\limits_{i=1}^{K}$	$\dfrac{[R-(1/2)n^*(N+1)]}{n}$
Anglo-American		19932.1
Latin-American		32119.1
Mediterranean Europe		35306.4
Central Europe		2.4
Scandinavia		31275.9
Indian Peninsula		6446.9
Southeast Asia		31570.0
Total		156652.8

Kruskal-Wallis Test Statistic = 68.63
Level of significance – Significant at the .001 level.

the .1 level for three of the cultural groupings, the Anglo-American group, the Mediterranean group, and the Scandinavian group. In the case of the Anglo-American group, most of the variation comes from the rankings in the Australian cells. In the case of the Mediterranean European group, most of the variation comes from the Italian cells, and in the Scandinavian group, the variation occurs between the more southern countries, Denmark and Sweden and the northern ones, Norway and Finland. Thus, while some variations exist within the cultural groupings, they are not very significant and usually the result of the differences in one country. Table 15.7 shows the result of the Kruskal-Wallis test for differences within the cultural groups.

Conclusions

The results of this study tend to confirm and strengthen the conclusion that cultural differences contribute to the significant country and minimal industry influences found in Stonehill and Stitzel [1969] and Collins and Sekely [1983]. The study shows the original results are reasonably stable since 14 countries and 214 companies were added to those examined by Collins and Sekely with consistent results.

Further, examination of the ranks of the debt ratios shows distinct groups of countries with respect to the country median rank. While these groupings do not conclusively prove the cultural impact on financial structure, they do give clear indication of the influence in that direction. The results also imply that cultural analysis may be of significant value in financial planning by multinational corporations.

Table 15.7 Results of Kruskal-Wallis test differences within cultural groups

Cultural group	Kruskal-Wallis test statistic	Level of significance
Anglo-American	8.51	.1
Latin-American	5.93	N.S.
Mediterranean Europe	4.84	.1
West Central Europe	2.14	N.S.
Scandinavia	6.25	.1
Indian Peninsula	2.59	N.S.
Southeast Asia	.80	N.S.

The present study found little industry impact on the debt ratios, which appears to contradict some earlier works. However, there are several reasons that might reconcile the current results with previous studies.

First, a partial explanation for the reduction of industry influence comes from an overall reduction of industry distinctions. The number of large, multinational companies that are engaged in activities in only one industry has continued to diminish over the past several decades. Thus, as Bowen points out, "there is a potential conglomeration effect which would tend to favor the null hypothesis of no industry influence" [Bowen, Daley, and Huber 1982].

Second, a significant increase in overall use of debt was found between the Stonehill and Stitzel study, using 1964 data, and the more recent studies that use 1980 data. However, the increase was not uniform across industries. The three industries that had the highest debt ratios in the earlier study increased by an average of 7.1%, while the three industries with the lowest ratios in the earlier study increased by 12.0%. This tended to diminish the industry influence on the debt ratio.

A third reason, especially concerning the differences between the Errunza results and those this study, were expressed in his summary. Errunza states that, "The assumptions of perfect and complete capital markets that underlie the modern theory of capital markets frequently do not hold in countries outside the U.S., especially in developing countries" [Errunza 1979]. Thus, one may find differences in capital structure between different industries occurring, not because of the industry influence, but because of the "desire to conform to local financial norms" [Errunza 1979].

The results of this research once again support the argument that there are country effects on capital structure and that these result, in part, from cultural differences. Further, there appear to be some inter-country influences caused by underlying cultural patterns among groups of countries. Such cultural patterns may influence the development of financial institutions, attitudes toward risk, and/or attitudes toward debt. The influence of culture strongly suggests that future research examine the effects of social and legal arrangements on capital structure. Whatever the link between culture and decisionmaking, these differences do cause capital structure to differ between countries, and must be considered by financial managers in the global environment.

Notes

1. The Kruskal-Wallis test is a nonparametric procedure used in the experimental situation where K random samples have been obtained, one from each of K possibly different populations, and we want to test the null hypothesis that all of the populations are identical against the alternatives that some of the populations tend to furnish greater observed values than other populations [Conover 1971]. The test statistic T is defined as:

$$T = \frac{12}{N(N+1)} \sum_{i=1}^{k} \frac{[R - (1/2)n^*(N+1)]}{n}$$

Where: T = Kruskal-Wallis test statistic
n = size of i random sample

$$N = \sum_{i=1}^{k} n$$

R = sum of the ranks assigned to sample i

2. Theoretically, 207 cells should have been developed. However, several countries did not have large companies in some of the industries.

References

Aggarwal, Raj. 1981. International differences in capital structure norms: An empirical study of large European companies. *Management International Review.* 75–88.

Bowen, Robert M., Lane A. Daley & Charles C. Huber. 1982. Evidence on the existence and determinants of inter-industry differences in leverage. *Financial Management.* Winter: 10–20.

Broek, Jan O.M. & J.W. Webb. 1973. *A geography of mankind.* New York: McGraw-Hill.

Conover, W.J. 1971. *Practical nonparametric statistics.* New York: John Wiley and Sons.

Child, John & Monir Tayeb. 1983. Theoretical perspectives in cross-national organizational research. *International Studies of Management and Organization,* Winter: 23–70.

Collins, J. Markham & William S. Sekely. 1983. The relationship of headquarters, country and industry classification to financial structure. *Financial Management,* Autumn: 45–51.

Errunza, Vihang, R. 1979. Determinants of financial structure in the central American common market. *Financial Management,* Autumn: 72–77.

James, Preston E. 1976. World view of major cultural regions. In Fred E. Dohis and Lawrence M Sommers, eds., *World Regional Geography: A Problem Approach.* New York: West Publishing Co.

Martin, Linda J. & Glenn V. Henderson. 1984. Industry influence on financial structure: A matter of interpretation. *Review of Business and Economic Research,* 19(2): 57–67.

Moody's Industrial Manual. 1981. New York, Moody's Investor Service, Inc.

Moody's International Manual. 1981. New York, Moody's Investor Service, Inc.

Remmers, Lee, Arthur Stonehill, Richard Wright & Theo Beekhuisen, 1974. Industry and size as debt ratio determinants in manufacturing internationally. *Financial Management,* Summer: 23–32.

Scott, David. 1972. Evidence on the importance of financial structure. *Financial Management,* Summer: 45–50.

—— & John D. Martin. 1975. Industry influence on financial structure. *Financial Management,* Spring: 67–73.

Stanley, Marjorie T., "Capital structure and the cost of capital for the multinational firm", *Journal of International Business Studies,* 12 (Spring/Summer 1981), pp. 103–120.

Stonehill, Arthur & Thomas Stitzel. 1969. Financial structure and multinational corporations. *California Management Review,* Fall: 91–96.

—— , Theo Beekhuisen, Richard Wright, Lee Remmers, Norman Toy, Antonio Pares, Alan Shapiro, Douglas Egan & Thomas Bates. 1975. Financial goals and debt ratio determinants: A survey of practice in five countries. *Financial Management,* Autumn: 27–41.

Toy, Norman, Arthur Stonehill, Lee Remmers, Richard Wright & Theo Beekhuisen. 1974. A comparative international study of growth, profitability, and risk as determinants of corporate debt ratios in the manufacturing sector. *Journal of Financial and Quantitative Analysis,* November: 875–886.

PART FOUR: Capital Budgeting

16

Capital Budgeting and the Multinational Corporation*

Arthur Stonehill and Leonard Nathanson

*Source: *California Management Review*, 11 (Summer 1968), pp. 39–54.

A better conceptual framework for evaluating foreign investments is needed. This article presents a survey of the methods currently being used by firms to evaluate multinational financing investments and suggests solutions to certain problems which occur when the theory of capital budgeting is applied to multinational operations.

The need for a normative theory. At the annual meetings of the American Finance Association in 1965, Stefan Robock stated the need for a normative theory in the following manner:

> The financial decision-making techniques being widely used in the newly international firms, and—I should add—still taught religiously in the leading schools of business, have not been extended to allow for global operations. They do not provide for systematically considering overseas financing alternatives and, therefore, do not include the additional variable involved when overseas alternatives are considered. A natural result is that most financial managers do not have an adequate conceptual framework and have not secured sufficient experience for dealing confidently and efficiently with overseas financing alternatives.[1]

Furthermore, he suggested that the principal differences between the multinational and uninational cases were caused by dissimilarities in financial attitudes, institutions, legal systems, governmental policies, and other environmental variables. More specifically, it is necessary to consider such new variables as exchange risks, differential inflation rates, taxes across national boundaries, effective versus nominal rates of interest, fringe benefits, joint ventures, special inducements, and developing local capital markets.[2] Other authors have also stated the need for a better conceptual framework for evaluating foreign investments. A. J. Merrett and Allen Sykes have emphasized the influence of differential tax rates on the decision to reinvest or repatriate overseas earnings.[3]

The *Harvard Business Review* has published a series of articles on various aspects of this problem. Among these, Dan Throop Smith discussed the following specific questions:[4]

- To what extent should different levels of income tax be taken into account in allocating funds?
- How should availability of separate sources of external funds influence investment decisions?
- How should different national standards in measuring and reporting corporate income be reconciled?

Paul O. Gaddis pointed out the need to evaluate carefully the income interrelationships that exist among various subsidiaries of the multinational corporation.[5] Millard Pryor discussed financial objectives and a method to compensate for differential risk.[6]

E. Bruce Fredrickson explored the effect of various methods of financial reporting by multinational corporations on the evaluation of their capital stocks by security analysts.[7] J. R. Bugnion used a theoretical capital budgeting approach to evaluate foreign investments.[8] Among other things, his article made an attempt to consider various methods of determining the cost of capital for foreign investment.

Empirical investigations of current business practices show a lack of uniformity. Even companies that use capital budgeting theory for evaluating domestic alternatives may not use it for foreign alternatives; if they do, there is no consistent way in which it is applied. The National Industrial Conference Board has recently published an outstanding empirical study, *U.S. Production Abroad and the Balance of Payments*; on the basis of one hundred detailed questionnaires and fifty interviews in depth, the authors conclude the following:

> Even in discussions of the technical application of various financial criteria the ever-present main point proved to be that considerations of market position *dominate* the decision-making process. They determine the need, the urgency, and the desirability of an investment, while financial evaluations are used mainly to test the validity of marketing assumptions and to determine both the financial requirements and the financial means for attaining marketing goals. Thus, for the most part, financial considerations are pertinent to the *how to* rather than to the *whether to* finance a foreign investment.[9]

Results of Surveys

Our own survey, which includes ninety-two American and eighteen foreign multinational corporations, confirms the Conference Board conclusion. Most of the corporations which were interviewed indicated that they separated capital requests into various categories similar to those originally described by Joel Dean.[10] Financial investment criteria were used most often in evaluating relatively small cost-saving projects, replacement projects, and other projects which would fall under the purview of local managers. For relatively large or strategic investments, however, financial investment criteria were used only as a rough screening device to prevent obviously unprofitable projects from wasting the time of the board of directors.

Foreign investment proposals were almost always relatively large and strategic. The decision at the board level was usually determined by the competitive situation, case by case, on the assumption that the financial homework had been done down the line.

Interviews with officers at different levels in the same corporation indicated that the financial homework was done, but with varying degrees of sophistication.

At the industrial engineering level the calculations were quite consistent with capital budgeting theory. The same generalization could be made about projects which were screened at lower levels of the financial organization.

As projects moved up the line for approval, however, theoretical financial investment criteria seemed to be less well understood and often subordinated to other considerations. In fact, officers at various levels of the same organization offered conflicting opinions as to the extent of use of financial investment criteria and rarely agreed on the exact way in which the actual calculations were made.

Despite the business world's lack of enthusiasm for financial investment criteria in the multinational case, it is possible to evaluate foreign investment alternatives within the familiar framework of capital budgeting theory if modifications are made.

One problem is to develop an operational objective function for foreign investments which is more closely related to a behavioral theory of the firm.

A second problem is to develop ways to quantify those risks which are peculiar to foreign operations but not relevant to domestic operations.

The Dominant Goal

An operational goal for capital budgeting. Operational foreign investment criteria must be established which are consistent with a behavioral theory of the firm. The economic theorist would presumably choose long-run profit maximization as the dominant investment criterion, despite the fact that, even in the classical entrepreneur-manager model of the firm, it is difficult to translate long-run profit into an operational criterion for investment decisions.

The separation of ownership from management in the large corporation of today has led organization theorists to construct a behavioral model of the firm.[11] A single goal of profit is replaced by a theory of goal conflict among the various individual and group participants in the organization. Richard Cyert and James March have found that the set of coalition goals usually includes commitments in the areas of production, inventory, sales, market share and profit, and that the goals or aspiration levels change over time as feedback from experience occurs.

In the case of multinational corporations, the Conference Board study and our own survey would support the Cyert and March behavioral hypothesis. The indications are that market share is the dominant goal of multinational corporations, though one can show that this will not necessarily lead to long-run profit maximization.[12]

Determining Market Value

Market value of common stock. Maximization of market value of common stock has serious defects as an operational criterion for multinational investment decisions. Even in the uninational case there is no agreement on a valuation model for common stock. Merton H. Miller and Franco Modigliani showed that earnings is the most important determinant, followed by the tax advantages of leverage, growth potential, and size.[13] Myron Gordon found that dividends, rate of growth of dividends, and earnings instability are the key determinants.[14] John Lintner argued that dividends and capital structure are the most important factors.[15] Other theorists have suggested liquidity, general price levels, monetary and fiscal policy, and a host of other financial and psychological variables.

None of the empirical studies has attempted to isolate the effect on market valuation of a substantial amount of foreign earnings, debt, growth, dividends, or other foreign variables. For example, empirical studies of the oil or mining industries might reveal some systematic differences in market valuation of the common stock of multinational companies compared to uninational companies in comparable "business risk" classes.

If we drop the empirical approach in favor of a normative model which

The decision rule would then be to accept all projects and use all sources of funds until the marginal cost of capital has risen to the point where acceptance of another project would show a negative net present value if its incremental returns were discounted by the marginal cost of capital.

In the real world, all projects and all sources of funds do not conveniently present themselves for appraisal at the right time. Investment and funding decisions are usually made sequentially. Many projects are nonpostponable.

Although we would like to borrow from the least expensive international source and invest in the most lucrative projects wherever they are located, free international transfer of long-term investment capital is the exception and not the rule. Sources of funds are not always independent of specific uses. Political considerations can be as important as the economic ones. Access to a foreign capital market may depend on the desirability of the project to be financed from the host country's viewpoint.

The amount of local loan capital available may depend on the amount of local equity participation. In fact, any number of restrictions may be placed on the availability and use of local capital. Even the United States has now instituted capital rationing of a sort through the voluntary balance of payments program. Furthermore, the United States Revenue Act of 1962 made the collection of funds from foreign subsidiaries in so-called "tax haven subsidiaries" less attractive for American multinational corporations.

Since a generalized international investment model is not possible with capital rationing, except under rather restrictive assumptions, we will proceed to analyze net present value within the less satisfactory framework of a two-country–two-corporation model.[19]

ABC-USA ABC-UK

Let us consider the hypothetical case of the ABC Aluminum Corporation (ABC-USA), a vertically integrated, multicorporate, multinational organization with headquarters in the United States, and foreign subsidiaries in many countries. ABC-USA is considering the establishment of a manufacturing joint venture in the United Kingdom (ABC-UK). ABC-USA would sell aluminum ingots to ABC-UK, where they would be fabricated and either sold in the British market or exported. ABC-USA would provide $16.8 million, of which $8.4 million would purchase £3 million of ABC-UK's common stock, and $8.4 million would be in the form of a ten-year dollar loan equivalent to £3 million. British investors would purchase the remaining £2 million of common stock in ABC-UK and establish trade credit for £2 million. Table 16.1 shows a starting pro-forma balance sheet.

A behavioral theory of the firm requires separate measures of net present value from the viewpoints of ABC-USA, ABC-UK, the United

Kingdom, and the United States. Minimum aspiration levels ͨ
in the organizational coalition must be met if the organization iᶳ
viable. From the financial viewpoint, this means that the aͨ
criterion should be a positive net present value to the owners of ABᷮ
and ABC-UK. From the economic and political viewpoints, the inveᷤ
should have a positive net present value to the United Kingdom anᴑ ͺᴵe
United States, which are important nonowner groups with a stake in the
organization.

Only net present value from the viewpoint of ABC-USA and ABC-UK
will be considered, but a cost-benefit analysis of economic returns to the
United Kingdom and United States should be made by the governments
concerned. For example, are market prices the same as national opportunity costs? This would depend on such factors as the use of unemployed
resources (low opportunity cost) and scarce foreign exchange (high
opportunity cost).

Spillover effects on the rest of the economy should also be considered.
For example, what use can be made of taxes collected (less subsidies)? Will
social overhead be built by the investor? Will there be noneconomic costs
incurred, such as pollution? What is the appropriate national discount rate
to apply to future returns? What is risk from a national viewpoint? If there
are more projects with positive net present values than economic resources
available for investment, how should a country resolve the rationing
problem?

It should be obvious that this kind of economic analysis is beyond the
capabilities of most multinational corporations, but they must recognize
that foreign investments will have to meet just such economic criteria, if
they are to be considered a net benefit to society and to be supported by
the governments concerned.

Net present value from the viewpoint of ABC-USA. The ABC-UK
project must have a positive net present value to ABC-USA. Cash is not a
homogeneous commodity. Pound sterling revenues earned by ABC-UK

Table 16.1 Pro-forma balance sheet of ABC-UK (£ millions)

Assets		Liabilities	
Cash	1	Accounts payable	2
Accounts receivable	2	Ten-year loan from ABC-USA	3
Inventory	2	Common stock (UK-held)	2
Plant and equipment	9	Common stock (USA-held)	3
Total assets	10	Total liabilities	10

would not necessarily have the same utility to owners of ABC-USA as equivalent dollar revenues earned in the United States. There would be differences in risk, liquidity, interest rates, legal requirements, and other environmental variables if the pounds were not repatriated to the United States, and additional costs for foreign exchange conversion and payment of deferred American taxes if the pounds were repatriated. The **incremental cash flows** would be:

Investment base. From the viewpoint of ABC-USA the initial cash outflow would consist of the entire $16.8 million.

Dividends. Dividends paid by ABC-UK to ABC-USA would be a dollar inflow; however, allowance must be made for the U.K. dividend withholding tax, the net U.S. tax liability or credit incurred on repatriation of earnings, and the cost of converting pounds to dollars.[20]

Management contracts, license fees, royalties, disclosure fees, and contribution to overhead. The various kinds of payment by ABC-UK to ABC-USA for "know-how" would be a dollar inflow. Additional costs incurred in ABC-USA to provide the services covered by such payments must be subtracted; however, most of the costs of gaining "know-how" are presumably "sunk costs" from the viewpoint of ABC-USA and, therefore, not incremental to the decision to invest in ABC-UK. Income management contracts, license fees, and royalties would be subject to the U.S. corporate income tax, but not the U.K. dividend withholding tax. Disclosure fees would be treated as capital gains by U.S. tax authorities. Contribution to overhead would not be taxed if it merely covered out-of-pocket costs of staff services. All of these inflows would incur the foreign exchange conversion cost.

Loan amortization and interest payments. Since the dollar loan to ABC-UK counted as a cash outflow, loan principal repayments and interest (less U.S. taxes) must count as a dollar inflow. Loan principal repayments can be thought of as a cash recapture of original investment which takes the place of depreciation. The eventual cost of foreign exchange conversion for these payments would be a cash outflow only from the viewpoint of ABC-UK.

Transfer prices. If ABC-USA has a purchase or sales relationship with ABC-UK, it might be possible to shift income from ABC-UK to ABC-USA through an arbitrary use of transfer prices (and vice versa). In practice, arbitrary shifting of income through transfer prices is not easily accomplished. The internal revenue experts of most countries are sophisticated enough to require separate calculation of transfer prices for tax purposes.[21] Thus, ABC-USA might record one set of transfer prices for administrative purposes, such as evaluation of performance, but ABC-USA would have to negotiate with local tax authorities over the transfer prices allowed for tax purposes. This is especially true for products which have no free market price or which are produced by industries considered to be oligopolistic.

It might be argued that one of the many cost-oriented formulas should be the basis for transfer prices, such as is generally the case domestically. This ignores the fact that the tax authorities in one country cannot audit cost calculations derived in another country.

Apart from tax considerations, misuse of transfer prices would be opposed by the U.K. government on the grounds that it would have an unfavorable effect on the the balance of payments, because it worsens the terms of trade. It would also be opposed by the British joint venture partners, because of the reduction of income in ABC-UK. In short, we do not feel transfer price "profits" should be considered, if ABC-USA expects to operate abroad in the long run.

Other incremental revenue and cost. From the viewpoint of ABC-USA there are likely to be other gains or losses from establishing ABC-UK. Unit production costs may be reduced in ABC-USA because of higher volume production of aluminum ingots. This may be offset by lower volume of production of fabricated products, if the U.K. market was previously supplied by exports from ABC-USA.

There may be financial or distribution economies of scale. If ABC-UK is not established there may be incremental costs due to loss of the U.K. market to other competitors or more stringent trade barriers.

ABC-UK may provide ABC-USA with quality management and technical personnel who can contribute to its pool of know-how and ability to perceive and develop new investment opportunities in the U.K., other Commonwealth countries, and E.F.T.A. On the other hand, ABC-UK may divert management talent in ABC-USA from more valuable tasks. The real question here is how to measure the intangible returns and how to "assign them" to ABC-USA or ABC-UK.

Reinvested earnings. The most difficult conceptual problem is how to treat reinvested earnings. Reinvested earnings in ABC-UK are obviously not a cash inflow into ABC-USA until they are repatriated. Apart from legal restrictions, the reason for not repatriating all earnings is that presumably reinvestment in the U.K. promises a larger net present value than if the same earnings were repatriated and invested in the U.S. Theoretically, each reinvestment decision would call for a new capital budgeting evaluation in the same manner as the original investment.

Potential lines of reasoning are: (1) reinvested earnings in ABC-UK should be treated as incremental revenue because they could be remitted to ABC-USA if desired; (2) reinvested earnings in ABC-UK should count as incremental revenue because they would be reflected eventually in an appreciation of the capital stock of ABC-USA in the same manner as reinvested earnings in the U.S.; (3) even if earnings reinvested in ABC-UK are not immediately reflected in the market value of the capital stock of

ABC-USA, they would increase the market (and book) value of ABC-UK. Eventually, this gain could be realized by ABC-USA if it chose to sell ABC-UK.[22]

The arguments about retained earnings have their counterpart in balance of payments accounting. Retained earnings of corporate subsidiaries do not count in the balance of payments account entitled "income from foreign investment," but dividends, branch profits and interest do count. On the other hand, reinvested earnings are added to accumulated net worth (book value) and new capital outflow to measure the investment position of the U.S. vis-à-vis the rest of the world, rather than using a market value estimation of these holdings.

We feel that the best way to treat reinvested earnings is to assume that they lead to a growth in the size of dividends and other cash inflow items. In addition, the "cash-out" or market value of ABC-UK at the time horizon for capital budgeting decisions could be calculated by capitalizing either the forecast dividend or earning streams for that horizon, using the U.K. capitalization rate for equivalent risk classes. This would be the liquidating dividend.

The Cost of Capital

What should the cost of capital be? What rate of discount should ABC-USA apply to the incremental dollar flows to and from ABC-UK? For United States investments the normal procedure would be for ABC-USA to use its American cost of capital. Setting apart for the moment the effect of differential risks for foreign operations, this would also be the appropriate rate for ABC-USA's foreign investment, unless acceptance of foreign investments actually caused a change in its American cost of capital.[23]

Access to foreign capital markets might alter the cost of debt to ABC-USA. If ABC-USA borrows dollars or pounds in London in its own name, or even through a fully consolidated foreign subsidiary, the debt would appear on its balance sheet in the same manner as any similar category of domestic debt. The optimal debt-equity ratio would remain unchanged, but if foreign debt were more expensive it would raise the average interest cost. Any interest payments by ABC-UK could not be consolidated for tax purposes, thereby further raising the aftertax cost of debt to ABC-USA.

The effect of loans made by a foreign subsidiary and guaranteed by ABC-USA is not altogether clear. Whether the foreign subsidiary is consolidated or not, the guarantee should be reported to the stockholders as a contingent liability. This is not always done. In any case, if the subsidiary is not consolidated, how should the guarantee affect the parent corporation's optimal debt-equity ratio? More empirical work is needed in this area.

Access to foreign capital markets might alter the cost of equity to ABC-USA. If ABC-USA sold its own common stock abroad, access to the additional source of foreign funds could lower its long-range cost of equity. This would depend on a comparison of its common stock with other common stocks available to the foreign investors.

On the other hand, American investors might view foreign operations as more risky than United States operations and, therefore, demand a higher rate of capitalization. Allowance for objective risks in foreign operations should be made by ABC-USA, but this may or may not offset the perceived risk as seen by the stockholders. Furthermore, the problems with financial disclosure, which were discussed earlier, cloud the whole issue of a rationally determined capitalization rate.

Uncertainty Absorption

In summary, foreign operations might affect the cost of capital for ABC-USA, but the evidence is inconclusive. Until empirical studies show that there is a significant relationship, we feel that the normal American cost of capital is sufficient.

When making a forecast of cash flows and the cost of capital in the multinational case, assumptions must be made about future business, financial, political, and foreign exchange conditions.

Use of a discount rate uniformly higher than the cost of capital to reflect **political and foreign exchange uncertainties** does not allow for the actual amounts at risk or for the time pattern of uncertainty. These uncertainties are a threat to the entire investment and not just the cash flows. Potential loss would depend on the value of the uncovered dollar investment, which would vary with reinvestment and financing policies. If the political or foreign exchange climates were expected to be unfavorable in the near future, it is unlikely that any investment would be acceptable. Such uncertainties relate to the more distant future. Thus, the early cash flows would be too heavily penalized for uncertainty and the distant cash flows not penalized enough.

A better way to allow for uncertainty in the multinational case would be to charge each period's incremental cash flows the cost of a program of uncertainty absorption for that period, whether or not the program was actually undertaken. Theoretically at least, that choice would depend on matching the certain costs of a program of uncertainty absorption against the uncertain value of losses prevented. If potential losses could be reduced to expected value (or utility) by assuming a probability distribution of various types of risks, the charge for uncertainty absorption should be a figure representing the lower of the cost of insurance or expected value of loss. Otherwise, if there is complete uncertainty, the cost of insurance would be a fair proxy for expected value of loss.

One method of uncertainty absorption would be for ABC-USA to purchase additional information about the future prospects of ABC-UK in order to convert a case of uncertainty into one of risk or even certainty. Information about the political and foreign exchange risks could be purchased by electing a politically prominent British citizen to the board of directors of ABC-UK. Information might also be gained from other multinational corporations in the United Kingdom, as well as from United States government offices.

A second method of uncertainty absorption would be for ABC-USA to minimize the amount of exposed dollar investment in ABC-UK. This would help protect ABC-USA from losses due to inflation or devaluation. One technique would be to replace ABC-USA's investment with local borrowing. Another would be to fix ABC-USA's claims on ABC-UK in dollar terms, although ABC-UK would then bear the risk. This was done in the case of the $8.4 million loan. Accounts receivable could be factored in the United Kingdom. The plant could be leased rather than purchased. Components and materials could be purchased locally to reduce the dollar liability for work-in-progress. Dollar investment need not be reduced to zero, because some assets, such as plant, equipment, and inventory, would presumably increase in local currency price in the event of inflation or devaluation.

ABC-USA could buy insurance which would compensate it for losses in ABC-UK. F.C.I.A. insurance could be purchased to cover sales of aluminum ingots and equipment to ABC-UK. It would cover political, commercial, and foreign exchange control risks (excluding inflation or devaluation). It would not be possible to buy an Agency for International Development investment guarantee because the United Kingdom is not an underdeveloped country, but this would be a possible program for other foreign investments.

ABC-USA could hedge expected pound sterling receipts, from such items as dividends or aluminum ingot sales, by selling pound sterling in the forward exchange market.

ABC-USA could also "negotiate the environment." For example, ABC-USA could maintain control over patents, key processes, marketing channels, and transportation. A concession agreement could be negotiated with the British government, whereby the two parties stipulate things they can and cannot do. By setting up a joint venture, ABC-USA might have a favorable political position in the United Kingdom, but this can work the other way if the aspiration level of local owners is not satisfied.

Even if ABC-USA chooses to be self-insured, it should conceptually reduce the forecasted incremental revenues by a charge which reflects what it would cost to absorb the uncertainties that pertain to a foreign operation. In this way, it makes the foreign investment alternative more nearly comparable to domestic American investment alternatives.

Value to British Partners

Net present value from the viewpoint of ABC-UK. The second financial investment criterion that must be satisfied is that ABC-UK should have a positive net present value to the British joint venture partners as seen from their viewpoint. The same factors should be considered from the viewpoint of ABC-UK.

From the viewpoint of ABC-UK the initial cash outflow would be £10 million, representing its starting stock of assets.

The main incremental revenues to ABC-UK would be earnings before depreciation, interest, and payments to ABC-USA for "know-how," but net of United Kingdom taxes.

Loan amortization and interest payments are not incremental costs to ABC-UK. As in uninational capital budgeting theory, they are relevant only to the choice of the method of financing, i.e., the cost of capital.

The relevant rate of discount for ABC-UK should not be the same as for ABC-USA, but should be a function of the local United Kingdom cost of capital. British investors and creditors would require ABC-UK to match or exceed other British companies in the same risk class. Otherwise, ABC-UK would be wasting real and monetary resources from the economic viewpoint of the United Kingdom and the financial viewpoint of British investors.

ABC-UK might have a relatively low cost of debt compared to British-owned companies in the same risk class. ABC-USA can guarantee British loans to ABC-UK or grant it credit directly. ABC-UK's optimal debt-equity ratio might also be somewhat higher, due to the financial strength of ABC-USA.

Non-British control of ABC-UK might increase the cost of British equity financing. Thus, it would be necessary to find a weighted average cost of equity to reflect the returns required by the two national sources of equity capital.

Political and foreign exchange uncertainties would depend on actions taken by ABC-USA. If American claims on ABC-UK are fixed in dollar terms, ABC-UK would have to bear the foreign exchange conversion risk. If ABC-USA is able to "negotiate the environment" to insure its control of key patents, processes, and operating decisions, the lack of such control by ABC-UK might be viewed as an increased political uncertainty from the British viewpoint. The voluntary American balance of payments program would be another political uncertainty from the British viewpoint.

The foreign exchange risks might be equivalent to the cost of hedging them in the forward exchange market, but the political uncertainties are uninsurable. Nevertheless, conceptually at least, an estimate of the expected value of loss due to political uncertainty should be made and charged against incremental cash flows.

Details of Survey

A survey of capital budgeting methods in multinational firms. A questionnaire was sent to 219 United States firms and 100 foreign firms, selected from *Fortune*'s list of the 500 largest American corporations and the 200 largest foreign corporations. Some had only a minor stake in foreign operations.

We were also granted interviews with officials of fourteen multinational industrial firms, either commercial banks, and the National Industrial Conference Board. Interviews with the industrial firms were designed to follow up the mail questionnaires. The banking survey will be reported in another article. The purpose of the National Industrial Conference Board interview was to check our results to see if they were consistent with the results of the N.I.C.B. study (see note 9). This proved to be the case.

Details of our survey and response to the questionnaires are presented in Tables 16.2 and 16.3.

Capital budgeting procedures (Table 16.4). From a procedural viewpoint, most foreign and domestic investment alternatives are apparently processed in about the same way, though the evidence is not conclusive.[23]

Income (Table 16.5). There seems to be a sharp difference in the way firms view foreign income. Over 29 per cent of the firms counted net foreign earnings (book value), whether or not they were repatriated. Nearly 48 per cent of the firms measured foreign income in terms of cash flow, but

Table 16.2 Survey data

	US firms	Foreign firms	Total
Questionnaire response			
Questionnaires mailed out	219	100	319
Questionnaires returned	119	36	155
Firms not multinational	19	16	35
Firm refused to answer	8	2	10
Questionnaires completed (incl. interviews)	92	18	110
Total combined foreign and domestic sales produced in foreign subsidiaries or affiliates			
Less than 10 per cent	35	8	43
Between 10 and 30 per cent	33	5	38
More than 30 per cent	19	5	24
No answer	5	–	5
Total number of firms	92	18	110

Table 16.3 Industry number key

Number used in survey	No. of firms with completed questionnaires	US SIC code (1957)	US input output table (1958) industry no.
1 Mining and petroleum	15	10–13, 29	5–8, 31
2 Food and tobacco	16	20, 21	14, 15
3 Lumber, paper and wood products	6	24, 26	20, 24
4 Chemicals, plastics and drugs	8	28	27, 28
5 Nonelectrical machinery and office equipment	10	35	43–52
6 Electrical machinery	5	36	53–58
7 Motor vehicles, aircraft, and other transportation equipment	9	37	59–61
8 Other	23	–	–
Total	92	–	–

a majority of these added reinvested earnings to cash flow as if the earnings had been repatriated and then reinvested. The remaining 23 per cent of the answers did not fit clearly into either the earnings or cash flow categories. The mining and oil companies favored the cash flow method, because most of their earnings are in dollars and they pay American taxes as income is earned, due to the use of the branch form of organization. Foreign firms and firms with over 30 per cent foreign sales also favored cash flow, but the reasons are not readily apparent.

Cost of capital (Table 16.6). Excluding the twenty-three which did not use cost of capital at all, over 64 per cent of the firms did not vary cost or capital for foreign investments. Use of some measure of local cost of capital was apparently significant only for the foreign firms, and the agricultural and forest products industries. About 80 per cent of the firms with more than 30 per cent of their sales from foreign subsidiaries did not vary their cost of capital for foreign investments.

Risk (Table 16.7). Nearly all of the firms claimed that they made an allowance for risk, but fully 38 per cent of the answers indicated that "subjective evaluation" was the method used. About 35 per cent of the answers stated that either a higher rate of return or a higher cost of capital was applied to foreign investment alternatives. Few answers suggested positive risk absorption methods, such as borrowing locally, buying insurance, or getting faster payback. Old-timers in international business such as mining, petroleum, motor vehicles, chemicals, drugs, and office equipment and the firms with over 30 per cent of sales from foreign subsidiaries tended to be much more subjective than the "newcomers."

Table 16.4 Capital budgeting procedure

In your capital budgeting procedure, how do you make a distinction between foreign and domestic investment alternatives?

	Survey industry number								Total US firms	Foreign firms
	1	2	3	4	5	6	7	8		
No distinction made	4	6	3	4	6	4	2	10	39	8
Vary required rate of return on investment	3	5	2	1	1	1	2	3	18	4
More critical of foreign	1						3		4	1
Subsidiary or divisional decision		2		1	1		1	5	10	2
No answer or not applicable	1	1		2				3	7	2
Other*	6	2	2		2		1	2	15	1
Total†	15	16	7	8	10	5	9	23	93	18

*Other answers were as follows: economic analysis (1), necessity (2), by project (3), geographical classification (1), availability of funds (1), long-range programs considered (1), judgement (2), operating return on operating assets (1), foreign investment limited to cash flow generated abroad (1), crude oil reserves are goal (1), depreciation plus one-half foreign earnings (1), when market cannot be served from US (1).
†Since some firms listed more than one criterion, the figures represent number of times mentioned.

Table 16.5 Potential income measurement

In analyzing potential income from foreign investments, how do you measure the various income streams (dividends, reinvested earnings, license fees, etc.)?

	Survey industry number								Total US firms	Foreign firms
	1	2	3	4	5	6	7	8		
Earnings										
Count all earnings after foreign taxes, regardless of currency	1	5		1	3			5	15	
Count all earnings after foreign taxes, except when there are currency restrictions								1	1	1
Book return on book investment	2	2	1	2	2	1	1	4	15	4
Cash Flow										
Count all cash inflows to the parent corp. after foreign and domestic taxes	1			1	1		4	1	8	5
Count all cash inflows to the parent corp. plus reinvested earnings adjusted for foreign and domestic taxes	3	1	3	2	1			6	16	3
Count all cash inflows to the parent corp. plus reinvested earnings, adjusted for foreign taxes only	3	2	1		1		3	4	14	1
Discounted cash flow	4	1		1		1	2		9	3
Other*	2	8	1	2	3	4		6	26	3
Total†	16	19	6	9	11	6	10	27	104	20

*Other answers were as follows: subjective evaluation (3), forecasting (2), volume of business (2), return on assets employed (2), payback analysis (4), assure adequate supply of raw materials (2), no answer or ambiguous (11).
†Since some firms listed more than one criterion, the figures represent number of times mentioned.

Consolidation (Table 16.8). Nearly all of the firms consolidated majority-owned foreign subsidiaries with domestic divisions. Most of the firms which answered that they did not consolidate had minority-owned affiliates only.

No Consistent Pattern

Conclusions. There is a need for a normative theory of capital budgeting which applies to foreign as well as domestic investment alternatives. The survey of methods currently being used by a sample of multinational firms shows no consistent pattern of foreign investment analysis.

A behavioral theory of goals is a better explanation of the observed objectives of multinational firms than the traditional economic goal of profit maximization. A goal of market share subject to various economic, political, and social constraints seems to typify the behavior of many multinational firms.

The usual financial objective of maximizing the market value of the shares of current owners is not entirely consistent with a behavioral theory of goals. The owners are only one of several important groups. Foreign joint venture partners are not always represented in the owner group, a fact which often causes problems with their governments.

It is difficult to build either an inductive or deductive model of market value determination. A number of different variables have been proposed, but there is no consensus. Foreign variables have been ignored as determinants of market value. Even if a satisfactory model could be built, accounting consolidation of foreign subsidiaries with domestic operations makes it nearly impossible for investment analysts to forecast any of the key variables for multinational firms.

Despite the weakness of a market value criterion, net present value is the best available method for analyzing foreign investments. In order to be consistent with the behavioural theory of the firm, the acceptance criterion should be a positive net present value, both from the viewpoint of the owners of the parent corporation and foreign joint venture partners. A cost benefit analysis of the investment should also show a positive net present value from the viewpoint of both the host country and the investing country.

Recommendations

Incremental cash inflow from the viewpoint of the parent corporation should include dividends, know-how payments, interest and loan repayments, export profits, any intangible gains, and the "cash-out" value of the

Table 16.6 Determining cost of capital

If you need a measure of capital, do you use a different rate for foreign than you do for domestic investment alternatives? If yes, please explain how you determine cost of capital in the different cases.

	Survey industry number								Total US firms	Foreign firms
	1	2	3	4	5	6	7	8		
Do not use cost of capital	1		2	1	4	4	5	5	22	1
Use cost of capital										
Do not vary cost of capital	10	10		7	6		3	12	48	8
Vary cost of capital subjectively	2							2	4	1
Use local cost of capital	1	5	3					1	10	3
Use local prime interest rate								2	2	4
Use cost of funds actually used		1				1	1	1	4	1
Other*	1		1						2	1
Total	15	16	6	8	10	5	9	23	92	18

*Other answers were as follows: 125 per cent of US cost of capital (1), 200 per cent of US cost of capital (1), greater than domestic rate (1).

Table 16.7 Risk allowance

How do you allow for varying degrees of risk in different countries?

	Survey industry number								Total US firms	Foreign firms
	1	2	3	4	5	6	7	8		
Subjective evaluation	8	4	1	7	6	1	6	11	44	6
Vary required rate of return on investment	7	7	3	1	2	3	2	8	33	7
Vary payback	1	2		1	1	1			6	
Borrow local funds where available	1		1		1	1		1	5	
Insure risks where possible	1	3	1	1	1			2	9	2
Adjust cost of capital in a present value analysis		1	1						2	4
No distinction made		1			1			3	5	
Other*	1	1					1	1	4	3
Total†	19	19	7	10	12	6	9	26	108	22

*Other answers were as follows: accrue reserves (1), avoid risk entirely (1), ambiguous or no answer (5).
†Since some firms listed more than one method, the figures represent number of times mentioned.

Table 16.8 Consolidating operations

In your financial reports to stockholders do you consolidate foreign and domestic operations: foreign operations only; do not consolidate; or other treatment?

| | Survey industry number | | | | | | | | Total US firms | Foreign firms |
	1	2	3	4	5	6	7	8		
Consolidate majority-owned foreign subsidiaries with domestic	14	12	6	6	7	4	8	18	75	8
Consolidate foreign operations only									0	0
Do not consolidate		2			1	1		1	5	6
Other treatment	1	2	—	2	2	—	1	4	12	4
Total	15	16	6	8	10	5	9	23	92	18

subsidiary at the time horizon for capital budgeting to reflect the value of reinvested earnings. Cash outflow should include both equity and loan capital provided to the subsidiary.

The parent corporation should discount the cash flows by its normal weighted average cost of capital under an "optimal" capital structure.

An allowance for political and foreign exchange uncertainty should be made by charging cash flows the cost of a program of uncertainty absorption, whether or not it is actually carried out. Methods of uncertainty absorption include purchasing more information, reducing the amount of uncovered home office investment, buying insurance where available, and negotiating the environment.

Incremental cash inflow from the viewpoint of the foreign subsidiary should include net earnings after local taxes but before depreciation, interest, and "know-how" payments. Cash outflows should be the original investment in assets.

The foreign subsidiary should discount its cash flow by its own weighted average cost of capital under an "optimal" capital structure. The optimal capital structure might be different than other local firms because of the financial backing of the parent corporation.

The foreign subsidiary should make an allowance for political and foreign exchange uncertainty by charging cash flows the cost of a program of uncertainty absorption. The cost and methods available will depend partly on what program is undertaken by the parent corporation.

Sights Set Too Low?

The survey of multinational firms did not show that they were following the analytical approach suggested here. In particular only 48 per cent of them used any kind of a cash flow technique. Over 29 per cent of them counted the full book value of net foreign earnings, regardless of currency or reinvestment policy. Only 17 per cent of the firms which used cost of capital required a foreign investment to yield more than some measure of the local cost of capital. About 38 per cent of the firms stated that they treat risk in a subjective way.

* * *

In our opinion, many of the multinational firms are setting their sights too low on required rate of return on foreign investment. By using book earnings to measure return on investment, they are not facing up to the fact that repatriation of foreign earnings has often been a costly affair. By not requiring a foreign investment to yield more than local cost of capital, they may be using local real and monetary resources in a less than optimal economic way from the viewpoint of the host country. By not quantifying risk, they are ignoring potential political and foreign exchange losses, except insofar as these are recognized as part of the strategic (as distinct from financial) desirability of a particular foreign investment.

If more rigorous financial investment criteria were adopted by the multinational firms, the capital outflow into direct foreign investments might be reduced.

On the other hand, if strategic considerations such as market share dominate the financial considerations, more rigorous financial analysis may not be worth the time and cost involved.

References

The authors received financial support for the research on which this article is based from the Ford Foundation Multinational Corporation Project and from the Institute of Business and Economic Research, University of California, Berkeley.

1. Stefan Robock, "Overseas Financing for U.S. International Business," *Journal of Finance*, May 1966, p. 298.
2. *Ibid.*, pp. 300–302.
3. A. J. Merrett and Allen Sykes, *The Finance and Analysis of Capital Projects* (London, England: Longmans Green and Company, Ltd., 1963), Chap. 13. Reprinted in Coyle and Mock, ed., *Readings in International Business* (Scranton, Pennsylvania: International Textbook Company, 1965), pp. 324–331.
4. Dan Throop Smith, "Financial Variables in International Business," *Harvard Business Review*, Jan.-Feb. 1966, p. 94.
5. Paul O. Gaddis, "Analyzing Overseas Investments," *Harvard Business Review*, May-June 1966, pp. 115–122.
6. Millard H. Pryor, "Planning in a Worldwide Business," *Harvard Business Review*, Jan.-Feb. 1965, pp. 130–139.
7. E. Bruce Fredrickson, "Security Analysis and the Multinational Corporation," *Financial Analysts Journal*, Sept.-Oct. 1965, pp. 109–117.
8. J. R. Bugnion, "Capital Budgeting and International Corporations," *Revue économiques et sociale*, Sept. 1965. Reprinted in *Quarterly Journal of A.I.E.-S.E.C. International*, Nov. 1965, pp. 30–54.
9. *U.S. Production Abroad and the Balance of Payments* (New York: National Industrial Conference Board, 1966), p. 63.
10. Joel Dean, *Capital Budgeting* (New York: Columbia Univ. Press, 1951).
11. See Richard Cyert and James March, *A Behavioral Theory of the Firm* (Englewood Clifs, N.J.: Prentice-Hall, Inc., 1963).
12. See William Baumol, *Economic Theory and Operations Analysis* (Englewood Cliffs, N.J.: Prentice-Hall, Inc., 1965), Chap. 13.
13. Merton H. Miller and Franco Modigliani, "Some Estimates of the Cost of Capital to the Electric Utility Industry, 1954–1957," *American Economic Review*, June 1966, p. 373.
14. Myron Gordon, *The Investment, Financing and Valuation of the Corporation* (Homewood, Ill.: Richard D. Irwin, Inc., 1962).

15. John Lintner, "Optimum Dividends and Corporation Growth Under Uncertainty," *Quarterly Journal of Economics*, Feb. 1964, pp. 49–95.
16. James T. Porterfield, *Investment Decisions and Capital Costs* (Englewood Cliffs, N.J.: Prentice-Hall, Inc., 1965), p. 17.
17. A recent example of government interference on behalf of its investors occurred in Norway in 1962. The Norwegian government renegotiated a direct investment concession agreement with Swiss Aluminum Ltd. The original concession was supposed to permit establishment of an aluminum smelter in Norway as a joint venture with 50 per cent Norwegian equity participation. The terms of payment for "know-how" to the Swiss company and the manner in which these terms were imposed on potential Norwegian investors made the eventual common stock offering in Norway so unpopular that only a fraction of the shares were sold. The Norwegian government eventually bought enough of the unsold shares to bring Norwegian ownership up to 20 per cent. Now the Swiss must operate as partners with the Norwegian government, rather than with Norwegian private investors.
18. As a rule, foreign subsidiaries cannot be consolidated with their parent corporation for tax purposes under U.S. laws. There are exceptions under certain conditions for Canada and Mexico.
19. For a mathematical programming approach, see H. Martin Weingartner, *Mathematical Programming and the Analysis of Capital Budgeting Problems* (Englewood Cliffs, N.J.: Prentice-Hall, Inc., 1963).
20. There would be a net tax liability to the U.S. if the tax credit for income and withholding taxes paid to the United Kingdom on the earnings of ABC-UK which have generated the dividend were less than the deferred United States tax on those earnings.
21. Section 482, U.S. Internal Revenue Code, allows tax authorities to reallocate income and expenses among related companies to reflect "arms length" prices.
22. To get a flavor of the controversy, see Ezra Solomon, *The Theory of Financial Management* (New York: Columbia Univ. Press, 1963) and Modigliani and Miller, "Corporate Income Taxes and the Cost of Capital: A Correction," *American Economic Review*, June 1963, pp. 433–443.
23. See Yair Aharoni, *The Foreign Investment Decision Process* (Boston: Harvard Graduate School of Business, Division of Research, 1966).

17

Capital Budgeting for the Multinational Corporation*

Alan C. Shapiro

*Source: *Financial Management*, 7 (Spring 1978), pp. 7–16.

Introduction

Multinational corporations (MNCs) evaluating foreign investments find their analyses complicated by a variety of problems rarely if ever encountered by domestic firms. This paper examines a number of such problems, including differences between project and parent company cash flows, foreign tax regulations, expropriation, blocked funds, exchange rate changes, inflation, and segmented capital markets. The major principle behind methods proposed to cope with these complications is to maximise the use of available information while reducing arbitrary cash flow and cost of capital adjustments. (A similar methodology, while not explicit, may lie behind some of the numerical examples in Rodriguez and Carter [13].) In practice, the methods usually involve adjusting a project's cash flows rather than its cost of capital. This is because there is normally more and better information on the specific impact of a given risk on a project's cash flows than on its cost of capital. Furthermore, adjusting a project's cost of capital to reflect incremental risk does not usually allow for adequate consideration of the time pattern and magnitude of the risk being evaluated. As Robichek and Myers [12] point out, using a uniformly higher discount rate to reflect additional risk involves penalizing future cash flows relatively more heavily than present ones.

Parent vs. Project Cash Flows

Substantial differences can exist between project cash flows and cash flows back to the parent firm because of tax regulations and exchange controls, for example. Furthermore, many project expenses such as management fees and royalties are returns to the parent company. In addition, the *incremental* revenue contributed to the parent MNC by a project can differ from total project revenues if, for example, the project involves substituting local production for parent company exports. In general, incremental cash flows to the parent can be found by subtracting world-wide parent company cash flows (without the investment) from post-investment parent company cash flows. Given such differences, the question arises as to the relevant cash flows to use in project evaluation.

One suggested position is that "to the extent that the corporation views itself as a true multinational, the effect of restrictions on repatriation may not be severe" [13, p. 341]. According to economic theory, though, *the value of a project is determined by the net present value of future cash flows back to the investor.* Thus, the parent MNC should value only those cash flows *which are or can be repatriated,* since only accessible funds can be used to pay dividends and interest, amortize the firm's debt, and be reinvested. This principle also holds, of course, for a domestic firm. For example, dividends received by a parent firm from an unconsolidated domestic subsidiary (less than 80% ownership) are taxed at a 15% rate and hence should only be valued at .85 of the original dividend paid. While the principle itself is simple, it can be complicated to apply. The next several sections use this principle to analyze the impact of taxation, expropriation, and exchange controls on cash flows to the parent.

Tax Treatment of Foreign Source Income

Since only after-tax cash flows are relevant, it is necessary to determine when and what taxes must be paid on foreign-source profits. While the tax treatment of foreign-source earnings is quite complex, there are several stages in the taxation of all income from foreign investments. First, the local government involved taxes profits. If tax concessions are granted, however, the tax rate can be zero. Ordinarily, the company then pays a withholding tax to the local government on that portion of profits which is repatriated in the form of dividends, interest, and fees and royalties. These withholding taxes can sometimes be avoided, however, if the company remits profits in the form of loan repayments, for example, rather than as dividends. Furthermore, the dividend withholding rate can actually be negative (as in Germany, which taxes retained earnings at 51% while earnings paid out as dividends are taxed at only 15% [14]). In addition, many countries, including the United States, tax income remitted from overseas operations. The United States is the only country which will also tax certain unremitted profits known as subpart F income. To further complicate tax analysis, the U.S. taxes income arising from operations in developed countries differently from those in less-developed countries. (For a good description of U.S. taxation principles and practices, see Price-

Waterhouse's "Information Guide for U.S. Corporations Doing Business Abroad" [11].)

To avoid double taxation, the U.S. government allows tax credits for foreign income and withholding taxes paid, but such credits can only be applied against U.S. taxes owed on other foreign-source income. The effective tax on foreign earnings thus depends on the local tax rate compared to the U.S. corporate income tax rate of 48%, the applicable withholding tax rate, and the availability of excess foreign tax credits. The actual withholding tax rate can still be substantially different from the nominal rate because of bilateral tax treaties.

To illustrate the complexities involved, assume an effective foreign income tax rate of t_f. Thus, each dollar of earnings abroad will provide $1-t_f$ dollars of retained earnings. If these earnings are then repatriated in the form of dividends, with a dividend withholding tax rate of t_d, the amount of money that gets through, per dollar of original earnings, will equal:

$.52, if either $T = t_f + t_d - t_f t_d < .48$ and no excess foreign tax credits are available, or if $T > .48$ and all foreign tax credits generated can be used elsewhere;

$1 - T$, if either $T < .48$ and excess foreign tax credits are available or if $T > .48$ and foreign tax credits are unusable. (These calculations only hold for developed countries. The applicable regulations for less developed countries can be found in the Price-Waterhouse guide [11].)

This computation becomes more complex if only some excess tax credits are available or if only a portion of the new tax credits generated can be used. The effective tax rate on repatriated dividends would then be a weighted average of .48 and T.

The actual tax on remitted funds would depend also on the transfer mechanism used, including adjustments in transfer prices, dividend flows, fee and royalty charges, and intracompany loan and credit arrangements. Rutenberg [14] analyzes these various fund shifting methods and their associated costs.

Let M_t be the after-local tax dollar cash flow in year t. If τ is the marginal rate of additional taxation on remitted funds, then the present value of these cash flows to the parent if remitted immediately equals $M_t(1 - \tau)/(1 + k)^t$ where k is the project's cost of capital. If $T > .48$ and foreign tax credits are usable, then τ will be negative.

Reinvested profits are more difficult to value. Let r be the after-local tax rate of return on the reinvested funds. Suppose that cash generated in year t will be repatriated in year $t + s$ along with all incremental returns earned on these reinvested funds. Then the present value of cash generated in year t should equal $M_t (1 + r)^s (1 - \tau)/(1 + k)^{t+s}$ where the marginal tax rate τ on remitted funds can vary from year to year. If all cash flows are expected to be reinvested locally, then a terminal value for the project will have to be estimated based on the assumption that complete repatriation will occur at the end of the planning horizon.

The project cost of capital may also have to be adjusted to reflect these cross-border tax effects[10]. For example, retained earnings abroad need yield only $(1 - \tau)k_e$ where k_e is the parent company's required return on equity capital. This is because the parent company will receive $1 - \tau$ dollars for each dollar originally remitted. Thus each dollar of remitted funds must yield the parent company $(1 - \tau)k_e$ annually or, in equilibrium, the return on retained earnings. Parent company funds must yield the firm's marginal cost of capital (provided that the foreign investment doesn't change the MNC's overall riskiness), and hence their cost is unaffected by foreign tax factors. The after-tax cost of local debt is, of course, dependent on local taxes. Furthermore, the cost of debt raised abroad is affected not only by local tax rates but also by the tax treatment of exchange gains and losses arising from foreign currency-denominated debt (see [3] and [16] for elaboration of these effects).

Political and Economic Risk Analysis

There are several methods by which multinational corporations can account for the added political and economic risks of overseas operations. One is to use a higher discount rate for foreign operations, another to require a shorter payback period. Neither approach, however, lends itself to a careful evaluation of a particular risk's actual impact on investment returns. Thorough risk analysis requires assessment of the magnitude of the risk's effects on cash flows as well as an estimate of the time pattern of the risk. For example, an expropriation five years from now is likely to be much less threatening then one expected next year. Thus, using a uniformly higher discount rate just distorts the meaning of a project's present value without obviating the necessity for a careful risk evaluation. Furthermore, the choice of a risk premium (or risk premia if the discount rate is allowed to vary over time) is an arbitrary one, whether it is 2% or 10%. Instead, adjusting cash flows makes it possible to fully incorporate all available information about a specific risk's impact on an investment's future returns.

The cash flow adjustments presented in this paper employ only expected values; that is, the analysis reflects only the first moment of the probability distribution of a given risk's impact. While this procedure does not assume that shareholders are risk-neutral, it does assume either that risks such as expropriation, currency controls, inflation, and exchange rate changes are nonsystematic or that foreign investments tend to lower a firm's systematic risk. In the latter case, adjusting only the expected values of future cash flows will yield a lower bound on the investment's value to the firm.

According to modern capital asset pricing theory, the use of expected values to reflect incremental risks is justified as long as the systematic risk of a proposed investment remains unchanged [2]. To the extent that the risks dealt with in this paper are unsystematic, there is no theoretical reason to adjust a project's cost of capital to reflect them. In fact, though, foreign investments appear to reduce a firm's systematic risk by supplying international diversification [1]. If anything, therefore, this approach under- rather than overestimates a project's present value. (This would seem to be desirable both in its own right and also because the results presented by Agmon and Lessard [1] are just barely statistically significant.)

It is unlikely, however, that management will be concerned solely with the systematic component of total risk. Furthermore, the parent and subsidiary company are likely to have differing attitudes towards these risks. It is likely that ignorance of the former and bias of the latter may cause conflicts in recognition of these risks. An alternative approach is to use the Robichek and Myers [12] certainty-equivalent method where risk-adjusted cash flows are discounted at the risk-free rate. However, this method requires generating certainty-equivalent cash flows, for which no satisfactory procedure has yet been developed. Furthermore, it involves losing some information on the valuation of future cash flows that is provided by shareholders in the form of their required yield on a typical firm investment.

Expropriation

The extreme form of political risk is expropriation. This is of course an obvious case where project and parent company cash flows diverge. A sophisticated cash flow adjustment technique recommended by Stonehill and Nathanson [22] is to charge each year's flows a premium for political risk insurance whether or not such insurance is actually purchased. (The United States government sells political risk insurance through the Overseas Private Investment Corporation (OPIC). Other nations, as well as private insurance companies such as Lloyd's, will also insure overseas investments against certain types of political risk.) This solution, however, does not really measure the effect of a given political risk on a project's present value. In the case of expropriation, political risk insurance normally covers only the book value, not the economic value, of expropriated assets. The relationship between the book value of a project's assets and the project's economic value as measured by its future cash flows is tenuous at best. It is worthwhile, of course, to compare the cost of political risk insurance with its expected benefits. Insurance though is no substitute for a careful evaluation of the impact of political risk on a given project.

The approach suggested here directly examines the impact of expropriation on the project's present value to the parent. Let X_t be the parent's expected after-tax dollar cash flow from the project in year t. If I_o is the initial investment outlay, then the project's present value to the parent firm equals

$$-I_o + \sum_{t=1}^{n} \frac{X_t}{(1 + k)^t},$$

where n is the life of the project and k the project cost of capital as before. Suppose now that an expropriation will take place with certainty during year h. Then, the new present value will equal

$$-I_o + \sum_{t=1}^{h-1} \frac{X_t}{(1 + k)^t} + \frac{G_h}{(1 + k)^h},$$

where G_h is the expected value of the net compensation provided. This compensation comes from several sources:

1. Direct compensation paid to the firm by the local government. (This compensation can be delayed, as in Chile, for example, where many MNCs were expropriated by the Allende government with little or no compensation. When Allende was overthrown, however, his successors began returning property and otherwise compensating these MNCs.).
2. Indirect compensation such as the management contracts received by oil companies whose properties were nationalized by the Venezuelan government. (Stephen Kobrin was gracious enough to point out to me the existence of these continuing arrangements.)
3. Payment received from political insurance. (Insurance payments may lag expropriation by several years as well.).
4. Tax deductions in the home country associated with such an extraordinary loss.
5. A reduction in the amount of capital that must be repaid by the project equal to the unamortized portion of any local borrowing. It is inconceivable that a firm which has had a foreign operation expropriated would pay back any local borrowing except as part of a total compensation package worked out with the local government. Suppliers of capital from outside the host country would normally be repaid by the parent company (whether or not loans were guaranteed) in order to preserve the parent's credit reputation.

Since it is unlikely that compensation will be provided immediately or even simultaneously from the different sources, G_h must be adjusted to reflect the various delays possible. Uncertainty regarding the magnitude of G_h will require specification of the likely range and probability of this compensation. G_h is therefore an expected value rather than a number generated with certainty. For a given period h, a MNC can determine how large G_h must be to still undertake a project.

Similarly, for a given level of compensation, a firm can determine beyond what period h^* expropriation will no longer affect the investment decision. For example, if $G = 0$, then h^* is the minimum value of j for which

$$\sum_{t=1}^{h} \frac{X_t}{(1 + k)^t} > I_o.$$

In this situation, h^* can be considered the present value payback period.

If the probability of expropriation equals P_h in year h and 0 in all other years, then the project's expected net present value (NPV_p) would equal

$$-I_o + \sum_{t=1}^{h-1} \frac{X_t}{(1 + k)^t} + (1 - P_h) \sum_{t=h}^{n} \frac{X_t}{(1 + k)^t} + P_h \frac{G_h}{(1 + k)^h}.$$

The term $(1 - P_h) \sum_{t=h}^{n} \frac{X_t}{(1 + k)^t}$

reflects the fact that if there is no expropriation in period h, with probability $1 - P_h$, cash flows will continue to be generated as originally anticipated. If expropriation does occur, though, future cash flows will be zero, save for compensation.

Determining an exact value for P_h is likely to be difficult if not impossible. While a number of commercial and academic political risk forecasting models are available, there is little evidence they can successfully forecast these risks. These models normally supply country indices which attempt to quantify the level of political risk in each nation (see, for example, the Business International Risk Index [3] and the Political System Stability Index in Haendel and West [7]). Their common weakness is that they assume each firm in a country is facing the same degree of political risk. Empirical evidence on the post-World War II experiences of U.S. and British MNCs, however, clearly indicates that industries differ in their susceptibilities to political risk [8,23]. For example, expropriation (or creeping expropriation) is more likely to occur in the extractive, utility, or financial service sectors of an economy than in the manufacturing sector. In general, it appears that the greater the perceived benefits to the local economy a given subsidiary provides, and the more expensive it would be to replace it with a purely local operation, the less risk it faces.

An alternative approach to use in incorporating information concerning the magnitude of P_h is break-even analysis. This involves determining the value of P^* where P^* is the solution to

$$NPV_p = 0 \text{ or } P^* = \frac{\sum_{t=1}^{n} \dfrac{X_t}{(1 + k)^t} - I_o}{\sum_{t=h}^{n} \dfrac{X_t}{(1 + k)^t} - \dfrac{G_h}{(1 + k)^h}}.$$

If $P_h < P^*$, then the project will have a positive net present value, provided that the project would be acceptable in the absence of expropriation. This probability break-even analysis is useful, since it is normally easier and requires less information to ascertain whether $P_h < P^*$ or $P_h > P^*$ than to decide on the absolute level of P_h. For example, if $P^* = .30$, then it is unnecessary to argue whether $P_h = .50$ or .60, since the result will not affect the decision (provided the decision is based on the project's expected net present value). The same is true for an argument as to whether $P_h = .10$ or .20. This break-even analysis can also tell a company when it is worthwhile to invest in more precise data concerning P_h.

In addition, since the firm's own actions can affect the probability of expropriation, this analysis can help a firm to compare the value of trying to change P_h (by entering into a joint venture or switching to local suppliers) with the costs of such actions. The size of the ultimate compensation package is also likely to be affected by these policies and can be included in the analysis. Thus, management can use this procedure to value available alternative strategies both before and after undertaking the investment.

For the general case, let P_t be the probability of expropriation in period t, given no previous expropriation. Then the project's expected net present value equals

$$-I_o + \sum_{t=1}^{n} \prod_{i=1}^{t} (1 - P_i) \frac{X_t}{(1 + k)^t} + \sum_{t=1}^{n} \prod_{i=1}^{t-1} (1 - P_i) \frac{P_t G_t}{(1 + k)^t}.$$

If $P_t \equiv P$, this expression reduces to

$$-I + \sum_{t=1}^{n} (1 - P)^t \frac{X_t}{(1 + k)^t} + \sum_{t=1}^{n} (1 - P)^{t-1} \frac{PG_t}{(1 + k)^t}.$$

This model formulation lends itself naturally to simulation of various political risk alternatives.

Illustration

Suppose a firm wishes to analyze an investment with a five-year life. The initial investment required is $1,000,000 with five annual cash inflows of $500,000 expected. With a cost of capital equal to 20%, the present value of this investment is $495,500. However, an expropriation during year 3 is considered possible. If the expropriation does take place, it is believed that compensation equal to $200,000 will be paid. Then the break-even probability required for this investment to have a positive expected present value equals .80. If the probability of expropriation is less than .80, the investment should be undertaken (if the decision is based on expected values). The break-even probability drops to .68 if the net compensation is 0.

Suppose, instead, that the expropriation is expected during the second

Exhibit 17.1 Effects of expropriation timing and compensation package on break-even probabilities

Investment cash flows		Break-even probability with compensation of	
Initial Outlay –	$1,000,000	$200,000	0
Year 1	500,000	$P_1^* = .37$	$P_1^* = .33$
Year 2	500,000	$P_2^* = .64$	$P_2^* = .45$
Year 3	500,000	$P_3^* = .80$	$P_3^* = .68$
Year 4	500,000	$P_4^* = 1.0$	$P_4^* = 1.0$
Year 5	500,000	$P_5^* = 1.0$	$P_5^* = 1.0$
Present value discounted at 20%		$495,500	

year. Then, even with compensation equal to $200,000, the investment should not be undertaken unless the probability of expropriation is less than .64. The break-even probability declines to .45, though, if $G_2 = 0$. Hence, the break-even probability P_2^* is much more sensitive to the degree of compensation than is P_3^*.

If an expropriation is not expected until year 4, the investment will automatically have a positive present value of $53,000 even if $P_4 = 1.0$ and $G_4 = 0$. (See Exhibit 17.1.)

Overall, the analysis reveals an investment that requires such a high probability of expropriation before it has a negative expected present value, particularly beyond the first year, that expropriation is probably not a relevant consideration. Any investment with a probability of expropriation of 45% in the second year, for example, would very likely not be considered in the first place.

Blocked Funds

The same methodology developed above can be applied to analyze the effects of various exchange controls. In discussing blocked funds, it must be pointed out that if all funds are expected to be blocked in perpetuity, then the value of the project to the parent is zero.

Assume that in year j all funds become blocked. These exchange controls will be removed in year n, at which time all available funds can be remitted to the parent. As before, let the return on reinvested funds equal r. Then the net present value of the project will equal

$$-I_0 + \sum_{t=1}^{j-1} \frac{X_t}{(1 + k)^t} + \sum_{t=j}^{n} \frac{X_t(1 + r)^{n-t}}{(1 + k)^n}.$$

If the probability of exchange controls equals α_j in year j and 0 in all other years, then the project's new expected present value NPV_a equals

$$-I_o + \sum_{t=1}^{j-1} \frac{X_t}{(1+k)^t} + (1-\alpha_j) \sum_{t=j}^{n} \frac{X_t}{(1+k)^t} + \alpha_j \sum_{t=j}^{n} \frac{X_t(1+r)^{n-t}}{(1+k)^n},$$

assuming that all blocked funds can be repatriated in year n. The break-even value for α_j, α^*, can be found by setting $NPV_a = 0$ and solving for α^*. Then,

$$\alpha^* = \frac{\displaystyle\sum_{t=1}^{n} \frac{X_t}{(1+k)^t} - I_o}{\displaystyle\sum_{t=j}^{n} \frac{X_t}{(1+k)^t} - \sum_{t=j}^{n} \frac{X_t(1+r)^{n-t}}{(1+k)^n}}.$$

The same approach set forth in the expropriation example can be used to incorporate the likelihood of the imposition of exchange controls in any future period t with probability α_t, along with a probability distribution about lifting of these controls. If blocked funds cannot be repatriated, then a compensation value would have to be described and included in the analysis.

In actuality, firms have many ways to remove blocked funds. These methods include transfer price adjustment on intracorporate sales, loan repayments, and fee and royalty adjustments, so funds are likely to be only partially blocked.

If Y_t dollars can be repatriated even when exchange controls exist, then the previous formula presented would be modified as follows:

$$-I_o + \sum_{t=1}^{j-1} \frac{X_t}{(1+k)^t} + \sum_{t=j}^{n} \frac{Y_t}{(1+k)^t} + (1-\alpha_j) \sum_{t=j}^{n} \frac{X_t - Y_t}{(1+k)^t}$$

$$+ \alpha_j \sum_{t=j}^{n} \frac{(X_t - Y_t)(1+r)^{n-t}}{(1+k)^n}$$

By using these formulas, a firm can see how sensitive its investment decision is to the probability and magnitude of blocked funds in any given year. If the present value turns out to be sensitive to the level of Y_t under exchange controls, the parent company can then structure its investment *in advance* so as to maximize the values of Y_t. This could include investing in the form of debt rather than equity, borrowing locally and setting high transfer prices on goods sold to the subsidiary while buying goods produced by the subsidiary at lower prices where legally possible. Numerous other mechanisms available for using blocked funds are described in Shapiro [18]. The important thing to note is that many of these methods require planning *prior* to the initial commitment of funds.

Incidentally, the automatic inclusion of depreciation in computing cash flows from domestic operations is questionable when evaluating a foreign project. Dividend payments in excess of reported profits will decapitalize the enterprise, thereby inviting closer host government scrutiny. On the other hand, using depreciation cash flows to service parent company debt would be more acceptable. Thus, while parent company funds, whether called debt or equity, require the same return, the cash flow from foreign projects could very well be affected by the form of this investment. Ordinarily, the tax and repatriation flexibility advantages of debt will prove decisive.

Illustration

Consider, for example, an investment requiring an initial outlay of $1,000,000 with expected cash inflows of $350,000 annually for the next five years. The present value of this investment discounted at 20% is $46,850. If exchange controls are anticipated just before the second year remittance, then, with full repatriation at the end of year 5, $a^* = .24$ if the blocked funds cannot be reinvested. In other words, the expected present value of the project is negative if the probability of exchange controls is greater than .24. If funds can be reinvested with an annual return of 5%, then a^* rises to .31 while $a^* = .46$, if the reinvestment rate is 10%.

If exchange controls are not expected until year 3, then these probabilities rise to .52, .60, and 1.0, respectively. In the latter case, the possibility of currency controls will not affect the investment decision.

This break-even analysis can be extended still further. Suppose that the probability of exchange controls in year 2 is .5 and that reinvestment is impossible. Then at least 51% of the funds must be removable each year via fee remittances, loan repayments, and transfer price adjustments (for example) for the investment to have a positive expected present value. This remittance percentage declines to .37 with a reinvestment rate of 5% and to .08 if a 10% reinvestment rate is assumed.

Exchange Rate Change and Inflation

We now turn to the evaluation of two major economic risks facing multi-nationals — inflation and exchange rate changes. Inflation and exchange risk are opposite side of the same coin. It is worthwhile, however, to analyze each effect separately since there is normally a lag between a given rate of inflation and the necessary exchange rate change [9]. This is particularly true when government intervention occurs, such as in a fixed rate system or a managed float. Furthermore, local price controls may not permit or may retard the effect of internal price adjustments.

Exchange Risk

As with political risk, many companies account for exchange risk by raising their discount rates. However, to the extent that exchange risk is unsystematic, the discount risk should not be adjusted. Rather, the expected value of cash flows should reflect the impact of exchange rate changes. The method advocated by Stonehill and Nathanson [22] is to adjust each period's dollar cash flow, X^t, by the cost of an exchange risk management program. Thus, if d_t is the expected forward discount in period t, for example, then the present value of period t's cash flow will be set equal to $X_t (1 - d_t) / (1 + k)^t$. This technique is fine if local currency cash flows are fixed, as (for instance) in the case of interest on a foreign currency-dominated bond.

Where income is generated by an on-going business operation, however, local currency cash flows themselves will vary with the exchange rate. Thus, multiplying each period's projected local currency cash flow, L_t, by the forecasted exchange rate, e_t, will overlook the fact that L_t itself is a function, $L_t(e_t)$, of the expected exchange rate. In fact, several recent articles have set forth the systematic and predictable changes to local currency cost and revenue streams of an exchange rate change (see [5] and [15]). The major conclusions of this work are that the sector of an economy in which a firm is engaged (export, import-competing, purely domestic) and the sources of its inputs (imports, domestic traded, domestic non-traded) are the major determinants of its susceptibility to exchange risk.

The recommended approach here is to isolate the different sources of a project's cash flows and to analyze each stream separately. This would involve identifying the impact of an exchange rate change on the project's revenues (what percentage of its sales is local as opposed to exports), its costs (what percentage of its inputs is domestic) and on depreciation. It is also necessary to isolate those revenues and costs that are contractually fixed in either local or foreign currency from those inputs and sales whose prices can adjust to a changed exchange rate. For example, while local currency devaluation can increase dollar profits, dollar cash flows from depreciation will unambiguously decline by the devaluation percentage unless indexation of fixed assets is permitted. However, indexation, where it exists, is generally tied to an inflation index related to the exchange rate only to the extent that a devaluation will increase local currency prices [6]. Furthermore, working capital requirements will probably change because of the changed competitive situation the firm faces. These changes would have to be incorporated in the analysis. If R_t, C_t and D_t are the local currency revenues, costs, and depreciation charges respectively of period t, then the project's expected after-local tax dollar cash flow in year t will equal

$$(1 - t_r)[R_t(e_t) - C_t(e_t)] \, e_t + D_t e_t + W_t(e_t)e_t,$$

where $W_t(e_t)$ is the net change in local currency working capital required with an exchange rate of e_t. In lieu of using expected exchange rates, it would be preferable to compute the above dollar cash flow for each possible exchange rate, assign a probability to each value, and then take the expected dollar cash flow over all possible exchange rates.

Illustration

Assume that a firm analyzing an overseas investment project anticipates a local currency (LC) devaluation of 10% at the end of the first year of plant operation. The relevant exchange risk factors are as follows: Output is sold in both domestic and export markets; imported and domestic raw materials are used; the unit cost of domestic raw materials will rise 8%; the unit cost of imported raw materials will increase 10%; the unit cost of labor will

Exhibit 17.2 Cash flow effect of a currency devaluation

	Exchange rate	
	LCI = \$.10	*LCI* = \$.09
Revenues (local currency)		
Sales (units)		
Domestic	100,000	105,000
Export	100,000	110,000
Price per unit	100	105
Gross revenue	20,000,000	22,575,000
Costs (local currency)		
Raw materials (cost per unit)		
Domestic	25	27
Imported	20	22
Labor (unit cost)	25	26
Variable cost per unit	70	75
Total variable costs	14,000,000	16,125,000
Fixed costs	2,000,000	2,100,000
Depreciation	1,000,000	1,000,000
Total costs	17,000,000	19,225,000
Profit before tax	3,000,000	3,350,000
Tax @ 50%	1,500,000	1,675,000
Net profit after tax	1,500,000	1,675,000
Depreciation	1,000,000	1,000,000
Total local currency cash flow	LC 2,500,000	LC 2,675,000
Dollar cash flow	\$ 250,000	\$ 240,750

increase 4%; fixed costs will rise 5%; domestic and export prices will be raised 5% in local currency terms; both export and domestic sales will increase due to the lower price relative to foreign competitors' prices. (Since the initial dollar price is $10.00, a 5% price increase to LC105 will reduce the dollar price to $9.45.)

Taking all these factors into account, local currency cash flow will increase from LC 2,500,000 to LC 2,675,000. Dollar cash flow declines by $9,250 from $250,000 to $240,750. Much of this reduction is due to the $5,000 decrease in the dollar value of depreciation-generated cash flows ($.5 \times 1,000,000 \times .10 - .5 \times 1,000,000 \times .09$). Exhibit 17.2 shows the calculation of these cash flows. The alternative method of reducing dollar cash flows by 10% would have led to a projected $25,000 reduction in cash flow.

In addition, working capital requirements are expected to increase by $50,000 to support the higher sales level. Therefore, the capital budget must be adjusted to reflect a yearly reduction in cash flow of $9,250 and a lump sum decrease of $50,000 at the end of the first year.

Inflation

Exchange rate changes are normally preceded by relatively higher or lower local rates of inflation than in the home country. As with exchange rate changes, a given inflation rate will not lead to a similar increase in profits or cash flows. Cash flows should be separated into their component parts to analyze each part on its own. The competitive as well as the cost effects of inflation can vary from firm to firm depending (as with exchange rate changes) on the location of a firm's markets as well as on the sources of its inputs (see Shapiro [15] for elaboration of these effects). For example, a firm selling locally at inflated prices will find profits rapidly increasing if a large percentage of its costs is fixed in terms of either the local or a foreign currency. Items such as rent, power, labor, and imported inputs will exhibit either fixed prices or prices whose increases may lag increases in the firm's product prices.

One danger faced by firms in many countries is a price freeze imposed either during rapid inflation or following devaluation of the local currency. Generally these price freezes are more effective in controlling a firm's output prices than in controlling its input costs, thus leading to a profit squeeze. Furthermore, a foreign firm is less likely or able to flout local price control measures since it is under certain subtle pressures to be a "good corporate citizen." In such a situation, a firm could raise its prices in advance of an anticipated price freeze and take on the burden of competing with inflated prices. When the price freeze occurs, however, and costs inevitably rise afterwards, the firm would be in a better position to continue operating profitably. This is especially true if imported materials are being used and a devaluation has occurred. Local companies that are unable to raise their prices when production costs rise will probably start producing inferior merchandise and cut back on service, sustain considerable losses, and/or go out of business. All these factors would have to be reflected through an adjustment of future cash flows [19].

Inflation will normally influence a firm's cash flows by causing a rise in working capital requirements. This is due to higher costs, increases in its required cash balances, and an easing of credit terms leading to higher accounts receivable.

Where indexation is permitted, dollar cash flows from depreciation should increase in times of inflation. As noted above, however, this benefit will disappear or at least be reduced following a devaluation.

Capital Market Segmentation

Multinational firms often finance overseas investments with project-specific funds. There are two approaches to evaluating a project whose financing is partially arranged in a segmented capital market. One way is to adjust the project's weighted cost of capital to include the cost of this debt. If k is the firm's marginal cost of capital applicable to the project, then the project's total cost of capital is I_0k, where I_0 is the total financing required. If F dollars of this total are now raised in the form of debt at an interest rate of i_1 rather than at the firm's normal cost of debt, i_0, then the project's new total cost of capital equals $I_0k - F(i_0 - i_1)$, which yields an adjusted marginal cost of capital of

$$k - \frac{F}{I_0}(i_0 - i_1) = k'.$$

The assumption here is that the firm's cost of capital k is based on a target worldwide debt ratio and hence that each dollar of debt raised abroad replaces one dollar of domestic debt. The cost of capital adjustment required if a firm leverages itself more highly abroad than domestically is presented in [17]. Using this method, the present value of period t's cash flow would equal

$$\frac{X_t}{(1 + k')^t}$$

The alternative method is to subtract the interest subsidy or penalty $F(i_0 - i_1)$ from the project's cash flows in each period. These adjusted cash flows would then be discounted at the firm's marginal cost of capital k. Thus, the adjusted present value of period t's cash flow would equal

$$\frac{X_t - F(i_0 - i_1)}{(1 + k)^t}$$

Obviously, a firm would never borrow at $i_1 > i_o$ if it had the option of borrowing at i_o. Capital controls can lead to this result, however. For example, during the period 1968–1974, regulations established by the U.S. Office of Foreign Direct Investment (OFDI) and the Federal Reserve Board restricted access to the U.S. capital market if funds were intended for loans or investments in developed countries. This forced U.S. multinational firms to borrow in the Euro-dollar market at rates of interest higher than in the U.S. to finance their foreign operations.

In a recent paper [21], Stonehill and Shapiro show that the correct discount rate is the marginal cost of unrestricted funds, because this figure more accurately reflects the firm's opportunity cost of funds. To maximize the present value of shareholder wealth, project cash flows should be discounted at "the yield foregone on the most profitable investment opportunity rejected, or the required rate of return, whichever is the higher" [24, pp. 99]. This opportunity cost of funds will normally equal the firm's marginal cost of capital. Where capital market segmentation exists, however, the firm's opportunity cost of funds may well differ from the project's marginal cost of capital. Adjusting the cost of capital implicitly assumes that all cash flows are reinvested at k′, while the adjusted cash flow method correctly assumes that cash flows are being reinvested at k. Thus, in the case of an interest subsidy, *i.e.*, $i_1 < i_o$, the correct discount rate is k, and cash flows should be adjusted by $F(i_o - i_1)$.

This result appears to contradict previous sections of the paper involving the analysis of taxation and blocked funds, where the return on reinvested funds was assumed to equal r rather than k. It is necessary to differentiate here, however, between returns on retained earnings and parent company returns. *The capital budgeting model presented here only recognized cash flows back to the parent, and it is the opportunity yield on these repatriated funds that is relevant.* This opportunity yield does equal K.

Summary and Conclusions

Capital budgeting for the multinational corporation presents many elements that rarely if ever exist in domestic capital budgeting. The primary thrust of this paper has been to adjust project cash flows instead of the discount rate to reflect the key political risks and economic risks that MNCs face abroad. Tax factors and segmented capital markets are also incorporated via cash flow instead of cost of capital adjustments. Cash flow adjustments are preferred on the pragmatic grounds that there is available more and better information on the effect of such risks on future cash flows than on the required discount rate.

References

[1] Tamir Agmon and Donald Lessard, "International Diversification and the Multinational Corporation: An Investigation of the Price Behavior of the Shares of U.S. Based Multinational Corporations on the N.Y.S.E.," *Journal of Finance*, forthcoming.

[2] Harold Bierman, Jr., and Jerome E. Hass, "Capital Budgeting Under Uncertainty: A Reformulation," *Journal of Finance* (March 1973), p. 119.

[3] Business International, *Business International Index of Environmental Risk*, Business International Corporation, New York, various dates.

[4] Business International, *Business International Money Report*, Business International Corporation, New York, October 1, 1976.

[5] Gunter Dufey, "Corporate Finance and Exchange Rate Variations," *Financial Management* (Summer 1972), p. 51.

[6] David K. Eiteman and Arthur I. Stonehill, *Multinational Business Finance*, Reading, Massachusetts, Addison-Wesley Publishing Co., 1973.

[7] Dan Haendel and Gerald West with Robert Meadow, *Overseas Investment and Political Risk*. Foreign Policy Research Institute Monograph Series, Philadelphia, Pennsylvania, 1975.

[8] Robert G. Hawkins, Norman Mintz, and Michael Provissiero, "Government Takeovers of U.S. Foreign Affiliates," *Journal of International Business Studies* (Spring 1976), p. 3.

[9] John S. Hodgson and Patricia Phelps, "The Distributed Impact of Price-Level Variations on Floating Exchange Rates," unpublished working paper, Norman, Oklahoma, University of Oklahoma, 1973.

[10] Walter N. Ness, Jr., "U.S. Corporate Income Taxation and the Dividend Remittance Policy of Multinational Corporations," *Journal of International Business Studies* (Spring 1975), p. 67.

[11] Price-Waterhouse, "Information Guide for U.S. Corporations Doing Business Abroad," New York, March, 1976.

[12] Alexander A. Robichek and Stewart C. Myers, *Optimal Financing Decisions*, Englewood Cliffs, New Jersey, Prentice-Hall, Inc., 1965.

[13] Rita M. Rodriquez and E. Eugene Carter, *International Financial Management*, Englewood Cliffs, New Jersey, Prentice-Hall, Inc., 1976.

[14] David P. Rutenberg, "Maneuvering Liquid Assets in a Multinational Corporation," *Management Science* (June 1970), p. 671.

[15] Alan C. Shapiro, "Exchange Rate Changes, Inflation and the Value of the Multinational Corporation," *Journal of Finance* (May 1975), p. 485.

[16] Alan C. Shapiro, "Evaluating Financing Costs for Multinational Subsidiaries," *Journal of International Business Studies* (Fall 1975), p. 25.

[17] Alan C. Shapiro, "Financial Structure and Cost of Capital in the Multinational Corporation," *Journal of Financial and Quantitative Analysis*, forthcoming.

[18] Alan C. Shapiro, "Management of Blocked Funds," University of Pennsylvania working paper, 1976.

[19] Alan C. Shapiro, "Protecting Against Anticipated Price Controls," University of Pennsylvania working paper, 1977.

[20] Alan C. Shapiro and David P. Rutenberg, "Managing Exchange Risks in a Floating World," *Financial Management* (Summer 1976), p. 48.

[21] Alan C. Shapiro and Arthur I. Stonehill, "Capital Budgeting With Segmented Capital Markets," University of Pennsylvania working paper, 1976.

[22] Arthur I. Stonehill, and Leonard Nathanson, "Capital Budgeting and the

Multinational Corporation," *California Management Review* (Summer 1968), p. 39.

[23] J. Frederick Truitt, "Expropriation of Foreign Investment: Summary of the Post World War II Experience of American and British Investors in Less Developed Countries," *Journal of International Business Studies* (Fall 1970), p. 21.

[24] James C. Van Horne, *Financial Management and Policy*, 4th ed., Englewood Cliffs, New Jersey, Prentice-Hall Inc., 1974.

18

Evaluating International Projects: An Adjusted Present Value Approach*

Donald R. Lessard[†]

*Source: Donald R. Lessard, ed., *International Financial Management: Theory and Application* (New York, Wiley, 1985), pp. 570–584.

In evaluating projects that cut across national boundaries, firms must deal with a variety of issues seldom encountered within a single country that affect the distribution of net operating cash flows available to the parent, as well as the valuation of these cash flows.[1] Factors influencing the statistical distribution of net operating cash flows, in addition to differences in fundamental economic and political conditions in various countries, include differing rates of inflation and volatile exchange rates that may or may not cancel each other, differences in tax rules and tax rates, and restrictions or taxes on cross-border financial transactions. Factors that may influence the valuation of operating cash flows with a given statistical distribution include incomplete and often segmented capital markets that result from controls on financial transactions both within and among countries; the dependence of net of tax cash flows available to the parent on the firm's overall tax and cash-flow position in various countries; the availability of project-specific concessional finance—loans, guarantees, or insurance against commercial or political risks; and, on occasion, requirements to issue securities—especially equity—within markets partially or totally isolated by barriers to internal or cross-border financial transactions. Further, the available cash flows and their value to the firm often depend on the specific financing of the project, not only because of concessional financing opportunities, but also because the costs or limits on cross-border transfers often depend on the nature of the financial transaction involved, e.g., interest or principal, fees, dividends, or payment for goods.

As a result of these various factors, it is often necessary to distinguish project and parent cash flows, to recognize interactions between the financing and valuation of a project, to take into account dependencies between project valuation and the corporation's overall tax and cash-flow situation, and to incorporate in the valuation criterion the perspectives of multiple investors not sharing a common capital market. Thus traditional weighted-average cost of capital rules that implicitly separate investment and financing decisions often are inapplicable or misleading,[2] as well as exceedingly complex.[3] A variety of alternative approaches have been put forward,[4] some involving multiple investment criteria,[5] others requiring the consideration of the "full-system" effects of the project in question,[6] and others providing relatively complex criteria reflecting the existence of multiple investors based in less than fully integrated capital markets.[7]

This paper seeks to show that an adjusted present value approach (APV), based on the value additivity principle (VAP) that holds for independent projects in complete capital markets, provides a relatively simple framework for evaluating most international projects consistent with state-of-the-art financial practice. It is restricted to projects wholly owned by the parent or whose equity is shared by investors having access to the same relatively complete capital markets. It does not address the valuation of projects by joint ventures in which equity is shared by investors based in markets segmented by barriers[8] or the relative valuation of particular projects by firms based in countries with relatively complete markets and by local firms operating in a more restricted capital market—a potential motivation for direct foreign investment.[9]

Special attention is given to the valuation of operating cash flows that are not denominated in any specific currency but that reflect the interaction of inflation rates and exchange rates and of nominal cash flows, such as depreciation tax shields and debt service that are contractually denominated in a specified currency.

The paper is organized in six sections. The second section describes the APV approach and discusses the circumstances under which it is applicable. The third section discusses the valuation of operating and contractual cash flows. The fourth section presents a general APV formula for foreign projects that distinguishes between operating and contractual cash flows and takes into account the effects of differing tax systems, exchange and credit restrictions, and concessional financing opportunities, together with their interactions with the structure of the project's cross-border inter-affiliate financing, as well as with the local subsidiary and parent firm's external financing. The fifth section discusses briefly the risk premiums applicable to the various cash flows, and the last section discusses the implementation of the APV approach, especially with regard to approaches involving multiple cash-flow estimates and simulation.

The Adjusted Present Value Approach

As a result of the "cost of capital revolution" of the 1960s, the dominant approach to project evaluation is to discount expected after-tax project cash flows by a weighted-average cost of capital,

$$\text{NPV} = \sum_{t=0}^{T} \frac{\overline{\text{CF}}_t}{(1 + \rho^*)^t}, \tag{1}$$

where NPV is net present value, $\overline{\text{CF}}$ is the expected total after-tax project cash flow in period t, and ρ^* is the weighted-average cost of capital. ρ^* in turn is usually defined as

$$\rho^* = (1 - \lambda)\rho^E + \lambda r(1 - \tau), \tag{2}$$

where λ is the weight of debt in the total capital structure, r is the pretax interest rate on debt, τ is the corporate tax rate, and ρ^E is the required rate of return on equity.

The advantage of the traditional approach is its simplicity. It imbeds in a single discount rate all financing considerations, thus enabling planners to focus on the project's investment characteristics. However, different discount rates are required for projects that differ from a firm's typical project in terms of either business risk or contribution to debt capacity, and equation (2) provides little guidance since ρ^E will be changed by an unspecified amount. Both conditions are the rule rather than the exception for foreign projects. Further, when the financing complications of foreign projects are introduced, the weighted-average approach becomes complex and cumbersome, removing its major advantage. In fact, when financing sources for foreign projects include limited amounts of restricted funds or project-specific concessionary credit, there will be different weighted-average costs for projects that differ only in scale. With capital structures that vary over time—which is typical of projects financed independently of the parent to minimize taxes, to take advantage of project-specific financing subsidies, or to minimize political risks—a different weighted average will be required in different years of the project's life.

Differences in project debt capacity can be incorporated via the alternative weighted-average formula developed by Modigliani and Miller:

$$\rho^* = \rho[1 - \tau\lambda], \tag{3}$$

where ρ is the "all-equity" required rate of return reflecting the project's business risk. Further, it can be generalized to situations where business risk differs as well. The *project* required rate of return, ρ_j^*, is given by

$$\rho_j^* = [r + \beta_j(\rho_m - r)][1 - \tau\lambda], \tag{4}$$

where β_j is the project's beta coefficient (adjusted to remove the effect of leverage) and $(\rho_m - r)$ is the risk premium on the market portfolio.

As noted by Myers [16], however, formulas (2) and (4) are exactly correct only if the cash flows are perpetual and λ is constant over time. In many cases where projects are financed from a common corporate pool, the errors are not serious. However, if the financial structures of specific foreign projects differ from those of the parent firm or vary over the project lives because of the availability of concessional finance, tax considerations, or efforts to reduce political or currency risks, even the generalized formula (4) is likely to be misleading.

To deal with the problem, Myers [16] suggests a return to the basic Modigliani-Miller equation underlying (3). Rather than implicitly incorporating financial factors in ρ^*, the approach values them explicitly in an adjusted present value equation:

$$\text{APV} = \sum_{t=0}^{T} \frac{\overline{CF_t}}{(1 + \rho_i)^t} + \sum_{t=0}^{T} \frac{TS_t}{(1 + r)^t}, \tag{5}$$

where the first term is the present value of the total expected operating cash flows discounted by ρ_j, the "all-equity" discount rate reflecting the project's business risk, and the second term is the present value of the tax shields arising from debt, discounted at the before-tax cost of debt, r. This is a direct application of the value additivity principle (VAP)—that in equilibrium the market value of any set of "risk-independent" cash flows available for distribution to security holders (after corporate taxes) is equal to the sum of the values of the individual components. [10]

Applicability of VAP to International Projects

Value additivity is a robust concept. Haley and Schall [11, pp. 230–237] show that it applies without exception for securities (claims to income streams) issued in complete, competitive capital markets with neutral personal taxes. Further, they argue that because of clientele effects, VAP will hold in general for individual firms even if personal taxes are not neutral in their treatment of interest, dividend, and capital gain income. Most importantly, they point out that even if markets are not complete (i.e., that there is no perfect substitute for one or more of the income streams provided by the firm or project), the potential for investor arbitrage will generally maintain value additivity. It breaks down when certain transactions are restricted or costly, and as a result the potential for investor arbitrage is impaired.

At first glance, this latter condition appears to rule out VAP for projects with income streams subject to cross-border costs or restrictions or to projects in countries with capital markets isolated by such barriers. However, VAP requires only that investors can engage in arbitrage among the various income streams available for distribution by the parent firm after corporate taxes. Thus any restrictions or taxes on cross-border transfers to the parent must be reflected in the income stream components, but will not affect the ability to combine or divide these remittable, net of corporate tax streams for valuation.

The fact that local capital markets are not competitive because of internal controls or lack of the necessary institutional infrastructure or are isolated from other markets by barriers to cross-border transactions is irrelevant in the valuation of projects by wholly owned ventures in such countries by firms based in countries with relatively open, competitive capital markets. These conditions may change the investment opportunity set facing the firm through their impact on the competition for projects resulting from differences in project valuation by local and international firms, but the appropriate context for the valuation of these flows is the base country capital market. Even in the case of joint ventures, these conditions will have no effect on the valuation of a given set of income streams by the international firm, although they may lead to different valuation criteria for the local firm and hence to lack of agreement between the participants regarding investment and financing decisions.[11]

Recognition of Inflation and Exchange Rate Changes

An individual international project may involve cash flows in several different currencies, some proportion of which will be contractually denominated in those currencies and the remainder of which will be determined by the interactions of future business conditions and changes in relative prices, price levels, and exchange rates. These flows can be viewed from four different perspectives as illustrated in Table 18.1: either in the base currency or the local currency valuation is that the discount rates used are consistent with the way the cash flows are stated—i.e., if current values are used, the discount rates must incorporate the relevant inflation premiums; if constant, the discount rates should not include inflation premiums.

Common practice in estimating and evaluating cash flows can be characterized as follows: Firms first project expected revenues and expenses in constant terms, linking present unit costs and revenues with future unit sales projections. These flows are transformed into current terms by inflating them at the anticipated general rate of inflation. If the flows are not already stated in the base currency, they then are translated into

Table 18.1 Alternative cash-flow perspectives

| | Treatment of inflation | |
Currency	Constant	Current
Local	I	II
Base	III	IV

current base currency units using projected exchange rates. This process involves moving from quadrant I in Table 18.1 to quadrant II and then to quadrant IV. Although there is nothing necessarily incorrect with this approach, it often is applied inconsistently, and important interdependencies between inflation and exchange rates and their impacts on operating and contractual cash flows are often overlooked. Further, it is difficult to extend this approach to accommodate a range of operating cash-flow estimates generated by simulation. Each scenario must incorporate explicit assumptions regarding inflation rates, exchange rates, and cash flows, while a simulation requires the joint distribution of the three sets of variables.

The basis for a simpler, yet more transparent approach is provided by the set of equilibrium relationships between interest rates, rates of inflation, and changes in exchange rates that (tend to) hold in efficient markets—purchasing power parity and the (domestic and international) Fischer effect.[12] Even when these relationships do not hold precisely, they serve to highlight the impact on cash flows of the interactions between inflation and exchange rates and to provide insights regarding the valuation of these flows.

It is useful to separate cash flows into two groups: (1) operating cash flows that are not contractually denominated in nominal terms and whose value in constant terms is relatively independent of inflation, and (2) contractual flows denominated in a particular currency whose value in current terms is relatively independent of inflation. A different treatment is appropriate for each of the two classes of flows.

Operating Cash Flows

The home currency value of operating cash flows in another currency is given by

$$V = \sum_{t=1}^{T} \frac{\overline{CF} \text{ (current)}_t {}^* \bar{S}_t}{(1 + \rho)^t} = \sum_{t=1}^{T} \frac{\overline{CF} \text{ (constant)}_t (1 + \bar{I})^{t} {}^* \bar{S}_t}{(1 + \rho)^t}, \qquad (6)$$

where $\overline{CF}$ (current) are expected cash flows in current local terms and $\overline{CF}$ (constant) are the expected flows in constant terms, and ρ is the all-equity rate appropriate for flows in the home currency with the project's risk.

This formula can be simplified substantially if the two key equilibrium relationships—purchasing power parity (PPP) and the Fisher effect (IFE)—are assumed to hold.[13] PPP implies that exchange rate changes and relative rates of inflation offset each other. As a result, the expected spot exchange rate for foreign currency (stated in terms of units of the base currency per unit of foreign currency) at time t is

$$\bar{S}_t = S_0 (1 + I)^t / (\bar{1} + \bar{I}^*)^t, \qquad (7)$$

where S_0 is the current spot rate, I the expected base currency inflation rate, and I^* the expected foreign currency inflation rate.[14,15] IFE implies that the nominal riskless interest rate, r, for a given currency, incorporates a premium for anticipated inflation. Thus $(1 + \rho)$ can be restated as

$$(1 + r_{\text{real}})(1 + I)(1 + \text{RP}) \tag{8}$$

when r_{real} is the real interest rate and RP is the risk premium.

Substituting into (6)[16]

$$V = \sum_{t=1}^{T} \frac{\overline{\text{CF}} \,(\text{constant})_t (1 + \bar{I}^*)^t S_0 (1 + \bar{I})^t / (1 + \bar{I}^*)^t}{[(1 + \rho_{\text{real}})(1 + \bar{I})]^t} \tag{9a}$$

$$= S_0 \sum_{t=1}^{T} \frac{\overline{\text{CF}} \,(\text{constant})^t}{(1 + \rho_{\text{real}})} \tag{9b}$$

The problem of cash flows in different currencies and discounts rates appropriate for each one collapses into a single currency calculation where the current exchange rate simply scales the flows to a common base.

Departures from PPP and IFE

Of course, PPP does not hold exactly, and interest rates do not provide exact guides to future exchange rate changes. However, there is little evidence for major currencies subject to market forces that deviations from these key relationships are persistent or that they can be forecast.[17] As a result, the simplified approach to cash-flow estimation and valuation based on these equilibrium tendencies is quite robust for single-point expected cash-flow estimates. If various distributions of cash flows are considered, the problem becomes more complex. *Ex post* deviations from IFE will have no effect on valuation if PPP continues to hold. However, departures from PPP are likely to alter cash flows stated in constant local terms, as well as the real exchange rate at which they can be converted into the base currency. This is because they result in changes in the relative prices of inputs or outputs sold or sourced in different countries. Further, the deviations themselves are likely to reflect changes in relative prices within countries, with important implications for cash flows.

It is much more likely that firms can forecast trends in relative prices of certain inputs and outputs as opposed to overall deviations from PPP, since relative price changes hinge on microlevel changes in productivity, scarcity, or substitutability of the good or factor in question. Furthermore, given the evidence that PPP holds quite well over the long run, these relative price shifts are likely to result in larger impacts on project values than divergences from PPP. These relative price shifts can be incorporated readily by changing project cash flows in either (9a) or (9b), but (9b) is more transparent since it abstracts from offsetting inflation and exchange rate changes.

Where exchange rates are forecast to diverge from PPP because of exchange controls or trade barriers, explicit joint estimates of the local currency cash flows and exchange rates are required. These can be stated in either real or nominal terms since the key element is the change in the real exchange rate (deviation from PPP) and not the absolute exchange rate and level of inflation. Typically, the impact of PPP deviations in such cases will not be symmetric, since price controls or other market interventions are likely to be systematically related to PPP departures.

Contractual Cash Flows

Contactual nominal cash flows including interest on debt and tax rebates based on historical cost depreciation can be discounted at a nominal rate appropriate to the currency in question and converted to the base currency by multiplying the resulting present value by the current spot rate,

$$V = S_0 \sum_{t=1}^{T} \frac{\overline{CF} \text{ (current)}_t}{|(1 + r)(1 + RP)|^t}, \tag{10}$$

where $(1 + r) = (1 + r_{real})(1 + I)$ and I is the rate of inflation for the currency in which the flows are denominated.

For major currencies, where interest rate parity and the Fisher effect tend to hold, market interest rates are appropriate. Where market interest rates do not reflect generally held inflation and exchange rate expectations as a result of credit controls or exchange restrictions, an offshore rate (if available) or an estimated rate must be used.

Deviations from IFE

Any unanticipated change in exchange rates, whether it represents a departure from PPP or not, changes the present value of contractual flows. Anticipated changes reflected in the interest rate will have no effect on the value of interest-bearing contractual claims, but will change the value of non-interest-bearing claims, such as depreciation and other tax shields based on historical cost allocations.[18]

Applying APV to Foreign Projects

The APV approach, outlined earlier, provides a "divide and conquer" approach to capital budgeting. Financial contributions to a project's value are recognized separately and explicitly, the total present value is the sum of the present value of the basic project cash flows, and the treatment of the various financial effects can be generalized to incorporate the special situations encountered in evaluating foreign projects. In particular, the cash flows can be separated into operating and contractual components, as well as into those components that can be estimated independently for the project and those that depend on systemwide cash-flow and tax interactions. This breakdown is illustrated in the following general equation:

Adjusted present value = APV   (11)

Noncontractual operating flows

Capital outlay

$$\sum_{i=1}^{N} S_0^i \sum_{t=0}^{T} \frac{I_t^i}{(1 + \rho_1)^t} \quad (11a)$$

+

Remittable after-tax operating cash flows

$$\sum_{i=1}^{N} S_0^i \sum_{t=1}^{T} \frac{\overline{CF_t^i}(1 - \tau)}{(1 + \rho_2)^t} \quad (11b)$$

+

Contractual flows

Contractual operating flows

$$\sum_{i=1}^{N} S_0^i \sum_{t=1}^{T} \frac{CONT_t^i(1 - \tau)}{(1 + \rho_3)^t} \quad (11c)$$

Depreciation tax shields

$$\sum_{i=1}^{N} S_0^i \sum_{t=1}^{T} \frac{DEP_t^i(\tau)}{(1 + \rho_1)^t} \quad (11d)$$

+

Tax shields due to normal borrowing

$$\sum_{i=1}^{N} S_0^i \sum_{t=1}^{T} \frac{INT_t^i(\tau)}{(1 + \rho_5)^t} \quad (11e)$$

+

Financial subsidies or penalties

$$\sum_{i=1}^{N} S_0^i \sum_{t=1}^{T} \frac{\Delta INT_t^i}{(1 + \rho_6)^t} \quad (11f)$$

+

Operating flows dependent on firm's overall tax and cash-flow position

Tax reduction or deferral via inter-affiliate transfers

$$\sum_{i=1}^{N} S_0^i \sum_{t=1}^{T} \frac{TR_t^i}{(1 + \rho_7)^t} \quad (11g)$$

+

Additional remittances via inter-affiliate transfers

$$\sum_{i=1}^{N} S_0^i \sum_{t=1}^{T} \frac{REM_t^i}{(1 + \rho_8)^t} \quad (11h)$$

where superscript i denotes currency i and $S_o{}^i$ is the current spot rate for currency i.

Each of the terms is discussed in greater detail below. We assume that operating flows are stated in constant terms and hence discounted at a real rate, while the contractual flows are stated in current terms and hence are discounted at the relevant nominal rate. Appropriate risk premiums for the various components are discussed later.

Capital Outlay (11a)

The elements of this term are unambiguous for items purchased by the firm, but are more complex for capital items sourced internally. The major obstacle in the latter case is calculating the true incremental cost to the system, which may differ substantially from the registered book value of the item in question. Contractual capital costs should be distinguished from noncontractual costs and discounted at nominal rates.

Capital expenditures often are paid out of accumulated funds from existing operations whose use is restricted by exchange controls or because special tax advantages will be forfeited or additional U.S. taxes imposed if the funds are remitted rather than reinvested. The APV framework lends itself readily to incorporating the incremental value of a project resulting from its ability to employ such funds. Since the operating cash-flow term already captures project cash flows that will be available for remittance, taxed as if they are remitted, the use of restricted funds simply reduces the investment outlays (11a) by the difference between their face value and the present value of these funds if remitted via the best alternative mechanism.

Operating Cash Flow (11b)

In the domestic case, there is little difficulty in defining after-tax operating cash flows. They are the total project cash flows less U.S. taxes. Whether they are reinvested in the project or not makes no difference, since all flows are deemed available to the corporate cash pool. With foreign projects, there are two major issues in defining operating cash flows: (1) whether to use project cash flows or only those flows remitted to the parent, and (2) what taxes to assume, since these will be a function of financing and remittance decisions. The first distinction arises because of foreign exchange restrictions and ceilings on profit remittances; the second because of the interactions of various national tax systems.

Clearly, the only cash flows of value to the parent are those available for remittance in one form or another, not necessarily those actually remitted. Furthermore, after-tax flows must take into account the incremental taxes to the entire corporation. However, the specific choice of ways to deal with the two issues is a question of managerial art—the solution should be straightforward, easy to apply, and likely to bring to management's attention the most critical issues.

There are two basic approaches. One is to begin with the most favorable set of assumptions regarding taxation and remittability and, in later terms of the APV equation, to subtract the present values of reductions due to specific restrictions or international tax interactions. The other is to start with conservative assumptions regarding remittability and taxation, later adding the present value of gains resulting from various mechanisms for circumventing restrictions or deferring taxes. I prefer the second alternative for the pragmatic reason that if a project is attractive under conservative assumptions, there is no need to proceed with the far more complex set of calculations regarding tax and remittance adjustments that require consideration of the total corporate cash flow and tax situation.[19]

The conservative approach includes in the first term only those cash flows available for remittance through normal channels—for example, amortization of investment and repatriation of earnings—but not those that can be obtained only through transfer pricing or other mechanisms for circumventing restrictions. The tax rate applied to these flows is either the parent rate or the foreign rate, whichever tax system imposes the largest tax liability. This implicitly assumes that all operating cash flows are remitted immediately to the United States and that the parent has no excess foreign tax credits. Any additional value derived by circumventing restrictions on cash remittances, deferring U.S. taxes, or offsetting excess foreign tax credits can be incorporated in additional terms. Since depreciation tax shields are captured in a separate term, after-tax cash flows are simply pretax flows multiplied by one minus the relevant tax rate.

A further and perhaps more serious issue in the computation of operating cash flows is the difficulty of measuring the true incremental cash flows of a project in an interdependent multinational system. For example, the establishment of a manufacturing plant in a country previously served by exports will result in an erosion of profits elsewhere in the system, but it may also create new profit opportunities for other parts of the system that provide intermediate or complementary products. This difficulty is exacerbated by departures from arm's length transfer pricing among units, some of which may result from conscious manipulation of tax and exchange control systems, but most of which result from the near impossibility of allocating the joint costs and benefits associated with "soft" factors of production, such as technology and managerial expertise used by more than one unit of the corporation. Clearly, an attempt should be made to measure incremental cash flows to the total system. Further, in keeping with conservative tax and remittance assumptions, interaffiliate flows should be valued as closely to an arm's length value as possible.[20]

Contractual Operating Flows (11c)

Some elements of operating costs or revenues, as well as capital costs, may be set contractually. Typically, this will be true only for a relatively short period, and the distinction is thus immaterial for capital budgeting. However, where long-term sourcing or sales contracts are involved, explicit recognition of the contractual cash flows is called for.[21]

Depreciation Tax Shields (11d)

This contractual cash flow is deterministic, subject to the corporation's ability to use or to sell the tax shield, given investment outlays. The relevant tax rate and set of tax rules that should be used are those binding at the margin, as noted above.

Interest Tax Shields (11e)

For a variety of reasons, including the availability of concessionary credit, the existence of tax or exchange considerations that favor remittances in the form of interest payments, and the desire to hedge currency or political risks, foreign projects are often financed with a different and typically higher proportion of debt than the corporation as a whole. Further, the debt issued to finance the project often exceeds the increment to overall debt capacity provided by the project. Thus approaches that directly utilize the project capital structure in computing a weighted-average cost of capital are likely to overstate the worth of the project, but a weighted average based on the total firm's capitalization also is likely to be misleading. In the APV equation, in contrast, the second term captures the tax shields associated with a project's incremental contribution to corporate debt capacity. The costs or benefits of "overborrowing" at the project level for reasons of currency risk, concessionary credit, or remittance restrictions are treated explicitly in later terms.

Financial Subsidies or Penalties (11f)

The value of subsidies in the form of concessionary credit or penalties resulting from local financing requirements can be computed by comparing the present value of the total pretax payments on the debt, including interest and principal, discounted at the rate that would apply if the same debt were issued to competitive capital markets with the face value of the debt. For example, if a project is eligible for a concessionary loan at 6 percent instead of a market rate of, say, 9 percent, (11f) would be the difference between the present value of the total pretax payments on the 6 percent debt discounted at 9 percent, and the face value of the debt.[22]

Ability to Reduce or to Defer Taxes (11g)

The base case operating cash flows, term (11b), incorporate conservative assumptions regarding the taxation of project cash flows—that they will be taxed at the U.S. rate or the local rate in the foreign country, whichever results in the greater tax liability. In many cases, an MNC can reduce taxes from this level by combining profits from countries with relatively low and high taxes, by shifting expenses and revenues among its affiliates, or simply by reinvesting profits in low-tax countries and deferring the additional U.S. taxes. In principle, the present value of these tax changes can be readily incorporated in an APV term, although computing them may require a complex corporate tax model. However, reversing the analysis to calculate a "break-even" value for term (11g) may show that a readily attainable degree of tax reduction is all that is required. Thus the full analysis can be avoided.

Ability to Circumvent Restrictions on Remittances (11h)

The base case operating flows, terms (11b), include only those operating flows available for remittance. Thus they will be less than project flows whenever there are binding remittance restrictions. In many cases, however, the restricted flows can be transfered out through interaffiliate pricing, management fees, special export programs, or other mechanisms. The value of these remittances, typically less than the face value of the funds in question, can be incorporated in another APV term. Again, a major advantage of the "divide and conquer" approach is that it makes explicit the impact on project value of remittance restrictions and alternative ways around them. Even where the exact possibilities for transferring restricted funds are not known, a "break-even" value for term (11h) can be computed, thus showing what proportion, in present value terms, of the restricted profits would have to be transferred to make the project marginally attractive.

Risk Premiums for Foreign Projects

Although the APV approach does not require that the effects of financial structure be reflected in the discount rate, the discount rate for each term must reflect both the rate of interest (real in the case of operating flows, nominal in the case of nominal flows) and a risk premium. According to current capital market theory, this risk premium should reflect only the systematic risk of the project. Depending on the openness of the base country capital market, this systematic risk should be measured relative to the firm's home country market portfolio or relative to the world market portfolio. As shown by Lessard [13], the systematic risk of projects in various countries differs substantially from U.S. and world perspectives, but much more so for other single-country versus world perspectives. From a single-country perspective, foreign projects will tend to have less systematic risk than domestic projects, although this may not be true if the more appropriate world base is used. In countries where local conditions are extremely uncertain, but not highly dependent on the world economy, the total risk of the project will be substantially greater than its systematic risk from any perspective other than the local one. Thus even apparently risky projects may not require greater than normal risk premiums.

The suggestion that cash flows from projects in politically unstable countries should not require large risk premiums is at odds with general practice. Many firms attach large risk premiums to such projects. However, the difference is often more semantic than real. A common approach to evaluating foreign projects is to discount most likely (modal) rather than expected (mean) cash flows at a risk-adjusted rate. For projects with a significant risk of expropriation or large losses due to changes in the economic structure of a country, the mean will be substantially lower than the mode. Thus the discount rate is being used to shift cash flows toward their expected values to discount them by a risk premium. Such "risk adjustments," however, introduce biases, and the more explicit approach that captures the effect of risks on expected cash flows, as well as on their valuation, is preferable.[23]

Appropriate discount rates for each major category of the APV terms are discussed below.

Noncontractual Flows (ρ_1 and ρ_2): Capital Outlays

Since these flows are not contractually fixed in any currency, but vary depending on the interactions of inflation and exchange rates, as well as on a host of other factors, I have argued that they should be stated in terms of units of constant purchasing power and discounted at the real rate of interest plus a risk premium reflecting their systematic risk. However, determining this systematic risk represents a major challenge. In many cases, there are no host country firms in the same industry with shares traded in an active market to provide beta estimates. Furthermore, formal or informal approaches for estimating fundamental betas are likely to be hampered by a lack of experience with similar projects. In addition, beta estimates estimated empirically will relate the volatility of equity values, reflecting both operating and contractual cash flows. Hence it is necessary to "back out" the relevant betas for the various components. This is not an insurmountable task, though, since the contractual flows are relatively safe and can be assumed to be discounted at a rate close to the riskless rate. Thus the adjustment involves "unlevering" beta, not only for financial leverage, but also for depreciation tax shields.

Contractucal Flows ($\rho_3 - \rho_6$)

The critical element in discounting these flows is determining the appropriate nominal interest rate for (near) riskless debt. Undoubtedly there is some risk of default associated with the various contractual flows, and hence a risk premium may be required. Nevertheless, as a first approximation, the corporation's borrowing rates in unregulated markets can be used. Technically, the depreciation tax shields are subject only to the risk that the firm cannot make use of them. This may be serious in certain cases, but in general if the firm cannot take the deductions directly, it can carry them forward or backward in time or, in the ultimate case, transfer them to another firm through mergers. Roughly speaking, then, ρ_4 will involve only a small risk premium and can be approximated by the interest rate on the firm's debt in the currency in question. Similar arguments apply to interest tax shields and financial subsidies.

System-Dependent Operating Flows (ρ_7 and ρ_8)

Although part of these flows are tax savings due to transfer pricing or earnings retention decisions, they are not contractually denominated except to the extent that the profit shifting also changes depreciation tax shields. Thus in practice it might be necessary to separate the term into an operating and contractual component, with the appropriate inflation and risk adjustments for each element. The amount available for remittance through these channels will depend directly on project operating cash flows and thus, although the risks of being able to remit these additional funds are unlikely to be highly systematic, the discount rate applicable to operating flows, ρ_2, appears to be a reasonable choice.

Conclusions

The APV approach provides a generalized framework capable of incorporating most of the special financial considerations that arise in evaluating foreign projects. Its attractiveness vis-à-vis traditional approaches, which attempt to force all these factors into a single term, rests only in part on its conceptual superiority. Much of its attraction lies in its transparency and simplicity of use in certain situations.

In practice, capital budgeting involves a great deal of trial and error with various "what if" questions. Furthermore, many uncertain outcomes are never reduced to specific cash flows, but instead are dealt with by testing the sensitivity of cash flows to changes in a particular assumption and by judging whether a particular variable is likely to exceed a "break-even" value. The ability to separate the various terms greatly facilitates such analyses. In most cases, only the operating cash-flow streams will need to be run under a variety of scenarios. Similarly, if there is uncertainty with respect to the appropriate discount rates, most of it will center on the risk premium for the operating cash flows, and thus sensitivity analysis can concentrate on these flows. The distinction between real and nominal flows allows a substantially simplified treatment of inflation and exchange rates, but it also serves to highlight the differential impact of these factors on the two types of flows.

While the assumptions of purchasing power parity and interest rate parity undoubtedly break down for certain countries or currencies, they provide the best set of base case single-point estimates. If deviations from these relationships are explicitly considered, a careful attempt to model the effect of these deviations on the cash flows themselves is called for. Treating them as independent in either a scenario or simulation approach is fallacious and is likely to result in more serious errors than assuming that the naive parity conditions hold. The explicit separation of contractual and noncontractual cash flows in various currencies lends itself to sensitivity or simulation approaches for determining the impact of exchange rate changes or a project's present value, valuable both for capital budgeting and foreign exchange exposure analysis.

While these considerations clearly favor the APV approach, they do not call for its use in all situations. Little will be lost in using a single discount rate that is roughly consistent with APV solutions for small, recurring projects with few or no financing interactions. However, even in this case, the APV framework provides the ideal basis for computing these hurdle rates for decentralized use. Any strategic decision that involves financial complexities, though, should be evaluated in the more complete fashion outlined.

Notes

† I am grateful to a large number of persons who have commented on the earlier versions of this paper, including Fischer Black, Gene Carter, Rich Cohn, Gunter Franke, Christine Hekman, Stewart Myers, Joel Ornstein, Jim Paddock, Alan Shapiro, and Kirit Vora. All remaining errors and arbitrary choices are, of course, my responsibility.

1. See Eiteman and Stonehill [6], Rodriguez and Carter [22], Shapiro [25], and Folks [7] for summaries of the factors distinguishing domestic and foreign projects. An early paper that raised most of these questions was Stonehill and Nathanson's [29].

2. Rodriguez and Carter [22] demonstrate how weighted-average measures using project or subsidiary capital structures are misleading when there is financial "layering" within the corporation.

3. Shapiro [26] provides a detailed derivation of a weighted-average rule for international projects that takes many of these factors into account. However, it is exceedingly complex, and the resulting hurdle rate is likely to differ across projects and over time.

4. Naumann-Etienne [17] provides a good review of the early literature on this topic.

5. Eiteman and Stonehill [6] suggested a dual hurdle rate approach. Although they have dropped it in their subsequent edition, it continues to be advocated by others.

6. See, for example, Pomper [20].

7. Alder [1] provides the most complete treatment of this issue.

8. See Adler [1] and Adler and Dumas [2] for a discussion of valuation in such cases. Although the APV from the viewpoint of a single investor will not in general

be the appropriate investment criterion for the joint venture, it will be appropriate for valuing that project from the single investor's viewpoint. In practice, there may be no rule that satisfies both participants in the joint venture. In such cases, project acceptance depends on bargaining among the participants, where each may use an APV measure to evaluate their share.

9. See, for example, Adler and Dumas [2,3], Agmon and Lessard [4], and Stapleton and Subrahmanyam [28].

10. The VAP, an extension of the first Miller-Modigliani proposition, was introduced by Schall [24] and, although not given the same name, by Myers [16]. For an excellent statement, see Haley and Schall [11, pp. 202–208].

11. In practice, virtually all international ventures can be considered joint ventures in the sense that the local government's income taxes are risky equity claims and locally issued debt typically carries some project-related risks. In these cases, the local government's valuation of a venture may differ from that of the international firm, but these effects will usually be swamped by other adjustments, such as shadow prices for foreign exchange and labor and the recognition of positive and negative externalities.

12. For a succinct definition of these relationships, see Giddy [9], Frenkel [8], and Solnik [27]. See Dornbusch [5] for a more complete discussion of the underlying economic theory.

13. For an excellent review of the theory and evidence regarding purchasing power parity, see Officer [18]. Levich [15] reviews the evidence regarding the degree to which the forward rate is an unbiased predictor of future spot exchange rates and of interest rate parity, conditions that jointly imply IFE.

14. The classical PPP relationship is defined in terms of certain, contemporaneous variables. Giddy [10] and Solnik [27] discuss the expectational form.

15. This formula can be altered readily to accommodate varying rates of inflation over time.

16. If PPP does not hold exactly, equation (9a) includes the covariances among cash flows, inflation, and exchange rates and does not reduce to (9b). However, if the cash flows in constant terms are (relatively) independent of inflation and the exchange rate, the approximation is satisfactory.

17. Roll [23], for example, finds no evidence that deviations from PPP persist or can be forecast.

18. The value of riskless contractual flows is unaffected by uncertainty regarding the exchange rate since it can be locked in by borrowing or lending an equivalent flow at the nominal market interest rate.

19. This assumption is analogous to the "default value" approach suggested by Folks [7].

20. Vernon and Wells [31] and Robbins and Stobaugh [21] provide further illustration of the difficulty of measuring incremental cash flows at a system level.

21. See Lessard [12, pp. 354–356] for a discussion of contractual and noncontractual cash flows and their implications for corporate exposure to exchange rate changes.

22. Pretax cash flows are used since it is assumed that the use of concessionary debt will require a matching reduction in other corporate borrowings. Thus the additional interest tax shields of the concessionary debt will be offset by reduced interest tax shields on corporate borrowing at market rates. The tax shields gained and lost will not match exactly if debt capacity is defined in terms of book values. Even if defined in terms of (net present value of) cash flows, the offset will be inexact since the proportion of the debt service flows that is interest will differ for the concessionary debt and borrowings at the market rate with the same present value. In most cases, however, the error is small.

23. Eiteman and Stonehill [6] follow a third approach, "adjusting" cash flows until they are of equivalent risk to those of domestic projects and then discounting them by the domestic cost of capital." This is similar to taking certainty equivalents of cash flows and discounting them by the riskless state. While in many ways it is theoretically more appealing than to discount expected cash flows by a risk-adjusted rate, there are no operational, yet reasonably precise ways to do this.

References

[1] Adler, M. "The Cost of Capital and Valuation of Two-Country Firm," *Journal of Finance* (March 1974).

[2] Adler, M., and Dumas, B. "Optimal International Acquisitions," *Journal of Finance* (March 1975).

[3] Adler, M., and Dumas, B. "The Microeconomics of the Firm in an Open Economy," *American Economic Review* (February 1977).

[4] Agmon, T., and Lessard, D.R. "Financial Factors and the International Expansion of Small-Country Firms," in Agmon and Kindleberger, eds., *Multinationals from Small Countries*. Cambridge, Mass.: M.I.T. Press, 1977.

[5] Dornbusch, R. "Monetary Policy under Exchange Rate Flexibility," in *Managed Exchange Rate Flexibility*. Boston: Federal Reserve Bank of Boston, Conference Vol., No. 20, 1979.

[6] Eiteman, D.K., and Stonehill, A.I. *Multinational Business Finance*, 2nd ed. Reading, Mass.: Addison-Wesley Publishing Company, 1979.

[7] Folks, W.R., Jr. "Critical Assumptions in Evaluating Foreign Investment Projects," paper submitted at Nijenrode conference, August 1979.

[8] Frenkel, J.A. "A Monetary Approach to the Exchange Rate: Doctrinal Aspects and Empirical Evidence," *Scandinaian Journal of Economics* (May 1976).

[9] Giddy, I. "The Cost of Capital in the International Firm," unpublished working paper, Columbia University, 1976.

[10] Giddy, I. "An Integrated Theory of Exchange Rate Equilibrium," *Journal of Financial and Quantitative Analysis* (December 1976).

[11] Haley, C.W., and Schall, L.D. *The Theory of Financial Decisions*. New York: McGraw-Hill Book Company, 1979.

[12] Lessard, D.R., ed. *International Financial Management*. New York: Warren, Gorham, & Lamont, 1979.

[13] Lessard, D.R. "World, Country and Industry Relationships in Equity Returns: Implications for Risk Reduction through International Diversification," *Financial Analysts Journal* (January/February 1976).

[14] Lessard, D.R., "Transfer Prices, Taxes, and Financial Markets: Implications of Internal Financial Transfers within the Multinational Firm," in R.B. Hawkins, ed., *Economic Issues of Multinational Firms*, JAI Press, 1979.

[15] Levich, R.M. "The Efficiency of Markets for Foreign Exchange," in Lessard, ed., *International Financial Management*.

[16] Myers, S.C. "Procedures for Capital Budgeting under Uncertainty," *Industrial Management Review* (Spring 1968).

[17] Naumann-Etienne, R. "A Framework for Financial Decisions in Multinational Corporations—A Summary of Recent Research," *Journal of Financial and Quantitative Analysis* (November 1974).

[18] Officer, L.H. "The Purchasing Power Theory of Exchange Rates: A Review Article," *IMF Staff Papers* (March 1976).

[19]   Ornstein, J., and Vora, K.T. "Foreign Investment Projects in Multinational Firms," Master's thesis, Sloan School of Management, M.I.T. (December 1978).

[20]   Pomper, C.B. *International Investment Planning: An Integrated Approach.* Amsterdam: North-Holland Publishing Company, 1976.

[21]   Robbins, S.M., and Stobaugh, R.B. *Money in the Multinational Corporation.* New York: Basic Books, 1973.

[22]   Rodriguez, R.M., and Carter, E.E. *International Financial Management.* Englewood Cliffs, N.J.: Prentice-Hall, 1979.

[23]   Roll, R. "Violations of Purchasing Power Parity and their Implications for Efficient International Commodity Markets," in M. Sarnat and G.P. Szego, eds., *International Finance and Trade*, Vol. 1. Cambridge, Mass.: Ballinger Publishing Company, 1979.

[24]   Schall, L.D. "Asset Valuation, Firm Investment, and Firm Diversification," *Journal of Business* (January 1972).

[25]   Shapiro, A.C. "Capital Budgeting for the Multinational Corporation," *Financial Management* (May 1978).

[26]   Shapiro, A.C. "Financial Structure and the Cost of Capital in the Multinational Corporation," *Journal of Financial and Quantitative Analysis* (November 1978).

[27]   Solnik, B. "International Parity Conditions and Exchange Risk," *Journal of Banking and Finance* (August 1978).

[28]   Stapleton, R.C., and Subrahmanyam, M.G. "Marketing Imperfections, Capital Market Equilibrium, and Corporation Finance," *Journal of Finance* (May 1977).

[29]   Stonehill, A.I., and Nathanson, L. "Capital Budgeting and the Multinational Corporation," *California Management Review* (Summer 1968).

[30]   Taggart, R.A., Jr. "Capital Budgeting and the Financing Decision: An Exposition," *Financial Management* (Summer 1977).

[31]   Vernon, R.A., and Wells, L.T. *Management in the International Economy*, 3rd ed., Englewood Cliffs, N.J.: Prentice-Hall, 1976.

Select Bibliography

Abuaf, Niso, "The nature and management of foreign exchange risk", *Midland Corporate Finance Journal*, 4 (Fall 1986), pp. 30–44.

—— , "Foreign exchange options: the leading hedge", *Midland Corporate Finance Journal*, 5 (Summer 1987), pp. 51–58.

Adler, Michael, "The cost of capital and valuation of a two-country firm", *Journal of Finance*, 29 (March 1974), pp. 119–132.

Adler, Michael, and Bernard Dumas, "Portfolio choice and the demand for forward exchange", *American Economic Review*, 66 (May 1976), pp. 332–339.

—— , "International portfolio choice and corporation finance: a synthesis", *Journal of Finance*, 38 (June 1983), pp. 925–984.

Aggarwal, Raj, "International differences in capital structure norms: an empirical study of large European countries", *Management International Review*, 21 (1981), pp. 75–88.

Agmon, Tamir, and Donald Lessard, "Investor recognition of corporate international diversification", *Journal of Finance*, 32 (September 1977), pp. 1049–1055.

Aliber, Robert Z., "The interest rate parity theorem: a reinterpretation", *Journal of Political Economy*, 81 (December 1973), pp. 1451–1459.

Aliber, R.Z., and C.P. Stickney, "Accounting measures of foreign exchange exposure: the long and short of it", *Accounting Review*, L (January 1975), pp. 44–57.

Babbel, David F., "Determining the optimum strategy for hedging currency exposure", *Journal of International Business Studies*, 14 (Spring/Summer 1983), pp. 133–139.

Baker, James C., "Capital budgeting in West European countries", *Issues in Financial Management*, 19 (1981), pp. 3–10.

Bilson, John F.O., "Rational expectations and the exchange rate", in Jacob A. Frenkel and Harry G. Johnson, eds., *The Economics of Exchange Rates* (Reading, Mass., Addison-Wesley, 1978), pp. 75–96.

Choi, Frederick D.S., Howard D. Lowe, and Reginald G. Worthley, "Accountors, accountants, and Standard No. 8", *Journal of International Business Studies*, 9 (Fall 1978), pp. 81–87.

Cohn, Richard A., and John J. Pringle, "Imperfections in international financial markets: implications for risk premia and the cost of capital to firms", *Journal of Finance*, 28 (March 1973), pp. 59–66.

Collins, J. Markham, and William S. Sekely, "The relationship of headquarters, country, and industry classification to financial structure", *Financial Management*, 12 (Autumn 1983), pp. 45–51.

Dornbusch, Rudiger, "Expectations and exchange rate dynamics", *Journal of Political Economy*, 84 (December 1976), pp. 1161–1176.

Dufey, Gunter, "Corporate finance and exchange rate variations", *Financial Management*, 1 (Summer 1972), pp. 51–57.

Dufey, Gunter, and Ian H. Giddy, "International financial planning: the use of market-based forecasts", *California Management Review*, 21 (Fall 1978), pp. 69–81.

———— , "Innovation in the international financial markets", *Journal of International Business Studies*, 12 (Fall 1981), pp. 33–51.

Eaker, Mark R., "Denomination decision for multinational transactions", *Financial Management*, 9 (Autumn 1980), pp. 23–29.

Errunza, Vihang R., and Lemma W. Senbet, "The effects of international operations on the market value of the firm: theory and evidence", *Journal of Finance*, 36 (May 1981), pp. 401–417.

Errunza, Vihang R., and Etienne Losq, "International asset pricing under mild segmentation: theory and test", *Journal of Finance*, 40 (March 1985), pp. 105–124.

Eun, Cheol S., and Bruce G. Resnick, "Currency factor in international portfolio diversification", *Financial Management*, 14 (Summer 1985), pp. 45–53.

———— , "Exchange rate uncertainty forward contracts, and international portfolio selection", *Journal of Finance*, 43 (March 1988), pp. 197–215.

Fama, Eugene F., "Forward rates as predictors of future spot rates", *Journal of Financial Economics*, 5 (October 1976), pp. 361–377.

Flood, Eugene, Jr., and Donald R. Lessard, "On the measurement of operating exposure to exchange rates: a conceptual approach", *Financial Management*, 15 (Spring 1986), pp. 25–36.

Folks, William R., Jr., "Decision analysis for exchange risk management", *Financial Management*, 1 (Winter 1972), pp. 101–112.

Folks, William R., and Stanley R. Stansell, "The use of discriminant analysis in forecasting exchange risk movements", *Journal of International Business Studies*, 6 (Spring 1975), pp. 33–50.

Garman, Mark B., and Steven W. Kohlhagen, "Foreign currency option values", *Journal of International Money and Finance*, 2 (December 1983), pp. 231=–237.

George, Abraham M., "Cash flow versus accounting exposures to currency risk", *California Management Review*, 20 (Summer 1978), pp. 50–55.

Germany, J. David, and John E. Morton, "Financial innovation and deregulation in foreign industrial countries", *Federal Reserve Bulletin*, 71 (October 1985), pp. 743–753.

Giddy, Ian H., "An Integrated theory of exchange rate equilibrium", *Journal of Financial and Quantitative Analysis*, 11 (December 1976), pp. 863–892.

———— , "Why it doesn't pay to make a habit of forward hedging", *Euromoney* (December 1976), pp. 96–100.

———— , "Exchange risk: whose view?", *Financial Management*, 6 (Summer 1977), pp. 23–33.

Giddy, Ian H., and Gunter Dufey, "The random behavior of flexible exchange rates: implications for forecasting", *Journal of International Business Studies*, 6 (Spring 1975), pp. 1–32.

Gordon, Sara L., and Francis A. Lees, "Multinational capital budgeting: foreign investment under subsidy", *California Management Review*, 25 (Fall 1982), pp. 22–32.

Grauer, Frederick A., Robert A. Litzenberger and Richard E. Stehle, "Sharing rules and equilibrium in an international capital market under uncertainty", *Journal of Financial Economics*, 5 (June 1976), pp. 233–256.

Grubel, Herbert G., "Internationally diversified portfolios: welfare gains and capital flows", *American Economic Review*, 58 (December 1968), pp. 1299–1314.

Grubel, Herbert G., and Kenneth Fadner, "The interdependence of international equity markets", *Journal of Finance*, 26 (March 1971), pp. 89–94.

Hekman, Christine R., "Don't blame currency values for strategic errors", *Midland Corporate Finance Journal*, 4 (Fall 1986), pp. 45–55.

Hodder, James E., "Evaluation of manufacturing investments: a comparison of U.S. and Japanese practices", *Financial Management*, 15 (Spring 1986), pp. 17–24.

Hughes, John S., Dennis E. Logue, and Richard J. Sweeney, "Corporate international diversification and market assigned measures of risk and diversification", *Journal of Financial and Quantitative Analysis*, 10 (November 1975), pp. 627–637.

Ibbotson, Roger C., Richard C. Carr, and Anthony W. Robinson, "International equity and bond returns", *Financial Analysts Journal*, 38 (July–August 1982), pp. 61–83.

Jacque, Laurent L., "Management of foreign exchange risk: a review article", *Journal of International Business Studies*, 12 (Spring/Summer 1981), pp. 81–101.

Jacquillat, Bertrand, and Bruno H. Solnik, "Multinationals are poor tools for diversification", *Journal of Portfolio Management*, (Winter 1978), pp. 8–12.

Jurgensen Report, *Report of the Working Group on Exchange Market Intervention*, Washington, D.C.: U.S. Treasury, 1983.

Kelly, Marie E. Wicks, and George C. Philippatos, "Comparative analysis of the foreign investment eevaluation practices by US-based manufacturing multi-national companies", *Journal of International Business Studies*, 13 (Winter 1982), pp. 19–42.

Kester, W. Carl, "Capital and ownership structure: A comparison of United States and Japanese manufacturing corporations", *Financial Management*, 15 (Spring 1986), pp. 5–16.

Khoury, Sarkis J., and K. Hung Chan, "Hedging foreign exchange risk: selecting the optimal tool", *Midland Corporate Finance Journal*, 1 (Winter 1988), pp. 40–52.

Kohlhagen, Steven W., "Forward rates as predictors of future spot rates", *Journal of International Business Studies*, 6 (Fall 1975), pp. 33–39.

——— , "A model of optimal foreign exchange hedging without exchange rate projections", *Journal of Interntional Business Studies*, 9 (Fall 1978), pp. 9–19.

Lee, Kwang Chul, and Chuck C.Y. Kwok, "Multinational corporations vs. domestic corporations: international environmental factors and determinants of capital structure", *Journal of International Business Studies*, 19 (Summer 1988), pp. 195–217.

Lee, Wayne Y., and Kanwal S. Sachdeva, "The role of the multinational firm in the integration of segmented markets", *Journal of Finance*, 32 (May 1977), pp. 479–492.

Lessard, Donald R., "World, national, and industry factors in equity returns", *Journal of Finance*, 29 (May 1974), pp. 379–391.

——— , "Evaluating international projects: an adjusted present value approach", in Donald R. Lessard, ed., *International Financial Management: Theory and Application* (New York, Wiley, 1985), pp. 570–584.

———— , "Finance and global competition: exploiting financial scope and coping with volatile exchange rates", *Midland Corporate Finance Journal*, 4 (Fall 1986), pp. 6–29.

Levich, Richard M., "Tests of forecasting models and market efficiency in the international money market", in Jacob A. Frenkel and Harry G. Johnson, eds., *The Economics of Exchange Rates* (Reading, Mass., Addison-Wesley, 1978), pp. 129–158.

———— , "Analyzing the accuracy of foreign exchange forecasting services: theory and evidence", in Clas Wihlborg and Richard Levich, eds., *Exchange Risk and Exposure: Current Developments in International Financial Development* (Lexington, Mass., Heath, 1980), pp. 99–127.

Levy, Haim, and Marshall Sarnat, "International diversification of investment portfolios", *American Economic Review*, LX (September 1970), pp. 668–675.

Logue, Dennis E., and George S. Oldfield, "Managing foreign assets when foreign exchange markets are efficient", *Financial Management*, 6 (Summer 1977), pp. 16–22.

Modigliani, Franco and Merton Miller, "The cost of capital, corporation finance and the theory of investment", *American Economic Review*, XLVIII (June 1958), pp. 261–297.

Oblak, David J., and Roy J. Helm, Jr., "Survey and analysis of capital budgeting methods used by multinationals", *Financial Management*, 9 (Winter 1980), pp. 37–41.

Remmers, Lee, Arthur Stonehill, Richard Wright and Theo Beekhuisen, "Industry and size as debt ratio determinants for manufacturing internationally", *Financial Management*, 3 (Summer 1974), pp. 24–32.

Robichek, Alexander A., and Mark R. Eaker, "Debt denomination and exchange risk in international capital markets", *Financial Management*, 5 (Autumn 1976), pp. 11–18.

Rodriguez, Rita M., "Corporate exchange risk management: theme and aberrations", *Journal of Finance*, 36 (May 1981), pp. 427–439.

Rutterford, Janette, "An international perspective on the capital structure puzzle", *Midland Corporate Finance Journal*, 3 (Fall 1985), pp. 60–72.

Sarathy, Ravi, and Sangit Chatterjee, "The divergence of Japanese and U.S. corporate financial structure", *Journal of International Business Studies*, 15 (Winter 1984), pp. 75–89.

Sekely, William S., and J. Markham Collins, "Cultural influences on international capital structure", *Journal of International Business Studies*, 19 (Spring 1988), pp. 87–100.

Shapiro, Alan C., "Exchange rate changes, inflation, and the value of the multinational corporation", *Journal of Finance*, 30 (May 1975), pp. 485–501.

———— , "Capital budgeting for the multinational corporation", *Financial Management*, 7 (Spring 1978), pp. 7–16.

———— , "Financial structure and cost of capital in the multinational corporation", *Journal of Financial and Quantitative Analysis*, 13 (June 1978), pp. 211–226.

Shapiro, Alan C., and David P. Rutenberg, "When to hedge against devaluation", *Management Science*, 20 (August 1974), pp. 1514–1530.

———— , "Managing exchange risks in a floating world", *Financial Management*, 5 (Summer 1976), pp. 48–58.

Solnik, Bruno H., "Note on the validity of the random walk for European stock market capital structure", *Journal of Finance*, 28 (December 1973), 1151–1159.

———— , "The international pricing of risk: an empirical investigation of the world capital market structure", *Journal of Finance*, 29 (May 1974), pp. 365–378.

——— , "Testing international asset pricing: some pessimistic views", *Journal of Finance*, 32 (May 1977), pp. 503–512.

Stanley, Marjorie T., "Capital structure and cost of capital for the multinational firm", *Journal of International Business Studies*, 12 (Spring/Summer 1981), pp. 103–120.

Stapleton, Richard C., and Marti Subrahmanyam, "Market imperfections, capital market equilibrium, and corporation finance", *Journal of Finance*, 32 (May 1977), pp. 307–319.

Stehle, Richard F., "An empirical test of the alternative hypothesis of national and international pricing of risk assets", *Journal of Finance*, 32 (May 1977), pp. 493–502.

Stonehill, Arthur, and Leonard Nathanson, "Capital budgeting and the multinational corporation", *California Management Review*, 11 (Summer 1968), pp. 39–54.

Stonehill, Arthur, and Thomas Stitzel, "Financial structure and multinational corporations", *California Management Review*, 12 (Fall 1969), pp. 91–96.

Stonehill, Arthur, Theo Beekhuisen, Richard Wright, Lee Remmers, Norman Toy, Antonio Parés, Alan Shapiro, Douglas Egan, and Thomas Bates, "Financial goals and debt ratio determinants: a survey of practice in five countries", *Financial Management*, 4 (August 1975), pp. 27–41.

Toy, Norman, Arthur Stonehill, Lee Remmers, Richard Wright, and Theo Beekhuisen, "A comparative international study of growth, profitability and risk as determinants of corporate debt ratios in the manufacturing sector", *Journal of Financial and Quantitative Analysis*, 9 (November 1974), pp. 875–886.

UNCTC, *World Investment Report 1991: The Triad in Foreign Direct Investment* (New York, United Nations, 1991).

Turnbull, Stuart M., "Swaps: a zero sum game?", *Financial Management*, 16 (Spring 1987), pp. 15–21.

Transnational Corporations and Management Division, *World Investment Report 1992: Transnational Corporations as Engines of Growth* (New York, United Nations, 1992).

Wheelwright, Steve, "Applying decision theory to improve corporate management of currency-exchange risks", *California Management Review*, 17 (Summer 1975), pp. 41–49.

Wright, Richard, and Sadahiko Suzuki, "Financial structure and bankruptcy risk in Japanese companies", *Journal of International Business Studies*, 16 (Spring 1985), pp. 97–110.

Name index

Subject index